Handbook of
Infant Perception

Volume 1
From Sensation to Perception

DEVELOPMENTAL PSYCHOLOGY SERIES

SERIES EDITOR
Harry Beilin

Developmental Psychology Program
City University of New York Graduate School
New York, New York

A complete list of titles in this series is available from the publisher.

Handbook of
Infant Perception

Volume 1
From Sensation to Perception

Edited by

Philip Salapatek

Institute of Child Development
University of Minnesota
Minneapolis, Minnesota

Leslie Cohen

Department of Psychology
The University of Texas at Austin
Austin, Texas

1987

ACADEMIC PRESS, INC.
Harcourt Brace Jovanovich, Publishers
Orlando   San Diego   New York   Austin
Boston   London   Sydney   Tokyo   Toronto

ACADEMIC PRESS, INC.
Orlando, Florida 32887

United Kingdom Edition published by
ACADEMIC PRESS INC. (LONDON) LTD.
24–28 Oval Road, London NW1 7DX

Library of Congress Cataloging in Publication Data

Handbook of infant perception.

(Developmental psychology series)
Includes bibliographies and index.
Contents: v. 1. From sensation to perception.
1. Perception in infants.   I. Salapatek, Philip.
II. Cohen, Leslie B.   III. Series.   [DNLM: 1. Perception
—in infancy & childhood. WS 105.5.D2 H236]
BF720.P47H36   1987   155.4'22   86-10788
ISBN 0-12-615151-2 (v. 1 : alk. paper)

PRINTED IN THE UNITED STATES OF AMERICA

86 87 88 89   9 8 7 6 5 4 3 2 1

Contents

4. Infant Color Vision and Color Perception

Davida Y. Teller and Marc H. Bornstein

5. Taste and Olfaction

Charles Crook

6. Touch, Motion, and Proprioception

Judith E. Reisman

Preface

It has been more than a decade since the publication of Cohen and Salapatek's two-volume compendium on infant perception. At that time research in the area of infant sensory and cognitive processes had proliferated to such an extent that a unified summary appeared both timely and necessary. Yet, the proliferation of knowledge was uneven. Individual investigators and laboratories had made remarkable strides in limited domains of inquiry, while many equally important areas of infant perception remained unexplored. Thus, the original *Infant Perception* books emerged as a collection of in-depth summaries of work of individual investigators, with some obvious substantive omissions, such as developmental anatomy, effector mechanisms in vision, the other senses, visual psychophysics, color perception, event perception, and cross-modal integration.

We felt in 1975 that while many of the foregoing omissions were important areas of infant perception, research on these topics was either scant or outdated. The field of infant perception had indeed grown at that time, but in an ungainly, adolescent fashion. Such is not the case at the present time. While new topics undoubtedly will be developed in infant perception, it is currently possible to draft two new volumes in which topics ranging from sensory to cognitive processes are treated systematically without many glaring omissions. Hence, the title, *Handbook of Infant Perception*.

In both current volumes, each contributor summarizes research in his/her area, and in addition introduces his/her most relevant findings. We believe the two volumes together provide a coherent picture of the current status of knowledge about infant perception, and while we had some reservations about splitting the handbook into separate volumes, the sheer quantity of information made it necessary. A convenient, although arbitrary distinction was made between the more sensory and psychophysical topics (Volume 1) and those that deal more with the relationship between perception and cognition (Volume 2).

Hickey and Peduzzi introduce Volume 1 with a rigorous account of the anatomical development of the human visual system and the relationship of its development to that of other species. The human data are of recent vintage, and a chapter such as this could not have been written in our earlier volume.

Aslin provides the bridge between anatomy and psychophysics in his chapter on effector mechanisms in infant vision. In this chapter the current wealth of data, much of it very recent, on visual accommodation, pupillary adjustments, and the various eye movement systems (saccadic, pursuit, vergence) are treated in a way that emphasizes the importance of these systems to visual intake.

On the more sensory side, Banks and Dannemiller consider the methodologies used to determine thresholds for pattern during human infancy. In addition to threshold techniques, spatial frequency analysis is outlined as a tool by which some aspects of both threshold and suprathreshold pattern detection may be understood.

Teller and Bornstein bridge the gap between sensory and more perceptual processes. On the one hand, they carefully outline the brightness and wavelength sensitivities of the infant. On the other hand, what is known about the categorical perception of color is also treated.

The volume concludes with chapters by Crook and by Reisman. Crook lays out the data on taste and smell in infants, while Reisman does the same for the other senses, namely, proprioception, vestibular sensitivity, touch, and pain.

Volume 2 begins with Dodwell, Humphrey, and Muir's treatment of infant shape and pattern perception. They discuss primarily two-dimensional shape from both a theoretical and an empirical point of view. There is a careful blending of traditional and current theory and data on the topic.

Yonas and Owsley extend the perception of shape to the third dimension, rigorously examining the nature of infant binocular vision and a variety of the other cues to depth. Nelson and Horowitz continue this extension in their chapter on infant visual motion perception.

Infant perception is advanced to a more cognitive level in the chapters by Harris and by Huttenlocher and Smyth-Burke. Harris considers various theoretical and empirical approaches to the question of how infants perceive the permanence of objects. The perception of objects is extended to the perception of simple and complex events by Huttenlocher and Smyth-Burke. They begin with the infant's simplest imitation acts and move toward the meaning of the first utterances.

Evidence for the integration of the senses is considered by Spelke in her contribution on cross-modal perception. She provides data indicating that from the earliest months, transfer of information takes place between the senses, and some perceptual attributes appear to be amodal.

Finally, Kuhl departs from visual perception to deal with infants' perception of speech and sound. She provides thorough treatment of speech-like sounds both cross species and cross culturally. The chapter covers everything from basic sensory processes to the perception of categorical information.

Because of our attempt to produce a comprehensive work on infant perception, these volumes were long in the making. However, it is with a good deal of satisfaction that we view the outcome in terms of both depth and scope. For this, of course, we must thank the dedication and patience of the contributors, whose manuscripts were a pleasure to read and to edit. We would also like to thank Michael Kuskowski and Linda Oakes for their help in preparing the final manuscripts. A special thanks goes to Linda, Phil's wife, for her love and support.

Memorial

Phil Salapatek died in March 1984, while the *Handbook of Infant Perception* was still in preparation. He was a good colleague and a close friend. Over the years we had occasion to teach together, room together, and play together. Phil had been ill for some time, but his death still came as a shock to those of us who knew him well and cared about him. Although we first became acquainted in the late 1960s, our close association and friendship really began with our joint editorship of *Infant Perception: From Sensation to Cognition,* which appeared in 1975. Phil's seminal contribution on infant pattern perception still stands as a model of scientific ingenuity and comprehensiveness. It clearly illustrated both his encyclopedic knowledge of infant perception and his dedication to furthering that knowledge. From Phil's earliest work on the precise measurement of infant scanning patterns to his latest investigations of event-related potentials to unexpected events, he has always been at the forefront of the field. His collection of superb graduate students at the University of Minnesota, who are now making their own major contributions to the understanding of infant perception, is another indication of his lasting contribution. In fact, four of his former students have contributed chapters to this handbook. Two of them, in particular, Dick Aslin and Marty Banks, deserve a special note of thanks for their aid in bringing these two volumes to completion. In a very real sense the *Handbook of Infant Perception* stands as a tribute to Phil; to his scientific contribution, his dedication to knowledge, and his ability to instill in others the same excitement he felt about the study of infant perception.

Leslie B. Cohen

Phil Salapatek died unexpectedly at the age of 43. To his students, Phil was more like a colleague than a senior professor. We learned and worked together, and his death caused each of us to ponder what we had lost. Shortly after his death, we gathered informally at a restaurant in New York City, during the biennial Infancy Conference, to attempt to understand what happened to Phil and to share our experiences as his students. Three days later, at a memorial service in Minneapolis, we joined Phil's family and colleagues in expressing more formally our feelings about his impact on our careers. While the intellectual contributions Phil made to the field of infant perception are numerous and profound (see his obituary in *Infant Behavior and Development,* 1984, *7,* 383–385), we all agreed that Phil's influence on our lives went beyond his role as scholar and mentor. From our collective impressions, covering over 15 years of graduate student supervision, we each volunteered the opinion that Phil's integrity, both professional and personal, was his most salient characteristic. Phil consistently went out of his way to support his students in ways we have since learned are very rare in the academic world. Despite his specific research interests, he was willing to embrace new ideas if convinced of their merit. Yet his support was not superficial or gratuitous. He made us work hard and think clearly until we were absolutely certain that our findings and interpretations were as solid as we could possibly make them. Reaching the correct conclusion was more important than collecting publishable data or protecting a former position. What we will miss most is the sage counsel, the reflective pauses, the good-natured joking, and the sailboat rides. As the major force in our professional careers, Phil gave us a gift we will value always. We can only hope to repay this gift by attempting to live up to his level of commitment as a scholar.

Phil Salapatek's students

Handbook of
Infant Perception

Volume 1
From Sensation to Perception

1

Structure and Development of the Visual System

T. L. HICKEY
JEAN D. PEDUZZI
School of Optometry, The Medical Center
University of Alabama at Birmingham
Birmingham, Alabama 35294

I. INTRODUCTION

This chapter is concerned with the structure and, to a more limited extent, the function of the adult and developing visual system. Since this chapter begins a book on infant perception, every attempt has been made to present findings concerned with the human visual system. However, in order to gain a better understanding of the visual system, it is often necessary to carry out invasive experiments that cannot be undertaken in humans. Therefore, some of this chapter is devoted to findings derived from studies using experimental animals. The findings from such studies are not presented in isolation, however. Rather, the knowledge gained from animal research is related to what we presently know about the human visual system.

Although our primary concern is the normal visual system, much can be learned from brains in which the normal processes of development have been altered. In humans, such alterations are generally the result of surgery, trauma, disease, or congenital anomalies. While brain tissue from such individuals can be quite useful in attempts to understand the human visual system, a more reliable source of abnormal material again

1

comes from studies of experimental animals. For our present purposes, the experimental alteration of most interest is visual form deprivation.

This chapter is not intended to cover all aspects of visual system structure, function, and development. Rather, it is intended to provide the reader with a better understanding of the primary visual pathway that extends from the retina, through the lateral geniculate nucleus, to the primary visual cortex (area 17) (see Figure 1). Most of what we presently know about the structure, function, and development of the visual system concerns this pathway. Given the focus of this book, it is particularly important that the reader have a thorough understanding of this retino-geniculo-cortical pathway since the development of this pathway occurs during, and is most likely related to, a critical period of visual system development, a period when the visual system is particularly susceptible to change. During this period of time, it is crucial that the organism experiences a normal visual environment. Any condition that degrades the organism's visual experience during such a period can result in permanent visual system deficiencies.

For more detailed descriptions of the entire human visual system, the reader is referred to such excellent sources as Polyak (1957), Duke-Elder

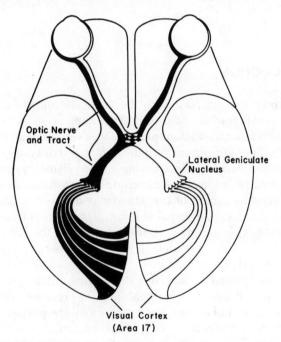

Figure 1. A simplified drawing of the retino-geniculo-cortical pathway in the human. (Modified from Polyak, 1957.)

and Wybar (1961), Brodal (1969), Moses (1981), and Carpenter (1983). Although some information about the structure of the eye is presented here, this very brief overview is meant only to acquaint the reader with the globe and its contents. More complete descriptions of the eye and orbit can be found in Walls (1942), Duke-Elder and Wybar (1961), Hogan, Alvarado, and Weddell (1971), and Rodieck (1973). A good general review of human nervous system development from a clinical point of view can be found in Dekaban (1970). An extremely thorough review of the visual pathways in normal and visually deprived cats has recently been provided by Sherman and Spear (1982).

II. THE EYE

A. Structure

The structure of the eye is best illustrated in photomicrographs or drawings of horizontal or sagittal sections. An example of one such drawing is shown in Figure 2. In this illustration, the various structures that make up the eye are shown quite clearly. The anterior segment of the eye contains the optical apparatus: the cornea, iris, lens, ciliary body (muscle), and zonule fibers. Although the cornea is the primary refractive surface of the eye, it is the lens that adjusts the path of the light rays so that objects located at different distances can be focused on the retina. The lens, a biconvex structure, is suspended behind the pupil (the circular opening in the iris) by the zonule fibers, which, in turn, are attached to the ciliary body and underlying ciliary muscle. The shape of the lens is determined to a large extent by the lens capsule, which tends to make the lens more spherical. The lens capsule is opposed in this action by the pull of the ciliary muscle, a pull transmitted to the lens by the zonule fibers. When a distant object is viewed, the ciliary muscle relaxes and is pulled toward the back of the eye by the inherent elasticity of the choroid. Since the zonule fibers are attached to the posterior part of the ciliary body, the relaxation of the ciliary body exerts a greater pull on these fibers, which in turn causes the lens to flatten. When a near object is viewed, however, contraction of the ciliary muscle moves the attachments of the zonule fibers forward and, thus, reduces their pull on the lens. Since the lens capsule is no longer opposed in its action, the lens becomes more spherical. By varying the amount of ciliary muscle contraction, it is possible to make fine adjustments in the shape of the lens, allowing us to focus on objects at different distances.

The posterior segment of the eye contains the vitreal chamber (vitreous humor) and the retina. The retina forms the inner layer, or tunic, of the

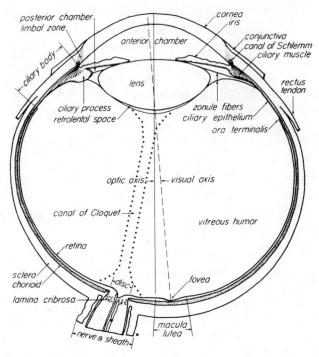

Figure 2. Line drawing of a horizontal section through the human eye. (From Walls, 1942.)

eye. It is surrounded externally by the choroid, a nutritive layer, and the sclera, a thick fibrous layer that provides both support and protection. The retina covers the internal surface of the posterior chamber, extending as far forward as the ora serrata (terminalis). Near the back of the eye it is interrupted briefly by the optic nerve fibers leaving the globe (optic disc). The retina is generally divided into the following layers, beginning at the choroid: pigment epithelium, photoreceptor layer (rod and cone outer segments), external limiting membrane, outer nuclear layer (rod and cone cell bodies), outer plexiform layer, inner nuclear layer, inner plexiform layer, ganglion cell layer, optic nerve layer, and internal limiting membrane. Since the transduction of light energy into electrical energy takes place in the photoreceptor outer segments, in most instances light must pass through eight of the 10 layers of the retina before a neural response is elicited. However, in the fovea, where one finds the greatest packing density of photoreceptors, the layers internal to the outer plexiform layer are displaced laterally. This displacement of many of the retinal layers allows light to reach the foveal cones with less distortion.

The neural elements involved in the retinal processing of visual information are the photoreceptors, the horizontal cells, the bipolar cells, the interplexiform cells, the amacrine cells, and the ganglion cells (see Figure 3). When light strikes the retina, a conformational change takes place in the visual pigment contained in the outer segments of the photoreceptors, the rods and cones (Hubbell & Bownds, 1979). In turn, this change results in the hyperpolarization of the photoreceptors. The wavelength of light absorbed depends on the type of visual pigment contained in the photoreceptor. The visual pigments of human rod photoreceptors, which are important in scotopic vision, are contained in the outer segment disc membranes and have maximum absorption of light at 500 μm (Bowmaker & Dartnall, 1980). The visual pigment of cones is contained in the outer segment folds of the cell membrane. Three types of cones can be found in humans. They have light absorption peaks at 435 μm (blue-sensitive), 540 μm (green-sensitive), and 560 μm (red-sensitive) (Bowmaker & Dartnall, 1980).

The first synaptic interaction in the retina occurs in the outer plexiform layer between the terminals of cones (cone pedicles) and rods (rod spherules) (Reale, Luciano, & Spitznas, 1978). This interaction allows the rod and cone signals to be mixed shortly after transduction has occurred. Besides making electrical connections with each other, rods and cones also contact horizontal cells and bipolar cells. The rod bipolar cell (RB) makes connections with several rods. All such connections occur at invaginated "ribbon synapses." Cone bipolar cells (CB), however, can make contact with cones at either invaginated ribbon synapses or at superficial synapses. Some cone bipolars contact many cones while others, the midget bipolars, contact only one cone each. In all, one type of rod bipolar and six types of cone bipolar cells have been identified in the primate retina (Boycott & Dowling, 1969; Kolb, 1970; Mariani, 1981, 1983).

While the photoreceptor–bipolar synapse represents a direct pathway through the retina, the photoreceptor–horizontal cell contact allows for lateral interaction in the retina. Of the two types of horizontal cells seen in the primate retina, the HI horizontal cell is contacted by cones and sends axon terminals to rods (Kolb, 1970), while the HII horizontal cell is contacted by cones and sends axon terminals to other cones (Kolb, Mariani, & Gallego, 1980). The outer plexiform layer also contains interplexiform cells which have processes in both the inner and outer plexiform layers and, thus, create a feedback loop between these two layers (Boycott, Dowling, Fisher, Kolb, & Laties, 1975).

Of the seven types of bipolar cells seen in the primate retina, some make synaptic contact in the inner sublamina (sublamina A) of the inner

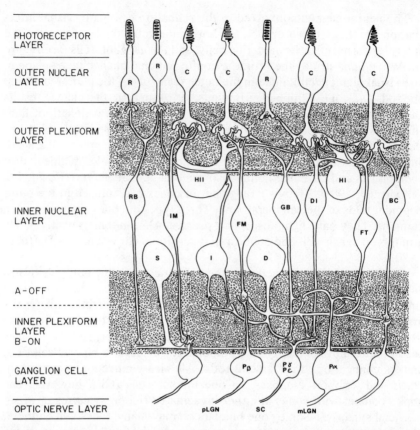

PHOTORECEPTOR LAYER

OUTER NUCLEAR LAYER

OUTER PLEXIFORM LAYER

INNER NUCLEAR LAYER

A-OFF

INNER PLEXIFORM LAYER
B-ON

GANGLION CELL LAYER

OPTIC NERVE LAYER

Figure 3. Schematic representation of the neural elements and interconnections in the primate retina. The photoreceptor layer contains the outer segments of the rods (R) and cones (C). The outer nuclear layer contains the cell bodies of the rods and cones. Interconnections between photoreceptors, photoreceptors and horizontal cells, and photoreceptors and bipolar cells are made in the outer plexiform layer. The dendrites of HI horizontal cells receive input from cones and send input to rods. Both the dendrites and axons of HII horizontal cells contact only cones. There are at least seven types of bipolar cells in the primate retina: rod bipolars (RB), invaginating midget bipolars (IM), flat midget bipolars (FM), giant bistratified bipolars (GB), diffuse invaginating cone bipolars (DI), flat-top bipolars (FT), and blue-cone bipolars (BC). Synaptic connections typical of each of these bipolar cell types are shown in this figure. The inner nuclear layer contains the cell bodies of horizontal cells, bipolar cells, interplexiform cells, and amacrine cells. Examples of stratified (S) and diffuse (D) amacrine cells are shown. These two amacrine cells differ with regard to the branching patterns of their processes in the inner plexiform layer, where synaptic connections are made between amacrine, bipolar, and ganglion cells. Three types of ganglion cells are shown. mLGN, Lateral geniculate nucleus magnocellular laminae; pLGN, lateral geniculate nucleus parvocellular laminae; SC, superior colliculus. (Adapted from Boycott & Dowling, 1969; Mariani, 1984.)

plexiform layer, while others synapse in the outer sublamina of the inner plexiform layer (sublamina B). While all rod bipolars end in sublamina B, cone bipolars can end in either sublamina (for review, see Mariani, 1984). The inner plexiform layer contains synaptic contacts between bipolar cells and ganglion cells, between bipolar cells and amacrine cells, between amacrine cells, and between amacrine and ganglion cells.

There are two broad classes of amacrine cells in the primate retina: diffuse and stratified amacrine cells (Boycott & Dowling, 1969; Polyak, 1941). Diffuse amacrine cells extend their processes throughout the inner plexiform layer. Stratified amacrine cells, on the other hand, send processes to distinct regions of the inner plexiform layer. Unfortunately, we still know relatively few details about the synaptic connections made in the inner plexiform layer of the primate retina.

At least three major morphological classes of ganglion cells have been found in the primate (Leventhal, Rodieck, & Dreher, 1981; Perry & Cowey, 1981, 1984; Perry, Oehler, & Cowey, 1984) and human (Boycott & Dowling, 1969; Polyak, 1941) retina. One class (type A: Leventhal et al., 1981; type Pα: Perry et al., 1984; parasol cell: Polyak, 1941; stratified diffuse cell: Boycott & Dowling, 1969) has a large cell body and a thick axon. A second class of ganglion cells (type B: Leventhal et al., 1981; type Pβ: Perry et al., 1984; midget ganglion cell: Boycott & Dowling, 1969; Polyak, 1941) have small cell bodies and small dendritic fields. A third class of ganglion cells represents a heterogenous group of cells (Pε and Pδ: Perry & Cowey, 1984; small diffuse: Polyak, 1941; and unistratified: Boycott & Dowling, 1969). These cells have small to medium-sized cell bodies with sparse dendrites and represent only 10% of all ganglion cells (Perry & Cowey, 1984).

In addition, retinal ganglion cells can be divided into a variety of classes based on their functional properties. While many ganglion cells exhibit concentrically organized (center-surround) receptive fields (e.g., Kuffler, 1953), the location of the excitatory and inhibitory regions in the receptive field can vary. Some cells increase their electrical activity when a spot of light falls on the center of their receptive field and decrease their level of activity when a spot of light falls on the surround portion of the receptive field. These ganglion cells are called on-center, off-surround cells. Other ganglion cells respond best when either the center portion of the receptive field is darkened or the surround illuminated. These cells have an off-center, on-surround receptive field organization. In the cat, ganglion cells with an off-center, on-surround receptive field organization receive input from bipolar cells that terminate in sublamina A of the inner plexiform layer; those with an on-center, off-surround receptive field receive input from bipolar cells that terminate in sublamina B of the inner plexiform layer (Nelson, Famiglietti, & Kolb, 1978). It is likely that a similar functional segregation exists in the inner plexiform layer of the primate retina (see Mariani, 1984).

Retinal ganglion cells in the monkey retina have been divided into several functional classes by de Monasterio (1978a, 1978b) and de Monasterio and Schein (1980), using the classification scheme originally devised by Wiesel and Hubel (1966) in their recordings of the monkey lateral geniculate nucleus. We will discuss only four of these classes. Type I ganglion cells have receptive fields in which the center and surround are sensitive to light of different wavelengths. Such cells are said to be color-opponent. Type II ganglion cells are also color-opponent, but lack a center-surround receptive field organization. Type III ganglion cells, also called broad-band cells, exhibit a center-surround receptive field organization in which both the center and the surround are sensitive to the same wavelength of light. Type IV ganglion cells are similar to Type III cells except that the center and surround portions of the receptive field are not sensitive to all of the same wavelengths of light. For example, a Type III ganglion cell might have a receptive field in which both the center and surround were sensitive to red and green light; the Type IV cell, on the other hand, would have a receptive field center sensitive to red and green light and a receptive field surround sensitive to only red light. Ganglion cells with concentric receptive field organization have also been found in the human retina (cells recorded in an eye removed because of a choroidal tumor) (Weinstein, Hobson, & Baker, 1971).

Retinal ganglion cells with center-surround receptive field organizations have also been classified as either X- or Y-cells (cat: Enroth-Cugell & Robson, 1966; monkey: de Monasterio, 1978a). Either cell type can exhibit on-center or off-center responses. In addition, retinal ganglion cells without center-surround organizations have been classified as W-cells. Since much less is known about W-cells, they will be discussed in less detail. The characterisitics of individual retinal ganglion cells that determine how they are functionally classified include, among others, the duration of their response to a stimulus that continuously illuminates the center of their receptive field. X-cells respond in a tonic or sustained fashion whereas Y-cells exhibit a phasic or transient response. X-cells tend to have smaller receptive field centers than Y-cells. X-cells exhibit linear summation within their receptive field center whereas Y-cells exhibit nonlinear summation. X-cells tend to have slower-conducting axons than Y-cells. X-cells usually respond to higher spatial frequencies than do Y-cells but Y-cells respond much better to lower spatial frequencies. Furthermore, with some qualifications, Y-cells respond better to high temporal frequencies than do X-cells. Type I cells in the monkey retina are believed to correspond to X-cells, type III and IV cells to Y-cells (de Monasterio, 1978a), and type II cells to W-cells (de Monasterio & Schein, 1980; also see Stone, 1983). Likewise, there is some evidence that type A ganglion cells correspond to Y-cells and type B ganglion cells to X-cells (Perry & Cowey, 1981, 1984; Perry et al., 1984). While retinal ganglion cells in humans cannot be functionally classified, an anatomical study by Stone and Johnston (1981) leaves open the very real possibility that the human retina also contains retinal ganglion cells with functional properties similar to X- and Y-cells.

B. Development

In comparison to the rest of the body, the size of the eye changes relatively little after birth. While the body as a whole increases in size about 20 times, the eye itself undergoes only a two- to threefold increase in size (volume) from birth to adulthood (Scammon & Wilmer, 1950; Wilmer & Scammon, 1950). Most of this growth takes place during the first two years of life, although some growth continues into childhood (Duke-Elder & Cook, 1963; Knighton, 1939; Larsen, 1971a-1971d). Also, not all parts of the eye undergo equal postnatal growth. While the anterior surface of the cornea increases in size by only 50%, the internal surface of the retina more than doubles, going from 590 mm^2 to 1250 mm^2 (Scammon & Wilmer, 1950). Even a twofold increase in the size of the eye can, however, have a dramatic effect upon the size of retinal images, especially if there is a substantial increase in axial length during development (See Rusoff & Dubin, 1977). In the human infant the axial length of the eye is approximately 16.5 mm (Blomdahl, 1979), whereas in the adult eye the axial length is some 24.5 mm (Larsen, 1971d); thus, there is an 8-mm increase in axial length during development, as determined by ultrasonic biometry. In addition, some recent findings have shown quite clearly that the development of the eye can be influenced by experimental manipulations of the visual environment. For example, visual deprivation resulting from either lid suture (McKanna & Casagrande, 1978, 1981; Sherman, Norton, & Casagrande, 1977; Wiesel & Raviola, 1977) or corneal opacification (Wiesel & Raviola, 1979) can result in structural changes that lead to severe myopia. These deprivation-induced structural changes include zonular dysplasia (poorly developed zonule fibers), lens hypoplasia (reduced lens size), and global hypertrophy (increase in the axial length of the eye).

Although we know a fair amount about the prenatal development of the human retina (Mann, 1964), we know less about its postnatal development. It appears that the more peripheral aspects of the human retina develop faster than the macular area (for references, see Abramov et al., 1982; Duke-Elder & Cook, 1963; Mann, 1964). Abramov et al. (1982) confirmed that the peripheral retina in the newborn infant is structurally quite mature while, at the same point in time, the central retina appears structurally immature. In an 11-month-old child, however, the foveal region was well developed, indicating, in agreement with earlier studies, that the entire retina achieves adult appearance sometime during the first year of life (Abramov et al., 1982). Myelination of the optic nerves begins first for those cells subserving the fovea and is complete for all ganglion cell axons by the beginning of the sixth postnatal month (Bembridge, 1956; Nakayama, 1967; Walton, 1978).

III. THE LATERAL GENICULATE NUCLEUS

A. Structure

The lateral geniculate nucleus is a thalamic relay station along the retino-geniculo-cortical pathway. As diagrammed in Figure 1, cells in this nucleus receive input via optic tract fibers and in turn send axons to the primary visual cortex. In most primates, including man, the lateral geniculate nucleus is located along the ventro-lateral border of the thalamus. Optic tract fibers enter the nucleus around its rostral pole and, to a lesser extent, along its rostro-lateral and dorso-lateral borders. Optic radiation fibers, that is, the axons of lateral geniculate nucleus cells, exit the nucleus along its dorsal, lateral, and caudal borders.

The lateral geniculate nucleus has been studied extensively in a variety of animals, including man. Anatomists, in particular, have long been fascinated by its distinctive pattern of lamination. The lateral geniculate nucleus is most often illustrated in textbooks as containing six quite distinct cellular laminae (layers) separated by relatively cell-free interlaminar zones. The two laminae nearest the ventral surface of the nucleus contain larger cells and are often referred to as magnocellular laminae. The remaining, more dorsal, laminae contain smaller cells and are generally referred to as parvocellular laminae. Typically, the individual laminae are identified by numbers. The two magnocellular laminae are numbered 1 and 2; the four parvocellular laminae are numbered 3–6. Based on experimental findings in nonhuman primates and upon postmortem analyses undertaken in the brains of humans that had lost one eye earlier in life (Balado & Franke, 1937; Goldby, 1957; Hickey & Guillery, 1979; Kupfer, 1962; Le Gros Clark, 1932; MacKenzie, 1934; Minkowski, 1920), we know that magnocellular lamina 1 and parvocellular laminae 4 and 6 receive input from the contralateral eye, while magnocellular lamina 2 and parvocellular laminae 3 and 5 receive input from the ipsilateral eye. Since the projections from the contralateral eye come from retinal ganglion cells located along the nasal retina and the projections from the ipsilateral eye come from retinal ganglion cells located in the temporal retina, each lateral geniculate nucleus processes information about stimuli located in the contralateral hemifield of visual space. We will return to the question of how the contralateral visual hemifield is represented in each nucleus, but first let us consider in more detail the three-dimensional structure of the human lateral geniculate nucleus.

Although the human lateral geniculate nucleus is usually illustrated as a six-layered structure, the laminar organization of the nucleus varies considerably across the rostro-caudal extent of the nucleus. Figure 4 contains several camera lucida drawings of frontal sections taken from throughout the rostro-caudal extent of the human lateral geniculate nucleus. Although the nucleus does contain six layers in more caudal regions, individual parvocellular laminae innervated by the same eye fuse in the lateral and rostral parts of the nucleus. While the laminar fusions in the lateral parts of the nucleus are quite evident in these drawings of frontal sections, the laminar fusions in the rostral parts of the nucleus are best illustrated in drawings of parasagittal sections (see Figure 5). Thus, over large parts of the nucleus the ipsilaterally innervated parvocellular laminae 3 and 5 fuse to form a single lamina 3/5 and the contralaterally innervated parvoceullar laminae 4 and 6 fuse to form a single lamina 4/6. Furthermore, in the most rostral parts of the nucleus, the contralaterally innervated parvocellular lamina 4/6 lies immediately adjacent to the contralaterally innervated magnocellular lamina 1. This region corresponds to the monocular segment of the nucleus since it contains no retinal projections from the ipsilateral eye. Thus, it is apparent that the overall laminar organization of the human lateral geniculate nucleus is more complicated than one is generally led to believe by textbook illustrations, as shown in the three-dimensional reconstructions in Figure 6.

Each visual hemifield is represented in the lateral geniculate nucleus in a very precise and orderly manner. Not only do adjacent points on one hemiretina project to adjacent points in the nucleus, but corresponding points in the nasal hemiretina of one eye and the temporal hemiretina of the other eye project to corresponding points in adjacent geniculate laminae. This projection makes sense when one remembers that any point in the central (binocular) part of the visual field is viewed by both eyes. If the point in visual space is to the left of the vertical meridian, an imaginary line that divides the visual field into left and right halves, corresponding points in the nasal hemiretina of the left eye and temporal hemiretina of the right eye will be stimulated. Ganglion cells activated in these regions

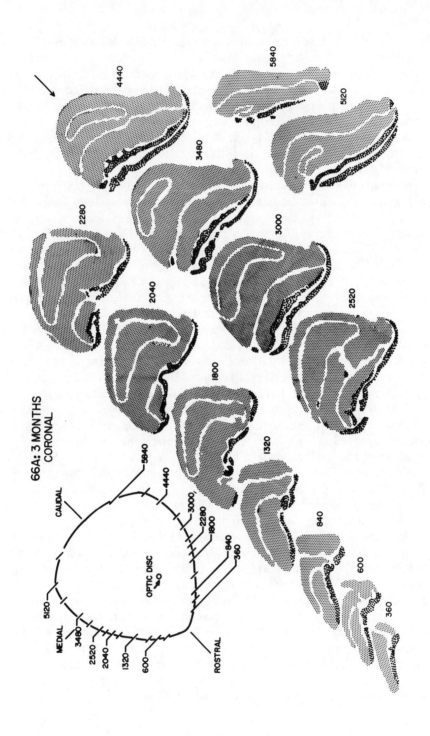

66A: 3 MONTHS
CORONAL

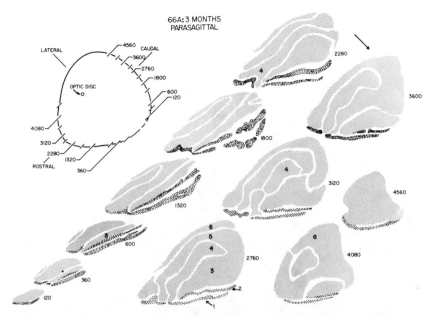

Figure 5. Camera lucida outlines of parasagittal sections through the human lateral geniculate nucleus. Conventions as for Figure 4. (From Hickey & Guillery, 1979.)

on the two retinae, in turn, activate rather discrete populations of cells in adjacent laminae of the lateral geniculate nucleus. These populations of geniculate cells form a projection column, which is centered around a "line of projection" (Bishop, Kozak, Levick, & Vakkur, 1962; Kaas, Guillery, & Allman, 1972; Malpeli & Baker, 1975; Sanderson, 1971) that passes perpendicular to the plane of the laminae. Thus, adjacent points in the visual field are represented in adjacent lines of projection through the

---

Figure 4. Camera lucida outlines of coronal sections through the human lateral geniculate nucleus. Coarse stippling represents the magnocellular layers, fine stippling, the parvocellular layers. Interlaminar zones are shown in white. The sections are arranged in rostrocaudal sequence and are numbered to show the distance, in micrometers, from the rostral tip of the nucleus. The medial parts of the sections are to the left and the lateral parts to the right.

A schematic outline of the nucleus is shown in the upper left corner of the figure. This has been drawn as it would appear when the nucleus is viewed from a dorsolateral angle, as indicated by the arrow in the upper right part of the figure. The lines that transect the schematic outline indicate the level from which each illustrated section was taken. The optic disc representation is a surface projection of the discontinuity seen in layer 6 at level 2280.

The lamination pattern seen in this brain from a 3-month-old infant does not differ significantly from patterns seen in adult brains. (From Hickey & Guillery, 1979.)

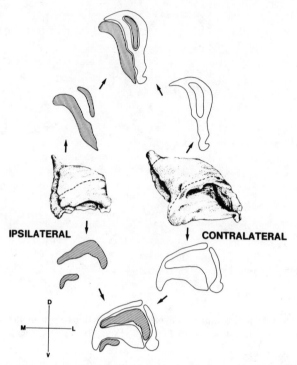

Figure 6.   Three-dimensional reconstruction of the parvocellular geniculate layers in the human. The magnocellular layers are not shown. The contralaterally innervated layers 4 and 6 are shown on the right, as they would appear if the other layers had been completely removed, and the ipsilaterally innervated layers 3 and 5 are shown on the left. In the upper and lower parts of the figure are shown two sections to illustrate how the reconstructions relate to the sections. Note that the break in layer 6 shown in the bottom figure corresponds to a hole in the reconstruction. A similar hole can be seen slightly more caudal in layer 4 of the reconstruction. These holes probably correspond to the optic disc representation. (From Hickey & Guillery, 1979.)

lateral geniculate nucleus. For points in the central (binocular) visual field, the lines of projection pass through both ipsilaterally and contralaterally innervated laminae. However, since the most peripheral parts of the visual field are viewed only by one eye (monocular), lines of projection subserving these parts of the visual field pass only through contralaterally innervated laminae. Many of these points are represented diagrammatically for the cat in Figure 7 and for the monkey in Figure 16.

The topographic projection of the visual field onto the lateral geniculate nucleus has been extensively mapped using electrophysiological techniques in both the cat (Sanderson, 1971) and the monkey (Malpeli &

Baker, 1975; Van Essen, Newsome, & Maunsell, 1984). In humans, in whom electrophysiological mapping studies are not possible, the general topography of the retinogeniculate projection can be inferred from some basic principles of geniculate organization (Kaas et al., 1972), from experiments using nonhuman primates (Malpeli & Baker, 1975), and from postmortem studies of normal and abnormal brain material (Hickey & Guillery, 1979). In general, the results of such studies show that the central visual field in humans is represented in the more caudal, six-layered part of the nucleus while the most peripheral (monocular) part of the visual field is represented at the rostral pole of the nucleus. There are two other landmarks in the human lateral geniculate nucleus that should be pointed out. In sections 2280 and 2520 in Figure 4 and sections 3120 and 4080 in Figure 5, there are breaks in laminae 4 and 6 that are oriented perpendicular to the plane of the laminae (also see Figures 8 and 9). These breaks correspond to the representation of the optic disc (blind spot) in the lateral geniculate nucleus. Since the optic disc corresponds to a point in visual space, its representation in the lateral geniculate nucleus falls along a line of projection and, as in the cat and monkey, this line of projection is oriented perpendicular to the plane of the laminae. (For a more in-depth discussion of lines of projection in the human lateral geniculate nucleus

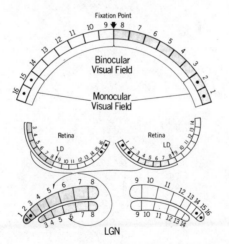

Figure 7. Schematic representation of the projection of the visual field onto a much simplified version of the retina and lateral geniculate nucleus. The contralaterally innervated layers (top) of the nucleus receive input from more of the retina and, thus, are more extensive. The most lateral part of this layer (dots) receives input only from one eye; that is, monocular segment. The lines that separate the numbered segments in the lateral geniculate nucleus roughly correspond to the lines of projection (From Kaas, Guillery, & Allman, 1972.)

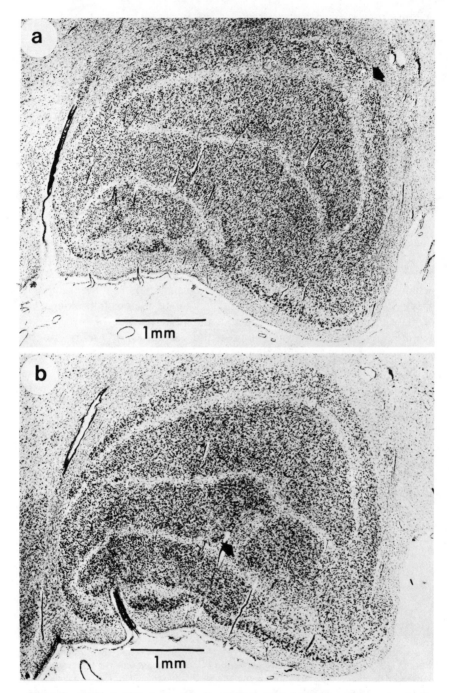

Figure 8. (a) Photomicrograph of section 2280 illustrated in Figure 4. Arrow marks the optic disc representation in layer 6. (b) Photomicrograph of section 2520 illustrated in Figure 4. Arrow marks the optic disc representation in layer 4. Cresyl violet. (From Hickey & Guillery, 1979.)

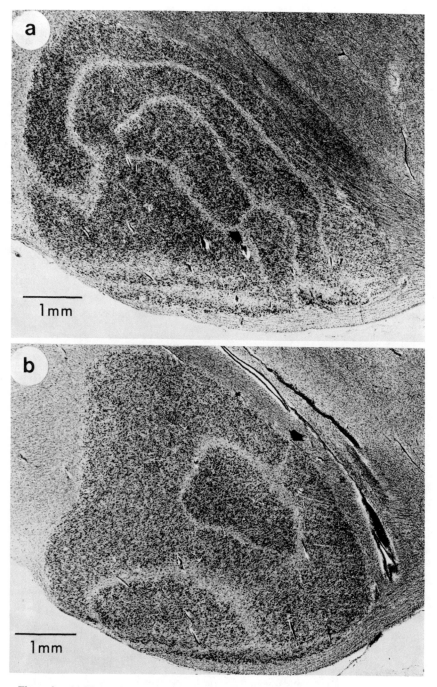

Figure 9. (a) Photomicrograph of section adjacent to section 3120 illustrated in Figure 5. Arrow marks optic disc representation in layer 4. (b) Photomicrograph of section 4080 illustrated in Figure 5. Arrow marks the optic disc representation in layer 6. Left–right orientation in both photomicrographs is reversed from Figure 5. Cresyl violet. (From Hickey & Guillery, 1979.)

see Hickey & Guillery, 1979.) Breaks corresponding to the optic disc representation are only found in contralaterally innervated laminae, since the optic disc is located in the nasal retina of each eye. Although the optic disc is located only 15° away from the fovea, its representation in the human lateral geniculate nucleus is located well inside the rostral half of the nucleus. Given that the fovea projects onto the most caudal parts of the nucleus, it appears that in the human, as in the rhesus monkey, the central 15° of the visual field are represented in over half the volume of the lateral geniculate nucleus. Although approximately 55° of each visual hemifield are viewed by one eye only, the monocular segment of the lateral geniculate nucleus contains only 7% of the volume of the nucleus (Hickey & Guillery, 1979). Thus the central portions of the retina project onto disproportionately large segments of the lateral geniculate nucleus.

Until recently little was known about the morphology of cells in the human lateral geniculate nucleus. Using Golgi-impregnated brain material, we (Hickey & Guillery, 1981) have described, in detail, the structure of neurons in both the magnocellular and parvocellular layers of the human lateral geniculate nucleus. In the magnocellular layers (Figure 10),

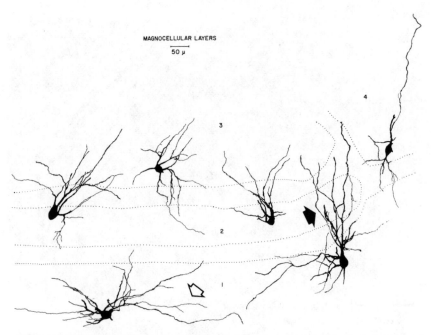

Figure 10. Camera lucida drawing of Golgi-impregnated nerve cells in the human lateral geniculate nucleus. The dotted lines represent laminar borders. The individual laminae represented are numbered according to the scheme outlined in the text.

PARVOCELLULAR LAYERS

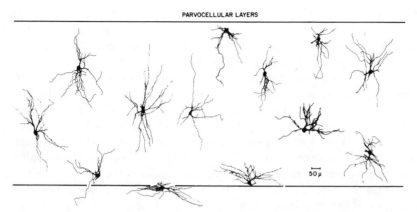

Figure 11. Camera lucida drawing of Golgi-impregnated nerve cells in the human lateral geniculate nucleus. The solid lines represent the borders of a parvocellular layer. The cells are drawn to show their dendritic orientation relative to the laminar borders. The cells and the lamina are not drawn to the same scale. Many of the vertically oriented dendritic trees would extend all the way across the lamina.

most cells are characterized by large cell bodies and relatively straight dendrites oriented either in the plane of the lamina (open arrow in Figure 10) or perpendicular to the plane of the lamina (solid arrow in Figure 10). Dendrites oriented in the plane of the lamina are usually confined to one lamina whereas dendrites oriented perpendicular to the plane of the lamina cross laminar borders freely. Such laminar crossings can occur between adjacent magnocellular laminae or between magnocellular and parvocellular laminae innervated by either the same or opposite eyes. Although a few parvocellular layer 3 and layer 4 cells extend their dendrites into adjacent magnocellular laminae (Figure 10), most parvocellular laminae cells confine their dendrites to their home lamina. Examples of some of the various types of parvocellular layer cells encountered in the human lateral geniculate nucleus are shown in Figure 11. Typically, parvocellular layer cells have smaller perikarya and more curved dendrites, which are oriented more or less perpendicular to the laminar borders. In addition, the dendrites of many parvocellular layer cells exhibit quite complex appendages (spines).

Thus, while there are basic differences between the morphology of magno- and parvocellular layer cells in the human lateral geniculate nucleus, besides the obvious differences in soma size, the most striking differences center around the orientation and laminar distribution of their dendrites. Parvocellular layer cells have dendrites that are most often oriented perpendicular to the laminar borders and do not extend into adjacent laminae. Magnocellular layer cells, on the other hand, have dendrites that can be oriented either parallel or perpendicular to the laminar borders and quite frequently extend into adjacent laminae. Based on these differences in morphology and given what we presently know about the lines of projection through the human nucleus (Hickey & Guillery, 1979; Hitchcock & Hickey, 1980b), one might predict that parvocellular layer cells with their dendrites oriented along the lines of projection would receive input from a smaller part of the visual field than would magnocellular layer cells. Furthermore, since magnocellular layers cells extend their dendrites across laminar borders, these cells could receive direct input from each eye (binocular) while parvocellular layer cells, with their dendrites most often confined to one lamina, would be unlikely candidates to receive binocular input.

The morphology of cells in both the magno- and parvocellular layers of the human lateral geniculate nucleus can be compared to Golgi-impregnated cells in both the monkey (Saini & Garey, 1981; Wilson & Hendrickson, 1981) and cat lateral geniculate nucleus (Famiglietti, 1970; Guillery, 1966; Hitchcock & Hickey, 1983; LeVay & Ferster, 1977; Tello, 1904; Updyke, 1979). Golgi impregnations of cells in the monkey lateral geniculate nucleus (Wilson & Hendrickson, 1981) showed relatively few striking morphological differences between cells in the magno- and parvocellular layers except, as in the human, cell body size and orientation and laminar distribution of dendrites. In most respects the distribution and orientation of magno- and parvocellular layer cell dendrites in the monkey were quite similar to the situation just described for the human.

From a functional standpoint, work concerned with the color-coding properties of rhesus monkey geniculate cells (Nothdurft & Lee, 1982; Schiller & Malpeli, 1978; Wiesel & Hubel, 1966) indicates that the parvocellular layer cells in the human lateral geniculate nucleus are involved in color vision. The vast majority of neurons in the parvocellular laminae of the monkey lateral geniculate nucleus have center-surround receptive field organizations and are color-opponent, type I cells. In addition, there are a small number of color-opponent, type II cells and a few broad-band, type III cells found in the parvocellular laminae. In contrast, neurons in the magnocellular laminae are broad-band, type III and type IV cells and are concerned with aspects of the visual environment other than color. Furthermore, there appears to be some segregation of on-center and off-center neurons in the primate lateral geniculate nucleus. Layers 3 and 4 contain predominantly off-center neurons whereas layers 5 and 6 contain primarily on-center neurons (see, for example, Schiller & Malpeli, 1978). Finally, the X- and Y-cell categories first used to describe retinal ganglion cells with different functional properties can also be used to describe the response properties of cells in the lateral geniculate nucleus. Several studies have shown that magnocellular layer cells in the primate lateral geniculate nucleus exhibit functional properties that are comparable to Y-cells and parvocellular layer cells have response properties that are like X-cells (Dreher, Fukada, & Rodieck, 1976; Rodieck & Dreher, 1979; Schiller & Malpeli, 1978; Sherman, Wilson, Kaas, & Webb, 1976; however, also see Blakemore & Vital-Durand, 1981; Kaplan & Shapley, 1982; Marrocco, McClurkin, & Young, 1982). This information, coupled with the anatomical studies of the human and monkey lateral geniculate nucleus described above, suggests that, in the human, parvocellular layer cells may well exhibit X-like functional properties and magnocellular layer cells Y-like functional properties. In addition, the translaminar distribution of monkey magnocellular layer cell dendrites may be related to Rodieck and Dreher's (1979) finding of binocular interactions for monkey Y-like (magnocellular) geniculate cells but not for X-like (parvocellular) geniculate cells.

B. Development

During prenatal development, the human lateral geniculate nucleus first appears as a distinct structure along the dorso-lateral wall of the thalamus around the 10th week of gestation (Dekaban, 1954; M. S. Gilbert, 1935; Okamura, 1957), although some descriptions place its appearance as early as the seventh embryonic week (Cooper, 1945). As a result of the enlargement of the pulvinar, the lateral geniculate nucleus is displaced down the lateral and caudal wall of the thalamus until it comes to lie along the ventro-lateral surface of the diencephalon (Hitchcock & Hickey, 1980b; Preobrazenskaya, 1965; Rakic, 1974, 1977a). During this displacement, the nucleus also undergoes a rotation along its rostro-caudal axis with more caudal parts of the nucleus being rotated more (see Figures 12 and 13) (Hitchcock & Hickey, 1980b; Rakic 1977a). The prenatal displacement and rotation of the human lateral geniculate nucleus is quite similar to that previously described for the rhesus monkey (Rakic, 1977a). As the human nucleus nears its final position along the ventro-lateral edge of the thalamus, the formation of cellular laminae begins around the 22nd week of gestation and is complete by the 25th week (Dekaban, 1954; Hitchcock & Hickey, 1980b). The formation of the optic disc representation in laminae 4 and 6 takes place during this same time period. During the prenatal development of the rhesus monkey lateral geniculate nucleus, lamination of the nucleus occurs as the input from the two eyes, that is, the distribution of retinogeniculate axon terminals, becomes segregated (Rakic, 1977b). It is likely that a similar situation holds for the human. At the time

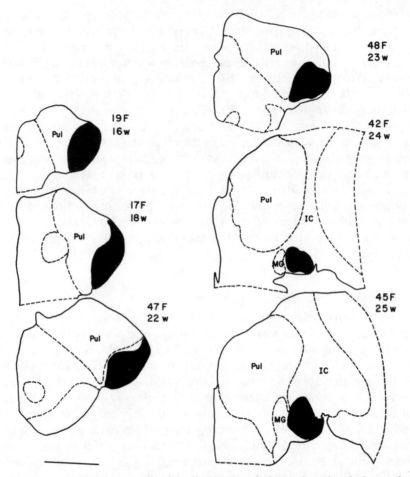

Figure 12. Schematic summary of the displacement the human lateral geniculate nucleus (shown in black) undergoes during prenatal development. The enlargement of the pulvinar (Pul) displaces the lateral geniculate nucleus laterally when viewed in coronal sections. MG, medial geniculate; IC, internal capsule. Medial is to the left, dorsal is at the top of the figure. Scale equals 4 mm. (From Hitchcock & Hickey, 1980b.)

lamination is occurring, most lateral geniculate nucleus cells are still quite immature. In fact, until the 30th week of gestation, most cells exhibit relatively little cytoplasm. However, during the last 10 weeks of gestation the growth of the cell body is quite rapid.

The lateral geniculate nucleus in the newborn infant exhibits many of the characteristics of the adult nucleus (Hickey & Guillery, 1979). The nucleus is well laminated with clearly defined interlaminar zones and the

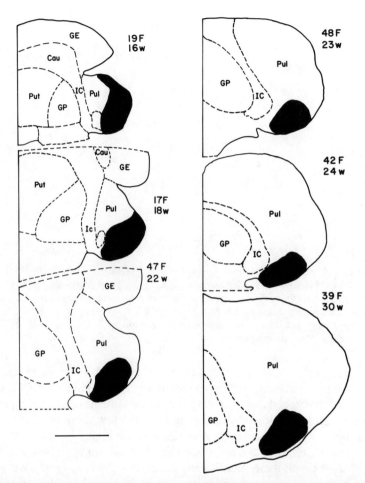

Figure 13. Schematic summary of the displacement the human lateral geniculate nucleus (shown in black) undergoes during prenatal development. The enlargement of the pulvinar (Pul) displaces the lateral geniculate nucleus caudally when viewed in parasagittal sections. GE, ganglionic eminence; Cau, caudate nucleus; IC, internal capsule; GP, globus pallidus. Anterior is to the left, dorsal is at the top of the figure. Scale equals 4 mm. (From Hitchcock and Hickey, 1980b.)

optic disc representation is well defined. The newborn human nucleus does differ from that in the adult, however, with the most obvious difference being the size of the geniculate cell bodies. Figure 14 compares the cross-sectional areas of cell bodies in newborn and adult human lateral geniculate nuclei. As can be seen, the cell bodies in the infant geniculate are considerably smaller than those in the adult. The time required for

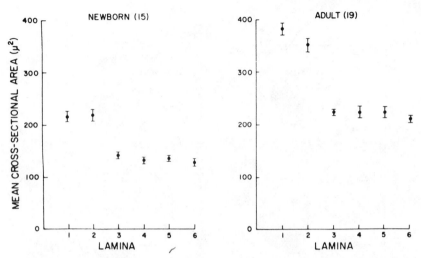

Figure 14. Average cross-sectional areas (± S.E.) of lateral geniculate nucleus cells in 15 newborn humans (left) and 19 older humans (right). Each point represents the average of either 15 or 19 means for each of the laminae. Since all geniculate cells have completed their growth by the end of the second postnatal year, the graph on the right presents data from humans that ranged in age from two to 40 years. The graph on the left represents data from humans ranging in age from newborn to one month postnatal. (From Hickey, 1978.)

human lateral geniculate nucleus cell bodies to reach adult size varies for cells in the parvocellular and magnocellular laminae (Hickey, 1977). Cells in both the parvocellular and magnocellular laminae undergo rapid increases in cross-sectional area during the first few months of life, with cells in the parvocellular layers approaching adult size by the end of the first 6 months. Cells in the magnocellular laminae do not reach a similar point in their development until near the end of the first year. Two years may be required before all geniculate cell body growth is complete in the human. In terms of dendritic morphology, however, there is some evidence that both parvocellular and magnocellular neurons in the human lateral geniculate nucleus are adultlike by the end of the first nine postnatal months (de Courten & Garey, 1982; Garey & de Courten, 1983).

It is interesting to compare normal geniculate cell growth in humans to the time course of geniculate cell growth in normal and visually deprived kittens (Guillery & Stelzner, 1970; Hickey, 1980; Hickey, Spear, & Kratz, 1977; Kalil, 1978, 1980; Wiesel & Hubel, 1963) (see Figure 15). The findings in the cat suggest that the time course of geniculate cell growth may be a reasonable predictor of the onset of the critical period. In cats, the end of the period of most rapid geniculate cell growth corresponds in time to both the beginning of cell shrinkage in the deprived layers of the lateral geniculate and the onset of the physiologically (Hubel & Wiesel, 1970) and behaviorally (Dews & Wiesel, 1970) defined critical period. If we extend these findings to the human, we see that the period of most rapid geniculate cell growth ends at round six months for cells in the parvocellular laminae and around 12 months for magnocellular laminae cells. If the relationship between geniculate cell growth and the onset of the critical period described for the cat also holds for humans, then the critical period in the development of the human visual system could begin within the first postnatal year of life. For a more in-depth discussion of this relationship see Hickey (1981).

IV. THE VISUAL CORTEX

A. Structure

Relay cells in the primate lateral geniculate nucleus send their axons, via the optic radiations, to the primary visual cortex (area 17) (see Figure 1). Since the geniculocortical fibers from each nucleus remain on the same side of the brain, the contralateral half of the visual field is represented in

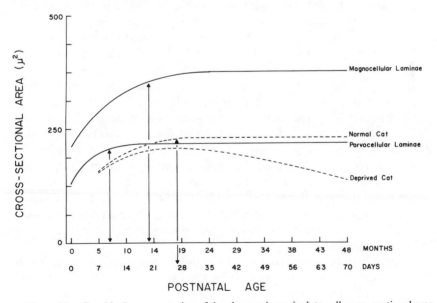

Figure 15. Graphical representation of the changes in geniculate cell cross-sectional area during normal development in humans (solid lines) and normal and visually deprived development in cats (broken lines). The vertical lines ending in arrows show the approximate point in development when the most rapid phase of geniculate cell growth is over. The postnatal ages are shown in months for humans and in days for cats. (From Hickey, 1981.)

each cortical hemisphere. As was true for the retinogeniculate projection, the geniculocortical projection is topographically organized, with cells in the more caudal parts of the lateral geniculate nucleus sending their axons to the more caudal parts of area 17. Thus the central parts of the visual field are represented near the caudal pole of the occipital lobe while the monocular crescent of the visual field is represented rostrally, quite close to the splenium of the corpus collosum. In humans most of area 17 is hidden from view in the calcarine sulcus, along the medial wall of each hemisphere. In some individuals the most caudal parts of area 17 extend around the occipital pole and onto the lateral surface of the brain. The parts of area 17 subserving the lower visual field extend beyond the edge of the calcarine sulcus and onto the cuneus gyrus above. In a similar manner, the parts of area 17 subserving the upper visual field extend onto the lingual gyrus below.

Within area 17, cortical neurons can be divided into two broad classes based on their structural characteristics: pyramidal cells and stellate cells (for example, see Lund, Henry, MacQueen, & Harvey, 1979, and Lund, Lund, Hendrickson, Bunt & Fuchs, 1975, for studies in cat and monkey; Conel, 1939, 1941, 1947, for studies in the human). Pyramidal cells have triangular cell bodies, a single apical dendrite, and several basal dendrites. The dendrites of pyramidal cells often have a large number of spines. Stellate cells generally have a more rounded cell body and dendrites that extend in all directions from the cell body. There are two main types of stellate cells in the visual cortex: smooth stellates and spiny stellates. The dendrites of smooth stellates are either spine-free or exhibit only a very few dendritic spines. Spiny stellates, however, have a large number of dendritic spines and are unique to the primary visual cortex. There are also other specialized cell types found in the primary visual cortex, including double bouquet cells and basket cells. The double bouquet cells were first described in the human brain by Cajal in 1911 (see Bro & Haycock, 1977, for English translation). Their dendritic arborization resembles a bouquet lying above and below the cell body and their axon forms a narrow column that extends across the cortical layers. The basket cell has an axon that surrounds the cell bodies of pyramidal cells in a basketlike fashion.

If the human primary visual cortex is cut perpendicular to its pial surface, six fairly distinct layers can be seen (E. Braak, 1982; H. Braak, 1976; Schkol'nik-Yarros, 1971). Layer I lies immediately below the surface of the brain. It contains few cell bodies but many dendritic and axonal processes. In monkey, this layer receives input from the pulvinar (Ogren & Hendrickson, 1979; Rezak & Benevento, 1979). Layers II and III contain many small-to-medium–sized pyramidal cells and smooth stellate cells. Layer IV, the most obvious of the six layers, contains many small spiny stellate cells as well as a number of quite large stellate cells. Layer IV also contains a thick band of myelinated axons known as the band or line of Gennari. The line of Gennari can be seen quite clearly in freshly cut brain and is responsible for this area often being referred to as the striate cortex. In monkeys the geniculocortical axons synapse, for the most part, in a subdivision of layer IV called layer IVC. Within this narrow cellular band, the inputs from the parvocellular and magnocellular laminae are segregated (Hubel & Wiesel, 1972; Hubel, Wiesel, & LeVay, 1977). Parvocellular layer geniculate cells project to the lower half of layer IVC (IVCβ) while magnocellular layer cells send their axons to the upper half of layer IVC (IVCα) (see Figure 16). In addition, layer IVA also

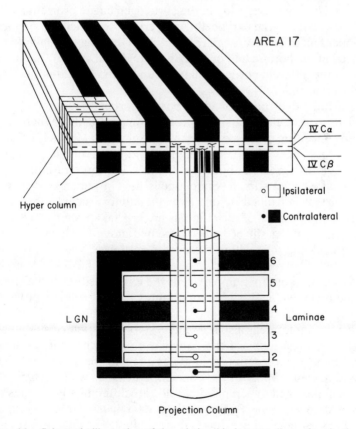

Figure 16. Schematic illustration of the relationship between lines of projection in the lateral geniculate nucleus and ocular dominance and orientation columns in the primary visual cortex. (Modified from Hubel & Wiesel, 1972.)

receives input from parvocellular layer geniculate neurons. Layer V contains small stellate cells and extremely large pyramidal cells called Meynert cells. Layer VI contains medium-sized pyramidal cells and smooth stellate cells and receives some input from both magno- and parvocellular layer geniculate neurons.

The axons of many of the pyramidal cells in layers II, III, V, and VI leave the primary visual cortex, destined for other cortical and subcortical areas. Cells in layers II and III send their axons to other cortical areas, whereas the cells in layers V and VI project to subcortical regions. In both cats (C. D. Gilbert & Kelly, 1975) and monkeys (Lund et al., 1975), layer V cells project to the superior colliculus via the corticotectal fibers and layer VI cells project to the lateral geniculate nucleus via the corticogeniculate fibers. As was the case for the geniculocortical projection in monkeys, there is some segregation in the corticogeniculate projection. Cortical cells projecting to the parvocellular layers of the geniculate are located in the upper half of layer VI; cells projecting to the magnocellular laminae are located in the bottom half of layer VI (Lund et al., 1975). A simplified drawing of the different cortical cell types and their efferent projections is shown in Figure 17.

From a functional point of view, visual cortical neurons have been grouped into four classes: simple cells, complex cells, hypercomplex cells, and concentric cells (see Hubel & Wiesel, 1962; Michael, 1978). The functional properties of simple, complex, and hypercomplex cells differ from one another in some, but not all, ways. All three respond to slit-, edge-, or bar-shaped stimuli. Simple cells have a rectangular receptive field center that is flanked by one or two inhibitory sidebands. Both the orientation and position of the stimulus are crucial for simple cells. They respond best when a slit of light is oriented along the long axis of the receptive field and falls within the center portion of the receptive field. Complex cells also respond to slits or edges. Again, the orientation of the stimulus is crucial but for complex cells the exact position of the stimulus within the receptive field is less important. Complex cell receptive fields do not show the distinct "on" and "off" regions characteristic of simple cells. Hypercomplex cells also respond best to well-oriented stimuli but in this instance, the lengths of the stimuli are also important. Concentric cells resemble the receptive field types seen in the retina and lateral geniculate nucleus. Many of the concentric cells, as well as some of the simple, complex, and hypercomplex cells, are differentially responsive to color (see Michael, 1981). So far, our understanding of structure–function relationships for cortical neurons is quite limited. The data that are available, however, suggest that this relationship may be complicated.

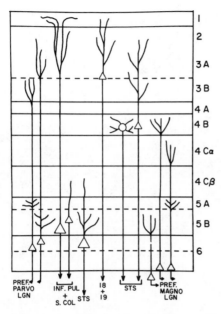

Figure 17. Schematic summary of the location of efferent cells in the rhesus monkey visual cortex (area 17). Small pyramidal cells in the upper and lower parts of layer 6 project to the parvocellular and magnocellular layers of the lateral geniculate nucleus, respectively. Pyramidal cells in layer 5 project to the inferior pulvinar and superior colliculus. Large pyramidal cells in layer 6 and small pyramidal cells and stellate cells in layer 4 project to the superior temporal sulcus (STS). Layer 3 pyramidal cells project to other visual cortical areas (18 and 19) (Adapted from Lund, Lund, Hendrickson, Bunt, & Fuchs, 1975.)

The primary visual cortex consists of a series of repeating units generally referred to as columns. Three of these columnar systems have received a great deal of attention during the last several years. They are ocular dominance columns, orientation columns, and color processing columns. We will discuss each separately. Within layer IV the geniculo-cortical axons are segregated into discrete left and right eye ocular dominance columns which extend across all six cortical layers and are oriented perpendicular to the cortical surface (Hubel & Wiesel, 1972). In each ocular dominance column, layer IV cells are controlled by one eye or the other, with cells in adjacent columns being controlled by opposite eyes. Cortical cells in the other layers are dominated by the geniculocortical input that controls the layer IV cells in that ocular dominance column. Although layer IV cells are only responsive to stimulation of one eye (monocular), most cells in the other cortical layers are influenced by both

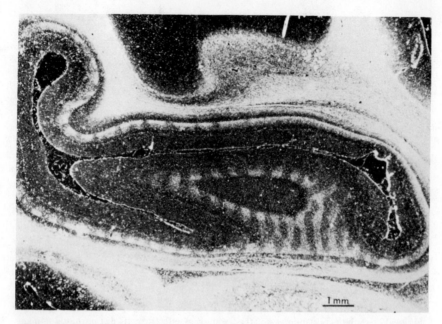

Figure 18. Darkfield photomicrograph of a parasagittal section through the calcarine cortex of a normal adult monkey that had received an intraocular injection of a radioactive proline–fucose mixture. Although short segments of ocular dominance columns can be seen at several points in the photomicrograph, they are best illustrated at the lower right where the layer IVc columns appear as parallel bands. When comparing these bands to those shown in the next figure, it must be remembered that the autoradiographic technique, as employed here, allows one to see only those ocular dominance columns innervated by one eye, in this case, the right eye. The silver staining technique illustrated in the next figure, however, allows one to see both left and right eye columns. Therefore, the spacing between adjacent ocular dominance columns will be quite different using the two different techniques. (From Hubel, Wiesel, & LeVay, 1977.)

eyes (binocular). In all cases, however, the eye that controls the layer IV cells dominates the cells in the other layers of the cortex.

In cats and monkeys, ocular dominance columns have been demonstrated using a variety of experimental techniques including electrophysiological recordings and degeneration and autoradiographic techniques (for example, see Hubel et al., 1977; Shatz, Lindström, & Wiesel, 1977) (also see Figure 18). None of these techniques are applicable to humans since they require some experimental intervention prior to the death of the animal. However, a silver staining technique was used to demonstrate ocular dominance columns in a normal rhesus monkey (LeVay, Hubel, & Wiesel, 1975). In general, this technique allowed the investigators to see an alternating pattern of wide dark bands and narrow light bands in area 17. The dark bands contained a large number of silver-stained axons while the adjacent light bands contained few such axons. By combining this staining technique with electrophysiological recordings, it was shown that the dark bands corresponded to the central regions of ocular dominance columns while the narrower light bands represented the interfaces between adjacent ocular dominance columns. Using a similar, though not identical, staining technique, we (Hitchcock & Hickey, 1980a) have demonstrated a banding pattern in area 17 of normal human visual cortex (see Figure 19) quite reminiscent of that seen in the rhesus monkey. Based on several pieces of evidence, including the facts that such bands have been seen in a number of human brains, are always confined to area 17, are fairly constant in width within any given brain, and align when viewed over serial sections, it seems quite likely that these bands are the morphological substrate of ocular dominance columns in the human. These findings have been confirmed and extended by Horton and Hedley-Whyte (1984). The demonstration of ocular dominance columns in the human is important since it allows us to extend, to humans, a basic principal of cortical organization seen in a number of subhuman animals.

A second columnar system seen in a variety of subhuman animals (Hubel & Wiesel, 1974; Hubel, Wiesel, & Stryker, 1978; Humphrey &

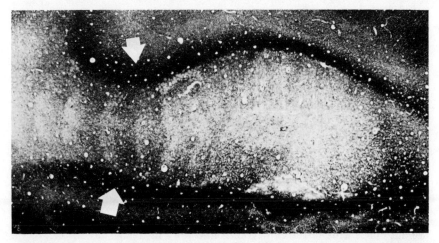

Figure 19. A low-power photomicrograph of a tangential section through a block of tissue from the posterior pole of area 17 of human cortex. A vertically oriented banding pattern, consisting of wide dark bands and narrow light bands, can best be seen in the left half of the photomicrograph. These bands intersect the line of Gennari (arrows) at almost right angles. Glees-reduced silver stain, frozen section at 25 μm. (From Hitchcock & Hickey, 1980a.)

Norton, 1980; Humphrey, Skeen, & Norton, 1980) is the orientation column (see Figure 16). As discussed earlier, while cells in the retina and lateral geniculate nucleus respond well to small spots of light directed onto their receptive fields, most cortical cells outside of layer IV are more selective in their stimulus requirements (for examples, see Dow, 1974; Dow & Gouras, 1973; Hubel & Wiesel, 1974; Schiller, Finlay, & Volman, 1976a, 1976b), responding best to lines or edges oriented at a preferred angle. Cells with similar preferred angles of stimulus orientation tend to be clustered together, forming what has become known as an orientation column. Cells in adjacent orientation columns prefer stimuli oriented at slightly different angles (see Figure 16). By combining several orientation columns and two adjacent ocular dominance columns, it is possible to analyze visual stimuli, at least in terms of all possible angles of stimulus orientation and location in the visual field. This combination of orientation columns and ocular dominance columns is called a hypercolumn, the "functional unit" of the visual cortex (Hubel & Wiesel, 1974). Stimuli emanating from a given point in visual space are analyzed by the cells in one hypercolumn, with adjacent points in visual space being analyzed in adjacent hypercolumns. The spatial relationship between orientation columns and ocular dominance columns has been simplified in Figure 16. The exact spatial relationship between the two columnar systems is more complicated and, in fact, remains to be completely worked out.

Finally, there is evidence for a columnar organization of color-coded cells in the primate visual cortex (Livingstone & Hubel, 1984; Michael, 1981). For example, Livingstone and Hubel (1984) have described a columnar system that appears to be less interested in the orientation of visual stimuli and more concerned with the color of those stimuli. This columnar system can be demonstrated using stain that is specific for the enzyme cytochrome oxidase. When area 17 of the monkey cortex is studied using this technique, darkly stained patches of tissue can be seen near the centers of each ocular dominance column. These patches are present in layers II, III, IVB, V, and VI in both monkeys and humans (Horton, 1984; Horton & Hedley-Whyte, 1984). In monkeys, Livingstone and Hubel (1984) showed that all neurons within these patches (their "blobs") were concentrically organized and lacked orientation selectivity. The majority of these neurons were color-opponent, including many double-opponent cells. This latter cell type, found only in the visual cortex, has a receptive field center that is excited by one wavelength (wavelength A) and inhibited by another (wavelength B). In turn, the receptive field surround of this cell is excited by wavelength B and inhibited by wavelength A. The spatial relationship of these patches, or "blobs," to orientation and ocular dominance columns is shown diagramatically in Figure 20.

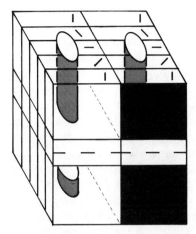

Figure 20. Schematic representation of the relationship between color-processing columns (tubular shaded regions), orientation columns, and ocular dominance columns. The segment of visual cortex illustrated corresponds to one hypercolumn as shown in Figure 16. (Adapted from Livingstone & Hubel, 1984.)

B. Development

Although we know a little about the postnatal development of the human visual cortex (Conel, 1939, 1941, 1947), research investigations in subhuman animals like the cat (LeVay, Stryker, & Shatz, 1978) and monkey (Hubel et al., 1977; Rakic, 1976, 1977b) again afford the greatest possibilities for studying those aspects of cortical development most closely related to the critical period of visual system development. During prenatal development and the first few weeks of postnatal development (Hubel et al., 1977; Rakic, 1976, 1977b), the geniculocortical projections from the two eyes overlap extensively in layer IV of the monkey visual cortex. This early overlap in the projections from the two eyes is quite similar to that seen during the prenatal development of the lateral geniculate nucleus (Rakic, 1977b), when retinogeniculate fibers from each eye project to the entire nucleus. In the last three weeks of fetal life, the geniculocortical projections begin to segregate. This partial separation of the inputs from the two eyes represents the first step in the development of ocular dominance columns. In both the rhesus monkey and the cat, ocular dominance column development is not complete at birth but rather continues during the first several weeks of postnatal life. Based on the findings of Horton and Hedley-Whyte (1984), it appears that ocular dominance columns in the human form during the first 6 months of postnatal life. Our own findings (T. L. Hickey & P. F. Hitchcock, unpublished observations) have shown well-formed columns in the cortex of a 6-

month-old human infant but rather poorly defined columns in the cortex of a 4-month-old infant.

The time course of ocular dominance column development in both cats and monkeys is quite interesting in that is seems to be related, at least in time, to the critical period of visual system development (Hubel et al., 1977). In fact, Hubel et al., (1977) first thought that the critical period of visual system development might simply reflect the time required for the ocular dominance columns to reach their final stage of development; that is, total segregation. However, it is now clear that while the formation of ocular dominance columns occurs during the most sensitive part of the critical period, this structural change is complete prior to the end of the critical period (LeVay, Wiesel, & Hubel, 1980).

Alterations in the visual environment, such as occur in lid suture experiments, disrupt the normal relationship between left and right eye ocular dominance columns since one eye is given a competitive advantage over the other (Wiesel & Hubel, 1965). The extent of the disruption depends upon the time at which the normal competitive interaction is altered. If the lids of one eye are sutured at birth, while the inputs from the two eyes still overlap to a large degree, the nondeprived eye is able to take over large areas of cortex normally controlled by the other eye (for examples, see Hubel et al., 1977; LeVay et al., 1980). This situation results in a pattern (visualized with the help of autoradiographic techniques) of alternating wide, nondeprived and narrow, deprived ocular dominance columns. If lid suturing is carried out later in development, when ocular dominance column formation is nearing completion, the relative gains by the nondeprived eye are less. After the development of ocular dominance columns is complete, lid-suturing does not alter the size of either the left or the right eye column. However, the results of other experiments suggest that a period of somewhat reduced sensitivity to environmental influences continues beyond this time. Even when changes in ocular dominance column width (as demonstrated using anatomical techniques) do not occur, some deprivation-induced changes in cortical cell physiology are still evident (Hubel et al., 1977; LeVay et al., 1980). During this period of reduced sensitivity, the visual system is still influenced by changes in its visual environment but not to the extent seen during the early part of the critical period.

V. EPILOGUE

A. Other Visual System Structures

In this brief look at the structure and development of the visual system, we have focused our attention on the retino-geniculo-cortical pathway.

There are, of course, many other regions in the brain involved in processing visual information. These regions include other parts of the cortex, other thalamic relay stations, and many brainstem structures. Even an extremely brief description of each of these other regions would require more space than is available for this chapter. Since one of our primary concerns has been the development of the visual system, it is quite reasonable to limit our discusison to the structures along the retino-geniculo-cortical pathway. At the present time, we know very little about the development of other visual system structures.

B. Directions for Future Research

The visual system remains a large and very complicated puzzle for which many individual pieces are yet to be identified and put into place. There are, however, a variety of experimental approaches that hold great promise for providing insights into the complex workings of the visual system. For example, much new information about nerve cell interactions and neurotransmitters has been gained through the use of tissue culture and brain slice preparations. Already antibodies to various chemical transmitters have identified neurotransmitters used by cells along the human visual pathway. New molecular biological techniques offer the potential of identifying mRNA that is unique to the visual system and, ultimately, will make it possible to identify the products of individual genes involved in visual system function. On a more global level, PET (positron emission tomography) scans already make it possible to view the functioning human visual system and provide valuable information about the sequence of information processing that takes place along the visual pathway. While much can be learned through judicious use of human postmortem material, experiments carried out in laboratory animals remain essential if we are to understand the human visual system. Along these lines, there are obvious needs for more animal studies concerned with the development of visual system structures both on and off the retino-geniculo-cortical pathway. We will not have a complete understanding of the visual system until we know more about these other structures, including the time course of their development. It is quite possible, if not likely, that there are several critical periods in the development of the visual system, each one related to a different aspect of visual behavior.

ACKNOWLEDGMENTS

My (T.L.H.) experiments were supported by N.I.H. Grants EY01338 and EY02159.

REFERENCES

Abramov, I., Gordon, J., Hendrickson, A., Hainline, L., Dobson, V., & LaBossiere, E. (1982). The retina of the newborn human infant. *Science, 217,* 265–267.

Balado, M., & Franke, E. (1937). Das Corpus Geniculatum Externum. *Monographs in Neurology and Psychiatry,* No. 62.

Bembridge, B. A. (1956). The problem of myelination in the central nervous system with special reference to the optic nerve. *Transactions of Ophthamological Societies of the United Kingdom, 76,* 311–322.

Bishop, P. O., Kozak, W., Levick, W. R., & Vakkur, G. J. (1962). The determination of the projection of the visual field on to the lateral geniculate nucleus in the cat. *Journal of Physiology (London), 163,* 503–539.

Blakemore, C. B., & Vital-Durand, F. (1981). Distribution of X- and Y-cells in the monkey's lateral geniculate nucleus. *Journal of Physiology (London), 320,* 17P–18P.

Blomdahl, S. (1979). Ultrasonic measurement of the eye in the newborn infant. *Acta Ophthalmologica, 57,* 1048–1056.

Bowmaker, J. K., & Dartnall, H. J. A. (1980). Visual pigments of rods and cones in a human retina. *Journal of Physiology (London), 298,* 501–511.

Boycott, B. B., & Dowling, J. E. (1969). Organization of the primate retina: Light microscopy. *Philosophical Transactions of the Royal Society of London, Series B, 255,* 109–184.

Boycott, B. B., Dowling, J. E., Fisher, S. K., Kolb, H., & Laties, A. M. (1975). Interplexiform cells of the mammalian retina and their comparison with catecholamine-containing retinal cells. *Proceedings of the Royal Society of London, Series B, 191,* 353–368.

Braak, E. (1982). On the structure of the human striate area. *Advances in Anatomy, Embryology and Cell Biology, 77,* 1–86.

Braak, H. (1976). On the striate area of the human isocortex. A Golgi and pigmentarchitectonic study. *Journal of Comparitive Neurology, 166,* 341–364.

Bro, S., & Haycock, J. W. (1977). Special translation: Visual cortex translated from *L'écorce cérébrale suivant les régions l'écorce visuelle.* Chapter 25 in *Histologie du système nerveux de l'homme et des vertébrés, 1911. Behavioral Biology, 21,* 508–528.

Brodal, A. (1969). *Neurological anatomy in relation to clinical medicine.* London & New York: Oxford University Press.

Carpenter, M. B. (1983). *Human neuroanatomy.* Baltimore, MD: Williams & Wilkins.

Conel, J. L. (1939). *The Postnatal Development of the Human Cerebral Cortex: Vol. 1. The cortex of the newborn.* Cambridge, MA: Harvard University Press.

Conel, J. L. (1941). *The Postnatal Development of the Human Cerebral Cortex: Vol. 2. The cortex of the one-month infant.* Cambridge, MA: Harvard University Press.

Conel, J. L. (1947). *The Postnatal Development of the Human Cerebral Cortex: Vol. 3. The cortex of the three-month infant.* Cambridge, MA: Harvard University Press.

Cooper, E. R. A. (1945). The development of the human lateral geniculate body. *Brain, 68,* 222–239.

de Courten, C., & Garey, L. J. (1982). Morphology of the neurons in the human lateral geniculate nucleus and their normal development. A Golgi study. *Experimental Brain Research, 47,* 159–171.

Dekaban, A. (1954). Human thalamus: An anatomical, developmental and pathological study. II. Development of the human thalamic nuclei. *Journal of Comparative Neurology, 100,* 63–98.

Dekaban, A. (1970). *Neurology of early childhood.* Baltimore, MD: Williams & Wilkins.

de Monasterio, F. M. (1978a). Properties of concentrically organized X and Y ganglion cells of macaque retina. *Journal of Neurophysiology, 41,* 1394–1417.

de Monasterio, F. M. (1978b). Properties of ganglion cells with atypical receptive field organization in retina of macaques. *Journal of Neurophysiology, 41,* 1435–1449.

de Monasterio, F. M., & Schein, S. J. (1980). Protan-like spectral sensitivity of foveal Y ganglion cells of the retina of macaque monkeys. *Journal of Physiology (London), 299,* 385–396.

Dews, P. B., & Wiesel T. N. (1970). Consequences of monocular deprivation on visual behavior in kittens. *Journal of Physiology (London), 206,* 437–455.

Dow, B. M. (1974). Functional classes of cells and their laminar distribution in monkey visual cortex. *Journal of Neurophysiology, 37,* 927–946.

Dow, B. M., & Gouras, P. (1973). Color and spatial specificity of single units in rhesus monkey foveal striate cortex. *Journal of Neurophysiology, 36,* 79–100.

Dreher, B., Fukada, Y., & Rodieck, R. W. (1976). Identification, classification and anatomical segregation of cells with X-like and Y-like properties in the lateral geniculate nucleus of old-world primates. *Journal of Physiology (London), 258,* 433–452.

Duke-Elder, S., & Cook, C. (1963). *System of opthalmology: Vol. 3. Normal and abnormal development. Pt. 1. Embryology.* St. Louis, MO: C. V. Mosby.

Duke-Elder, S., & Wybar, K. C. (1961). *System of ophthalmology. Vol. 2. The anatomy of the visual system.* St. Louis, MO: C. V. Mosby.

Enroth-Cugell, C., & Robson, J. G. (1966). The contrast sensitivity of retinal ganglion cells of the cat. *Journal of Physiology (London), 187,* 517–552.

Famiglietti, E. V. (1970). Dendro-dendritic synapses in the lateral geniculate nucleus of the cat. *Brain Research, 20,* 181–191.

Garey, L. J., & de Courten, C. (1983). Structural development of the lateral geniculate nucleus and visual cortex in monkey and man. *Behavioral Brain Research, 10,* 3–13.

Gilbert, C. D., & Kelly, J. P. (1975). The projections of cells in different layers of the cat's visual cortex. *Journal of Comparative Neurology, 163,* 81–106.

Gilbert, M. S. (1935). The early development of the human diencephalon. *Journal of Comparative Neurology, 62,* 81–116.

Goldby, F. (1957). A note on transneuronal atrophy in the human lateral geniculate body. *Journal of Neurology, Neurosurgery and Psychiatry, 20,* 202–207.

Guillery, R. W. (1966). A study of Golgi preparations from the dorsal lateral geniculate nucleus of the adult cat. *Journal of Comparative Neurology, 128,* 21–50.

Guillery, R. W., & Stelzner, D. J. (1970). The differential effects of unilateral lid closure upon the monocular and binocular segments of the dorsal lateral geniculate nucleus in the cat. *Journal of Comparative Neurology, 139,* 413–422.

Hickey, T. L. (1977). Postnatal development of the human lateral geniculate nucleus: Relationship to a critical period for the visual system. *Science, 198,* 836–838.

Hickey, T. L. (1978). Postnatal development of the human lateral geniculate nucleus. In S. J. Cool & E. L. Smith, III (Eds.), *Frontiers in visual science* (Springer series in optical sciences). Berlin & New York: Springer-Verlag.

Hickey, T. L. (1980). Development of the dorsal lateral geniculate nucleus in normal and visually deprived cats. *Journal of Comparative Neurology, 189,* 467–481.

Hickey, T. L. (1981). The developing visual system. *Trends in Neurosciences, 4,* 41–44.

Hickey, T. L., & Guillery, R. W. (1979). Variability of laminar patterns in the human lateral geniculate nucleus. *Journal of Comparative Neurology, 183,* 221–246.

Hickey, T. L., & Guillery, R. W. (1981). A study of Golgi preparations from the human lateral geniculate nucleus. *Journal of Comparative Neurology, 200,* 545–577.

Hickey, T. L., Spear, P. D., & Kratz, E. (1977). Quantitative studies of cell size in the cat's dorsal lateral geniculate nucleus following visual deprivation. *Journal of Comparative Neurology, 172,* 265–282.

Hitchcock, P. F., & Hickey, T. L. (1980a). Ocular dominance columns: Evidence for their presence in humans. *Brain Research, 182,* 176–179.

Hitchcock, P. F., & Hickey, T. L. (1980b). Prenatal development of the human lateral geniculate nucleus. *Journal of Comparative Neurology, 194,* 395–411.

Hitchcock, P. F., & Hickey, T. L. (1983). Morphology of C-laminae neurons in the dorsal lateral geniculate nucleus of the cat: A Golgi impregnation study. *Journal of Comparative Neurology, 220,* 137–146.

Hogan, M. J., Alvarado, J. A., & Weddell, J. E. (1971). *Histology of the human eye.* Philadelphia, PA: Saunders.

Horton, J. C. (1984). Cytochrome oxidase patches: A new cytoarchitectonic feature of monkey visual cortex. *Philosophical Transactions of the Royal Society of London, Series B, 304,* 199-253.

Horton, J. C., & Hedley-Whyte, E. T. (1984). Mapping of cytochrome oxidase patches and ocular dominance columns in human visual cortex. *Philosophical Transactions of the Royal Society of London, Series B, 304,* 255–272.

Hubbel, W. L., & Bownds, M. D. (1979). Visual transduction in vertebrate photoreceptors. *Annual Review of Neuroscience, 2,* 17–34.

Hubel, D. H., & Wiesel, T. N. (1962). Receptive fields, binocular interaction and functional architecture in the cat's visual cortex. *Journal of Physiology (London), 160,* 106–154.

Hubel, D. H., & Wiesel, T. N. (1970). The period of susceptibility to the physiological effects of unilateral eye closure in kittens. *Journal of Physiology (London), 206,* 419–436.

Hubel, D. H., & Wiesel, T. N. (1972). Laminar and columnar distribution of geniculo-cortical fibers in the macaque monkey. *Journal of Comparative Neurology, 146,* 421–450.

Hubel, D. H., & Wiesel, T. N. (1974). Sequence regularity and geometry of orientation columns in the monkey striate cortex. *Journal of Comparative Neurology, 158,* 267–294.

Hubel, D. H., Wiesel, T. N., & LeVay, S. (1977). Plasticity of ocular dominance columns in monkey striate cortex. *Philosophical Transactions of the Royal Society of London, Series B, 278,* 377–409.

Hubel, D. H., Wiesel, T. N., & Stryker, M. P. (1978). Anatomical demonstration of orientation columns in macaque monkey. *Journal of Comparative Neurology, 177,* 361–380.

Humphrey, A. L., & Norton, T. T. (1980). Topographic organization of the orientation column system in the striate cortex of the tree shrew (*Tupaia glis*) I. Microelectrode recording. *Journal of Comparative Neurology, 192,* 531–547.

Humphrey, A. L., Skeen, L. C., & Norton, T. T. (1980). Topographic organization of the orientation column system in the striate cortex of tree shrew (*Tupaia glis*) II. Deoxy-glucose mapping. *Journal of Comparative Neurology, 192,* 549–566.

Kaas, J. H., Guillery, R. W., & Allman, J. M. (1972). Some principles of organization in the dorsal lateral geniculate nucleus. *Brain, Behavior and Evolution, 6,* 253–299.

Kalil, R. (1978). Development of the dorsal lateral geniculate nucleus in the cat. *Journal of Comparative Neurology, 182,* 265–292.

Kalil, R. (1980). A quantitative study of the effects of monocular enucleation and deprivation on cell growth in the dorsal lateral geniculate nucleus of the cat. *Journal of Comparative Neurology, 189,* 483–524.

Kaplan, E., & Shapley, R. M. (1982). X and Y cells in the lateral geniculate nucleus of macaque monkeys. *Journal of Physiology (London), 330,* 125–143.

Knighton, W. S. (1939). Development of normal eye in infancy and childhood. *Sightsaving Review, 9,* 3–10.

Kolb, H. (1970). Organization of the outer plexiform layer of the primate retina: Electron microscopy of Golgi-impregnated cells. *Philosophical Transactions of the Royal Society of London, Series B, 258*, 261–283.

Kolb, H., Mariani, A., & Gallego, A. (1980). A second type of horizontal cell in the monkey retina. *Journal of Comparative Neurology, 189*, 31–44.

Kuffler, S. W. (1953). Discharge patterns and functional organization of mammalian retina. *Journal of Neurophysiology, 16*, 37–68.

Kupfer, C. (1962). The projection of the macula in the lateral geniculate nucleus of man. *American Journal of Ophthalmology, 54*, 597–609.

Larsen, J. S. (1971a). The sagittal growth of the eye. I. Ultrasonic measurement of the depth of the anterior chamber from birth to puberty. *Acta Opthalmologica, 49*, 239–262.

Larsen, J. S. (1971b). The sagittal growth of the eye. II. Ultrasonic measurement of the axial diameter of the lens and the anterior segment from birth to puberty. *Acta Opthalmologica, 49*, 427–440.

Larsen, J. S. (1971c). The sagittal growth of the eye. III. Ultrasonic measurement of the posterior segment (axial length of the vitreous) from birth to puberty. *Acta Opthalmologica, 49*, 441–453.

Larsen, J. S. (1971d). The sagittal growth of the eye. IV. Ultrasonic measurement of the axial length of the eye from birth to puberty. *Acta Opthalmologica, 49*, 873–886.

Le Gros Clark, W. E. (1932). A morphological study of the lateral geniculate body. *British Journal of Ophthalmology, 16*, 264–284.

LeVay, S., & Ferster, D. (1977). Relay cell classes in the lateral geniculate nucleus of the cat and the effects of visual deprivation. *Journal of Comparative Neurology, 172*, 563–584.

LeVay, S., Hubel, D. H., & Wiesel, T. N. (1975). The pattern of ocular dominance columns in macaque visual cortex revealed by a reduced silver stain. *Journal of Comparative Neurology, 159*, 559–576.

LeVay, S., Stryker, M., & Shatz, C. J. (1978). Ocular dominance columns and their development in layer IV of the cat's visual cortex: A quantitative study. *Journal of Comparative Neurology, 179*, 223–244.

LeVay, S., Wiesel, T. N., & Hubel, D. H. (1980). The development of ocular dominance columns in normal and visually deprived monkeys. *Journal of Comparative Neurology, 191*, 1–51.

Leventhal, A. G., Rodieck, R. W., & Dreher, B. (1981). Retinal ganglion cell classes in the old-world monkey: Morphology and central projections. *Science, 213*, 1139–1142.

Livingstone, M. S., & Hubel, D. H. (1984). Anatomy and physiology of a color system in the primate visual cortex. *Journal of Neuroscience, 4*, 309–356.

Lund, J. S., Henry, G. H., MacQueen, C. L., & Harvey, A. R. (1979). Anatomical organization of the primary visual cortex (area 17) of the cat. A comparison with area 17 of the macaque monkey. *Journal of Comparative Neurology, 184*, 599–618.

Lund, J. S., Lund, R. D., Hendrickson, A. E., Bunt, A. H., & Fuchs, A. F. (1975). The origin of efferent pathways from the primary visual cortex, area 17, of the macaque monkey as shown by retrograde transport of horseradish peroxidase. *Journal of Comparative Neurology, 164*, 287–304.

MacKenzie, I. (1934). Degeneration of the lateral geniculate bodies: A contribution to the pathology of the visual pathways. *Journal of Pathology, 39*, 113–139.

Malpeli, J. G., & Baker, F. H. (1975). The representation of the visual field in the lateral geniculate nucleus of *Macaca mulatta*. *Journal of Comparative Neurology, 161*, 569–594.

Mann, I. C. (1964). *The development of the human eye*. London: British Medical Association.

Mariani, A. P. (1981). A diffuse invaginating cone bipolar cell in primate retina. *Journal of Comparative Neurology, 197*, 661–671.

Mariani, A. P. (1983). Giant bistratified bipolar cells in monkey retina. *Anatomical Record, 206*, 215–220.

Mariani, A. P. (1984). The neuronal organization of the outer plexiform layer of the primate retina. *International Review of Cytology, 86*, 285–320.

Marrocco, R. T., McClurkin, J. W., & Young, R. A. (1982). Spatial summation and conduction latency classification of cells of the lateral geniculate nucleus of macaques. *Journal of Neuroscience, 2*, 1275–1291.

McKanna, J. A., & Casagrande, V. A. (1978). Reduced lens development in lid-suture myopia. *Experimental Eye Research, 26*, 715–723.

McKanna, J. A., & Casagrande, V. A. (1981). Zonular dysplasia in myopia. In T. Sato & R. Yamaji, *Proceedings of the Second International Conference on Myopia* (pp. 21–32). Yokohama: Sato Eye Clinic.

Michael, C. R. (1978). Color vision mechanisms in monkey striate cortex: Dual opponent cells with concentric receptive fields. *Journal of Neurophysiology, 41*, 572–588.

Michael, C. R. (1981). Columnar organization of color cells in monkey's striate cortex. *Journal of Neurophysiology, 46*, 587–604.

Minkowski, M. (1920). Über den Uerlauf, die Endigung und die zentrale Repräsentation von gekrenzten und ungekrenzten Sehnervenfasern bei einigen Säugethieven und beim Menschen. *Schweizer Archiv fur Neurologie und Psychiatrie, 6*, 201–252.

Moses, R. A. (1981). *Adler's physiology of the eye. Clinical application* (7th ed.). St. Louis, MO: C. V. Mosby.

Nakayama, K. (1967). Studies on the myelinization of the human optic nerve. *Japanese Journal of Ophthalmology, 11*, 132–140.

Nelson, R., Famiglietti, E. V., Jr., & Kolb, H. (1978). Intracellular staining reveals different levels of stratification for on- and off-center ganglion cells in cat retina. *Journal of Neurophysiology, 41*, 472–483.

Nothdurft, H. C., & Lee, B. B. (1982). Responses to coloured patterns in the macaque lateral geniculate nucleus: Analysis of receptive field properties. *Experimental Brain Research, 48*, 55–65.

Ogren, M. P., & Henrickson, A. E. (1979). The structural organization of the inferior and lateral subdivisions of the *Macaca* monkey pulvinar. *Journal of Comparative Neurology, 188*, 147–178.

Okamura, N. (1957). On the development of the medial and lateral geniculate body in man. *Arbeiten aus der zweiten Abteilung des anatomischen Institutes der Universität zn Tokushima, 2*, 129–216.

Perry, V. H., & Cowey, A. (1981). The morphological correlates of X- and Y-like retinal ganglion cells in the retina of monkeys. *Experimental Brain Research, 43*, 226–228.

Perry, V. H., & Cowey, A. (1984). Retinal ganglion cells that project to the superior colliculus and pretectum in the macaque monkey. *Neuroscience, 12*, 1125–1137.

Perry, V. H., Oehler, R., & Cowey, A. (1984). Retinal ganglion cells that project to the dorsal lateral geniculate nucleus in the macaque monkey. *Neuroscience, 12*, 1101–1123.

Polyak, S. L. (1941). *The retina*. Chicago, IL: University of Chicago Press.

Polyak, S. L. (1957). *The vertebrate visual system*. Chicago, IL: University of Chicago Press.

Preobrazenskaya, N. S. (1965). Occipital area, lateral geniculate body, pulvinar and other sub-cortical structures of the visual analyzer. S. A. Sarkisov, Ed., In *Development of the child's brain*. Leningrad: Medicine. (in Russian)

Rakic, P. (1974). Embryonic development of the pulvinar - LP complex in man. In I. S. Cooper, M. Riklon, & P. Rakic, Eds., *Pulvinar - LP complex*. Springfield, IL: Charles C. Thomas.

Rakic, P. (1976). Prenatal genesis of connections subserving ocular dominance in the rhesus monkey. *Nature (London), 261*, 467–471.

Rakic, P. (1977a). Genesis of the dorsal lateral geniculate nucleus in the rhesus monkey: Site and time of origin, kinetics of proliferation, routes of migration and pattern of distribution of neurons. *Journal of Comparative Neurology, 176*, 23–52.

Rakic, P. (1977b). Prenatal development of the visual system in rhesus monkey. *Philosophical Transactions of the Royal Society of London, Series B, 278*, 245–260.

Reale, E., Luciano, L., & Spitznas, M. (1978). Communicating junctions of the human sensory retina. A freeze-fracture study. *Albrecht von Graefes Archiv fuer Klinische und Experimentelle Opthalmologie, 208*, 77–92.

Rezak, M., & Benevento, L. A. (1979). A comparison of the organization of the projections of the dorsal lateral geniculate nucleus, the inferior pulvinar and adjacent lateral pulvinar to primary visual cortex (area 17) in the macaque monkey. *Brain Research, 167*, 19–40.

Rodieck, R. W. (1973). *The vertebrate retina. Principles of structure and function*. San Francisco, CA: Freeman.

Rodieck, R. W., & Dreher, B. (1979). Visual suppression from nondominant eye in the lateral geniculate nucleus: A comparison of cat and monkey. *Experimental Brain Research, 35*, 465–477.

Rusoff, A. C., & Dubin, M. W. (1977). Development of receptive-field properties of retinal ganglion cells in kittens. *Journal of Neurophysiology, 40*, 1188–1198.

Saini, K. D., & Garey, L. J. (1981). Morphology of neurons in the lateral geniculate nucleus of the monkey. A Golgi study. *Experimental Brain Research, 42*, 235–248.

Sanderson, K. J. (1971). The projections of the visual field to the lateral geniculate and medial interlaminar nuclei in the cat. *Journal of Comparative Neurology, 143*, 101–118.

Scammon, R. E., & Wilmer, H. A. (1950). Growth of the components of the human eyeball. II. Comparison of the calculated volumes of the eyes of the newborn and of adults, and their components. *Archives of Ophthalmology, 43*, 620–637.

Schiller, P. H., Finlay, B. L., & Volman, S. F. (1976a). Quantitative studies of single-cell properties in monkey striate cortex. I. Spatiotemporal organization of receptive fields. *Journal of Neurophysiolgoy, 39*, 1288–1319.

Schiller, P. H., Finlay, B. L., & Volman, S. F. (1976b). Quantitative studies of single-cell properties in monkey striate cortex. II. Orientation specificity and ocular dominance. *Journal of Neurophysiology, 39*, 1320–1333.

Schiller, P. H., & Malpeli, J. G. (1978). Functional specificity of lateral geniculate nucleus laminae of the rhesus monkey. *Journal of Neurophysiology, 41*, 788–797.

Shatz, C. J., Lindström, S., & Wiesel, T. N. (1977). The distribution of afferents representing the right and left eyes on the cat's visual cortex. *Brain Research, 131*, 103–116.

Sherman, S. M., Norton, T. T., & Casagrande, V. A. (1977). Myopia in the lid-sutured tree shrew (*Tupaia glis*). *Brain Research, 124*, 154–157.

Sherman, S. M., & Spear, P. D. (1982). Organization of visual pathways in normal and visually deprived cats. *Physiological Reviews, 62*, 738–855.

Sherman, S. M., Wilson, J. R., Kaas, J. H., & Webb, S. V. (1976). X- and Y-cells in the dorsal lateral geniculate nucleus of the owl monkey (*Aotus trivirgatus*). *Science, 192,* 475–477.

Shkol'nik-Yarros, E. G. (1971). *Neurons and interneuronal connections of the central visual system.* New York: Plenum.

Stone, J. (1983). *Parallel processing in the visual system: The classification of retinal ganglion cells and its impact on the neurobiology of vision.* New York: Plenum.

Stone, J., & Johnston, E. (1981). The topography of primate retina: A study of the human, bushbaby, and new- and old-world monkeys. *Journal of Comparative Neurology, 196,* 205–223.

Tello, F. (1904). Diposicion microscopia y estructural del cuerpo geniculado externo. *Trabajos del Laboratorio de Investigaciones Biologicas Universidad de Madrid, 3,* 39–62.

Updyke, B. V. (1979). A Golgi study of the class V cell in the visual thalamus of the cat. *Journal of Comparative Neurology, 186,* 603–620.

Van Essen, D. C., Newsome, W. T., & Maunsell, J. H. R. (1984). The visual field representation in striate cortex of the macaque monkey: Asymmetries, anisotropies and individual variability. *Vision Research, 24,* 429–448.

Walls, G. L. (1942). *The vertebrate eye and its adaptive radiations.* Bloomfield Hills, MI: Cranbrook Press.

Walton, D. S. (1978). The visual system. In U. Stave (Ed.), *Perinatal physiology* (pp. 739–750). New York: Plenum.

Weinstein, G. W., Hobson, R. R., & Baker, F. H. (1971). Extracellular recordings from human retinal ganglion cells. *Science, 171,* 1021–1022.

Wiesel, T. N., & Hubel, D. H. (1963). Effects of visual deprivation on morphology and physiology of cells in the cat's lateral geniculate body. *Journal of Neurophysiology, 26,* 978–993.

Wiesel, T. N., & Hubel, D. H. (1965). Comparison of the effects of unilateral and bilateral eye closure on cortical unit responses in kittens. *Journal of Neurophysiology, 28,* 1029–1040.

Wiesel, T. N., & Hubel, D. H. (1966). Spatial and chromatic interactions in the lateral geniculate body of the rhesus monkey. *Journal of Neurophysiology, 29,* 1115–1156.

Wiesel, T. N., & Raviola, E. (1977). Myopia and eye enlargement after neonatal lid fusion in monkeys. *Nature (London), 266,* 66–68.

Wiesel, T. N., and Raviola, E. (1979). Increase in axial length of the macaque monkey eye after corneal opacification. *Investigative Ophthalmology and Visual Science, 18,* 1232–1236.

Wilmer, H. A., & Scammon, R. E. (1950). Growth of the components of the human eyeball. I. Diagrams, calculations, computations and reference tables. *Archives of Ophthalmology, 43,* 599–619.

Wilson, J. R., & Henrickson, A. E. (1981). Neuronal and synaptic structure of the dorsal lateral geniculate nucleus in normal and monocularly deprived *Macaca* monkeys. *Journal of Comparative Neurology, 197,* 517–539.

2

Motor Aspects of Visual Development in Infancy

RICHARD N. ASLIN
Department of Psychology
University of Rochester
Rochester, New York 14627

I. INTRODUCTION

The visual system, perhaps more than any other sensory modality, relies on several sophisticated motor mechanisms to orient the receptors and optimize the quality of information available for perceptual analysis. For over two decades, investigators of human infants have depended almost exclusively on ocular fixations and eye movements to characterize visual development. However, very little systematic research has been directed to the study of developmental aspects of oculomotor control. Two other motor systems involved in visual processing—accommodation of the lens and changes in pupil size—have also received very little empirical study in the human infant.

Studies of motor systems provide an important perspective on visual development. In adults, the control of ocular fixations, accommodation, and pupil size constrain the quality of visual information available to the retina. As a result, any inefficiency in visuomotor control may lead to a loss of visual information. In infants, the maturity of these motor systems may also affect the quality of visual information. Thus, age-related improvements attributed to sensory or perceptual systems may be based, at least in part, on improvements in motor control. It is important, therefore,

43

to identify which mechanisms—sensory, motor, or sensorimotor—are responsible for developmental improvements in visual functioning.

The purpose of this chapter is to provide a review of research and theory on motor aspects of visual development. Three motor systems related to visual perception—eye movements, accommodation, and pupillary responses—will be examined in an attempt to define both the known and potential constraints placed by these sytems on visual processing. In addition, technological developments in the recording of these motor responses will be reviewed.

II. THE ACCOMMODATIVE RESPONSE SYSTEM

A major determinant of the quality of information available to the visual system is the transformation of light through the optics of the eye to the retina. There are a number of factors that can affect the optical quality of the retinal image. The most obvious factor is the overall refractive power of the eye. Refractive power refers to the amount of bending that occurs as light travels through the surfaces and media of the eye. The adult eye typically has a refractive power of approximately 60 diopters[1] (Bennett & Francis, 1962). Thus, an object at optical infinity is brought into clear focus approximately 24 mm behind the front surface or cornea of the eyeball, a distance that corresponds to the mean axial length of the adult eyeball. If the eyeball is relatively long, the image will generally be in focus in front of the retina, and if the eyeball is relatively short, the image will generally be in focus behind the retina. Furthermore, an object located nearer than optical infinity is brought into focus farther than 24 mm behind the cornea. To compensate for these variations in retinal image position, the eyeball contains a variable lens that can alter the refractive power by approximately 10 diopters. The motor system that controls these changes in optical quality by altering the shape of the crystalline lens of the eye is called accommodation.

Accommodation is accomplished by a complex system involving the ciliary muscle, the ciliary body, and the zonule that encapsulates the lens tissue. As shown in Figure 1, relaxation of the ciliary muscle results in a posterior movement of the ciliary body, a tightening of the zonule, and a flattening of the lens that reduces its refractive power. In contrast, innervation of the ciliary muscle results in an anterior movement of the ciliary body that relaxes tension on the zonule and, in turn, allows the lens to increase in thickness and in refractive power.

[1] A diopter is the reciprocal of stimulus distance in meters. Thus, 1 diopter is equivalent to 1 m, 2 diopters to 0.5 m, etc.

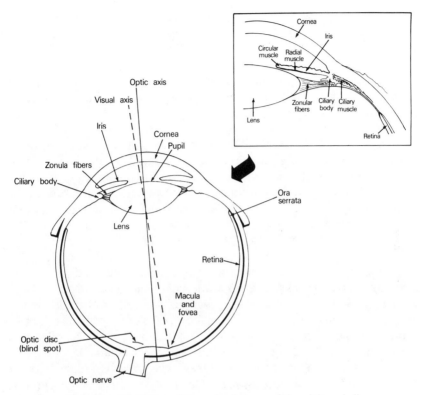

Figure 1. Illustration of the major features of the adult eyeball.

A. Spherical Refractive Errors and Accommodation

The focus of the retinal image is determined by the accuracy of accommodation to a stimulus at different viewing distances and the presence of refractive errors. A refractive error refers to the mismatch between the focal plane of the retinal image and the plane of the retinal photoreceptors. Typically, refractive errors are assessed after the administration of a cycloplegic drug that paralyzes the ciliary muscle in its most relaxed position, thereby minimizing the refractive power of the lens. Refractive errors are of two types: spherical and astigmatic. In the case of purely spherical refractive errors, the curvature of the refracting surfaces of the eye are equivalent for all stimulus orientations, and the focal plane of the retinal image is displaced a constant distance from the retina. Thus, a hyperopic (farsighted) eye refracts light too little and the retinal image is focused behind the retina, whereas a myopic (nearsighted) eye refracts light too much and the retinal image is focused in front of the retina. In the case of an astigmatic error, the refracting surfaces of the eye have different radii of curvature, and the focal plane of the retinal image is located at different distances from the retina depending on which stimulus orientations are refracted more (or less) by the eye's optics.

For purely spherical refractive errors, the focal plane of the retinal image can be brought into optimal focus on the retina if the range of accommodation can overcome the refractive error at a given viewing distance. In an emmetropic eye (no refractive error when the ciliary muscle is totally relaxed), the 10-diopter range of accommodation allows a visual stimulus located at any distance between 10 cm and infinity to be brought into optimal focus on the retina. In a hyperopic eye, in which accommodation is required to focus a visual stimulus even when it is at infinity, the 10-diopter amplitude of accommodation saturates at a more distant position. In a myopic eye, in which accommodation cannot be relaxed enough to focus distant objects, the 10-diopter amplitude of accommodation is restricted to a nearer range of stimulus distances. For astigmatic refractive errors, it is impossible for accommodation to bring all stimulus orientations into focus at the same time. Thus, either a single orientation is brought into optimal focus and all other orientations are blurred, or accommodation moves the focal plane of the retinal image to a compromise position that minimizes the total amount of blur for all stimulus orientations. The effectiveness with which the accommodative system maintains optimal focus of the retinal image, therefore, is a function of (1) sensorimotor factors (detecting image blur and programming an appropriate change in lens curvature), (2) the type and magnitude of refractive errors, and (3) the range through which the accommodative system can operate.

The empirical study of accommodation in young infants was preceded historically by numerous reports of the magnitude of refractive errors during the early postnatal period (e.g., Santonastaso, 1930; see also Banks, 1980b; Howland, 1982). If young infants were grossly hyperopic or myopic, the range of target distances within which a stimulus could be accurately focused on the retina would be reduced (assuming there is an amplitude of accommodation comparable to the 10 diopters found in young adults). The average spherical refractive error is approximately 2 diopters of hyperopia in the newborn, which increases slightly during the first few postnatal weeks and then shows a gradual decline to zero or emmetropia (see review in Banks, 1980b).

The presence of hyperopia in young infants may be the partial result of several measurement errors. The device used to measure refractive errors is called a retinoscope. This device contains a light whose beam is projected into the subject's eye while the experimenter observes the reflection of that beam from the retina as it emerges from the eye. Typically, the subject's eye is treated with a cycloplegic drug to relax accommodation. Two facts are critical for a precise measurement of refractive error under these conditions. First, the experimenter must direct the retinoscope beam in line with the subject's visual axis (a line from the fovea to the retinoscope light). If the beam enters the eye from an off-axis angle, the measurement tends to be more myopic and astigmatic in adults. Second, if the cycloplegic drug does not totally relax accommodation, the measurement also tends to be more myopic. Finally, it has been hypothesized by Glickstein and Millodot (1970) that the retinoscope beam reflects from a plane slightly discrepant from the photoreceptor layer. The plane of reflection was calculated to be in front of the photoreceptor layer, resulting in approximately a ⅓-diopter overestimate of hyperopia in adults as assessed by retinoscopy. In addition, the magnitude of this error attributed to the layer of reflection is greater in small eyes. Thus, in the newborn infant the overestimation of hyperopia may be as much as 1 diopter. Nevertheless, small amounts of hyperopia may not lead to focusing errors if the infant can accommodate sufficiently to bring the retinal image into optimal focus. For those infants with high amounts of hyperopia or myopia, however, the accommodative system may not be able to maintain optimal retinal image focus throughout a large range of viewing distances. If the accommodation system were not functional in early infancy, the retinal image would be in focus only at a single viewing distance.

B. Accommodative Accuracy in Infants

The first empirical report of accommodation in human infants was by Haynes, White, and Held (1965). They employed dynamic retinoscopy to assess changes in accommodation to a small target placed at different viewing distances. In dynamic retinoscopy no cycloplegic drugs are used since they freeze accommodation in a relaxed state. Figure 2(a) shows the results of the Haynes et al. study. The focal distance of the eye is plotted as a function of the distance of the stimulus from the infant. Thus, perfectly accurate accommodation is indicated by a 45° line with a slope of 1, whereas fixed accommodation is indicated by a flat line with zero slope. Note that infants did not begin to accommodate appropriately until the second postnatal month; that is, changes in target distance were not accompanied by changes in accommodation. In early infancy, accommodation appeared to remain fixed at a near viewing distance of approximately 20 cm. By the fourth postnatal month, however, the accuracy of accommodation was nearly adultlike.

The evidence from Haynes et al. (1965) of a fixed focal distance in

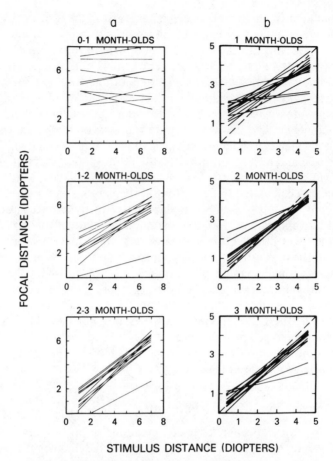

Figure 2. Accommodative response functions in 1- to 4-month-old infants as a function of stimulus distance. (a) Data from Haynes, White, and Held (1965) and (b) data from Banks (1980b). (Redrawn from Banks, (1980b).)

young infants implied that the retinal image was blurred for stimuli located at distances other than 20 cm. In adults, such evidence of retinal blur would imply the loss of visual information prior to the processing of the retinal image by neural mechanisms. However, studies of visual acuity by Fantz, Ordy, and Udelf (1962) and Salapatek, Bechtold, and Bushnell (1976) provided evidence that contradicted this implication for infants. Salapatek et al. assessed visual acuity in 1- and 2-month-olds at viewing distances near the 20-cm fixed focal distance as well as at greater viewing distances. If the infants did not accommodate, one would expect a decline in acuity as viewing distance increased. However, no differences in acuity were found in this study for either age group. Either the Haynes et al. data on accommodation had underestimated the young infants' ability to accommodate, or the effect of blurring on the retinal image was less significant in young infants than in adults. Subsequent research has indicated that both of these alternatives are partially correct.

Evidence that Haynes et al. (1965) had underestimated accommodative accuracy in young infants was provided by Banks (1980a) who replicated and extended the Haynes et al. (1965) study with the addition of an important control. Haynes et al. used a small visual stimulus as the accommodation target. At near viewing distances the stimulus was clearly above the youngest infants' acuity threshold (approximately 40 min of arc). However, as the stimulus was positioned at greater viewing distances, its retinal size decreased. Thus, beyond approximately 50 cm, the accommodative stimulus may have been below the youngest infants' acuity threshold. In the absence of patterned retinal input, accommodation in adults tends to revert to a resting position of approximately 80 cm (Owens & Leibowitz, 1980). In young infants, this resting position of accommodation may be even closer, possibly accounting for the apparent fixed focal distance of 20 cm reported by Haynes et al. Banks (1980a) employed stimuli that maintained a constant angular size at all viewing distances. As shown in Figure 2(b), the resultant accommodation functions obtained with dynamic retinoscopy were more adultlike than those reported by Haynes et al. Nevertheless, there was a clear developmental improvement in the accuracy of accommodation during the first three postnatal months. Similar findings have been reported by Braddick, Atkinson, French, and Howland (1979), using a different measurement technique (see discussion on photorefraction in Section IV,C,2).

The second factor contributing to the absence of an acuity loss for more distant stimuli in young infants involves the sensitivity of the visual system to blur. As discussed in Banks and Dannemiller (this volume), an overall characterization of the pattern processing ability of the visual system is provided by the contrast sensitivity function (CSF). The CSF is measured by presenting a pattern of light–dark bars whose luminance is sinusoidally modulated in one spatial dimension. The resultant pattern is a grating (set of light–dark bars) characterized by three parameters: spatial frequency, contrast, and orientation.[2] Spatial frequency refers to the number of bars per unit of visual angle (cycles/degree). Contrast refers to the difference in luminance between the light and dark bars (light–dark/

---

[2] Two other parameters are important to a full characterization of a sinewave stimulus: mean luminance and phase. Mean luminance refers to the average intensity of the light and dark bars across the entire extent of the grating. Phase refers to the relative position of the light and dark bars on the retina or with respect to a reference point.

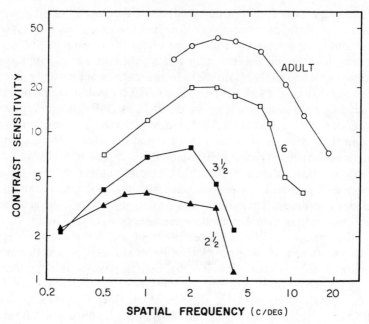

Figure 3. Contrast sensitivity functions for infants between 2½ and 6 months of age and for adults. (Reprinted from Banks, 1982.)

light+dark). Orientation refers to the direction in which the grating is positioned (e.g., vertical, horizontal, or oblique). As shown in Figure 3 for both infants and adults, the contrast required for a grating to be just detectable is lowest (i.e., contrast sensitivity is highest) when the bars in the grating are medium-sized. Contrast sensitivity is poor at both low and high spatial frequencies, that is, only gratings of high contrast are detected. Figure 3 also illustrates that (1) sensitivity to contrast is considerably poorer in 2-month-olds than in adults, (2) the peak in the CSF shifts toward higher spatial frequencies during development, and (3) the entire CSF shows a consistent developmental improvement during the first postnatal year.

The relevance of these data on the infant CSF for the detection of stimulus blur can be inferred from data on the effect of artificially induced blur on the adult CSF (Green & Campbell, 1965). Lenses whose blurring effect could not be overcome by accommodation were placed in front of subjects as they viewed gratings of different spatial frequencies. Figure 4 shows that at high spatial frequencies the blurring lenses led to a significant loss of contrast sensitivity. However, at low spatial frequencies there was little or no loss of contrast sensitivity. The range of low spatial frequencies within which a minimal effect of blurring was present in adults corresponds to the range of spatial frequencies that young infants can detect under optimal (i.e., nonblurred) conditions (see Figure 3). These findings suggest that the young infant's CSF is not significantly affected by small amounts of blur. Support for this suggestion comes from studies by Powers and Dobson (1982) and Boltz, Manny, and Katz (1983) who found that acuity in young infants is not significantly affected by small amounts of blur induced with positive lenses (up to 6 diopters in 6-week-olds and 2 diopters in 3- to 7-month-olds). Thus, there may be little functional advantage to accurate accommodation until sensitivity to higher spatial frequencies emerges in the middle of the first postnatal year. In adults, a similar reduction in the magnitude of accommodative responses occurs when blurring lenses degrade the fine details of a visual stimulus (Heath, 1956) or when the spatial frequency of the stimulus is reduced (Charman & Tucker, 1977; Owens, 1980).

The young infant's insensitivity to small amounts of blur may be the primary determinant of inaccurate accommodation prior to the third post-

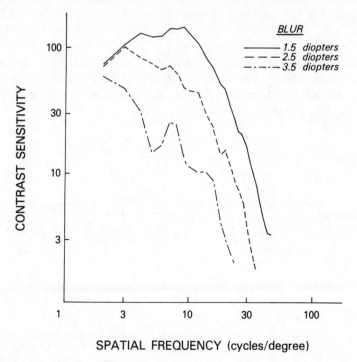

SPATIAL FREQUENCY (cycles/degree)

Figure 4.   The effect of stimulus blur on the adult contrast sensitivity function. (Redrawn from Green & Campbell, 1965.)

natal month. This possibility has been proposed by Banks (1980a) based on a model developed by Green, Powers, and Banks (1980). Green et al. (1980) provided data from a number of species that supported the notion of a larger depth of focus in small eyeballs. Depth of focus refers to the amount of change in stimulus distance under conditions of *fixed* accommodation that is required to just detect a change in stimulus blur. If young infants have a large depth of focus compared to adults, the stimulus for making an accurate accommodative response may be degraded or absent.

Depth of focus is primarily a function of two parameters: the spatial resolution (acuity) of the visual system and the size of the pupil. As discussed earlier, a visual system that cannot resolve fine details (high spatial frequencies) is insensitive to small amounts of blur. Pupil size affects the depth of focus by altering the size of the blur circle on the retina. As shown in Figure 5, a spot of light located at a distance less than optical infinity will create a focused image behind the retina (assuming emmetropia and relaxed accommodation). Thus, the spot of light creates a blur circle on the retina, and the size of the blur circle is directly proportional to the size of the pupil. If we now consider identical spots of light located at two different distances from the eye, two blur circles of differing size will be created on the retina. Depth of focus refers to the limit of resolution for detecting this size difference in the two blur circles.

Banks (1980a) has provided evidence that the accommodative inaccuracies of young infants, who have much poorer acuity than adults and a slightly smaller pupil size, are primarily accounted for by a larger depth of focus. That is, if one stimulus is placed at the current focal distance (i.e.,

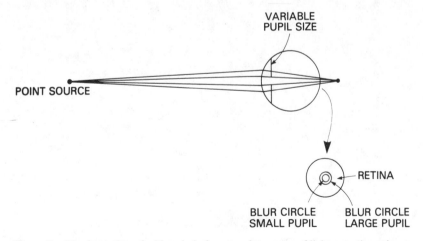

Figure 5.   The formation of a blur circle from a point source of light onto the retina as a function of pupil size.

the position of accommodation) and a second identical (i.e., of equivalent retinal size) stimulus is placed at a distance slightly nearer or farther than the current focal distance, the infant's visual system is not capable of detecting a difference between the two stimuli. As the second stimulus is moved away from the current focal distance, a position is reached at which this stimulus appears blurred compared to the first stimulus. This threshold for detecting a difference in stimulus blur defines the depth of focus for the infant's visual system. In all cases examined by Banks (1980a), the accommodative inaccuracies in 1- to 3-month-olds were within the estimated depth of focus of the infant's visual system. Thus, the control of accommodation in young infants can be accounted for largely by sensory rather than motor factors.

These findings from Banks (1980a) do not imply that motor factors are irrelevant to the control of accommodation. Several aspects of accommodation in infants, such as the latency, direction, velocity, and time course of accommodative responses, have not been studied because they require a continuous measurement of changes in accommodation. Thus, although infants may in general require less accommodation than adults to achieve optimal retinal image quality (given poor "neural" spatial resolution), the motor system controlling these changes in accommodation may be very inefficient. An example of this possible motor inefficiency was provided by Sokol, Moskowitz, and Paul (1983), who used the visual evoked potential (VEP) to assess accommodative accuracy in 14- to 16-week-olds. In adults, the latency of the VEP increases with increasing stimulus blur. Sokol et al. found that the infants' VEP latency increased when as little as 2 diopters of minus lens was placed in front of the viewing eye. Adults are able to accommodate to overcome the blurring effect of a minus lens that is considerably greater in power than 2 diopters. Based on dynamic retinoscopy and photorefraction, infants in the age range tested are also capable of accommodative responses of at least 2 diopters. In Sokol et al.'s study of lens-induced blur, however, the infants apparently did not fully engage their accommodative capacity.

The influence of motor control factors on the accuracy of accommodation in adults has received extensive study. In adults, the latency of the accommodative response is approximately 250–350 msec, the velocity is 2–10 diopters/sec, and the resultant time course is up to 2–3 sec depending on the magnitude of the response (Campbell & Westheimer, 1960; Tucker & Charman, 1979). In addition, the direction of the initial accommodative response is somewhat controversial. Some investigators have claimed that, because the size of the blur circle is the same whether the retinal image is focused in front of or behind the retina by an equivalent distance, the initial accommodative response should be in the correct direction only half the time (Stark, 1968). Other investigators have claimed that stimulus factors such as spherical and chromatic aberration, as well as contributions from the binocular vergence system (see Section IV,C), provide information that clarifies the direction of the focusing error (Fincham, 1951). Furthermore, some models of accommodation incorporate the fact that the accommodation response shows a spontaneous oscillation of small amplitude (0.2 diopters) with a peak frequency of 2 Hz (Campbell, Robson, & Westheimer, 1959). These spontaneous changes in accommodation presumably modulate the retinal contrast of the stimulus, thereby providing a cue to the appropriate direction of the larger accommodative response. Since these spontaneous fluctuations are very rapid in comparison to the latency and response time of the accommodative system, such an error detection system could be quite efficient (see reviews in Charman & Tucker, 1978; Toates, 1972). However, at present there is no empirical evidence that such an error-detecting mechanism actually guides the adult accommodation response. There are currently no data on the dynamic properties of infant accommodation.

Despite the relatively large depth of focus of the infant eye, there are circumstances under which accommodative inaccuracies can lead to significant decrements in image quality. As mentioned earlier, the ability of the accommodative system to maintain optimal retinal image focus is a function of the sensitivity to blur, the presence of refractive errors, and the amplitude of accommodation. Only one study has examined the relation between refractive errors and accommodative accuracy in young infants. Brookman (1983) employed dynamic retinoscopy to assess longitudinally the accommodative accuracy of 2- to 20-week-old infants as they viewed a high-contrast grating at 10, 12.5, 16.7, 25, and 50 cm. As in the Banks (1980a) study, Brookman controlled for the angular size of the grating at all viewing distances. In general, the results of this study were identical to Banks (1980a) in that accommodative accuracy improved with age and even 2-week-olds showed better performance than previously reported by Haynes et al. (1965). Brookman also measured refractive errors in each infant at 20 weeks of age using cycloplegia and retinoscopy. One infant, whose refractive error was highly hyperopic, showed little or no evidence of accommodation during the first 5 postnatal months. However, as shown in Figure 6, this same infant, when subsequently fitted with corrective lenses, showed a normal accommodation response. Although other infants with similar refractive errors did not exhibit this poor accommodation performance in the absence of corrective lenses, it is apparent that some infants are susceptible to disruptions in image blur that are not overcome with a low level of accommodative effort. In addition, it was clear that infants with myopia were unable to relax accommo-

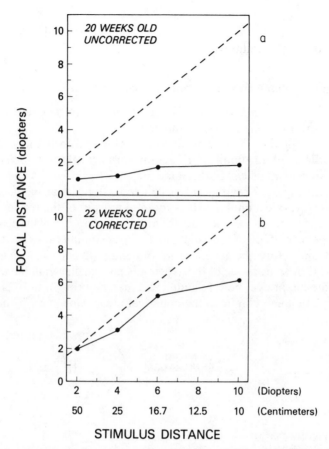

Figure 6. Accommodative response functions in an infant whose hyperopia was (a) uncorrected and (b) corrected by lenses. (Reprinted from Brookman, 1980.)

dation sufficiently to obtain clear image focus for distant objects once the depth of focus diminishes in size in the second six months after birth. Thus, infants with high levels of hyperopia or myopia may be at risk for the development of accommodative inaccuracies and the resultant loss of acuity and contrast sensitivity. Ingram, Traymar, Walker, and Wilson (1979) have provided evidence that refractive errors at 12 months of age are predictive of later ocular and oculomotor difficulties. It remains unclear, however, whether refractive errors *per se* place infants at risk for ocular anomalies or whether a restricted amplitude of accommodation is the mediating factor. For example, an infant with 5 diopters of hyperopia may fail to accommodate accurately to a stimulus at 50 cm (2 diopters) if the amplitude of accommodation is less than 7 diopters. Detailed measurements of refractive errors and accommodative amplitudes are needed to clarify these possibilities.

C. Astigmatic Refractive Errors and Accommodation

To this point we have only considered spherical refractive errors and the role of accommodation in optimizing the focus of the retinal image. Astigmatic refractive errors are also quite common in infancy. As discussed earlier, not all stimulus orientations are brought into focus by the optics of an astigmatic eye at the same distance behind the cornea. Thus, as shown in Figure 7 for the case of mixed astigmatism, if there is no spherical error, one stimulus axis is focused in front of the retina and the other axis is focused behind the retina. However, if a spherical error exceeds the magnitude of the astigmatism, both stimulus axes are focused either in front of (myopic astigmatism) or behind (hyperopic astigmatism) the retina. If the magnitude of the astigmatism is smaller than the depth of focus of the infant eye, both stimulus axes can be brought into focus and accommodation can eliminate the spherical error. However, if the astig-

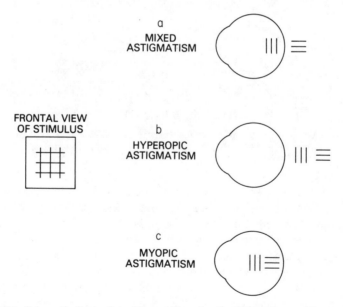

Figure 7. Schematic illustration of the position of optimal image focus with respect to the retina for a stimulus composed of horizontal and vertical lines when the eye is astigmatic. Astigmatism may occur in combination with (a) no spherical error, (b) hyperopia, or (c) myopia.

matism is larger than the depth of focus, the accommodation system can deal with the refractive error in one of two ways: (1) one stimulus axis can be selected and accommodation can bring that axis into clear focus on the retina, or (2) accommodation can position the focus of the retinal image so that the refractive error for the two stimulus axes is divided equally on either side of the retina. Both alternatives assume that the amplitude of accommodation is sufficient to alter the position of the retinal image. In the case of myopia and a distant stimulus, accommodation cannot be relaxed and the focus of the stimulus axes will be determined by the refractive error itself. In the case of high hyperopia and a near stimulus, accommodation may saturate before either stimulus axis is brought into clear focus. Finally, if the retina splits the stimulus axes, the accommodative system may oscillate between the axes to alternate clear focus of the two stimulus orientations.

Much of the data on infant astigmatism has been summarized by Banks (1980b). Across studies, the incidence of astigmatism of significant magnitude (>1 diopter) has been reported to range from 4% to 63% in newborns, from 13% to 82% in 1- to 6-month-olds, and from 17% to 51% in 6- to 12-month-olds. Within studies, the incidence of astigmatism appears to be considerably higher in the first six postnatal months and to decline throughout the first three postnatal years. For example, Mohindra, Held, Gwiazda, and Brill (1978) reported that the incidence of astigmatism rose from 9% to 57% between birth and 20 weeks of age before falling to 37% at 40 weeks of age. Howland, Atkinson, Braddick, and French (1978) and Atkinson, Braddick, and French (1980) reported that the incidence of astigmatism rose from 27% to 64% between birth and 1 month of age before falling to 34% by 9 to 12 months of age and to 5% by 2 to 3 years of age. Fulton et al. (1980) also reported that the incidence of astigmatism rose from 20% to 25% between birth and 30–40 weeks of age before falling to 16% at 1 year and 15% at 2 years of age. In summary, the incidence of astigmatism in the first postnatal year is considerably higher than the 10% or less incidence in later childhood and adulthood.

There are a number of factors involved in the measurement of astigmatic refractive errors that raise doubts about the accuracy of estimates of higher incidence of astigmatism in young infants (see Banks, 1980b). For example, retinoscopy is limited to an assessment of astigmatism in one axis at a time. Thus, if accommodation is allowed to vary freely, as in the Mohindra et al. (1978) study, the magnitude of the refractive error in orthogonal axes could change over time. This criticism does not apply to the use of retinoscopy with cycloplegic drugs, as in the Fulton et al. (1980) study, because accommodation is fixed (and presumably relaxed completely). The use of photorefraction, as in the Howland et al. (1978) study, also precludes any between-axis changes in accommodation because a single photograph simultaneously captures the magnitude of astigmatism in two axes. Both retinoscopy and photorefraction require that the subject fixate in line with the measurement device, since off-axis viewing leads to measurement errors biased toward greater amounts of astigmatism (Bennett & Francis, 1962). In retinoscopy, the decision regarding the infant's fixation must be made by the experimenter as data are being collected. In photorefraction, this decision can be made objectively from auxillary photographs taken simultaneously with a second camera. However, in both cases the judgment of fixation is based on the direction in which the center of the subject's pupil is oriented. Unfortunately, the center of the pupil (the optic axis) is not coincident with the line of sight (the visual axis). This discrepancy between the optic and visual axes (see Figure 1) is from 3 to 5° in adults and from 5 to 8° in young infants (Slater & Findlay, 1972). Thus, if data on astigmatism are collected when the infant appears to be fixating the measurement device, when in fact fixation is to the nasal side of the measurement device, the estimate of astigmatism will be inflated. Such a measurement error would predict greater refraction of the vertical stimulus axis, but only Fulton et al. (1980) have reported such an asymmetry in the first postnatal year. In addition, as the discrepancy between the optic and visual axes declines during the first postnatal year, one would predict a decline in the incidence of erroneous astigmatism. Nearly all the studies of infant astigmatism have noted a significant *increase* in the incidence of astigmatism between birth and 6 months of age before the incidence declines in the second 6 months after birth. Thus, although it is unclear whether the absolute magnitude of astigmatic refractive errors has been estimated correctly in young infants, it seems clear that the greater incidence of astigmatism in early infancy is not simply the result of measurement errors.

The relevance of astigmatic refractive errors to visual resolution involves the depth of focus of the eye and the ability of the accommodative system to bring one of the stimulus axes into clear focus on the retina. Banks (1980a) has estimated the depth of focus of the 1-month-old to be approximately ±1 diopter. Thus, if the infant were accommodated to a distance of 1 m, the depth of focus would extend from 50 cm to optical infinity. In contrast, the 3-month-old's depth of focus was estimated to be approximately ±0.4 diopters, and the resultant range of equivalent visual resolution would extend from 80 cm to 140 cm if the infant were accommodated to 1 m. If the infant were accommodated to 50 cm, the depth of focus for the 1- and 3-month-old would correspond to ranges of 33 to 100 cm and 42–63 cm, respectively. From these estimates, one would predict that any astigmatic error greater than 1 diopter would create a significant loss of visual resolution. Atkinson and French (1979) and Held (1978) have shown that infants preferentially fixate gratings oriented orthogonally to the axis of the astigmatic error. Thus, the functional result of astigmatism greater than 1 diopter is measurable in early infancy.

The loss of acuity associated with astigmatism in infancy is presumably the result of accommodative inaccuracies. For example, consider a hyperopic infant with 2 diopters of astigmatism (Figure 7b) such that the vertical stimulus axis is focused closer to the retina than the horizontal stimulus axis. If gratings of different orientations were presented at a 33-cm viewing distance, the infant would need to accommodate 3 diopters in addition to any spherical refractive error to bring the vertical stimulus axis into focus (recall that 3 diopters is 33 cm from optical infinity). Because of the 2 diopters of astigmatism, the infant would need to accommodate 5 diopters to bring the horizontal stimulus axis into focus. Thus, the infant may show either equivalent acuity for both horizontal and vertical gratings because accommodation is engaged appropriately when either stimulus orientation is presented alone, or the infant may show poorer acuity for the horizontal grating because accommodation is more accurate for the stimulus axis that requires the lesser amount of effort to attain clear focus. This example shown in Figure 7b is in contrast to an infant who has myopic astigmatism (Figure 7c), in which both stimulus axes are focused in front of the retina. If such an infant had an average of 3 diopters of myopia across all meridians and the gratings were presented at 33 cm, no accommodation would be required to "split" the two stimulus axes around the retina. In this case, because of the 2 diopters of astigmatism, only 1 diopter of accommodation is required to bring the more distant stimulus axis into clear focus and 1 diopter of relaxation of accommodation to bring the over-refracted stimulus axis into clear focus. Again, this infant may show no difference in acuity to the two grating orientations if (1) accommodation is increased or relaxed appropriately to the two gratings or (2) accommodation is simply not altered. In this latter case the infant may simply revert to the most effortless position of accommodation because it splits the difference between the two stimulus axes. In the earlier example, in which both stimulus axes were hyperopic, this was not possible.

A study by Dobson, Howland, Moss, and Banks (1983) assessed the accuracy of accommodation among astigmatic 3-months-olds as they viewed either horizontal or vertical gratings. Accommodation in the majority of the infants was near the distance of the grating. However, the vertical stimulus axis was in better focus in 14 of the 16 infants regardless of the orientation of the grating. It appeared that although 12 of these infants were capable of accommodating appropriately to bring the horizontal stimulus axis into clear focus, they preferred to exert only the minimal accommodative effort, thereby bringing the vertical stimulus axis with the lesser error into clear focus. Surprisingly, they did this for both stimulus orientations. One hypothesis considered by Dobson et al. is that the infants focused on some other aspect of the stimulus display than the grating. Another hypothesis was that the infants were biased to keep their accommodation close to the resting position (which was near the viewing distance of 55 cm). Because Dobson et al. provided no further tests of these hypotheses, these data on the accuracy of accommodation to particular grating orientations must await further detailed study.

In summary, the accommodative system plays an important part in optimizing the quality of visual information received at the retina for processing by neural mechanisms. In early infancy, accommodative responses are either absent or of minimal magnitude and, as a result, the retinal image is frequently out of focus. However, the poor spatial resolving powers of the infant visual system render these optical errors of little functional significance. That is, the blur induced by accommodative errors does not lead to a reduction in acuity or contrast sensitivity for stimuli containing low spatial frequency information. A large part of the young infant's poor accommodative accuracy appears to be the result of a degradation in the ability to detect blur. As sensitivity to higher spatial frequencies emerges in the first six postnatal months, the sensitivity to blur improves and accommodative errors are reduced.

Refractive errors also play a large part in determining the quality of the retinal image. The accommodative system cannot overcome focusing errors at all viewing distances if the infant is highly myopic or hyperopic. Although the mean spherical refractive error is 2 diopters of hyperopia at birth, those infants with spherical errors greater than 3 to 4 diopters may be incapable of accommodating appropriately if the amplitude of accommodation is less than 7 to 8 diopters. Astigmatic refractive errors greater than 1 diopter also impair visual resolution for certain stimulus orientations because all stimulus orientations cannot be brought into clear focus at the same time. Astigmatism appears to increase in the first postnatal year before its incidence declines in the second and third years. Unfortunately, until more detailed measurements are made of accommodative accuracy to different stimuli at different viewing distances, and of the relation of accommodative accuracy to refractive errors and accommodative amplitude, many of the dynamic aspects of the infant's accommodative system will remain unclear.

III. THE PUPILLARY RESPONSE SYSTEM

A. Anatomy, Optics, and Adaptation

As shown in Figure 1, the pupil of the eye is actually a variable aperture defined by the iris, a pigmented annulus of connective tissue located anterior to the lens. The pupil varies in diameter by the reciprocal action of a dilating muscle (the radial muscle) and a constricting muscle (the circular muscle), which are innervated by the sympathetic and parasympathetic branches, respectively, of the autonomic nervous system. Because of this dual innervation, the pupil varies in diameter in response to differences in luminance, emotional state, and arousal level, as well as showing cyclical fluctuations of small magnitude and variable frequency. Except in cases of neurological damage or monocular instillation of a dilating (mydriatic) drug, the two pupils respond consensually even to monocular luminance increments or decrements (see review in Lowenstein & Loewenfeld, 1969).

The two major functions of the pupil are to regulate the amount of light reaching the retina and to vary the depth of focus of the eye.[3] A description of the increase in depth of focus with decreases in pupil size has been presented earlier (see Section II,B). The intensity of light energy reaching the retina is a function of the *area* of the pupil. Thus, a doubling of the diameter of the pupil results in a fourfold increase in the intensity of the retinal image. In adults, the range of pupil diameters is approximately 2–8 mm. Thus, a pupillary dilation from 2 to 8 mm results in a 16-fold or 1.2-log unit increase in the intensity of the retinal image. Although this may seem to be a large effect, it is only a fraction of the 8–10 log unit sensitivity range of the adult visual system. Similarly, the change in depth of focus resulting from a pupillary constriction from 8 to 2 mm is only 0.3 diopters, an insignificant amount in comparison to the 10-diopter amplitude of accommodation in adults.

Given these figures on the minimal functional effect of changes in pupil size for modulating light intensity and depth of focus, one might question

---

[3] A third result of a decrease in pupil size is a reduction in chromatic and spherical aberration (see Cornsweet, 1970). Chromatic aberration refers to the fact that different wavelengths of light are refracted by different amounts as they travel through the optics of the eye. Spherical aberration refers to the fact that rays entering the eye at different distances from the optic axis are not refracted equally. Both chromatic and spherical aberration result in a spread of the image of a point source at the plane of the retina. As in the case of depth of focus and the size of the blur circle, a smaller pupil diameter reduces both chromatic and spherical aberration. However, in adults, neither type of aberration is greatly affected by the normal range of pupil sizes.

the utility of a variable pupil for the human visual system. However, Woodhouse and Campbell (1975) have provided evidence that changes in pupil size offer two significant advantages to visual processing. First, the fact that the fully dilated pupil leads to a 16-fold increase in the intensity of the retinal image means that the visual system is more sensitive under darkened conditions if the pupil is dilated rather than constricted. This advantage of a dilated pupil is diminished at higher levels of background illumination because 1.2 log units is a small difference except when the background is total darkness. At higher levels of background illumination, very large changes in sensitivity are accomplished by a process called light adaptation. That is, if there is a large increase or decrease in background illumination, the visual system changes its range of sensitivity to maximize the detection of intensity variations near the new background level. This process of adapting to a new level of background illumination is mediated primarily by neural mechanisms in the retina (see review by Bartlett, 1965). A study of light adaptation in infants (Dannemiller & Banks, 1983) suggests that the process of light adaptation does not become adultlike until 3 months after birth. The pupillary system does not seem to contribute significantly to these developmental differences in adaptation (Dannemiller & Banks, 1983).

A second functional advantage of a variable pupil is to increase the sensitivity of the visual system to small intensity differences by constricting the pupil during steady illumination. For example, if the background illumination is constant (e.g., in a normally illuminated room), a constriction of the pupil reduces the amount of light reaching the retina. This reduction in intensity by the pupil induces a slow adaptation to a lower level of background illumination. As a result, when there is a sudden decrease in background illumination, the level of adapation has been biased toward lower intensities, resulting in a 10-fold increase in sensitivity and a 4- to 10-min reduction in the time course of dark adaptation. Woodhouse and Campbell (1975) found no evidence of a complementary facilitation of sensitivity to *increases* in background illumination, suggesting that the more rapid time course of light adaptation (compared to dark adaptation) is not greatly affected by a bias toward pupillary dilation. In summary, the variable size of the pupil, at least in adults, facilitates the sensitivity of the visual system to *decreases* in background illumination.

B. Pupillary Responses in Infants

There are two aspects of the pupillary response to increments or decrements in luminance: (1) the phasic response magnitude (amount of constriction or dilation) and (2) the tonic or resting level of pupil size after the phasic response and subsequent adaptation effects have been completed. In adults, the pupillary response has a latency of approximately 300–500 msec, maximally constricts or dilates within 1 sec of stimulus onset, and may not reach a steady resting size for several minutes (in the case of large increments or decrements in luminance). There are no published reports on the dynamic characteristics of the phasic pupillary response in infants. This situation is undoubtedly the result of the great difficulty in recording and measuring the size of the infant's pupil at high sample rates. Recently, a variety of video recording techniques have been developed that enable the on-line recording of pupil size in young infants. Figure 8

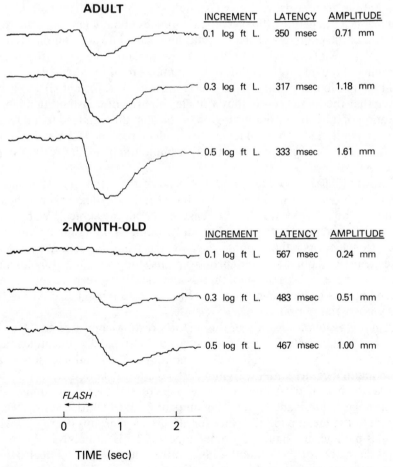

Figure 8. Pupillary responses in an infant and an adult to 500-msec increments in luminance.

illustrates phasic pupillary responses recorded in my laboratory from a 2-month-old infant and an adult following 500-msec luminance increments of 0.1, 0.3, and 0.5 log units. Note the sluggishness of the infant's responses, including the longer latencies and the smaller magnitudes, compared to the adult's responses. Based on evidence from the preferential looking technique that 2-month-olds are sensitive to 0.1-log unit increments or less (Peeples & Teller, 1975), it would appear that at least some of the development in pupillary responsiveness between 2 months and adulthood is the result of improvements in the motor system itself.

The resting level of the infant's pupil has been studied extensively (see review in Peiper, 1963). Unfortunately, pupil size in young infants is susceptible to a wide variety of stimuli that do not differ markedly in luminance (Fitzgerald, 1968). Thus, inferences about changes in the resting size of the pupil to a visual stimulus must take into account the state or arousal level of the infant as well as the meaningfulness of the visual stimulus to the infant. In addition, the stimulus used to establish a level of light adaptation (unless total darkness) must be of sufficient size to guarantee that the infant continuously fixates an area of constant luminance. Fixation of a lighter or darker region of the stimulus can lead to a fluctuation in pupil size. These fluctuations, unless recorded in detail, could mask or bias a single measure (e.g., a photograph) of the resting pupil size.

Banks (1980a) recorded the resting size of the pupil in 1-, 2-, and 3-month-olds as well as in adults as they viewed a large checkerboard pattern. Photography was used to ensure that all the subjects were fixating the same region of the stimulus, and a rating scale of infant state was used to select only those photographs taken while the infant was alert. The mean pupil diameters obtained from this study were 4.2, 4.6, 4.6, and 5.2 mm for the 1-, 2-, and 3-month-olds and the adults, respectively. Thus, there appears to be a significant increase in resting pupil size during the early postnatal period.

A more systematic study of the infant's resting pupil size to different levels of illumination was conducted by Salapatek, Bechtold, and Bergman (1977). One-month-olds, 2-month-olds, and adults viewed an even luminance field after a 10-min dark adaptation period. Every 30 sec the luminance of the stimulus field was increased by 0.5 log units. The total range of luminances was 3 log units (0.6 ftL to 60 ftL). As shown in Figure 9, the mean pupil diameter for all three age groups decreased with increasing field luminance. At luminances of 2 ftL and above, the mean pupil diameters of the 2-month-olds and the adults were identical. However, at lower luminances the adults showed larger mean pupil diameters. In contrast, the mean pupil diameters of the 1-month-olds were consist-

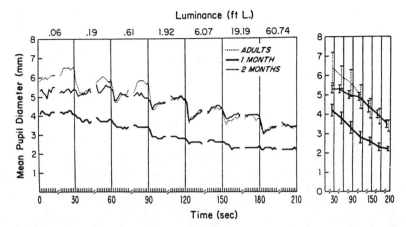

Figure 9. Mean pupil diameters in adults, 1-month-olds, and 2-month-olds as a function of increasing background luminance following dark adaptation. (Reprinted from Salapatek & Banks, 1978.)

ently smaller than those of the 2-month-olds at all luminance levels. Although this difference between the 1- and 2-month-olds may indicate a true developmental difference in pupillary responsiveness, it may also indicate a contribution of state to the smaller pupil sizes in the younger infants. As noted by Banks (1980a), the infants in the Salapatek et al. (1977) study viewed the highest luminances after a lengthy period of dark adaptation and successive light adaptation. The pupil tends to decrease in size during periods of inattention and just before the onset of sleep (Lowenstein & Loewenfeld, 1969). Thus, although there may be a developmental difference in pupil size at low luminances (<2 ftL), the apparent developmental difference at high luminances may be an artifact of state variables. As in the case of the dynamic properties of the pupillary response, the resting size of the infant's pupil at different levels of light adaptation has simply not been investigated in great detail.

In summary, the study of pupillary responses in infants could provide important information relevant to issues in visual perception. For example, Banks and Munsinger (1974) employed pupillometry to study the photopic spectral sensitivity of a 4-year-old. Pupillometry could prove useful in assessments of photopic and scotopic spectral sensitivity as well as light and dark adaptation in infants. In addition to these potential applications of pupillometry to the study of infant vision, the pupillary system may also be important to developmental differences in the regulation of retinal image intensity and the magnitude of the depth of focus of the eye. Based on current evidence, these developmental differences appear to receive only a minimal contribution from the pupillary system. However, until the dynamic characteristics of the infant's pupillary response system are studied in detail, the relative importance of pupil size to visual processing will remain uncertain.

IV. EYE MOVEMENT RESPONSE SYSTEMS

The traditional assumption among researchers of infant vision is that the fovea is the retinal region with highest spatial resolution. Only a small portion of the visual field is imaged on the foveal and parafoveal regions of the retina at any given time. Thus, even if accommodation and pupillary responsiveness in the infant were adultlike, the ability to process detailed visual information would be largely determined by the manner in which the eyes were directed to specific regions of the visual field. The control of eye movements and the interaction between eye and head movements are clearly critical aspects of the young infant's ability to access visual information. In this section, the three major types of eye movements—saccadic, pursuit, and vergence—will be reviewed. The saccadic and pursuit systems are concerned primarily with monocular aspects of oculomotor control, whereas the vergence system is concerned with binocular eye movements. For all three systems, both the characteristics of the motor responses and their implications for visual perception will be discussed.

A. The Saccadic System

1. Foveation of Peripheral Targets

Perhaps the most basic aspect of oculomotor control is the ability to move the line of sight from one region of the visual field to another. In adults, the line of sight is coincident with the fovea and visual resolution for stimuli imaged on the fovea is much better than for stimuli imaged on extrafoveal retinal regions (Riggs, 1965). In the absence of eye movements, the projection of different regions of the visual environment onto the fovea could be accomplished by head and body movements. However, the eyes can rotate within the orbits at a much higher velocity than the head can rotate on the neck. Thus, it is more efficient, at least within the central region of gaze where the eye muscles are in relative balance, to employ rapid changes in fixation via eye movements rather than head or body movements.

As shown in Figure 10, the position of the eye in each orbit is determined by a set of six extraocular muscles innervated by the oculomotor

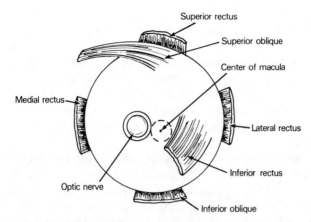

Figure 10. The six extraocular muscles and their relative positions with respect to the back of the eyeball. (Redrawn from Noback & Demarest, 1975.)

nuclei of the brainstem. The six extraocular muscles operate primarily in pairs to move the eye horizontally, vertically, or torsionally. If the fixation target is positioned at a constant distance from the subject, both eyes move conjugately; that is, the right and left eyes move in the same direction and through an equivalent angular extent. However, if the fixation target undergoes a change in distance, the eyes move nonconjugately so that the two lines of sight intersect at the distance of the target. Conjugate eye movements are either of very high velocity (saccadic) or of slow velocity (smooth pursuit). Nonconjugate or disjunctive eye movements are of slow velocity (convergence or divergence).

An important aspect of saccadic eye movements is that their neural programming is ballistic. That is, once the neural impulse has been initiated from the central nervous system to the oculomotor nuclei of the brainstem, the saccadic movement cannot be canceled or modified until the eye has come to a new position in the orbit (Westheimer, 1954). It is also important to note that the termination of a saccadic movement is not accomplished by a braking effect from the antagonist extraocular muscle (Robinson, 1964). This situation is in marked contrast to most other skeletal muscle groups which operate in tandem (1) to initiate a change in limb position by activation of the agonist muscle and relaxation of the antagonist muscle and (2) to terminate the change in limb position by activation of the antagonist muscle and relaxation of the agonist muscle. Once the final limb position has been reached both the agonist and antagonist muscles are activated to maintain a constant endstate. For saccadic eye movements, however, the agonist muscle receives a very brief neural impulse (approximately 10–40 msec in duration) that exerts much more force than is needed to hold the eyeball in its new orbital position. The antagonist muscle relaxes with the onset of this agonist innervation and remains relaxed until the eyeball decelerates to its new position in the orbit. At this point the antagonist and agonist muscles are in balance to hold the eyeball in its new orbital position. In summary, a saccade consists of an acceleration of the eyeball by a very brief neuromuscular pulse and deceleration by the friction or damping characteristics of the eyeball within the orbital tissues.

Despite the seemingly formidable neural programming factors involved in saccadic eye movements, the saccades of adults are remarkably accurate. As shown in Figure 11a, a sudden displacement of the fixation target is followed, after a latency of 200 to 250 msec, by a saccade whose velocity is up to 900°/sec and whose amplitude is within 5 to 10% of the requirement for accurate foveation (Alpern, 1969). The presence of one or more small corrective saccades that accurately position the target on the fovea follow the initial saccade by 150 to 200 msec. If the peripheral target undergoes a change in position prior to the onset of the initial saccade, or if the peripheral target disappears, the presence of a saccade to the original peripheral location is dependent on the timing of the change in the peripheral target (Komoda, Festinger, Phillips, Duckman, & Young, 1973; Wheeless, Boynton, & Cohen, 1966). For example, if the peripheral target disappears within 100 msec of its onset, the saccade will be canceled. However, if the peripheral target disappears just prior to the onset of the saccade, the saccade cannot be canceled and the line of sight terminates on a peripheral position indistinguishable from a saccade to a

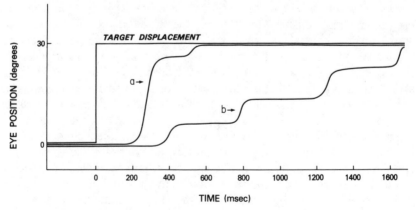

Figure 11.   The time course and form of a saccadic eye movement to the sudden appearance of a peripheral target in (a) an adult and (b) a 2-month-old.

peripheral target that did not disappear (Becker & Fuchs, 1969). If the peripheral target changes position during the saccadic latency period, the magnitude of the saccade is directed either to (1) the first peripheral position, (2) the second peripheral position, (3) or a position intermediate between the first and second peripheral positions (Becker & Jurgens, 1979). In summary, the magnitude of a saccade is dependent on the position of the peripheral target and the timing of any changes in peripheral target position relative to the latency of the initial saccade.

The foregoing general characteristics of saccades in adults raise a number of interesting developmental questions. First, it may seem straightforward that a peripheral target located in the right visual field triggers a rightward saccade. However, this peripheral target is imaged on the left hemiretina because of the inversion of the retinal image by the optics of the eye. In addition, there is no simple neural pathway from a particular extrafoveal retinal location to the initiation of a direction- and magnitude-appropriate eye movement for target foveation. Thus, it is quite possible that at birth the infant visual system is confronted with the problem of mapping stimulation at a particular retinal locus onto a motor response coordinate system. In short, the immature visual system may require experience in making saccades to "learn" which motor commands (i.e., "left" or "right") are required to foveate a peripheral target that stimulates the right or left hemiretina. Second, whether saccades in young infants are directionally appropriate or not, the magnitude of the initial saccade may require information about extraocular muscle strength, eyeball mass, and the damping characteristics of the orbital tissues. This information may not be available without some experience, such as trial and error attempts at peripheral target localization.

The directional appropriateness of infant saccades was studied initially by determining whether a peripheral target was eventually fixated. Peiper (1963) summarized a variety of anecdotal evidence that young infants rarely appear to change their gaze to fixate a target in the peripheral visual field. During the first few postnatal months, the tendency to change fixation suddenly toward a peripheral target seems to increase in frequency. Tronick (1972) referred to this developmental improvement as the growth of the infant's "effective visual field" and quantified it by presenting a target at varying retinal eccentricities from a central fixation stimulus. Both the central stimulus and the peripheral targets were fairly large (6°) and were either stationary or rotated about their midline axis to create a more salient stimulus for the infants. During the 2- to 20-week postnatal period, Tronick (1972) reported that the infant's effective visual field increased from ±15° to ±40° if the central stimulus did not rotate. Rotation of the central stimulus apparently limited the growth of the effective visual field in 20-week-olds to ±25°. Thus, in general, older infants appear to be more attentive to visual stimuli that are located at a greater angular distance in the peripheral visual field than younger infants. However, this conclusion is subject to an alternative interpretation because Tronick (1972) always presented the peripheral target while the infant was engaged in fixation of the central stimulus. It seemed possible that younger infants were in fact capable of detecting the presence of the peripheral targets at greater eccentricities, but their tendency to relinquish fixation of a currently attended stimulus may have been less than that of older infants (who perhaps encoded the central stimulus more quickly). Finlay and Ivinskis (1984) have provided evidence that 4-month-olds show a cardiac orienting response to the onset of a peripheral target regardless of whether a saccade was initiated to localize the target.

The tendency of young infants to maintain fixation of a central stimulus rather than changing fixation to a peripheral stimulus was examined directly by Harris and MacFarlane (1974) and Aslin and Salapatek (1975). Both sets of investigators employed illuminated targets that could be rapidly turned on and off. One experimental condition was a replication of the Tronick (1972) study in that a central fixation stimulus remained on in the visual field while a peripheral stimulus was introduced. The new experimental condition consisted of the offset of the central stimulus coincident with the onset of the peripheral stimulus. In this latter condition there was no competition between two stimuli (central and peripheral), and one could assess the ability of the infant's visual system to detect the peripheral target and program a directionally appropriate saccade. It is important to note that both of these studies employed a more rigid scoring criterion than Tronick (1972). Tronick (1972) had accepted any sequence of eye movements that eventually resulted in fixation of the peripheral target as evidence of localization. Thus, some of the fixations of peripheral targets undoubtedly occurred by chance. In the Harris and Mac-Farlane (1974) and Aslin and Salapatek (1975) studies, however, only the *first* change in fixation from the central stimulus was used to assess the directional appropriateness of the saccadic system.

The results of these two studies of saccadic localization, as well as several subsequent studies (see below), provided several important facts about infant saccades. First, the probability of initiating a directionally appropriate first saccade to a peripheral target decreases with retinal eccentricity. Second, the probability of peripheral target localization increases with postnatal age. Third, the presence of a central fixation stimulus during peripheral target presentation greatly reduces the probability of peripheral target localization. Thus, very young infants are capable of detecting a peripheral target and moving the line of sight to fixate that target as far as 25 to 30° from a central fixation stimulus. However, infants are less likely to make a saccade toward a peripheral target if the central fixation stimulus remains in the visual field. Moreover, part, but not all, of the developmental increase in the size of the infant's effective visual field is the result of a greater tendency to "give up" fixation of a central stimulus as the infant gets older.

Another important aspect of these data on infant saccades is the fact that by the second postnatal week the line of sight is reliably directed toward a peripheral target. One could argue that this process of peripheral target localization is learned through a very limited period of postnatal experience based on the results of saccades that were initially directed randomly.[4] However, three studies of newborns (Harris & MacFarlane, 1974; Lewis, Maurer, & Kay, 1978; MacFarlane, Harris, & Barnes, 1976) provide evidence that such a "learning" effect must occur in the very first hours after birth. Consequently, it seems quite implausible to argue for an experiential effect in the *directional* aspect of saccadic programming. Rather, it seems likely that the sensorimotor linkage between stimulation of retinal hemifield and direction of saccadic eye movement is specified innately.

Of the studies mentioned thus far on saccadic eye movements in infants, only Aslin and Salapatek (1975) recorded in detail the dynamic characteristics of the saccades themselves. Electrooculography (EOG) was used to record the horizontal direction and magnitude of the infants' saccades. EOG consists of recording the electrical potential between the cornea and the retina from surface electrodes placed near the orbit of one or both eyes. Rotation of the eye within the orbit alters the corneal-retinal potential with respect to the fixed electrodes. Under most conditions, EOG cannot provide an accurate indication of the direction of gaze within the visual field because of head movements. However, saccades typically occur before the head moves, and thus the EOG signal prior to subsequent head movements provides a reasonably accurate indication of the magnitude of saccades. Aslin and Salapatek (1975) discovered that infants

---

[4] Any model that assumes the visual system could "learn" to make directionally appropriate saccades must also assume that two aspects of the eye movement are stored from one saccade to the next: (1) the direction in which the saccade occurred, and (2) the angular distance from the line of sight to the peripheral target both before and after the saccade. For example, if a saccade results in an improvement of visual resolution for the peripheral target, then the motor command which resulted in the saccade must be stored for effective use in similar situations in the future (e.g., similar extrafoveal stimulus locations). In addition, if the direction of the saccade is stored, but the visual system cannot recall if the result of the saccade has brought the line of sight closer to the peripheral target, then the mapping of retinal loci onto a saccadic motor map cannot occur.

do not make a single saccade with a smaller corrective saccade to localize a peripheral target. Rather, as shown in Figure 11b, 1- and 2-month-olds execute a *series* of saccadic movements, and each saccadic step in the localizing sequence is of approximately equal magnitude. This apparent limitation on the magnitude of individual saccades is not simply the result of an inability to make large saccades because infants frequently make large saccades in the dark. It would appear that the young infant's visual system is actively programming a sequence of small saccades, presumably because of an underlying sensory or motor constraint.

There are several possible explanations of multiple saccades in young infants. First, one could argue that young infants are simply not interested in or motivated to localize a peripheral target and, as a result, execute an inefficient series of saccades. Although one can never rule out attentional and motivational factors as a partial explanation of infants' poor performance, this explanation does not appear to account completely for the presence of multiple saccades. The high likelihood of making a directionally appropriate first saccade indicated that the infants were attentive. In addition, the summed magnitudes of the EOG signal for all saccades in a localization series were linear out to a 20° target eccentricity, indicating that the targets were fixated with a consistent region of the retina. Finally, although the mean latencies to initiate a series of saccades were longer in infants than in adults, the shortest latencies were nearly as short as those recorded from highly trained and motivated adults (240 versus 200 msec). Thus, the infants gave the appearance of being highly motivated to localize the peripheral targets, even though they were not instructed to respond rapidly and accurately. If attentional and motivational factors are relevant to the presence of infants' multiple saccades, they cannot offer a complete explanation of the phenomenon.

A second class of possible explanations of the presence of multiple saccades in infants involves the quality of sensory information available to the infant's visual system for saccadic programming. It is clear that the peripheral targets were suprathreshold, that is, of sufficient size and intensity to trigger directionally appropriate saccades. However, it is possible that the retinal image of these peripheral targets was degraded, either optically or neurally. For example, the optics of the eye induce a spatial spreading of the image of an object on the retina through the combined effects of chromatic and spherical aberration, cloudy media, and diffraction. As a result, a small visual stimulus actually stimulates a somewhat larger region of the retina (see Westheimer & Campbell, 1962). In addition, degradation could result from a spread of neural activation over large regions of the peripheral retina despite stimulation of a small retinal locus. Both of these effects, optical and neural, would lead to a spreading of the excitation of the peripheral target's image at the level of the retina. Despite this spreading effect, however, the saccadic system would not be expected to execute a saccade that was smaller in magnitude than that required to localize the edge of the target's image that was nearest to the current line of sight. After this initial undershooting saccade, the target would be located closer to the fovea and the spreading effect should be diminished. Thus, one would expect the second saccade to be consistently smaller in magnitude than the first. However, this was not observed in the infant's EOG recordings.

Another sensory constraint on saccadic programming is the possibility that the infant's visual system cannot accurately specify relative visual direction. In adults, the angular distance of a peripheral target from the current line of sight can be judged quite accurately. For example, a peripheral target at 10° appears to be half the angular distance from a fixation point as a peripheral target at 20°. In infants, however, this mapping of retinal locus onto a spatial coordinate system may be poorly specified. As a result, a peripheral target at 10° may signal a 7° saccade and a target at 20° may signal a 9° saccade. There is some support for this possibility in the data of Aslin and Salapatek (1975). They reported that within the range of peripheral target distances where the EOG signal was linear (±20°), the magnitude of each saccade in a multiple series was significantly greater when the peripheral target was at 20° compared to 10°. This finding implies that the infant's visual system has some information about the angular extent of the peripheral target, but perhaps the calibration of this information is not refined enough to result in magnitude-appropriate initial saccades.

A third class of possible explanations of the presence of multiple saccades concerns the purely motor side of oculomotor control. We have already discussed reasons for eliminating some simple motor control explanations. Infants *are* capable of making large saccades in the dark, and the magnitude of saccades in a localizing attempt are related, at least in a qualitative way, to the angular distance of the peripheral target. However, it is possible that the repetitive, almost stereotyped, nature of the infant's multiple saccades is the result of a motor control strategy. That is, infants may be unable to control finely the duration of the neural pulse that triggers a saccade. There may, however, be a minimum duration of that neural pulse that can be initiated reliably by the oculomotor system. Thus, it may be more efficient to program a minimum pulse duration, one that leads to a predictable outcome, rather than attempting to program a variable pulse duration whose outcome cannot be controlled accurately.

If the magnitude of infant saccades were finely controlled, one would expect that visual feedback after each saccade in a multiple saccade series would specify the direction and magnitude of subsequent saccades in the series. If visual feedback during a multiple saccade series were irrelevant to the direction and magnitude of the saccades, one would expect the subsequent saccades to continue despite disappearance of the peripheral target after the initial saccade. Salapatek, Aslin, Simonson, and Pulos (1980) conducted a study of 2-month-olds' multiple saccades to a peripheral target that was extinguished after the initial saccade. Surprisingly, the most frequent response was a continuation of the multiple saccade series, even when the peripheral target was briefly presented only 10° from the previously visible central fixation stimulus. As a result, up to five or six additional saccades were made in the same direction as the initial directionally appropriate saccade. Obviously, these saccades brought the line of sight through an angular extent well beyond the original location of the peripheral target. These results would seem to indicate that the entire series of saccades was preprogrammed prior to the initial saccade, and that visual feedback in the intersaccade interval did not alter the initial direction or magnitude of subsequent saccades. However, despite a constant intersaccade interval after the peripheral target was extinguished and no change in the relative magnitude of subsequent saccades, it is possible that the saccadic system did note the absence of the peripheral target. A reasonable strategy to follow when a target disappears is simply to continue the search for the target. Thus, a continuation of the multiple saccade series would be a sensible search strategy, provided that the original specification of peripheral target distance was not very accurate (if it were accurate, one might simply cease the series of saccades). A definitive answer to this question of information processing during intersaccadic intervals will require movement of the peripheral target to a new location after the initial saccade.

A second motor control mechanism that may lead to multiple saccades is the interaction between eye and head movements. Recordings from the monkey's eye and neck muscles by Bizzi, Kalil, and Tagliasco (1971) have shown that under most circumstances the eye begins to rotate in the orbit prior to the onset of head rotation. However, the onset of neck muscle activity precedes that of extraocular muscle activity. The delay in the onset of head rotation is the result of the head's greater mass compared to the eyeball. As the head begins to rotate, the position of the eye in the orbit changes. This change must be compensated for by a counter-rolling of the eye in the orbit during the latter stages of the saccade. As illustrated in Figure 12, the compensation in the magnitude of the saccade for the rotation of the head is very finely coordinated in the mature monkey. It seemed possible that the infant's oculomotor system "expected" the head to rotate immediately after the onset of the saccade. However,

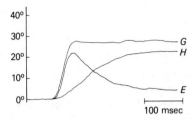

Figure 12. The time course and form of a change in gaze (G) by a monkey, including a saccadic eye movement (E) and a head movement (H). (Reprinted from Morasso, Bizzi, & Dichgans, 1973.)

the presence of head restraint in Aslin and Salapatek's (1975) study prevented the execution of such a rotation. If this were true, and the head failed to rotate, the counter-rolling might occur despite the absence of a head movement and thereby reduce the magnitude of the saccade. As a result, the presence of multiple saccades may be the result of restraining the head to obtain an accurate EOG recording.

This eye–head interaction hypothesis was examined in detail by Regal and Salapatek (1982). They recorded eye movements using EOG and head movements using a potentiometer attached to a cap on top of the infant's head. Their results indicated that 2- to 5-month-olds show a pattern of multiple saccades that is nearly identical to those recorded by Aslin and Salapatek (1975) under conditions of head restraint. Multiple saccades were also present under unrestrained conditions in which the infants employed head movements in combination with eye movements to localize a peripheral target. In addition, the saccades in a multiple saccade series were approximately equal in magnitude. Thus, although eye–head coordination may be poor in young infants, the programming of eye and head movements does not appear to account for the presence of multiple saccades.

The fourth potential explanation of the presence of multiple saccades concerns developmental changes in sensorimotor control. It is possible that the sensory information specifying stimulation of a particular retinal locus is adultlike, and that the motor system is capable of executing a saccade of appropriate direction and magnitude to foveate the peripheral target. However, the mapping of retinal locus onto motor output may be confounded by the changing anatomy of the retina. In monkeys, Hendrickson and Kupfer (1976) have shown that the photoreceptors within the foveal region of the retina increase in packing density during postnatal development as extrafoveal photoreceptors migrate toward the foveal depression. Because the total number of photoreceptors remains constant during postnatal development, the relation between a given photoreceptor and its corresponding locus in the visual field must change during this period of neural migration.[5] In other words, a stimulus located 10° from the optic axis in the newborn monkey will stimulate a different set of photoreceptors as the animal matures and as the photoreceptors alter their relative spatial positions on the retina.[6]

Figure 13a illustrates how this migration of photoreceptors toward the fovea could explain the presence of multiple saccades in human infants. First, it is necessary to assume that each photoreceptor is linked innately to a specific motor response (i.e., a saccade of a particular direction and magnitude). Second, it is necessary to assume that the infant employs the center of the fovea as the line of sight. Third, it is necessary to assume that the optics of the eye change proportionally during postnatal development. Given these three assumptions, consider the case shown in Figure 13b of an adult eyeball and a peripheral target that is presented 10° from the line of sight. The image of the peripheral target stimulates a small region of photoreceptors located 10° from the fovea and adults typically program and execute a 10° saccade to foveate the target. However, if this small region of photoreceptors migrated to its adult position on the retina from a position more distant from the fovea, the peripheral target would have to be located more than 10° from the fovea in infancy to trigger a 10° saccade. Similarly, a peripheral target located 10° from the fovea in early infancy would trigger a saccade of less than 10°. Thus, the migration of photoreceptors toward the fovea during development could explain the presence of consistent undershoots in infants' multiple saccades. The migration hypothesis does not, however, explain why each saccade in a multiple saccade series is of approximately equal magnitude.

In summary, the migration hypothesis is based on three assumptions that cannot at present be verified. We do not know if an innate sensorimo-

---

[5] I am indebted to Martin Banks for bringing to my attention the developmental implications of photoreceptor migration for pattern vision.

[6] The surface area of the human retina increases by 50% between birth and the second postnatal year (Robb, 1982). Because the number of retinal photoreceptors remains constant during postnatal development, the overall density of photoreceptors per square millimeter must decrease. However, the optics of the eyeball may compensate for this decrease in photoreceptor density because the axial length of the eyeball also increases by 50% during the first two postnatal years. Nevertheless, this optical compensation is unlikely to be linear across the retina. For example, Mastronarde, Thibeault, and Dubin (1980) have shown in the kitten retina that the density of ganglion cells decreases more rapidly in the peripheral retina compared to the central retina. In summary, many of the optical and neural aspects of retinal growth have not been described in enough detail to evaluate the possibility of a changing sensorimotor map from retinal locus to saccade magnitude.

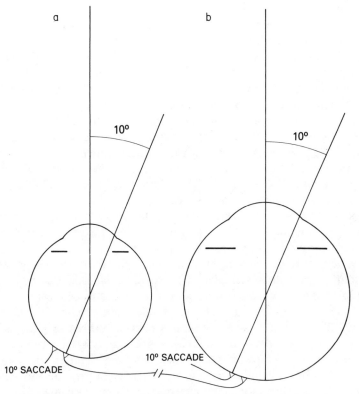

Figure 13. A model of photoreceptor migration during early retinal development illustrating the diminished magnitude of an extrafoveal eye position signal in infants (a) compared to adults (b).

tor linkage is present between specific photoreceptors and specific saccadic responses. Electrophysiological studies in cats and monkeys that could document this sensorimotor linkage have not been conducted on developing animals. We also do not know if the young infant employs a consistent line of sight nor if this line of sight is coincident with the fovea. Anatomical evidence from Abramov et al. (1982) has confirmed the earlier observations of Mann (1964) that the foveal depression is quite crude at birth. Thus, it is quite possible that newborns employ a line of sight that is highly variable or possibly located on an extrafoveal region of the retina. Finally, we do not know if the optics of the eye change proportionally between birth and adulthood. Although a schematic eye for the newborn has been proposed by Lotmar (1976), based largely on the ultrasound measurements of Larsen (1971a–1971d), there is not a consistent description of optical development, nor is there good evidence that all the refractive surfaces and dimensions of the eyeball undergo a proportional change during postnatal development. Until these three assumptions are verified, the validity of the hypothesis of photoreceptor migration as an explanation of multiple saccades will remain unclear.

A second sensorimotor explanation of multiple saccades concerns what has been called the saccadic dead zone (Young, 1981). In adults, a target fixated within the fovea can undergo a small displacement without triggering a saccade. The magnitude of this dead zone is quite small (approximately 0.3°), although some investigators have argued that it is an artifact of the poor resolution of some eye movement recording techniques. For example, Timberlake, Wyman, Skavenski, and Steinman (1972) showed that adults can make voluntary saccades as small as 10 min of arc. The small size of the saccadic dead zone is undoubtedly determined in part by the very rapid falloff in visual resolution outside the fovea. In infants, the proportional falloff in visual resolution as a function of retinal eccentricity has not been studied. Nevertheless, it seems likely that the young infant's poor acuity (presumably mediated by foveal areas) does not fall off as much in peripheral vision as it does in adults. As a result of this hypothesized gradual falloff in visual resolution, one might predict that the saccadic dead zone would be larger in infants because the sensory information available from the fixation stimulus is not significantly degraded as a result of small eye movements. A fixation target that is suddenly displaced by a small distance on the retina may not provide the saccadic system with a stimulus for initiating a corrective eye movement. Once the target displacement has exceeded the dead zone, the saccadic system would begin to program an eye movement. Unfortunately, this notion of a saccadic dead zone does not account for the presence of equal magnitude saccadic steps in infants' localization attempts. A larger dead zone in infants would simply predict a larger variance in fixation around a stationary target and perhaps a longer latency to initiate a saccade to a central stimulus that moved slowly into the periphery (see Section IV,B on pursuit movements). The larger dead zone would, however, predict the absence of small corrective saccades if a preceding saccade brought the peripheral target within the dead zone. This prediction has not as yet been investigated.

Much of the uncertainty regarding the mechanisms underlying infants' saccades is the result of the absence of any systematic manipulation of peripheral target characteristics (size, intensity, flicker, movement, spatial frequency). Across a variety of studies of infant vision, many of which were not concerned with eye movements *per se,* it seems clear that young infants (1) are less attentive to small stimuli, (2) tend to fixate moving or flickering stimuli rather than stationary or steadily illuminated ones, and (3) tend to fixate and localize high-contrast and high-luminance stimuli rather than low-contrast and low-luminance ones. One aspect of stimulus size that has not been investigated is the role of spatial summation in the control of saccades. In adults, the detectability of a small stimulus remains constant even when its diameter is increased, provided that the total energy within the stimulus remains constant. As stimulus diameter is increased, a size is reached beyond which spatial summation does not operate and detectability falls even when a constant stimulus energy is maintained. This critical size varies as a function of retinal eccentricity. In peripheral vision, the critical size is much larger than in central vision. Thus, detectability of a peripheral target is enhanced by simply increasing its size. Hamer and Schneck (1984) have reported that the critical size for spatial summation in 2-month-olds is much larger than in adults (up to 10° versus 2°). Thus, the capture of stimulus energy by the peripheral retina may extend over a very large area, effectively requiring a large stimulus for peripheral detection unless the stimulus is of high luminance.

Another reason that many questions remain to be answered about infants' saccadic programming is the uncertainty concerning foveal functioning. As mentioned earlier, it is not clear what region of the retina is used for fixation (the line of sight) and whether the infant has a functioning fovea. Lewis et al. (1978) provided evidence that newborns will fixate a vertical bar that is only 8 min of arc in width (compared to highly variable fixations of a blank field). They concluded that newborns have a functioning central retina. However, their results could have been obtained if the infants used a consistent but nonfoveal line of sight for fixation of the stimulus, particularly since the vertical extent of the bar was 24°. A follow-up study by Lewis and Maurer (1980) showed that newborns will fixate a 4° dot more steadily than a blank field. Again, the authors could only conclude that a region of the retina very close to the fovea was used for fixation. As long as the infant shows steady fixation of a target, regardless of the target's size, it will be unclear whether the fovea or some other near-foveal region of the retina was used as the line of sight.

In summary, the saccadic eye movement system is an extremely complex sensorimotor mechanism that enables adults to move the fovea efficiently to fixate (and presumably process information contained within) limited regions of the visual field. The infant visual system is faced with the developmental task of calibrating the saccadic system by coordinating the locus of retinal stimulation with the neuromotor command required to initiate a saccade of very high velocity and accuracy. At birth, the general mapping of visual direction within the saccadic system appears intact. However, the magnitude of saccades is grossly hypometric, requiring

oculomotor experience and/or neural maturation during the first few postnatal months. Possible explanations of these magnitude-inappropriate
saccades in young infants were discussed, but at present none of the
alternatives has received strong empirical support.

2. Scanning of Visual Patterns

The foregoing discussion of the infant's saccadic eye movement system
was limited to a consideration of saccades elicited by single, small visual
targets rather than the complex array of visual stimuli present in the
natural visual environment. The use of a single target rather than a complex visual array or configuration of visual contours was motivated by a
concern for the basic characteristics of the saccadic system. A complex
visual pattern introduces many contours that could compete for the infant's attention, confounding a study of the infant's basic oculomotor
abilities with other variables such as preference, motivation, and visual
memory. Nevertheless, a significant portion of the literature on infant eye
movements involves the description of scanpaths directed to complex
visual stimuli. Although this literature on infant scanning is beyond the
scope of the present chapter, several critical issues relevant to basic
characteristics of the saccadic system will be reviewed. Readers interested in a more comprehensive discussion of infant scanning are directed
to several recent reviews (Aslin, 1985; Bronson, 1982; Haith, 1980).

Partially as a result of our knowledge of adult fixation strategies, such
as those present in reading, investigators have been interested in the
individual fixations made by infants while viewing a visual stimulus. The
development of infrared corneal photography enabled a small group of
researchers to gather detailed records of the scanpaths made by infants
presented with a variety of simple and complex stimuli. Since adults tend
to direct the foveal region of the retina to view specific features of a
complex visual stimulus, it seemed reasonable to expect that scanpaths
obtained from young infants would tell us a great deal about visual processing. However, after several initial demonstrations of the newborn's
tendency to fixate contours (Kessen, Salapatek, & Haith, 1972; Salapatek, 1968; Salapatek & Kessen, 1966), it became unclear exactly what the
implications of scanning data were. In addition, several researchers realized that certain basic assumptions underlying the accuracy of the scanpaths were questionable. For example, the inference that the center of the
pupil was coincident with the fovea was shown to be incorrect in many
cases, inducing measurement errors as large as 8 to 10° (Slater & Findlay,
1972). Thus, it was not even clear that the infant's scanpaths based on
corneal photography were an accurate representation of the details of
individual fixations of the visual stimulus.

As researchers in the area of visual scanning grappled with these methodological problems, a number of more basic interpretive issues emerged to further challenge the users of this technique. For example, the view that a scanpath represents the translation of the fovea over a visual stimulus implied to some investigators that no other portion of the retina was involved in visual processing. This "tunnel vision" view of scanpaths is clearly unwarranted in light of many facts from the adult literature which document that pattern processing can occur across a fairly large extrafoveal region of the retina (e.g., Day, 1957). Since acuity in adults is so much greater in the foveal area, it seemed natural to assume that this relation would also apply to infants. In fact, however, there are no data from infants on visual acuity as a function of retinal eccentricity. Based on the infant's poor acuity (see review by Dobson & Teller, 1978), and anatomical data on the developing retina (Abramov et al., 1982; Mann, 1964), it would appear reasonable to conclude that the proportional decrease in acuity from the fovea to the periphery is greater in adults than in infants. However, we have no data on the size of the region surrounding the line of sight (foveal or extrafoveal) that is involved in the processing of visual information during a fixation.

Another interpretive problem with the scanning technique is the assumption that a fixated stimulus is actually processed and encoded. Again, it is seductive to draw parallels between adult and infant fixations. Faced with a task like reading, in which acuity limits the retinal region within which letters can be recognized, adults systematically move the fovea to encompass the entire sequence of words in the text (Rayner, 1978). However, in the case of an infant viewing a large two-dimensional shape or a photograph of a face, it is not at all clear that visual processing necessarily occurs during each individual fixation. Clearly, adults can recognize familiar stimuli without an extensive scanpath (e.g., in tachistoscope studies) by relying on extrafoveal areas of the retina (Sperling, 1960). If asked to search for details in a complex stimulus, however, adults will produce a comprehensive scanpath in an attempt to process all of the visual information present in the stimulus (Noton & Stark, 1971; Yarbus, 1967).

The interpretive issues facing users of scanning as a measure of visual processing in infants can be summarized as follows. First, we do not know the size of the area surrounding the line of sight that performs visual processing and/or encoding. It seems likely that this area is of variable size depending on the type of stimulus presented to the subject and the task demands of the situation. Second, we do not know whether a currently fixated stimulus region is in fact being processed, and we do not know whether stimulus information once processed during a fixation is encoded for later recognition. Finally, we do not know if a scanpath is even necessary for visual processing and/or encoding of the stimulus. In adults, there are circumstances in which eye movements are unnecessary, since the critical information can be processed in a single fixation. Thus, there are certainly situations, at least for adults, in which scanning of the stimulus is not a prerequisite for visual processing. This raises the possibility that large portions of a scanpath are unrelated to the specific characteristics of the stimulus.

This rather pessimistic view of the scanning technique should not be taken as an argument for abandonment. On the contrary, there are some circumstances in which scanning data can provide important information concerning visual processing by infants. In addition, researchers have only recently begun to tackle the interpretive problems underlying the use of the scanning technique. These interpretive issues have been addressed both in interactive studies of scanning (see Bronson, 1982), in which the stimulus undergoes a change, and in basic studies of eye movement control (see preceding section on saccades). In addition, the strategy of incorporating both global and detailed measures of visual fixation in the same experiment would seem to be a fruitful avenue for balancing the two methodological approaches. The usefulness of scanning as a measure of visual processing in infants must await the careful implementation of these methodological approaches.

B. The Pursuit System

Most species with a fovea also have an oculomotor system that allows the fovea to maintain fixation of a slowly moving target. This target-tracking ability is called smooth pursuit because the eyes move conjugately at a constant velocity to match the velocity of the moving visual stimulus. An apparently more basic target-tracking system, optokinetic nystagmus (OKN), is present in both foveate and nonfoveate species. If the entire visual field (or a large portion of it) moves at a constant velocity, the eyes tend to move smoothly to match the velocity of the moving visual field. In the case of a single target, the smooth pursuit movement is terminated when the target moves out of the animal's visual field. However, in the case of whole-field movement, the stimulus triggering a tracking response is continuously present. Thus, the smooth tracking response is interrupted by a saccade that moves the line of sight in the direction opposite to the whole-field movement. This alternation of smooth following and saccadic returns to a more central orbital position is OKN. The function of smooth pursuit movements is presumably to allow the fovea to process details of a moving stimulus. However, because the presence of a

fovea is not a requirement for OKN, this type of tracking eye movement presumably functions to provide the retina with a temporarily stable image of the entire visual field. The response characteristics and perceptual implications of these two tracking systems will now be reviewed.

1. Optokinetic Nystagmus

OKN has been observed in infants as young as several hours after birth, although the consistency of the smooth or slow phase of OKN increases dramatically during the first few months after birth (McGinnis, 1930). Interestingly, OKN in infants has been used primarily to study various aspects of pattern perception, including visual acuity (Dayton, Jones, Aui et al., 1964; Fantz et al., 1962; Gorman, Cogan, & Gellis, 1957), brightness discrimination (Doris & Cooper, 1966), apparent motion (Tauber & Koffler, 1966), and binocular vision (Atkinson & Braddick, 1981; Naegele & Held, 1982). Only recently have investigators attempted to study the details of the OKN response itself. Kremenitzer, Vaughan, Kurtzberg, and Dowling (1979) used electrooculography (EOG) to record OKN from 28 1- to 3-day-old infants. The visual field consisted of alternate black and white stripes (subtending 6° each) that moved at constant velocities between 9°/sec and 40°/sec. Although the use of EOG precluded an absolute calibration of eye velocity, the slope of the slow phase of OKN did increase as the velocity of the striped field increased from 9°/sec to 25°/sec. However, above 25°/sec the slope of the slow phase of OKN did not show a consistent increase (and in some cases actually decreased), whereas in adults slow phase velocity increased monotonically between 9°/sec and 40°/sec. In general, then, OKN can be elicited from very young infants, but there appears to be some sensory or motor constraint on the peak velocity of the slow phase of OKN.

Developmental investigations of OKN across the first postnatal year have typically confounded improvements in sensory abilities with potential improvements in the motor aspects of the OKN response. For example, it is typically assumed that because OKN can be elicited at birth with large stripes, the decrease in threshold stripe width for eliciting OKN in older infants is solely the result of sensory development (i.e., an improvement in visual acuity). However, recent work on monocular assessments of OKN in infants raises the possibility that OKN may not be a "motor-free" measure of sensory development. A study of monocular OKN in developing cats (Van Hof-Van Duin, 1978) showed that there is an asymmetry in temporalward versus nasalward OKN in very young kittens and in older cats who were deprived of normal binocular vision during early life. This asymmetry consisted of a younger onset age for OKN elicited by nasalward stimulus movement than by temporalward movement. Atkinson and Braddick (1981) found a similar developmental OKN asymmetry in human infants younger than 3 months of age and in infants with various binocular sensory anomalies. These findings from Atkinson and Braddick (1981) were based primarily on direct observation of the infants' eye movements, although EOG was used in some instances. A more quantitative study of the development of asymmetrical OKN in human infants was recently reported by Naegele and Held (1982). They used EOG to record both binocular and monocular OKN elicited by stripes that moved either nasalward or temporalward. Their index of asymmetry was the ratio of slow phase velocity for temporalward compared to nasalward stimulus movement. They reported that this ratio increased linearly from approximately 0.2 in 1-month-olds to 1.0 (i.e., symmetrical) in 5-month-olds. Although the mechanisms underlying asymmetrical OKN, as well as its relation to binocular vision, are not understood at present, these results provide a clear quantitative example of the fact that OKN is not mature as an oculomotor system in early infancy.

Further quantification of OKN responses in infancy has been provided by Hainline, Lemerise, Abramov, and Turkel (1984). They employed an infrared corneal reflection system to record binocular OKN from 21- to 184-day-old infants. The stimulus display consisted of a 30 × 22° field of alternate black and white stripes that moved either horizontally or vertically at 7°/sec. The most striking finding was the fact that OKN was more frequently elicited by stripes that moved vertically than by stripes that moved horizontally. Infants at all ages tested showed clear instances of vertical OKN, but only infants older than 2 to 3 months showed robust evidence of horizontal OKN.[7] In addition, the latency between onset of stimulus movement and onset of OKN was very long for horizontal movement but almost immediate for vertical movement. These results indicate that motor factors are involved in at least the directional nature of OKN.

It is also possible that binocular viewing of the moving stripes created a conflict for the younger infants because of the monocular asymmetry described above. That is, horizontal stripe movement generates nasalward motion in one eye and temporalward motion in the other eye and may interfere with the programming of symmetrical (conjugate) OKN found in older infants and adults. Presumably, no asymmetry in vertical OKN is present in early infancy because both upward and downward stimulus movement elicit vertical OKN that is equivalent in the two eyes. Thus, the use of OKN as a sensory assessment technique in the first few

---

[7] The fact that other investigators have reported horizontal OKN in much younger infants probably resulted from the relatively small field size of the striped pattern used to elicit OKN in the Hainline et al. (1984) study.

postnatal months requires careful evaluation of possible nonsensory developments, such as motor asymmetries.

2. Smooth Pursuit

Although OKN responses in human infants have only recently been described with the aid of objective recording techniques, OKN has been observed in a qualitative manner by numerous investigators. In contrast, smooth pursuit movements have rarely been studied in developing infants, either with or without objective recording techniques. The first quantitative description of the development of smooth pursuit in infants was provided by McGinnis (1930). The eye movements of infants were filmed as a black vertically oriented bar on a white background was moved laterally through the field of view. McGinnis reported that infants' tracking of this target was totally saccadic until the sixth postnatal week. However, the film records of each infant's face were judged by adult observers. Thus, the conclusion regarding the absence of smooth pursuit in young infants was based on a rather global observation rather than on a detailed record of the infants' eye movements.

The first quantitative studies of infant tracking were reported by Dayton and Jones (1964) and Dayton, Jones, Steele, and Rose (1964). They used EOG to record the tracking responses of young infants who viewed a single 15° diameter black dot on a white background. The target traveled across the field of view (180°) at a constant velocity of 16°/sec. The Dayton et al. studies, like that of McGinnis 30 years earlier, demonstrated that infants' tracking was totally saccadic until the end of the second postnatal month. However, these studies used only a single target velocity. A recent study by Kremenitzer et al. (1979) also used EOG to study infants' tracking of a large target (12° diameter), but the target was moved at several velocities (9°–40°/sec). They reported that even newborns show brief segments of smooth pursuit (typically 300–400 msec in duration) interspersed among saccades. Although the EOG signal could not be calibrated to provide an absolute measure of the velocity of the eye during these segments of smooth pursuit, there was an increase in the slope of the EOG signal as target velocity increased from 9 to 19°/sec. Beyond 19°/sec, however, smooth pursuit velocity (estimated from the slope of the EOG signal) did not increase.

The results of the Kremenitzer et al. (1979) study appear to demonstrate that newborns are capable of some limited form of smooth pursuit. However, it is possible that at some velocities a large target elicits smooth segments of tracking via the OKN system. Unfortunately, this possibility is difficult to verify because target size and velocity have not been varied systematically to determine whether it affects adults' smooth pursuit per-

formance. However, if newborns do not have a fovea with superior resolving powers (as suggested by Abramov et al., 1982), infants may fixate
a single target with some portion of the extrafoveal retina. A target that is
small compared to the angular extent of the infant fovea would not provide a salient fixation stimulus. A very large target, however, would provide contours that extended well into the peripheral retina. These peripheral contours would provide a salient stimulus for eliciting an OKN
response. Of course, it is possible that a young infant who fixated a *small*
target with an extrafoveal portion of the retina might also employ the
OKN system to track the target smoothly. Thus, the distinction between
smooth tracking in infants that is mediated by the OKN system rather
than by the smooth pursuit system may be largely semantic. Nevertheless, the ability to track a small target is certainly relevant to any description of the OKN and smooth pursuit systems.

A detailed description of the development of smooth pursuit requires a
measurement technique that is more accurate than EOG. The primary
measurement problem with EOG is the fact that the recording electrodes
are placed on the head. Thus, if the head rotates while the eyes maintain
fixation on a stationary target, the EOG signal changes. Because it is
impossible to eliminate infants' head movements, the accuracy of the
EOG signal is quite poor unless very brief segments of the record are
sampled. An alternative to EOG is a recording system based on the relative positions of one or more corneal reflections. The primary advantage
of corneal reflection systems is that small head movements do not alter
the system's accuracy, provided that the video camera and light source
are fixed and the infant's eye is within a very restricted field of view (3 cm
square). Recently, a number of infrared video-based recording systems
have been developed to measure eye movements in infants. These new
systems have two main advantages over past systems. First, a single
infrared light source is aligned coaxially with the camera lens to create a
bright pupil from the light reflected back from the retina. This bright pupil
enhances the contrast between the infant's iris and pupil, thereby improv-
ing the accuracy of estimating the center of the pupil. Second, on-line
circuitry has been developed to detect the position of the corneal reflection with respect to the center of the pupil. It is possible, therefore, to
obtain a measure of horizontal and vertical eye position, as well as pupil
size, at a rate of 60 Hz.

These new video recording and analysis techniques were used by Aslin
(1981) to record the tracking movements of 32 infants between 22 and 115
days after birth. Each session of data collection consisted of a series of
trials during which a black vertical bar (2° wide, 8° high) on a white
background was moved through a 20° excursion across a television

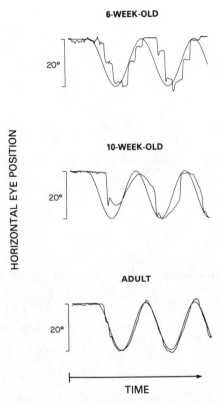

Figure 14. Target-tracking eye movements in 6- and 10-week-old infants and adults illustrating the saccadic tracking prior to 8 weeks and the onset of smooth pursuit interspersed among saccades after 8 weeks of age. (Redrawn from Aslin, 1981.)

screen. The target oscillated sinusoidally in a horizontal path at average target velocities ranging from 10 to 40°/sec. Representative target-tracking responses from infants at different ages are illustrated in Figure 14. Note that despite the low target velocity (16°/sec or less), none of the infants younger than 8 weeks showed any evidence of smooth pursuit. Rather, their target-tracking responses consisted entirely of saccades. Infants older than 6 weeks showed brief segments of smooth pursuit interspersed among saccades and the proportion of smooth pursuit increased with age. Thus, although smooth pursuit appears to emerge during the 6- to 8-week age range, as McGinnis (1930) stated 50 years ago, the accuracy of these movements is poor because the velocity of the eye does not match the velocity of the target.

Figure 15 illustrates how the smooth pursuit system breaks down as

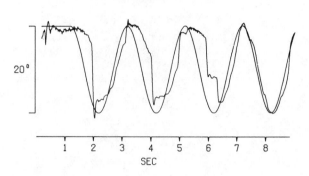

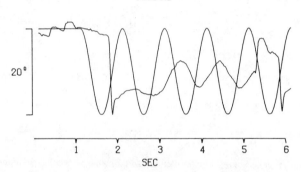

Figure 15. The effect of target velocity on smooth pursuit in a 10-week-old illustrating an increase in phase lag and a decrease in magnitude. (Redrawn from Aslin, 1981.)

target velocity increases. This 10-week-old was presented with a target that moved through one complete right–left cycle (±20°) in either 2 sec or 1 sec. At the slower target velocity, fixation closely matched the position of the moving target after three oscillations. However, at the faster target velocity, the latency of the initial saccade placed the eye well behind the position of the target and the smooth pursuit system never "caught up" with the target's oscillations. Rather, the phase lag remained approximately 180° and the amplitude of the eye's oscillations was reduced. In this case, the smooth pursuit system of an infant who could track fairly accurately at lower target velocities failed to keep the target fixated for more than a few brief moments as the paths of the eye and the target crossed. Clearly, between infancy and adulthood the smooth pursuit system develops significantly, because adults tested under identical conditions showed much greater accuracy in their smooth pursuit of a target traveling at the faster velocity of 40°/sec.

There are several possible explanations for the absence of smooth pursuit in young infants. As summarized by Aslin (1981), smooth pursuit may be absent because of (1) attentional/motivational factors, (2) anatomical and neuromuscular factors, (3) sensory mechanisms, or (4) sensorimotor control mechanisms. The eye movement records shown in Figures 14 and 15 provide evidence that the young infants were highly attentive and sufficiently motivated to track the moving target consistently. Thus, a simple attentional or motivational deficit does not appear to account for the absence of smooth pursuit in young infants. The presence of the slow phase of OKN indicates that any anatomical or neuromuscular constraints are not severe enough to prevent the young infant's eyeball from rotating smoothly. Thus, the sensory and the sensorimotor explanations appear to offer the most likely account for the absence of smooth pursuit in infants under 8 weeks of age.

Sensory mechanisms that are known to develop rapidly during the first few postnatal months include acuity and contrast sensitivity (see Banks & Dannemiller, this volume). However, we know that adults who view a target that has been optically degraded with lenses do not show significant reductions in smooth pursuit accuracy, and they certainly do not revert to saccadic tracking (Feustel, Hanna, & Aslin, 1981). Two related areas of sensory processing that have not received extensive study in young infants are temporal resolution and velocity analysis. If the young infant's visual system was sluggish at updating the time course of changes in retinal image position, then the programming of tracking eye movements would consistently fall behind the movement of the target. Finally, even if we assume that the young infant's sensory mechanisms are mature, the manner in which this sensory information is utilized to control the movement of the eyes by the extraocular muscles could be inaccurate.

Although both sensory and sensorimotor control factors may be involved in the absence of smooth pursuit in young infants,[8] I would like to offer an alternative explanation that incorporates many of the features of

___

[8] An example of an interesting sensorimotor factor that could lead to the absence of smooth pursuit in young infants involves the relative contributions of central and peripheral regions of the retina to motion perception. Harris, Cassel, and Bamborough (1974) reported that 2- to 4-month-olds track a target only if the velocity of the target is different from the velocity of a patterned background that fills the visual field. Because a rightward eye movement induces a leftward translation of the image of the patterned background, accurate tracking of a single target requires suppression of motion information from the peripheral retina. Thus, if a salient background is present during target movement, younger infants may be unable to ignore the translation of the background across the retina and attend solely to the movement of the target.

the explanation of multiple saccades illustrated in Figure 13. Recall that anatomical evidence suggests that retinal photoreceptors migrate toward the fovea during development. Thus, assuming a proportional increase in the optical properties of the developing eyeball, a target that is located 10° from the fovea at an early age will stimulate a set of photoreceptors that will eventually be located closer to the fovea. If the link between retinal locus and extraocular muscle output is established innately, the extrafoveal target in early infancy will trigger a smaller saccade than the same extrafoveal target in adulthood. If a similar model is applied to the pursuit system, the velocity of a target that moves from the fovea toward the peripheral retina will be underestimated. When the moving target has reached a retinal location 10° from the fovea, the photoreceptors stimulated by the target are ones that will eventually migrate to a location closer to the fovea. Thus, the velocity computation (change in retinal position per unit time) will systematically underestimate the actual velocity of the moving target.

An additional assumption is required for this explanation based on velocity errors to account for the absence of smooth pursuit. There must be some region surrounding the fovea within which velocity computations are made and outside of which the saccadic system interrupts these computations to bring the fovea closer to the moving (or stationary) target. Without this final assumption, we would expect to find rudimentary smooth pursuit in newborns, but the velocity of these pursuit movements would simply be very low compared to the velocity of the target. The complete absence of smooth pursuit in infants under 8 weeks of age, however, suggests that the velocity computation is never completed until the target displacement has exceeded a saccadic dead zone. The eventual intermixing of smooth pursuit movements (of low velocity) with saccades in the tracking of 10-week-olds (see Fig. 14) is consistent with this notion of a saccadic dead zone.

This model of young infants' saccadic and tracking eye movements is based on a number of as yet unverified assumptions. Not only must we assume that the optics of the eye change proportionally during development and that young infants utilize the central fovea as the line of sight, but we must also assume an innate linkage between the retinal locus stimulated by a peripheral target and the motor command to the extraocular muscles. This latter assumption has received some support from a study of newborn kittens by Stein, Clamann, and Goldberg (1980). They electrically stimulated neurons in the superior colliculus (SC) of kittens prior to the age of eye opening (<10 days postnatally). They found that neurons in the SC were topographically organized as in the adult cat. Contralateral saccades were elicited by stimulation of the right or left SC and saccade magnitudes were proportional to stimulation intensity. However, stimulation thresholds for evoking saccades in newborn kittens were three times higher than in the adult cat SC, and saccades in newborn kittens rarely exceeded 10°. Thus, there appears to be an innate sensori-motor linkage between retinal locus and the direction and magnitude of saccades. However, there may also be a developmental change in this linkage which compensates for the migration of retinal photoreceptors. Although there are animal models of the human visual system (e.g., macaques) that could provide empirical tests of the effects of neural migration within the retina on the programming of saccades and smooth pursuit, these models have not as yet been exploited to address this hypothesized explanation of multiple saccades and saccadic tracking in young infants.

C. The Vergence System

The importance of accurately aligning the two lines of sight during binocular fixation is supported by two lines of evidence. First, in normal adults the failure to maintain simultaneous fixation of a target with the two foveas results either in diplopia (double images) or in suppression of the input to one of the two eyes. Inconsistent or inaccurate binocular alignment, therefore, leads to a severe loss of binocular depth perception (stereopsis) as well as the possible presence of diplopia and its resultant confusion in specifying a target's visual direction. Second, evidence from nonhumans indicates that eye misalignment during an early postnatal sensitive period leads to a permanent reduction in the proportion of binocular neurons in the visual cortex as well as deficits in stereopsis (see review by Movshon & Van Sluyters, 1981). Similarly, both clinical (von Noorden, 1980) and experimental (Banks, Aslin, & Letson, 1975; Hohmann & Creutzfeldt, 1975) evidence in humans has shown that binocular misalignment during an early postnatal sensitive period results in the permanent loss of fusion and stereopsis.

In light of these findings from humans and nonhumans, it is of considerable functional significance to describe the accuracy of binocular fixation and vergence eye movements in young infants. The primary question is whether both foveas (the two lines of sight) are aligned simultaneously to fixate a single visual target. If young infants did not show accurate bifoveal fixation, then either fusion and stereopsis must be absent or some underlying mechanism supporting fusion and stereopsis in infants must be different from the adult visual system. Problems of measurement have made it almost impossible to describe the accuracy of binocular fixation and vergence eye movements in young infants. In addition, vergence eye movements are driven by two major types of stimulus information—diplopia (fusional vergence) and blur (accommodative vergence)—that are difficult to vary independently, particularly with infant subjects. In this final section, the empirical evidence currently available on the control of vergence eye movements in infants will be reviewed, and particular attention will be directed to those methodological issues that have confronted researchers in this area.

1. Fusional Vergence

In adults, the presence of diplopia is a sufficient stimulus for initiating vergence eye movements to restore fusion. The neural mechanisms underlying diplopia are beyond the scope of this chapter (see review by Aslin & Dumais, 1980), but the attainment of fusion despite dual retinal inputs from a single visual target is attributed to corresponding retinal points. As shown in Figure 16, all possible pairs of corresponding retinal points define a surface, called the horopter, that intersects the point of bifoveal fixation. Thus, if a single visual target stimulates a pair of corresponding retinal points (i.e., on the horopter), the target is perceived as single or fused. A target that is positioned so that noncorresponding reti-

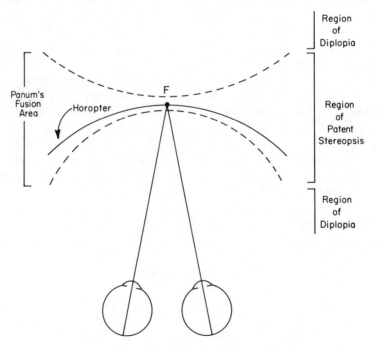

Figure 16. The relative positions of the horopter and Panum's fusion area with respect to the point (F) of binocular fixation. (Reprinted from Aslin & Dumais, 1980.)

nal points are stimulated leads to the perception of diplopia unless the target lies very close to the horopter. Interestingly, if the amount of noncorrespondence is small, the target will still be perceived as fused. That is, there is a small area in front of and behind the horopter, called Panum's fusion area, where stimulation of noncorresponding retinal points does not lead to diplopia.

A number of studies have shown that adults precisely control their vergence eye movements to realign the two foveas onto a single visual target. For example, Westheimer and Mitchell (1969) presented different targets to each eye of adults using a mirror haploscope. By varying the angle of the haploscope mirrors, they altered the relative retinal positions of the two targets so that noncorresponding points were stimulated. It had been known for many years that adults confronted with this stimulus situation simply program a convergent or a divergent eye movement to fuse the two targets, provided that the targets are nearly identical in shape and size (i.e., that they are fusable). However, Westheimer and Mitchell (1969) displaced the targets briefly onto noncorresponding retinal points so that the vergence response would not be completed. In this way, they could record the initial direction of the vergence movement (convergence versus divergence) even for targets that were not fusable. Their results showed that adults always made a vergence movement in the appropriate direction, despite the fact that the two targets (one viewed by each eye) were quite different in shape (nonfusable). A number of theories of binocular vision (e.g., Marr, 1982) have incorporated this finding by hypothesizing that vergence eye movements are triggered by low spatial frequency information. In addition, Schor, Wood, and Ogawa (1984) documented the fact that Panum's fusion area is much larger when the spatial frequency content of the target is low-pass filtered. Thus, although high spatial frequencies are required for the fine vergence movements leading to bifoveal fixation by the central fovea, low spatial frequency information is sufficient to program directionally appropriate vergence movements for a target located off the horopter. In addition, if the visual target only contains low spatial frequency information (e.g., blurred edges), or if the visual system can only resolve low spatial frequencies, the size of Panum's fusion area is expanded and the stimulus for accurate vergence movements (i.e., diplopia) may be degraded.

Data on the accuracy of bifoveal fixation and vergence eye movements in infants is not only sparse but is also subject to a number of methodological problems. Newborns appear wall-eyed in that the two pupil centers tend to be directed temporally even during periods of apparent attentiveness (Rethy, 1969). Two studies using corneal photography (Maurer, 1975; Wickelgren, 1967) have verified this wall-eyed appearance in newborns who have no known ocular abnormalities. Both studies reported that the centers of the two pupils (the estimated lines of sight) are directed temporally on either side of a visual stimulus. However, the use of corneal photography to estimate the position of the two lines of sight may be inaccurate. Slater and Findlay (1972, 1975b) provided evidence that the center of the pupil is not an accurate estimate of the line of sight. As shown in Figure 1, the center of the pupil (the optic axis) is displaced temporally with respect to the actual line of sight connecting the fovea to the target (the visual axis). This displacement was estimated to be as large as 8 to 10° in newborns, with a gradual developmental decline to 3 to 4° by adulthood. Thus, in the absence of an objective technique for measuring the line of sight, it appeared that corneal reflection photography would not be able to determine if infants exhibit accurate bifoveal fixation or whether the wall-eyed appearance of infants is more than simply a measurement artifact.

Two additional studies of young infants using the corneal reflection technique have provided a partial answer to the question of binocular fixation and vergence eye movement control. Slater and Findlay (1975a) reasoned that although an absolute measurement of the line of sight with corneal photography could not be obtained from each infant, one could apply a group correction factor to compensate for the discrepancy between the optic and visual axes. In addition, one could present a target at different viewing distances. If binocular fixation was maintained at all viewing distances, application of the correction factor should indicate that the change in vergence was appropriate for the change in target distance. Slater and Findlay (1975a) reported that newborns who viewed a target at 25 cm had a vergence angle (the angle formed by the intersection of the estimated lines of sight) that was greater than the vergence angle to a target presented at a 50-cm viewing distance. However, when the target was positioned at a 12-cm viewing distance, the estimated vergence angle was highly variable and tended to return to the value obtained for the 50-cm viewing distance. Thus, newborns appeared on average to converge appropriately to a target at 25 and 50 cm, but not to a target at 12 cm.

Aslin (1977) employed a similar measurement strategy to study the vergence movements of 1-, 2-, and 3-month-olds as they viewed a target that moved from a 50-cm to a 15-cm viewing distance. Corneal photography was used to assess binocular fixation, but the visual target itself created the corneal reflection (rather than a set of fixed marker lights). In this way, consistent binocular fixation would be indicated by an invariant relation between the centers of the two pupils and each corneal reflection. As shown in Figure 17, vergence angle (estimated by the measure of interpupillary distance) increased as the target approached the infants.

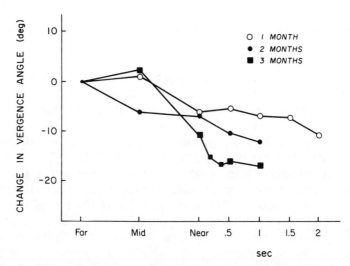

Figure 17. Mean convergence responses in 1-, 2-, and 3-month-olds to a target approaching from a 50-cm to a 15-cm viewing distance. The magnitude of convergence required for accurate binocular fixation is 13.4°. (Redrawn from Aslin, 1977.)

However, for the youngest infants the corneal reflection of the target did not remain in an invariant position on the two pupils at the near viewing distance. The average change in vergence angle required to maintain binocular fixation in this situation was 13.4°, but the youngest infants did not show changes in convergence that consistently met this criterion, even though the direction of their vergence movements was nearly always appropriate. From these results and those of Slater and Findlay (1975a), it seems clear that at best binocular fixation in young infants is intermittent, particularly for near targets. In addition, we are not certain that in young infants the two foveas are used as the lines of sight (e.g., a consistent extrafoveal location on each retina may be used as the line of sight), even though by 3 months of age changes in vergence are magnitude appropriate.

Although there are a number of possible explanations for the inaccuracies recorded in young infants' vergence eye movements, neither a simple attentional explanation nor a simple range of motor movement explanation seems plausible. For example, as in most studies of infant eye movements, even the best (i.e., most attentive) segments of data indicate that the magnitude of vergence movements is reduced in young infants. In addition, the range of orbital positions through which each eye can rotate is considerably greater than the positions required for accurate binocular fixation to both far and near targets. These arguments do not imply that attentional and motor control issues are irrelevant to the accuracy of binocular fixation in young infants. However, three other possible explanations appear more promising in accounting for the development of vergence eye movement control.

The first aspect of fusional vergence that may account for the developmental improvement in the accuracy of binocular fixation is the possibility that Panum's fusion area is effectively larger in young infants and gradually diminishes in size during postnatal development. This possibility was raised by Aslin (1977) based on the results of an experiment designed to measure small changes in binocular alignment. Aslin (1977) introduced small wedge prisms in front of one eye while the infant was binocularly fixating a target. A wedge prism placed base-out (thick edge temporally) before one eye displaces the visual direction of the retinal image and creates diplopia. Normal adults typically initiate a corrective eye movement to realign the two foveas on the target and restore fusion. As shown in Figure 18, the infants tested by Aslin (1977) did not consistently realign the eyes after the introduction of the prism until they were between 4.5 and 6 months of age. Thus, a displacement of the target's image from the horopter by 2.5 or 5° was not sufficient to trigger a vergence eye movement until the fifth postnatal month.

The results illustrated in Figure 18 appear to contradict the finding that by 3 months of age infants on average make magnitude-appropriate ver-

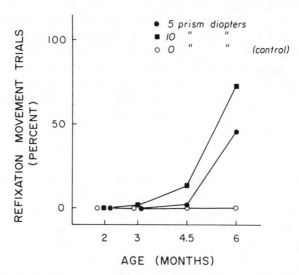

Figure 18.   Mean proportion of trials during which infants between 2 and 6 months of age showed a refixation response to prism-induced binocular misalignments. (Redrawn from data in Aslin, 1977.)

gence movements as a target moves from 50 cm to 15 cm (see Fig. 17). Why do infants not show evidence of a realignment of the two lines of sight when a small displacement is induced with prisms? Although there are a number of possible explanations for this apparent discrepancy (see Aslin, 1977), the hypothesis that Panum's fusion area shrinks developmentally provides a plausible alternative. When a target moves from 50 cm to 15 cm, the change in vergence angle required for accurate binocular fixation is 13.4°. If we assume that the size of Panum's fusion area is initially quite large at birth (e.g., 5–6°), then the smaller magnitude of convergence for 1-month-olds shown in Figure 17 is explained by the absence of a stimulus (diplopia) for making a larger vergence response. That is, diplopia is absent as long as the level of noncorrespondence is less than the size of Panum's fusion area, and one would predict an "undershooting" of the vergence response of approximately 5–6°. In older infants, Panum's fusion area is presumably smaller, but not as small as in adults. Thus, a prism that would induce a vergence response in adults does not trigger a response in infants, even though a larger stimulus (e.g., the 13.4° change in the target-tracking experiment) does trigger a vergence response. If this explanation based on a developmental shrinkage of Panum's fusion area is correct, we would expect a further reduction after 6 months of age in the minimum prism size needed to induce a realignment of the eyes.

As in the adult study by Schor et al. (1984) showing that targets containing low spatial frequencies effectively increase the size of Panum's fusion area, the hypothesized shrinkage of Panum's fusion area may result solely from the developmental improvement in sensitivity to high spatial frequencies. Alternatively, as suggested by Held, Birch, and Gwiazda (1980), sensitivity to binocular disparity may improve more rapidly than sensitivity to high spatial frequencies. Regardless of the underlying sensory mechanism, however, the hypothesis of a developmental shrinkage in Panum's fusion area generates a testable prediction regarding the accuracy of binocular fixation as a function of viewing distance. As shown in Figure 19, there is a consistent relation in adults between viewing distance and vergence angle indicated by the function with a slope of unity and an asymptote at the vergence near point. This adult function assumes that the size of Panum's fusion area is very small and that the target contains some high spatial frequencies. In contrast, the functions with the shallower slopes indicate the predicted change in vergence angle if the size of Panum's fusion area were larger. In each case (1-, 2-, and 3-month-olds), as Panum's fusion area becomes smaller with increasing age, the accuracy of the vergence response would increase. This hypothesis that the sensory component of the fusional system accounts for developmental im-

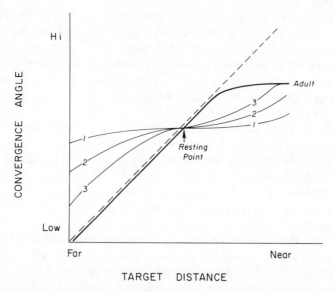

Figure 19. Hypothetical vergence response functions to different target-viewing distances in adults and in 1-, 2-, and 3-month-olds if the size of Panum's fusion area decreases during development.

provements in vergence accuracy is similar to the hypothesis concerning the accommodative system (see Section II,B).

Note that in Figure 19 there is a single intermediate viewing distance at which binocular fixation is very accurate, while at viewing distances progressively more discrepant from this position fixational accuracy diminishes. This intermediate distance corresponds to the position of rest of the vergence system. Thus, a target located beyond the resting position requires effort to diverge the two lines of sight and a target located in front of the resting position requires effort to converge the lines of sight. In the absence of a fixational stimulus (e.g., darkness), the two lines of sight revert to an average resting position in adults that corresponds to a viewing distance of 120 cm (Owens & Leibowitz, 1980). Similarly, under conditions of reduced illumination, as high spatial frequency information is lost, binocular fixation is less accurate and is biased toward the resting position of vergence (Ivanoff & Bourdy, 1954). The hypothetical vergence response functions for infants shown in Figure 19 were drawn under the assumption that the resting position of vergence does not change during development. However, if the resting position of vergence was much more distant than in adults, as suggested by the wall-eyed appearance of newborns, we might expect some limitation on the accuracy of convergence responses to a near target.

The second possible explanation of developmental improvements in binocular fixation, therefore, is that the resting position of vergence in young infants is more distant than in adults. This possibility was investigated by Aslin and Jackson (1981) using corneal photography to measure interpupillary distance (an estimate of vergence angle) in total darkness. A sample of 18 infants ranging in age from 5 to 20 weeks of age showed a mean resting position of vergence of 31 cm, a distance that is considerably different from the reported adult mean of 120 cm. A followup study by Aslin and Jackson (1982) showed that the average resting position of vergence increased to 51 cm in 5- to 12-month-olds, 48 cm in 18- to 36-month-olds, and 80 cm in adults.[9] Thus, the possibility that young infants fail to fixate a near target accurately because the resting position of vergence is at a far distance appears to be incorrect. In contrast, the findings of the Aslin and Jackson (1981, 1982) studies indicate that the viewing distance that requires the least amount of neuromuscular effort for accurate binocular fixation is in the 30–50 cm range.

A third possible explanation of inaccurate binocular fixation of near targets by young infants is the migration of photoreceptors discussed earlier (see Figure 13). Consider the example shown in Figure 20, in which a subject is fixating a target that suddenly jumps to a location in front of the horopter. For an adult, this target displacement creates diplopia because the target image stimulates noncorresponding retinal points, and an appropriate convergence eye movement is executed to restore fusion. For an infant, however, the signal for making a convergence eye movement may be reduced in magnitude if the calculation of retinal disparity (the magnitude of noncorrespondence) is based on the eventual location of the photoreceptors. As discussed earlier, if we assume that the optics of the eyeball increase proportionally during development and that the central fovea corresponds to the line of sight, a migration of photoreceptors toward the fovea would result in an underestimation of the angular displacement of a target from the line of sight. As illustrated in Figure 20, if a target is displaced suddenly from 50 to 40 cm, the disparity signal for initiating a convergence movement would be 0.9° in an adult but only 0.6° in a newborn, simply because of the developmental increase in interocular separation. Any developmental migration of photoreceptors toward the

---

[9] The nearer estimate of dark vergence in adults (80 cm) obtained by Aslin and Jackson (1982) compared to the 120 cm estimate obtained by Owens and Leibowitz (1980) probably resulted from the use of a photographic (objective) measurement technique in the former study compared to the nonius alignment (subjective) measurement technique used in the latter study. Kertesz, Hampton, and Sabrin (1983) recently reported that subjective techniques underestimate the magnitude of shifts in vergence compared to an objective eye movement recording technique. This underestimation presumably results from the fact that fusion can occur within at least 15 min of arc of the horopter (see Figure 16).

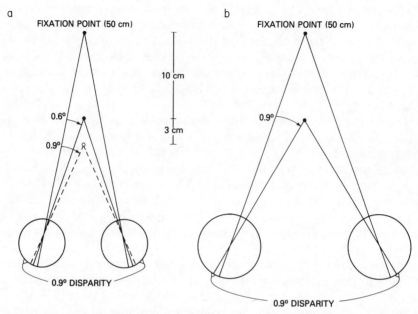

Figure 20. A model of photoreceptor migration during early retinal development illustrating the reduced disparity signal in infants (a) compared to adults (b).

fovea would further diminish the magnitude of the disparity signal in infants for initiating the convergence movement. Thus, the same model that was proposed as an explanation for the inaccuracies in saccadic and smooth pursuit eye movements in young infants appears to offer a reasonable account for the larger effective size of Panum's fusion area and the "undershooting" of vergence movements for a near target viewing distance. A test of this model of photoreceptor migration must await empirical studies using an animal model of oculomotor development.

2. Accommodative Vergence

Fusional (or diplopic) stimuli are only one of two primary types of information that can trigger a vergence eye movement. Muller (1826/1943) was the first to describe the role of accommodation in the control of vergence eye movements. He noted that the eyes converge to an approaching visual target even under monocular viewing conditions. In this case, the fusional stimulus for convergence has been eliminated by occluding one eye (i.e., diplopia can only be present under binocular viewing conditions). The explanation offered to account for convergence under monocular viewing conditions was that the increase in accommodation induced a change in vergence. Similar findings have been reported under conditions of lens-induced accommodation, which eliminate potential cues to convergence from the increase in target size.

There is considerable debate concerning the relative importance of fusional and accommodative factors in the control of vergence eye movements (see review in Semmlow, 1981). Although classic theories such as those offered by Maddox (1886) proposed that accommodative factors are primary and fusional factors are only involved in finely aligning corresponding retinal points at the termination of a vergence response, more recent models of vergence control favor the primacy of fusional vergence (see Semmlow & Heerema, 1979). Consider the case of a target located at a 50-cm viewing distance. In adults, the minimum detectable change in stimulus blur is approximately $\frac{1}{4}$ diopter, or a target displacement from 50 to 44 cm. In contrast, the minimum detectable change in stimulus disparity is less than 1 min of arc, or a target displacement from 50 to 49.8 cm. In addition, the blur stimulus is ambiguous with respect to the direction of target displacement (i.e., 50 cm $\pm$ 6 cm), whereas the disparity stimulus contains a magnitude and a sign (crossed disparity equals nearer; uncrossed disparity equals farther). These facts provide indirect support for the primacy of fusional stimuli in the control of vergence eye movements.

If accommodative factors influence the accuracy of vergence movements in maintaining binocular fixation, young infants may show poor vergence movements because their accommodative system is inaccurate. This hypothesis that accommodative insufficiency creates a conflict for the young infant's vergence system and thereby reduces the magnitude of convergence responses to near targets was proposed by Slater and Findlay (1975a). Their hypothesis rested on two assumptions: (1) accommodation to near targets is inaccurate (or absent) in very young infants and (2) the link between accommodation and vergence is present in very young infants. The first assumption was based on the findings of poor accommodative accuracy in newborns reported by Haynes et al. (1965). However, as we have seen in Section II,B, these findings somewhat underestimated the accommodative responses of young infants. Nevertheless, there does appear to be a developmental improvement in accommodative accuracy, and the assumption that accommodative errors are greater in young infants appears to be generally correct.

The second assumption was not verified empirically until Aslin and Jackson (1979) reported the first study of accommodative convergence in young infants. They obtained a measure of vergence angle using corneal photography while infants monocularly viewed a target at two different distances. A pair of red–green filters was placed in front of the two eyes using a set of spectacle frames and either a red and black or a green and

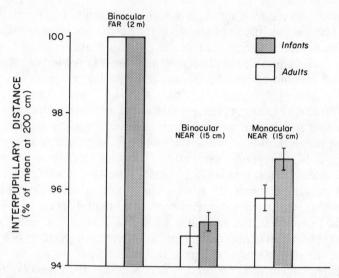

Figure 21. Mean convergence responses (indicated by decreases in interpupillary distance) in adults and infants as a function of target distance. Data under monocular viewing conditions indicate the presence of accommodative convergence. (Data replotted from Aslin & Jackson, 1979.)

black checkerboard was presented as a fixation target. Because the chromatically filtered targets could only be seen by one eye, and infrared photography could measure interpupillary distance through both filters, a measure of accommodative convergence was obtained. As shown in Figure 21, the infants between 2 and 6 months of age showed convergence to the near target under monocular viewing conditions. Thus, infants as young as 2 months, the age when accommodative accuracy becomes nearly adultlike, show the link between accommodation and vergence found in adults.

The hypothesis that accommodative insufficiency prevents accurate convergence to near targets may be a viable explanation of the data from newborns and 1-month-olds. However, it does not appear to offer a good explanation of the subsequent development in sensitivity to prism-induced binocular misalignments (see Fig. 18), because accommodation is reasonably accurate after the second postnatal month. An alternative explanation of the vergence inaccuracies in infants older than 1 month of age involves the resting positions of accommodation and vergence. It is clear from the studies by Aslin (1977) and Aslin and Jackson (1979) that fusional vergence is present by the fifth postnatal month and accommodative vergence is present by the third postnatal month, even though both systems may show improvements during subsequent development. Given the finding from Aslin and Jackson (1981) that the resting position of vergence corresponds to a much nearer viewing distance in infants than in adults, it is important to study the relation between this vergence resting position and the resting position of accommodation. In adults, the average resting position of accommodation is approximately 80 cm (Owens & Leibowitz, 1980), a viewing distance that is significantly different from the average resting position of vergence (120 cm).

It would appear that any large discrepancy between the resting positions of vergence and accommodation could create a conflict between these systems under normal binocular viewing conditions and lead to binocular misalignments. As shown in Figure 22, the resting position of vergence is either coincident with, in front of, or behind the resting position of accommodation. If the two resting positions are coincident (i.e., within the depth of focus and Panum's fusion area), then a target placed at this viewing distance induces neither an accommodative nor a vergence response. However, consider the case in which the subject has been placed in total darkness and the two systems are allowed to revert to discrepant resting positions. If a target is suddenly presented at the accommodative resting position and one eye is occluded, no accommodative effort is needed to keep the target in focus and no accommodative vergence is induced. Thus, the vergence angle remains at its resting position rather than at the distance of the monocularly fixated target. If the occluded eye is suddenly unoccluded, fusional vergence will be activated

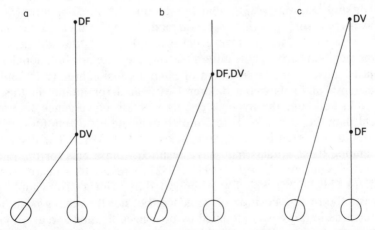

Figure 22. Illustration of three possible relations between the resting positions of vergence and accommodation: (a) vergence nearer than accommodation, (b) vergence coincident with accommodation, and (c) vergence farther than accommodation.

to eliminate the diplopia that exists because the resting position of vergence is either in front of or behind the resting position of accommodation.

This discrepancy between the resting positions of vergence and accommodation would be trivial if these two systems did not interact. However, as discussed earlier, a change in accommodation leads to a change in vergence. In addition, studies of adults (Fincham & Walton, 1957) that have held stimulus blur constant despite changes in accommodation have shown that a change in vergence induces a change in accommodation. Thus, any large discrepancy between the two resting positions creates a conflict between the clarity of the target (affected by blur-induced accommodation and vergence-induced accommodation) and fusion of the target (affected by fusional vergence and accommodative vergence). If the discrepancy is too large, either clarity or fusion must be sacrificed. The only evidence on the relation between the two resting positions in infants comes from a study by Aslin and Dobson (1983). They obtained a measure of the resting position of vergence using corneal photography and the resting position of accommodation using photorefraction. Photorefraction is a technique for assessing the refractive state of the eye by measuring the spread of light reflected from the retina. Photographs are taken of the infant's eyes from a fixed camera distance. If the infant is focused at the camera distance, the spread of light from the retina is minimal. However, if the infant is focused either in front of or behind the camera, the spread of light from the retina will be larger in proportion to the amount of defocus (see Atkinson et al., 1981; Howland & Howland, 1974).

Aslin and Dobson (1983) found in a group of 3- to 12-month-olds that the average resting position of accommodation was 70 cm, whereas the average resting position of vergence was 102 cm. Although these two resting positions are significantly different, they are not functionally different because of the large extent of Panum's fusion area ($\pm 1°$) and the large depth of focus (± 0.5 diopters) estimated for infants in this age range. In addition, the average resting position of vergence was more distant than the 31 cm for 1- to 5-month-olds and the 51 cm for 5- to 12-month-olds reported by Aslin and Jackson (1981, 1982). The discrepancies among these studies may have resulted from a bias for the infants tested by Aslin and Jackson (1981, 1982) to revert to a nearer resting position. This latter possibility is supported by evidence from adults that suggests the resting position of vergence, but not the resting position of accommodation, is easily modified by prolonged fixation at a given viewing distance (Schor, 1979a, 1979b). Nevertheless, any shift in the resting position of vergence resulting from near-target viewing would argue against the documented difficulties shown by young infants in maintaining accurate binocular fixation of near targets. Thus, at present the most plausible explanation for the inaccuracies in vergence eye movements among young infants can be summarized as (1) a large Panum's fusion area that gradually diminishes in size during the first postnatal year and (2) an inaccurate accommodative system that fails to trigger accurate vergence eye movements via accommodative vergence until accommodative accuracy improves by the third postnatal month.

V. SUMMARY AND CONCLUSIONS

The three major types of motor systems that influence the quality of visual information available to the infant retina—accommodation, pupillary changes, and eye movements—were reviewed. In each case, a variety of developmental improvements in motor system accuracy and efficiency were noted, particularly during the first three postnatal months. These improvements in motor control imply that much of the information available to the infant visual system is constrained by nonsensory factors. The accommodative system is initially quite inaccurate in maintaining a clearly focused retinal image. However, because of the poor resolving power of the newborn's visual system, differences in stimulus blur are probably not detected and, as a result, the major stimulus for accommodation is degraded. Thus, although refractive errors or a restricted amplitude of accommodation can significantly degrade the quality of the retinal image, the long-term effects of inaccurate accommodation during early infancy are probably minimal.

Differences in pupil size also affect the quality of the retinal image by modulating the amount of light reaching the photoreceptors and by influencing the depth of focus. Unfortunately, very little research has been conducted on the dynamic properties of the infant's pupillary responses. It is clear from current evidence that the motor system controlling pupillary responses is quite sluggish in early infancy. However, neither the absolute size of the infant's pupil nor the effect of pupil size on depth of focus appears to lead to significant deficits in visual processing. Nevertheless, the small magnitude of pupillary influences on the overall sensitivity of the infant's visual system could combine with a number of other nonsensory factors and lead to a significant loss in visual processing.

The eye movement systems that direct the two foveas to fixate different regions of the visual array are perhaps the most influential motor factors in visual processing. Although the saccadic system is capable of responding in a directionally appropriate manner at birth, the magnitude and sequencing of saccades is inefficient until at least the fifth postnatal month. Not only are young infants less likely to redirect their gaze to a peripheral target while another target is being fixated, but the presence of multiple saccades reduces the speed with which peripheral targets are foveated. Similarly, the tracking of a moving target is accomplished solely by the saccadic system until the end of the second postnatal month. When smooth pursuit movements emerge developmentally, their velocity is slow and they rarely match the velocity of the moving target. Finally, vergence eye movements in newborns are sluggish and of reduced magnitude. Although in the third postnatal month large vergence movements are on average magnitude appropriate, a small binocular misalignment induced by prisms is not typically overcome. Accommodative vergence is present by the second postnatal month, but there appears to be a significant change in the resting position of vergence from a very near viewing distance in early infancy to an intermediate distance in adulthood.

All of the motor systems discussed in this chapter have been studied with measurement techniques that are at best crude when compared to the techniques used in studying adult accommodation, pupillary responses, and eye movements. These limitations on the accuracy of measurement have led to a number of controversies and questions that may be impossible to answer without the aid of an animal model of oculomotor development. For example, the hypothesized migration of retinal photoreceptors during development was incorporated into an explanation of the inaccuracies observed in saccadic, pursuit, and vergence eye movements during early infancy. However, it will remain unclear whether this explanation is viable until a detailed animal model of the developing retina, as well as the link between photoreceptor stimulation and oculomotor output, are explored. Although improvements in techniques for more accurately recording the motor aspects of human visual development will provide some answers to the questions raised in this chapter, it is more likely that significant advances will require the neurophysiological and behavioral study of nonhuman species during early development.

ACKNOWLEDGMENTS

Preparation of this chapter was made possible by a Research Career Development Award from NIH (HD-00309) and by research grants from NSF (80-13075) and NICHHD (HD-11915). The helpful comments provided by Martin Banks, Philip Salapatek, and Sandra Shea are gratefully acknowledged.

REFERENCES

Abramov, I., Gordon, J., Hendrickson, A., Hainline, L., Dobson, V., & LaBossiere, E. (1982). The retina of the newborn human infant. *Science, 217,* 265–267.

Alpern, M. (1969). Types of movement. In H. Davson (Ed.) *The eye* (2nd ed., Vol. 3). New York: Academic Press.

Aslin, R. N. (1977). Development of binocular fixation in human infants. *Journal of Experimental Child Psychology, 23,* 133–150.

Aslin, R. N. (1981). Development of smooth pursuit in human infants. In D. F. Fisher, R. A. Monty, & J. W. Senders (Eds.), *Eye movements: Cognition and visual perception.* Hillsdale, NJ: Erlbaum.

Aslin, R. N. (1985). Oculomotor measures of visual development. In G. Gottlieb & N. Krasnegor (Eds.), *Measurement of audition and vision during the first year of postnatal life: A methodological overview.* Norwood, NJ: Ablex.

Aslin, R. N., & Dobson, V. (1983). Dark vergence and dark accommodation in human infants. *Vision Research, 23,* 1671–1678.

Aslin, R. N., & Dumais, S. T. (1980). Binocular vision in infants: A review and a theoretical framework. In H. W. Reese & L. P. Lipsitt (Eds.), *Advances in child development and behavior* (Vol. 15). New York: Academic Press.

Aslin, R. N., & Jackson, R. W. (1979). Accommodative-convergence in young infants: Development of a synergistic sensory-motor system. *Canadian Journal of Psychology, 33,* 222–231.

Aslin, R. N., & Jackson, R. W. (1981). Dark vergence in human infants. *Investigative Ophthalmology and Visual Science, Supplement, 20,* 47(6).

Aslin, R. N., & Jackson, R. W. (1982, March). *Development of dark vergence.* Paper presented at the biennial meeting of the International Conference on Infant Studies, Austin, TX.

Aslin, R. N., & Salapatek, P. (1975). Saccadic localization of visual targets by the very young human infant. *Perception & Psychophysics, 17,* 293–302.

Atkinson, J., & Braddick, O. (1981). Development of optokinetic nystagmus in infants: An indicator of cortical binocularity? In D. F. Fisher, R. A. Monty, & J. W. Senders (Eds.), ·*Eye movements: Cognition and visual perception.* Hillsdale, NJ: Erlbaum.

Atkinson, J., Braddick, O., Ayling, L., Pimm-Smith, E., Howland, H. C., & Ingram, R. M. (1981). Isotropic photorefraction: A new method for refractive testing of infants. *Documenta Ophthalmologica Proceedings Series, 30,* 217–222.

Atkinson, J., Braddick, O., & French, J. (1980). Infant astigmatism: Its disappearance with age. *Vision Research, 20,* 891–893.

Atkinson, J., & French, J. (1979). Astigmatism and orientation preference in human infants. *Vision Research, 19,* 1315–1317.

Banks, M. S. (1980a). The development of visual accommodation during early infancy. *Child Development, 51,* 646–666.

Banks, M. S. (1980b). Infant refraction and accommodation. *International Ophthalmology Clinics, 20,* 205–232.

Banks, M. S. (1982). The development of spatial and temporal contrast sensitivity. *Current Eye Research, 2,* 191–198.

Banks, M. S., Aslin, R. N., & Letson, R. D. (1975). Sensitive period for the development of binocular vision. *Science, 190,* 675–677.

Banks, M. S., & Munsinger, H. (1974). Pupillometric measurement of difference spectra for three color receptors in an adult and a four-year-old. *Vision Research, 14,* 813–817.

Bartlett, N. R. (1965). Dark adaptation and light adaptation. In C. H. Graham (Ed.), *Vision and visual perception*. New York: Wiley.

Becker, W., & Fuchs, A. F. (1969). Further properties of the human saccadic system: Eye movements and correction saccades with and without visual fixation points. *Vision Research, 9*, 1247–1258.

Becker, W., & Jurgens, R. (1979). An analysis of the saccadic system by means of double step stimuli. *Vision Research, 19*, 967–983.

Bennett, A. G., & Francis, J. L. (1962). The eye as an optical system. In H. Davson (Ed.), *The eye* (Vol. 4). New York: Academic Press.

Bizzi, E., Kalil, R. E., & Tagliasco, V. (1971). Eye-head coordination in monkeys: Evidence for centrally patterned organization. *Science, 173*, 452–454.

Boltz, R. L., Manny, R. E., & Katz, B. (1983). The effects of induced blur on infant visual acuity. *American Journal of Optometry and Physiological Optics, 60*, 100–105.

Braddick, O., Atkinson, J., French, J., & Howland, H. C. (1979). A photorefractive study of infant accommodation. *Vision Research, 19*, 1319–1330.

Bronson, G. (1982). The scanning patterns of human infants: Implications for visual learning. *Monographs on infancy* (Whole No. 2). Norwood, NJ: Ablex.

Brookman, K. E. (1980). *Ocular accommodation in human infants*. Unpublished doctoral dissertation, Indiana University, Bloomington, Indiana.

Brookman, K. E. (1983). Ocular accommodation in human infants. *American Journal of Optometry and Physiological Optics, 60*, 91–99.

Campbell, F. W., Robson, J. G., & Westheimer, G. (1959). Fluctuations of accommodation under steady viewing conditions. *Journal of Physiology (London), 145*, 579–594.

Campbell, F. W., & Westheimer, G. (1960). Dynamics of the accommodation response of the human eye. *Journal of Physiology (London), 151*, 285–295.

Charman, W. N., & Tucker, J. (1977). Dependence of accommodation response on the spatial frequency spectrum of the observed object. *Vision Research, 17*, 129–139.

Charman, W. N., & Tucker, J. (1978). Accommodation as a function of object form. *American Journal of Optometry and Physiological Optics, 55*, 84–92.

Cornsweet, T. N. (1970). *Visual perception*. New York: Academic Press.

Dannemiller, J. L., & Banks, M. S. (1983). The development of light adaptation in human infants. *Vision Research, 23*, 599–609.

Day, R. H. (1957). The physiological basis of form perception in the peripheral retina. *Psychological Review, 64*, 38–48.

Dayton, G. O., & Jones, M. H. (1964). Analysis of characteristics of fixation reflexes in infants by use of direct current electrooculography. *Neurology, 14*, 1152–1156.

Dayton, G. O., Jones, M. H., Aui, P., Rawson, R. A., Steele, B., & Rose, M. (1964). Developmental study of coordinated eye movements in the human infant. I. Visual acuity in the newborn human: A study based on induced optokinetic nystagmus recorded by electrooculography. *Archives of Ophthalmology, 71*, 865–870.

Dayton, G. O., Jones, M. H., Steele, B. & Rose, M. (1964). Developmental study of coordinated eye movements in the human infant. II. An electrooculographic study of the fixation reflex in the newborn. *Archives of Ophthalmology, 71*, 871–875.

Dobson, V., Howland, H. C., Moss, C., & Banks, M. S. (1983). Photorefraction of normal and astigmatic infants during viewing of patterned stimuli. *Vision Research, 23*, 1043–1052.

Dobson, V., & Teller, D. Y. (1978). Visual acuity in human infants: A review and comparison of behavioral and electrophysiological studies. *Vision Research, 18*, 1469–1483.

Doris, J., & Cooper, L. (1966). Brightness discrimination in infancy. *Journal of Experimental Child Psychology, 3*, 31–39.

Fantz, R. L., Ordy, J. M., & Udelf, M. S. (1962). Maturation of pattern vision in infants during the first six months. *Journal of Comparative and Physiological Psychology, 55,* 907–917.

Feustel, T. C., Hanna, T., & Aslin, R. N. (1981). Pursuit of blurred targets: Implications for infant tracking. *Investigative Ophthalmology and Visual Science, Supplement, 20,* 26(41).

Fincham, E. F. (1951). The accommodation reflex and its stimulus. *British Journal of Ophthalmology, 35,* 381–393.

Fincham, E. F., & Walton, J. (1957). The reciprocal actions of accommodation and convergence. *Journal of Physiology (London), 137,* 488–508.

Finlay, D., & Ivinskis, A. (1984). Cardiac and visual responses to moving peripheral stimuli presented either successively or simultaneously to the central and peripheral visual fields in four-month-old infants. *Developmental Psychology, 20,* 29–36.

Fitzgerald, H. E. (1968). Autonomic pupillary reflex activity during early infancy and its relation to social and nonsocial visual stimuli. *Journal of Experimental Child Psychology, 6,* 470–482.

Fulton, A. B., Dobson, V., Salem, D., Mar, C., Petersen, R. A., & Hansen, R. M. (1980). Cycloplegic refractions in infants and young children. *American Journal of Ophthalmology, 90,* 239–247.

Glickstein, M., & Millodot, M. (1970). Retinoscopy and eye size. *Science, 168,* 605–606.

Gorman, J. J., Cogan, D. G., & Gellis, S. S. (1957). An apparatus for grading the visual acuity of infants on the basis of optokinetic nystagmus. *Pediatrics, 19,* 1088–1092.

Green, D. G., & Campbell, F. W. (1965). Effect of focus on the visual response to a sinusoidally modulated spatial stimulus. *Journal of the Optical Society of America, 55,* 1154–1157.

Green, D. G., Powers, M. K., & Banks, M. S. (1980). Depth of focus, eye size, and visual acuity. *Vision Research, 20,* 827–836.

Haith, M. M. (1980). *Rules that babies look by.* Hillsdale, NJ: Erlbaum.

Hainline, L., Lemerise, E., Abramov, I., & Turkel, J. (1984). Orientational asymmetries in small-field optokinetic nystagmus in human infants. *Behavioral Brain Research, 13,* 217–230.

Hamer, R. D., & Schneck, M. E. (1984). Spatial summation in dark-adapted human infants. *Vision Research, 24,* 77–85.

Harris, P. L., Cassel, T. Z., & Bamborough, P. (1974). Tracking by young infants. *British Journal of Psychology, 65,* 345–349.

Harris, P. L., & MacFarlane, A. (1974). The growth of the effective visual field from birth to seven weeks. *Journal of Experimental Child Psychology, 18,* 340–348.

Haynes, H., White, B. L., & Held, R. (1965). Visual accommodation in human infants. *Science, 148,* 528–530.

Heath, G. G. (1956). The influence of visual acuity on accommodative responses of the eye. *American Journal of Optometry and Archives of the American Academy of Optometry, 33,* 513–524.

Held, R. (1978). Development of visual acuity in normal and astigmatic infants. In S. J. Cool & E. L. Smith (Eds.), *Frontiers in visual science.* Berlin & New York: Springer-Verlag.

Held, R., Birch, E., & Gwiazda, J. (1980). Stereoacuity of human infants. *Proceedings of the National Academy of Sciences of the U.S.A., 77,* 5572–5574.

Hendrickson, A., & Kupfer, C. (1976). The histogenesis of the fovea in the macaque monkey. *Investigative Ophthalmology, 15,* 746–756.

Hohmann, A., & Creutzfeldt, O. D. (1975). Squint and the development of binocularity in humans. *Nature (London), 254,* 613–614.

Howland, H. C. (1982). Infant eyes: Optics and accommodation. *Current Eye Research, 2,* 217–224.

Howland, H. C., Atkinson, J., Braddick, O., & French, J. (1978). Infant astigmatism measured by photorefraction. *Science, 202,* 331–333.

Howland, H. C., & Howland, B. (1974). Photorefraction: A technique for study of refractive state at a distance. *Journal of the Optical Society of America, 64,* 240–249.

Ingram, R. M., Traymar, M. J., Walker, C., & Wilson, J. M. (1979). Screening for refractive errors at age 1 year: A pilot study. *British Journal of Ophthalmology, 63,* 243–250.

Ivanoff, A., & Bourdy, C. (1954). Le comportement de la convergence en nocturne (The behavior of convergence in night vision). *Annales d' Optique Ocularei, 3,* 70–75.

Kertesz, A. E., Hampton, D. R., & Sabrin, H. W. (1983). The unreliability of nonius line estimates of vertical fusional vergence performance. *Vision Research, 23,* 295–297.

Kessen, W., Salapatek, P., & Haith, M. M. (1972). The visual response of the human newborn to linear contour. *Journal of Experimental Child Psychology, 13,* 9–20.

Komoda, M. K., Festinger, L., Phillips, L. J., Duckman, R. H., & Young, R. A. (1973). Some observations concerning saccadic eye movement. *Vision Research, 13,* 1009–1020.

Kremenitzer, J. P., Vaughan, H. G., Kurtzberg, D., & Dowling, K. (1979). Smooth-pursuit eye movements in the newborn infant. *Child Development, 50,* 442–448.

Larsen, J. S. (1971a). The sagittal growth of the eye. I. Ultrasonic measurement of the depth of the anterior chamber from birth to puberty. *Acta Ophthalmologica, 49,* 239–262.

Larsen, J. S. (1971b). The sagittal growth of the eye. II. Ultrasonic measurement of the axial diameter of the lens and the anterior segment from birth to puberty. *Acta Ophthalmologica, 49,* 427–440.

Larsen, J. S. (1971c). The sagittal growth of the eye. III. Ultrasonic measurement of the posterior segment (axial length of the vitreous) from birth to puberty *Acta Ophthalmologica, 49,* 441–453.

Larsen, J. S. (1971d). The sagittal growth of the eye. IV. Ultrasonic measurement of the axial length of the eye from birth to puberty. *Acta Ophthalmologica, 49,* 873–886.

Lewis, T. L., & Maurer, D. (1980). Central vision in the newborn. *Journal of Experimental Child Psychology, 29,* 475–480.

Lewis, T. L., Maurer, D., & Kay, D. (1978). Newborns' central vision: Whole or hole? *Journal of Experimental Child Psychology, 26,* 193–203.

Lotmar, W. (1976). A theoretical model for the eye of new-born infants. *Albrecht v. Graefes Archiv Puer Klinsche und Experimentelle Ophthalmologie, 198,* 179–185.

Lowenstein, O., & Loewenfeld, I. E. (1969). The pupil. In H. Davson (Ed.), *The eye* (Vol. 3). New York: Academic Press.

MacFarlane, A., Harris, P., & Barnes I. (1976). Central and peripheral vision in early infancy. *Journal of Experimental Child Psychology, 21,* 532–538.

Maddox, E. (1886). Investigations in the relation between convergence and accommodation of the eyes. *Journal of Anatomy, 20,* 475–508, 565–584.

Mann, I. (1964). *The development of the human eye.* London: British Medical Association.

Marr, D. (1982). *Vision.* San Francisco, CA: Freeman.

Mastronarde, D. N., Thibeault, M. A., & Dubin, M. W. (1980). How ganglion cells redistribute during postnatal growth of the cat retina. *Investigative Ophthalmology and Visual Science, Supplement, 20,* 70(5).

Maurer, D. (1975). The development of binocular convergence in infants (Doctoral dissertation, University of Minnesota, 1974). *Dissertation Abstracts International B, 35,* 6136-B (University Microfilms No. 75-12, 121)

McGinnis, J. M. (1930). Eye movements and optic nystagmus in early infancy. *Genetic Psychology Monographs, 8,* 321–430.

Mohindra, I., Held, R., Gwiazda, J., & Brill, S. (1978). Astigmatism in infants. *Science, 202,* 329–331.

Morasso, P., Bizzi, E., & Dichgans, J. (1973). Adjustment of saccade characteristics during head movements. *Experimental Brain Research, 16,* 492–500.

Movshon, J. A., & Van Sluyters, R. C. (1981). Visual neural development. In M. R. Rosenzweig & L. W. Porter (Eds.), *Annual Review of Psychology* (Vol. 32). Palo Alto, CA: Annual Reviews, Inc.

Muller, J. (1943). *Physiologie des Gesichtsines* (*Elements of physiology*) (W. Baly, Trans.). Philadelphia, PA: Lea & Blanchard. (Original work published 1826).

Naegele, J. R., & Held, R. (1982). The postnatal development of monocular optokinetic nystagmus in infants. *Vision Research, 22,* 341–346.

Noback, C. R., & Demarest, R. J. (1975). *The human nervous system.* New York: McGraw-Hill.

Noton, D., & Stark, L. (1971). Eye movements and visual perception. *Scientific American, 224,* 34–43.

Owens, D. A. (1980). A comparison of accommodative responsiveness and contrast sensitivity for sinusoidal gratings. *Vision Research, 20,* 159–167.

Owens, D. A., & Leibowitz, H. W. (1980). Accommodation, convergence, and distance perception in low illumination. *American Journal of Optometry and Physiological Optics, 57,* 540–550.

Peeples, D., & Teller, D. Y. (1975). Color vision and brightness discrimination in two-month-old human infants. *Science, 189,* 1102–1103.

Peiper, A. (1963). *Cerebral function in infancy and childhood.* New York: Consultants Bureau.

Powers, M. K., & Dobson, V. (1982). Effect of focus on visual acuity of human infants. *Vision Research, 22,* 521–528.

Rayner, K. (1978). Eye movements in reading and information processing. *Psychological Bulletin, 85,* 618–660.

Regal, D., & Salapatek, P. (1982). Eye and head coordination in human infants. *Investigative Ophthalmology and Visual Science, Supplement, 22,* 85(12).

Rethy, I. (1969). Development of the simultaneous fixation from the divergent anatomic eye-position of the neonate. *Journal of Pediatric Ophthalmology, 6,* 92–96.

Riggs, L. A. (1965). Visual acuity. In C. H. Graham (Ed.), *Vision and visual perception.* New York: Wiley.

Robb, R. M. (1982). Increase in retinal surface area during infancy and childhood. *Journal of Pediatric Ophthalmology and Strabismus, 19*(4), 16–20.

Robinson, D. A. (1964). The mechanics of human saccadic eye movement. *Journal of Physiology* (*London*), *174,* 245–264.

Salapatek, P. (1968). Visual scanning of geometric figures by the human newborn. *Journal of Comparative and Physiological Psychology, 66,* 247–258.

Salapatek, P., Aslin, R. N., Simonson, J., & Pulos, E. (1980). Infant saccadic eye movements to visible and previously visible targets. *Child Development, 51,* 1090–1094.

Salapatek, P., & Banks, M. S. (1978). Infant sensory assessment: Vision. In F. D. Minifie & L. L. Lloyd (Eds.), *Communicative and cognitive abilities: Early behavioral assessment.* Baltimore, MD: University Park Press.

Salapatek, P., Bechtold, A. G., & Bergman, J. (1977, November). *Pupillary response in 1-and 2-month-old infants.* Paper presented at the annual meeting of the Psychonomic Society, Washington, DC.

Salapatek, P., Bechtold, A. G., & Bushnell, E. W. (1976). Infant visual acuity as a function of viewing distance. *Child Development, 47,* 860–863.

Salapatek, P., & Kessen, W. (1966). Visual scanning of triangles by the human newborn. *Journal of Experimental Child Psychology, 3,* 155–167.

Santonastaso, A. (1930). La rifrazione oculare nei primi anni di vita. *Annali di Ottalmologia e Clinica Oculista, 58,* 852–885.

Schor, C. M. (1979a). The influence of rapid prism adaptation upon fixation disparity. *Vision Research, 19,* 757–765.

Schor, C. M. (1979b). The relationship between fusional vergence eye movements and fixation disparity. *Vision Research, 19,* 1359–1367.

Schor, C. M., Wood, I., & Ogawa, J. (1984). Binocular sensory fusion is limited by spatial resolution. *Vision Research, 24,* 661–665.

Semmlow, J. L. (1981). Oculomotor responses to near stimuli: The near triad. In B. L. Zuber (Ed.), *Models of oculomotor behavior and control.* Boca Raton, FL: CRC Press.

Semmlow, J. L., & Heerema, D. (1979). The synkinetic interaction of convergence accommodation and accommodative convergence. *Vision Research, 19,* 1237–1242.

Slater, A. M., & Findlay, J. M. (1972). The measurement of fixation position in the newborn baby. *Journal of Experimental Child Psychology, 14,* 349–364.

Slater, A. M., & Findlay, J. M. (1975a). The corneal-reflection technique and the visual preference method: Sources of error. *Journal of Experimental Child Psychology, 20,* 240–247.

Slater, A. M., & Findlay, J. M. (1975b). Binocular fixation in the newborn baby. *Journal of Experimental Child Psychology, 20,* 248–273.

Sokol, S., Moskowitz, A., & Paul, A. (1983). Evoked potential estimates of visual accommodation in infants. *Vision Research, 23,* 851–860.

Sperling, G. (1960). The information available in brief visual presentations. *Psychological Monographs, 74,* (Whole No. 498).

Stark, L. (1968). *Neurological control systems.* New York: Plenum.

Stein, B. E., Clamann, H. P., & Goldberg, S. J. (1980). Superior colliculus: Control of eye movements in neonatal kittens. *Science, 210,* 78–80.

Tauber, E. S., & Koffler, S. (1966). Optomotor response in human infants to apparent motion: Evidence of innateness. *Science, 152,* 382–383.

Timberlake, G. T., Wyman, D., Skavenski, A. A., & Steinman, R. (1972). The oculomotor error signal in the fovea. *Vision Research, 12,* 1059–1064.

Toates, F. M. (1972). Accommodation function of the human eye. *Physiological Review, 52,* 828–863.

Tronick, E. (1972). Stimulus control and the growth of the infant's effective visual field. *Perception & Psychophysics, 11,* 373–376.

Tucker, J., & Charman, W. N. (1979). Reaction and response times for accommodation. *American Journal of Optometry and Physiological Optics, 56,* 490–503.

Van Hof-Van Duin, J. (1978). Direction preference of optokinetic responses in monocularly tested normal kittens and light deprived cats. *Archives of Italian Biology, 116,* 471–477.

von Noorden, G. K. (1980). *Burian-vonNoorden's binocular vision and ocular motility: Theory and management of strabismus* (2nd ed.). St. Louis, MO: C. V. Mosby.

Westheimer, G. (1954). Mechanism of saccadic eye movements. *Archives of Ophthalmology, 52,* 710–724.

Westheimer, G., & Campbell, F. W. (1962). Light distribution in the image formed by the living human eye. *Journal of the Optical Society of America, 52,* 1040–1045.

Westheimer, G., & Mitchell, D. E. (1969). The sensory stimulus for disjunctive eye movements. *Vision Research, 9,* 749–755.

Wheeless, L., Boynton, R., & Cohen, G. (1966). Eye-movement responses to step and pulse-step stimuli. *Journal of the Optical Society of America, 56,* 956–960.

Wickelgren, L. (1967). Convergence in the human newborn. *Journal of Experimental Child Psychology, 5,* 74–85.

Woodhouse, J. M., & Campbell, F. W. (1975). The role of the pupil light reflex in aiding adaptation to the dark. *Vision Research, 15,* 649–653.

Yarbus, A. L. (1967). *Eye movements and vision.* New York: Plenum.

Young, L. R. (1981). The sampled data model and foveal dead zone for saccades. In B. L. Zuber (Ed.), *Models of oculomotor behavior and control.* Boca Raton, FL: CRC Press.

3

Infant Visual Psychophysics

MARTIN S. BANKS
School of Optometry and
*   Department of Psychology*
University of California
Berkeley, California 94720

JAMES L. DANNEMILLER
Department of Psychology
University of Wisconsin
Madison, Wisconsin 53706

I. INTRODUCTION

The mature visual system is a marvelous device. It gathers information about a wide variety of environmental properties, represents the information efficiently, and allows the perceiver to respond appropriately. All of these things occur reliably in spite of dreadfully complicating factors such as changes in the source of illumination, movement of objects under inspection or of the perceiver, changes in the context in which objects are presented, and so forth.

Recently, the development of the visual system has drawn much theoretical and empirical attention. This interest arises from our natural curiosity about how sophisticated devices come to be, but there are additional reasons. For one, the cognitive and social capabilities of young infants have also come under increasing scrutiny. The study of early cognitive and social skills generally involves visual stimulation, so it has become important to know what infants can and cannot see in order to ensure that immature performance can be ascribed to cognitive or social immaturities rather than to an inability to discern the stimuli used.

Another reason for the recent interest in infant vision arose from findings in the basic research field of neurophysiology and the clinical field of pediatric ophthalmology. The presence of ocular abnormalities early in

115

life (cataracts, crossed eyes, myopia, etc.) cause seemingly permanent deficits in various visual capabilities (e.g., Awaya, et al., 1973; Banks, Aslin & Letson, 1975; Freeman, Mitchell, & Millodot, 1972; Hubel & Wiesel, 1965; Wiesel & Hubel, 1965). This susceptibility of infants and young children to ocular abnormalities means that early diagnosis and treatment are required for effective eye care. Much research has, therefore, been devoted to describing how normal visual development proceeds, so that abnormality can be spotted, and to developing sensitive assessment techniques.

This volume presents work that was spawned by the recent interest in visual development. Our chapter has two fairly specific purposes. First, we describe and evaluate the psychophysical approach to the study of visual development. What is psychophysics? What are its strengths and weaknesses as a scientific methodology? What experimental techniques does the approach offer? How are psychophysical procedures implemented in infant research? Second, we review specific psychophysical findings concerning the development of pattern vision and temporal vision in human infants.

II. PSYCHOPHYSICS AND ITS TECHNIQUES

Psychophysics attempts to relate the physical properties of the external world to one's experience of it. The senses are considered the bridge between the external world and the inner world of experience, so psychophysics concentrates on sensory capabilities. The basic question asked in classical psychophysics is, what are the limits of sensory capability? Exploration of this question takes two routes: what is the smallest detectable energy (the absolute threshold)?; and, what is the smallest detectable change (the difference threshold)? These sound like rather uninteresting questions, but they are not because they are normally used as vehicles to explore the mechanisms that underlie sensory capabilities. We will return to this point shortly, but first we describe other defining characteristics of psychophysics.

Psychophysicists are most concerned with sensory mechanisms and those mechanisms are assumed to be low-level and indifferent to cognitive strategies. The performance of these mechanisms is also generally assumed to be dependent primarily upon the physical properties of stimulation. These two assumptions have led to two other common features of psychophysical research. First, because physical properties of stimulation are assumed to be important, the field is characterized by its careful attention to stimulus measurement. In visual psychophysics, for example, the luminance, wavelength composition, size, temporal duration, and any other relevant physical dimension are usually specified precisely. The stimuli used are often quite simple as well. Second, because higher-level, cognitive mechanisms are not of primary interest, psychophysicists try to minimize their impact on performance by making the subject's task as simple as possible. Thus, the response asked for is generally very simple. ("Press this button if you see it, and the other button if you don't.") Subjects are also usually given any information that might aid performance without introducing experimental bias. Hence, they are typically given comprehensive instructions, lots of practice, rest periods as needed, and trial-by-trial feedback on their performance. To minimize the effects of variations in attentiveness, subjects are often allowed to initiate trials themselves.

Psychophysics is commonly portrayed as the discipline concerned with sensory thresholds. Indeed, the field's reliance on threshold data has been criticized on the grounds that sensory thesholds have little relevance for everyday perception. This point is certainly valid because the visual environment is populated by objects whose contours and features are well above threshold. Sensory thresholds only have a significant impact on perception in certain situations: for example, the ability to read a distant highway sign or to detect an aircraft in a dense fog (Ginsburg, 1978). Nonetheless, criticism of psychophysical research because it relies on threshold data misses the point of most research in this field. Sensory thresholds are generally measured not because the the thresholds themselves are of interest but rather because they reveal the characteristics of underlying sensory mechanisms. In this sense, psychophysics resembles geophysics. A geophysicist maps the complex of direct and indirect shock waves produced by surface explosions in order to determine the shape, depth, and composition of underlying layers of rock. The psychophysicist maps the space of sensory experience under different conditions in order to ascertain the character of underlying sensory mechanisms.

This argument tells us why the psychophysicist attempts to relate the physical properties of stimulation to their sensory effects, but it does not tell us why the threshold region in the space of sensory experience is chosen. Why not a point 10 times higher than threshold? We believe thresholds are used because they are easy to find accurately and reliably. The subject can easily provide reliable data on the location of the transition from experience to no experience. It would be much more difficult to

design techniques that would reliably locate the region of sensory experience that is 10 times higher than threshold.[1]

Let us describe a hypothetical psychophysical experiment to illustrate
how thresholds are typically used to map sensory space and to reveal
underlying mechanisms. The experiment involves determining the relationship between the wavelength and the visibility of a light. The experiment is most concerned with rod vision, so it is conducted under dim,
scotopic illumination levels. Conceivably, one could use two strategies—
input or output mapping—to chart this relationship between wavelength
and visibility.

Output mapping strategies involve the presentation of a constant intensity value and the measurement of a variable output or response. In our
example, one might present a dim, fixed-intensity flash of light and ask the
subject to report a number corresponding to its perceived intensity. If this
was done for a number of wavelengths, a curve plotting perceived intensity (a psychological dimension) as a function of wavelength (a physical
dimension) could be determined. The problem with this strategy is that
the characteristics of psychological scales, such as perceived intensity,
are often difficult to ascertain. Are there floor and ceiling effects? Is the
scale a ratio scale, an interval scale, or an ordinal scale?

The input mapping strategy, which is characteristic of psychophysical
research, avoids this difficulty to a great extent. It involves varying the
intensity of the stimulus in order to achieve some criterion output or
response. In our example, we might present a variety of intensities at each
wavelength and again ask the subject to report, for each intensity, a
number corresponding to its perceived intensity. Following the input
mapping strategy, we would summarize our findings by plotting the physical intensity required at each wavelength to elicit a constant perceived
intensity. We could choose any level of perceived intensity to serve as
criterion and thus avoid potential floor and ceiling effects and other
sources of error. For reasons stated above, the best choice for the criterion level would probably be a threshold. Our summary graph would then
plot the threshold intensity (a physical dimension) as a function of wavelength (another physical dimension). The beauty of this approach is that it

[1] This argument is not valid for all psychophysical experiments. At least one class of
experimental questions is concerned with the actual value of thresholds. These are investigations of the visual system's optimal performance. For example, Green (1970) and Williams
(1985) measured visual acuity and contrast sensitivity in adults and quantitatively related the
threshold values to the spacing and size of photoreceptors. Another example is the experiment of Hecht, Schlaer, and Pirenne (1942). They measured the absolute threshold of the
visual system under optimal conditions and then used the threshold value to deduce that a
single quantum of light can be an effective visual stimulus.

sidesteps the problem of using indeterminant psychological scales; the only scales involved in the ultimate description are physical scales whose properties are known. The only assumption involved is that the criterion output—in this case, the threshold value—represents a similar sensory effect across wavelengths.[2]

It is interesting to note that input and output mapping strategies are both common in perceptual research. Input mapping is characteristic of adult and infant psychophysical research whereas output mapping is characteristic of most perceptual research concerned with higher-order mechanisms (e.g., Bornstein, Kessen, & Weiskopf, 1976; Ruff & Birch, 1974). The advantage of the input mapping strategy is its psychometric and logical simplicity. The disadvantage of the input mapping strategy is that it requires much more time to collect the data. In our hypothetical example, this strategy demands that several intensity levels at each wavelength be presented in order to find the intensity that elicits a criterion response. The output mapping strategy requires only one intensity level at each wavelength.

The hypothetical example developed above yields a psychophysical map of the relationship between the visibility and the wavelength of a light under dim illumination conditions. This map, which is called the scotopic (rod) spectral sensitivity curve, has proven very useful. The scotopic spectral sensitivity curve, once corrected for absorption by the ocular media, has the same shape as the curve that describes the way rhodopsin absorbs light of different wavelengths. It is reasonable to assume, then,

---

[2] The experimenter using an output mapping strategy has to be concerned with the rules that different subjects follow when relating input magnitude to response. For example, consider the use of the duration of fixation measure in studies of infant perception. Two infants may look for differing amounts of time at the same magnitude of a stimulus. So far, this creates no problems. Suppose, however, that when the stimulus is increased in magnitude, the two infants scale their fixation times according to different rules. One infant's fixation durations may increase fairly linearly with stimulus magnitude while the other infant's fixations may increase logarithmically. The underlying sensory responses are obscured by the indeterminate nature of the relationship between physical magnitude and response magnitude.

The use of an output mapping strategy in these studies bears some resemblance to a similar technique in audio engineering. For example, to determine the fidelity (frequency response) of a stereo system, an audio engineer can use the output mapping strategy of probing the system with a constant amplitude signal of various frequencies. The output amplitude at each of these frequencies is then measured and the effect (attenuation) of the system on each input frequency can be specified. The choice of an input amplitude is somewhat arbitrary because the system is approximately linear; the scale that relates input amplitude to output amplitude is a ratio scale, that is, the doubling of input amplitude leads to a doubling of response amplitude. No such *a priori* assumption can be made about the psychological scales that arise when the output mapping strategy is used in psychophysics.

that the psychophysical sensitivity curve and the absorption curve are intimately related. Since rhodopsin is the photopigment of rods, we can conclude that vision under dim illumination is mediated entirely by rods. This and many other examples illustrate the potential utility of using threshold data to determine the functional characteristics of sensory mechanisms.

The next topic we consider is methods used to measure thresholds. The term psychophysics generally refers to behavioral work. That is to say, psychophysical techniques are those that involve voluntary behavioral responses such as button presses and verbal reports. Electrophysiological techniques like visually evoked potentials and electroretinography are generally not considered psychophysical techniques. Psychophysics is also characterized by its emphasis on repeated measures. Specifically, most experiments involve hundreds or even thousands of trials per subject. For this reason, most psychophysical publications present data from only a handful of subjects.

The psychophysicist has several specific methods at his disposal: (1) method of adjustment; (2) method of limits; (3) method of constant stimuli; and (4) adaptive staircase techniques. These methods are distinguished by the manner in which the stimuli are presented and by the responses required of the subject. We discuss only two of them here—the method of constant stimuli and adaptive staircases—because the others are not currently applicable to infant research.

The method of constant stimuli is a very common psychophysical technique. This method places the control of stimulus level in the experimenter's hands. Several levels that span the subjects' estimated threshold are chosen beforehand. A number of trials are then presented at each level during the experimental session. Very frequently, the two-alternative forced-choice paradigm is used. In this paradigm the stimulus appears in one of two positions on each trial and the subject responds by indicating in which position (e.g., left) he/she thought the stimulus appeared. The subject's responses at each level are converted into a percentage correct score. Thus, percentage correct scores are obtained at each stimulus level. These percentages as a function of stimulus level are called the psychometric function. In the two-alternative, forced-choice procedure outlined above, the psychometric function generally extends from 50%, or chance performance, at low stimulus levels to 100%, or perfect performance, at high levels. The exact shape of the psychometric function depends on experimental conditions, but the cumulative normal distribution (ogive) is most frequently assumed.

Since psychometric functions change smoothly from 50%, the point at which the subject presumably cannot detect the stimulus, to 100%, the point at which subject always detects the stimulus, how does one determine the location of threshold? Clearly the determination is somewhat arbitrary because any point between 50% and 100% would be a possibility. Most researchers have defined the 70% or 75% point as threshold, in part because the psychometric function is steepest in that region.[3] Various techniques have been used to estimate either of these points. They can be estimated using graphical interpolation, but a more rigorous approach is to use a curve-fitting routine such as probit analysis (Finney, 1971).[4]

Adaptive staircase procedures (Wetherill & Levitt, 1965) are also commonly used for psychophysical measurement. These procedures differ from the method of constant stimuli in several respects. In staircase procedures, the level of the stimulus on each trial depends upon the observer's response(s) on the previous trial(s). Because stimulus levels are determined by the subject's performance, they tend to cluster around the point to be estimated on the psychometric function. For this reason, staircases allow accurate estimation of thresholds without requiring unreasonably large numbers of trials.

A large number of staircase procedures exist. Different versions are distinguished by four characteristics: (1) the rules used to determine changes from trial to trial in the level of the stimulus, (2) the step size by which the level is increased or decreased from trial to trial, (3) the rule used to terminate the staircase, and (4) the algorithm used to estimate threshold from the resulting data. The most common procedure is the two-down, one-up staircase of Wetherill and Levitt (1965). The change rule of this procedure requires two consecutive correct judgments before the stimulus level for the next trial is decremented (detection is made more difficult). Any incorrect judgment results in an increment in stimulus level on the next trial (detection is made easier). The step size of these increments and decrements is usually fixed, but several techniques have additional provisions for changing the step size as the staircase progresses (e.g., Pollack, 1968). The two-down, one-up staircase is generally terminated once a prespecified number of reversals (a change from incrementing to decrementing the level or vice versa) has occurred. Threshold is

---

[3] The experimenter generally assumes that the shapes and slopes of psychometric functions are roughly the same for different stimuli. If this assumption is valid, the shape of derived sensitivity functions does not depend on the choice of threshold criterion. If this assumption is invalid, however, the shape of derived sensitivity functions varies with threshold criterion. This is a particular problem when the slopes of psychometric functions are shallow. Since shallow slopes are the rule in infant work, the validity of this assumption should be checked whenever possible.

[4] Probit analysis is available on the SAS statistical package for IBM computers.

estimated simply by averaging the stimulus levels at each reversal. The two-down, one-up procedure estimates the 70.7% point on the subject's psychometric function. The statistical properties of staircase estimators have been reported by Rose, Teller, and Rendleman (1970).

It is important, of course, to use a psychophysical method that yields the most accurate estimate of threshold. In infant work, it is obviously desirable to require as few trials as possible. Two sorts of issues are important to evaluating whether the method of constant stimuli or adaptive staircases are better for infant psychophysical work. First the statistical accuracy of the procedures is important. We consider this issue by asking, under *ideal conditions*, how accurate are the two techniques in estimating threshold given a fixed number of trails? Second, the relative efficiencies of the techniques *in practice* are important. We consider this issue by asking, how useful are the two techniques in estimating thresholds under typical infant testing conditions?

We consider statistical accuracy under ideal conditions first. The accuracy of any psychophysical method depends on efficient placement of observations. This amounts to an efficient selection of stimulus levels. As might be expected, what constitutes efficient placement depends on the experimental question. For example, if one wants to estimate the slope of the psychometric function, it is best to distribute levels widely (Levitt, 1971). If, on the other hand, one wishes to determine a single point, such as the 70% point, it is better to cluster observations near the point being estimated (Levitt, 1971). The goal of most infant psychophysical work has been to estimate one point, so we will focus on that problem.

The method of constant stimuli makes optimal placing of observations difficult. The experimenter must choose the position and spacing of stimulus values prior to the experimental run. Since one often does not know the subject's capability beforehand, one has to make somewhat arbitrary choices. This presents a problem. One might, for example, choose stimulus levels that are all too low for the subject and only obtain points around the 50% level. A threshold could not be estimated with any accuracy in this case. Adaptive procedures, however, are designed to use information gained during the course of a session to improve the placing of stimulus levels. In that way, the majority of levels are placed near the threshold value so that most trials contribute significantly to the final computed value.

These considerations imply that adaptive staircases may estimate threshold in a given number of trials more accurately than the method of constant stimuli does. This is an empirical question, however, so let us investigate it in that fashion. There are two measures of accuracy that are important: bias and variability. Bias is simply the difference between the true and estimated thresholds. Variability is the dispersion of individual cases of estimated thresholds about the mean threshold estimate. Bias can be partialed out if it is known, but variability cannot. Therefore, we concentrate here on the variability of threshold estimates.

Which method—method of constant stimuli with probit analysis or two-down, one-up adaptive staircase—yields the lesser variability in threshold estimates? Unfortunately, this question cannot be answered simply. One approach has been to use computer simulations to compare the two methods. These simulations are first approximations to these methods in actual use because most simulations make assumptions that are probably not true in actual psychophysical work. This is particularly true with infants because performance may not be stable across trials. Nonetheless, McKee, Klein, and Teller (1985) have argued that the variability of threshold estimates with adaptive staircase procedures can in principle be no less than the variability of threshold estimates from the method of constant stimuli with *optimum placement of trials*. Their computer simulations appear to support this assertion in that the variability of threshold estimates is about the same for the two methods when trials are placed optimally in the method of constant stimuli. But when trials are not placed optimally, adaptive staircases provide less variable threshold estimates than the method of constant stimuli. This occurs because staircases, given a reasonable number of trials, automatically place the majority of trials near the threshold value. In other words, adaptive staircases seem, on statistical grounds, to be a better choice than the method of constant stimuli.

The second important consideration is how these two procedures work in practice. We consider three problems that all argue in favor of using the method of constant stimuli, given our current state of knowledge. First, the criteria for rejecting poor experimental data sets are clearer with the method of constant stimuli: an infant who fails to respond near 100% correct with a highly visible target is probably not attending sufficiently to allow a meaningful estimate of threshold. The criteria for rejecting a poor staircase run are not as clear (see Manny & Klein, 1985), for a suggested criterion for rejecting poor staircase runs). Second, the upper asymptote of the infant's psychometric function may not be 100%. This presents no particular problems for the method of constant stimuli beyond those introduced if probit analysis is run with the assumption of an upper asymptote of 100%. However, asymptotes below 100% present problems for staircases. In particular, low asymptotes decrease the probability that two consecutive correct trials will occur as required by the rules of the two-down, one-up staircase. This reduces the probability that the staircase will converge quickly on the appropriate stimulus level. Finally, because a two-down, one-up staircase converges on the 70.7% point on the psychometric function, a majority of the trials presented to the infant may be at or near threshold. We have used staircase procedures in our laboratory and our distinct impression is that infants' attention wanes when a number of near-threshold trials are presented consecutively. This is not as serious a problem with the method of constant stimuli because this method often presents numerous trials well above threshold. One way to alleviate the problem with the staircase procedure is to present levels well above threshold on a random schedule or when the experimenter thinks that they are necessary to maintain the infant's attention. These "easy" trials should not be used to compute changes in the direction of the staircase. Of course, if one has to present too many "easy" trials, the advantage of staircase procedures for required number of trials would diminish.

Human infants are, of course, nonverbal and this fact poses a number of problems for psychophysical testing. In particular, infants cannot be instructed to perform at the limit of their sensory capacity nor to respond in an unambiguous fashion. The developmentalist's only recourse is to rely on existing response systems. In psychophysical work, these response systems usually involve visual attending behaviors. These include general orienting behaviors to peripheral stimuli, such as eye movements and head turns, and visual following behaviors, such as smooth pursuit. Other responses, such as optokinetic nystagmus (OKN), electroretinography (ERG), and visually evoked potentials (VEP), have been used in related research but, according to our earlier definition, these are not conventional psychophysical response measures.

Two behavioral techniques that use visual orienting behaviors are most common in infant psychophysical work. They are the preferential looking technique (Fantz, 1958, 1965) and the forced-choice preferential looking technique (Teller, 1979). Both techniques rely on the tendency of young infants to fixate a patterned field rather than a blank field when given the choice. Fantz, Ordy, and Udelf (1962) and others have used the preferential looking technique (PL) to measure pattern detection thresholds. This is accomplished by simultaneously presenting a patterned field and a blank field of equal hue, luminance, and size. The infant's direction of first fixation, number of fixations, or total fixation time on each field is recorded. If significantly more or longer fixations are observed to the pattern, one can conclude that the infant can detect the pattern. The forced-choice preferential looking technique (FPL) is a variant of the PL technique. As in PL, two stimuli—a patterned and an unpatterned field— are generally presented on each trial, one to the left and one to the right. An adult observer, who is unaware of the location of the patterned stimulus, is asked to judge its location based on the infant's behavior. The observer is allowed to use any aspect of the infant's behavior to make this judgment. In order to learn which behaviors are most informative for each infant, the observer is given practice and trial-by-trial feedback. So, if direction of first fixation is most informative for one infant, the observer should learn this and use that behavior to guide his judgments. If facial expressions are most informative for another infant and the observer notes this, that behavior would be used. When the observer in an FPL experiment is able to judge the pattern's location more often than expected by chance, one can conclude that the infant can detect the pattern.

We now consider the relationship between the results from PL and FPL experiments and infants' sensory thresholds. Any estimation of threshold requires information about what stimulus levels are above threshold and what levels are below threshold. Unfortunately, poor performance (negative results) is weak evidence that a stimulus is below threshold. Consequently, PL and FPL threshold estimates are ambiguous: they only indicate that threshold must be at the estimated value or lower. The difficulties arise because the dependent measures used (in PL, direction, number, or duration of fixations and in FPL, the adult observer's percentage correct) are at least two steps removed from the variable of interest, the sensory threshold. One step is between the infant's detection of the stimulus and the production of overt behavior in response to it. The other step is between the overt behavior and the actual dependent measure. These two steps, which we will call nonsensory factors, can be thought of as noisy channels in the transmission of information from the infant to the experimenter. They can only cause a loss of information (i.e., an elevation of the threshold estimate) and an increase in variability (i.e., a decrease in the slope of the psychometric function). These factors hamper the interpretation of infant psychophysical data because one generally cannot determine how much information is lost at each stage.

We can illustrate this ambiguity with an example. Consider a PL experiment in which an infant's number of fixations did not differ between a striped pattern and a blank field. The experimenter presumably wants to know if the striped pattern was below the infant's sensory threshold but cannot tell because she cannot answer the following questions. Could the infant simply not detect the stimulus? Or could he detect it, but failed to produce overt behavior indicative of detection? Because these ambiguities affect the estimation of sensory thresholds, it is very important to minimize the magnitude of information lost in these two steps. Consequently, developmental psychophysicists control behavioral state as well as possible in order to maximize the probability that overt behavior will be elicited by a detected stimulus. Likewise, sensitive dependent measures are chosen to minimize information loss due to a mismatch between the overt behavior and the dependent measure. The FPL technique probably minimizes information loss due to this mismatch better than the PL procedure does. In PL experiments, the only useful overt behavior is the particular aspect of fixation recorded (say, first fixation). FPL experiments, in contrast, allow the observer to learn which behaviors are most informative for each infant and to guide his judgments accordingly. If some infants' most informative behaviors include other responses like the steadiness of fixation or facial expressions, the FPL procedure should be a more sensitive measure of threshold. Atkinson, Braddick, and Moar (1977a) have confirmed this expectation. They showed that lower contrast threshold estimates (higher contrast sensitivities) were obtained when the observer make an FPL judgment rather than a first fixation judgment.

We have discussed a number of important points in the last few paragraphs, so let us summarize them before moving on. The estimation of threshold requires information about which stimulus levels are above and below threshold. However, poor performance at low stimulus levels is ambiguous. It may indicate that the level is actually below threshold. But it might also result from information loss at two steps between the infant's threshold and the experimenter. It is very difficult to ascertain how much each step is responsible for the poor performance, so one must conclude that threshold estimates are lower-bound estimates of the true sensory threshold. Nonetheless, any psychophysical experiments should strive to minimize information loss at the two nonsensory steps.

The ambiguity of psychophysical threshold estimates in infants renders estimates of visual capacity at a given age uncertain. It also makes age comparisons quite difficult. This second point has not been fully appreciated in the infant psychophysical literature, so we describe it in some detail here. Suppose we conducted an FPL experiment to measure grating acuity thresholds in infants from 1 to 6 months of age. Suppose further that the thresholds obtained were 2 cycles/degree (c/deg) at 1 month and 6 c/deg at 6 months. Could we conclude that acuity improves by that amount over that age range? Not with any certainty. Performance in an FPL task may reflect the contribution of sensory thresholds (the variable of interest) and nonsensory factors. Consequently, a change in performance with age could be due to age changes in threshold, age changes in nonsensory factors, or both. Is it plausible that these nonsensory factors change with age and thus contaminate age comparisons? Unfortunately, it is. For example, it is plausible that the relationship between stimulus detection and the production of overt behavior changes. The behavioral repertoire and reactivity of human infants undergo significant changes with age (Kessen, Haith, & Salapatek, 1970). Thus, an age-related change in performance cannot necessarily be ascribed to a change in sensory threshold.

If threshold measurements at one age and comparisons of thresholds across age are uncertain, the reader might wonder why one should bother to collect psychophysical data from infants at all.[5] Not surprisingly, we believe that it is worth the effort. Even though psychophysical techniques yield uncertain estimates of sensory thresholds in infants, there are several ways to increase one's confidence that the threshold estimates reflect the behavior of sensory mechanisms rather than nonsensory factors. In the remainder of this section we briefly describe four approaches or sorts of information that are useful in this regard. We call them verification techniques. They are (1) the use of thresholds as relative rather than absolute information; (2) stimulus convergence; (3) response convergence; and (4) good performance relative to some known optimal performance. (The first technique does not have the same status as the others; indeed, we will describe cases in which is it subsumed under the second and third techniques.) We define these four techniques briefly here. More detailed discussions of them are provided in Sections III–VI below on visual acuity, contrast sensitivity, light and dark adaptation, and temporal vision.

First, consider the use of threshold data as relative rather than absolute information. The error introduced into threshold estimates by the intrusion of simple nonsensory factors may not be crucial for a large class of problems in visual development. Consider, for example, the often-replicated result that infants are less sensitive than adults in visual detection tasks. How much of this sensitivity difference is attributable to the intrusion of nonsensory factors such as low motivation to respond to a detected stimulus? If the problem under investigation involves an absolute comparison between infants and adults (e.g., stimulus intensity at threshold), one cannot answer this question without some means of estimating the magnitude of nonsensory contributions. However, if the problem involves a comparison between infants and adults in terms of relative,

---

[5] Similar interpretive difficulties exist in all infant work. For example, when an infant fails to dishabituate to a novel stimulus in a habituation experiment, it is weak evidence that they cannot detect the stimulus change. Similarly, when an infant fails to search for a hidden object in an object permanence experiment, one cannot conclude with assurity that the infant does not know that the object still exists. Indeed, these sorts of interpretive difficulties exist, in a presumably less severe form, in adult psychophysical work, too. The relationship between an adult's true sensory threshold and his performance is known to vary with nonsensory factors such as perceptual set, response criterion, and stimulus–response compatibility. Psychophysicists who study adults do their best to minimize the impact of these factors, but one cannot measure how much all such factors contribute. Consequently, their effects on performance cannot be partialed out.

within-age sensitivity to different values along some stimulus dimension, then the effects of simple nonsensory factors present no particular problems. For example, consider scotopic spectral sensitivity. Here the question is a relative one: how sensitive are infants to different wavelengths of light at absolute threshold? Despite large differences between infants and adults in absolute sensitivity, the shapes of their scotopic spectral sensitivity curves (a relative comparison) are essentially identical (Powers, Schneck, & Teller, 1981). Of course, even these types of relative comparisons carry with them the assumption that some nonsensory factor such as motivation will not differentially interact with the stimulus dimension that constitutes the independent variable.

The concept of stimulus convergence was described by Yonas and Pick (1975). In the current context, stimulus convergence refers to the ability of a model of sensory mechanisms to predict thresholds for one sort of stimulus (e.g., faces) from thresholds obtained with another sort of stimulus (e.g., gratings). The same response measure (e.g., FPL) is used for both sorts of stimuli. If the predictions of the sensory model are accurate, our confidence that the data reflect sensory behavior is increased. In other words, the presence of stimulus convergence is reasonably persuasive evidence that infants' performance depends primarily on sensory rather than nonsensory factors and that the stimuli used tap the same sorts of sensory mechanisms. We give examples of such cases below under contrast sensitivity. The absence of stimulus convergence is more difficult to interpret because two possibilities exist: (1) stimulus convergence was not observed because of significant contributions by nonsensory factors (e.g., a stronger motivation to look at faces than at gratings), and (2) stimulus convergence was not observed because an inappropriate model of the sensory mechanisms involved was used.

The concept of response convergence was also described by Yonas and Pick (1975). In the current context, response convergence refers to the ability to obtain similar threshold estimates using different response measures. The same sorts of stimuli (e.g., gratings) are used for each response measure. Response convergence should be observed if the response measures reflect the behavior of the same sensory mechanisms. So, for example, FPL and visually evoked potentials (VEPs), if they reflect the behavior of the same sensory mechanisms, should yield similar estimates of visual acuity for gratings. If the thresholds are similar, one's confidence that the data reflect sensory behavior is increased because the contribution of nonsensory factors would presumably vary from one response measure to another. We provide examples of attempts to examine response convergence below under visual acuity, contrast sensitivity, and temporal vision. We argue in the first of those sections that several attempts to assess response convergence have been misguided. We suggest a different strategy that should minimize problems encountered previously.

The final source of information that can increase one's confidence in infant threshold estimates is good performance relative to some theoretically optimal performance. The intrusion of nonsensory factors such as poor motivation to respond to a detected stimulus can only degrade performance. Consequently, if one could show that infants performed at the optimal level expected for sensory performance, we could safely conclude that nonsensory factors did not contaminate the results. A hypothetical example illustrates this. Suppose an FPL experiment yielded an acuity estimate of 2 c/deg at 1 month. One could conceivably calculate the maximum level of performance expected given the optical quality and photoreceptor density of the young eye. If the observed acuity was similar to the predicted optimum, our confidence in the accuracy of the threshold estimates would be strengthened considerably. We describe examples of this approach in our sections on visual acuity and temporal vision.

This concludes our general discussion of psychophysics and its application to the study of infant vision. The remainder of this chapter reviews developmental research that exemplifies the psychophysical approach.

One topic considered is the development of pattern vision. The ability to recognize, classify, and identify objects on the basis of pattern information is arguably the most complex and sophisticated of our visual capabilities. This point is corroborated by the difficulty computer scientists have had in producing general pattern recognition devices (e.g., Dodwell, 1970; Marr, 1982). For this reason, the study of the development of pattern vision has traditionally attracted more experimental and theoretical attention than any other topic in infant perception. We review basic findings concerning early pattern vision in the next three sections, visual acuity, contrast sensitivity, and light and dark adaptation. The last section, temporal vision, has been included because, in our opinion, spatial-temporal interactions are crucial to pattern vision.

In our discussion of each topic, we briefly review relevant adult psychophysical work and then describe and evaluate developmental studies. We concentrate on behavioral studies but occasionally include electrophysiological results that aid the interpretation of developmental findings.

III. VISUAL ACUITY

A fundamental visual function is to represent pattern information in a manner that allows the recognition and identification of objects and determination of their spatial layout. This function depends on the ability to detect differences in intensity or wavelength composition because such differences create the contours of patterns in the first place. It is not enough, however, to just detect intensity or wavelength differences. Object recognition and determination of spatial layout also depend on the ability to encode the spatial distribution of such differences. The study of visual acuity concerns the accuracy of this encoding of spatial distribution.

Measures of visual acuity generally involve high-contrast black and white patterns. An observer's performance is assessed as the separation is varied between two contours within the pattern. The separation for which the subject is just able to detect or resolve the pattern serves as the measure of visual acuity and is expressed in degrees of visual angle.

Different acuity tasks use different sorts of patterns. We will discuss three: minimum visible acuity tasks, minimum separable acuity tasks, and vernier acuity tasks. The stimuli used in each of these tasks are depicted in Figure 1. As one might expect, the just-detectable separation of contours varies among these tasks.

Minimum visible tasks involve a single black line on a white background (or a single white line on a dark background). Adults can, under optimal conditions, detect such a line when its width is only $\frac{1}{2}$ sec of arc (Hecht & Mintz, 1939). Minimum visible acuity measurements, however, are highly dependent on the intensity discrimination capacity of the eye (Riggs, 1965). Consequently, they probably should not be regarded as measures of acuity.

Minimum separable acuity tasks require the subject to respond to a separation between elements of a pattern. The most common pattern is a series of alternating black and white stripes of equal width (a square wave grating). The finest grating the subject can resolve is taken as the measure of acuity. It is generally expressed in terms of spatial frequency, the number of pattern repetitions per degree of visual angle. (Other units for

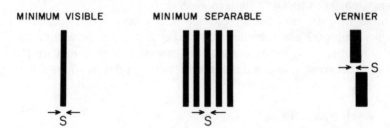

MINIMUM VISIBLE   MINIMUM SEPARABLE   VERNIER

Figure 1.   Stimuli typically used in minimum visible, minimum separable, and vernier acuity tasks. In each task, the measure of visual acuity is the minimum separation of contours that the subject can detect. Those separations (S) are indicated by the arrows.

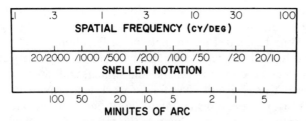

Figure 2. Scales for representing minimum separable acuity thresholds. From top to bottom the scales represent the spatial frequency in cycles per degree (or stripes per degree), Snellen notation, and stripe width in minutes of arc.

expressing acuity are displayed in Figure 2). Adult minimum separable acuity under optimal conditions is 45–60 c/deg, which corresponds to a stripe width of $\frac{1}{2}$ to $\frac{2}{3}$ min of arc.

Vernier acuity tasks require the subject to discriminate displacements of one line with respect to another. Generally, one must distinguish whether an upper vertical line is displaced to the left or right of a lower vertical line. The just-discriminable offset under optimal conditions is about 2 sec of arc for adults (Berry, 1948). This precision is remarkable because 2 sec is less than $\frac{1}{10}$ the diameter of photoreceptors in the fovea. Westheimer (1979, 1982) has argued that minimum separable and vernier acuity tasks actually tap different visual mechanisms. This is an intriguing idea to which we return below.

We would like to point out an important implication of the fact that different sorts of tasks yield widely different estimates of visual acuity. Because the resolution threshold varies from one pattern to another, one cannot use an acuity estimate obtained with one sort of pattern to predict the threshold for another sort of pattern. This has important implications for infant research. Several investigators have used estimates of minimum separable acuity (specifically, the angular subtense of one stripe when the grating is at threshold) to argue that the pattern elements in another stimulus (for example, the individual features in a schematic face) are resolvable. This is in general inappropriate because, as we have described here, acuity estimates actually vary strikingly from one pattern to another and hence cannot be used to predict one another in any simple way. Section IV on contrast sensitivity considers an approach that offers solutions to this problem.

One motivation for studying visual acuity (and, as we shall see, for studying the growth of visual acuity) is the expectation that it will provide insight into optical, anatomical, and physiological influences on visual performance. In tests of visual acuity, the visual system's ability to encode the spatial distribution of stimulation is pushed to the limit. Accurate processing is required from many stages beginning with the eye's optics and proceeding to central neural networks. Psychophysical estimates of acuity have helped delineate quantitative relationships between adults' visual performance on the one hand and optical and neural mechanisms on the other. A brief discussion of such work will provide a background and framework for much of the infant work on acuity development.

Two classical observations illustrate the influence of optical and neural factors on adults' visual acuity. First, minimum visible, minimum separable, and vernier acuity all depend heavily on the average luminance of the stimulus. For example, adults' minimum separable acuity increases more than 100-fold from dark scotopic to bright photopic conditions (Shlaer, 1937). Second, all three measures of acuity depend significantly on the retinal eccentricity of the target (retinal eccentricity refers to the angular distance from the fovea to the retinal region being tested). For example, adults' minimum separable acuity is highest in the fovea and falls dramatically, but steadily, as the target is moved into the periphery (Mandelbaum & Sloan, 1947). We consider the optical and neural factors that contribute to the luminance- and eccentricity-dependence of adults' visual acuity below.

The increase in acuity with higher luminance appears to be caused by both optical and neural factors. Consider first the contribution of optical factors. As luminance is increased, the pupil constricts. This improves the sharpness of the retinal image (and thereby improves visual acuity) because restricting light to the center of the cornea and lens minimizes the defocusing effects of spherical and chromatic aberrations (see Campbell & Gubisch, 1966, for details).[6] Neural factors, however, are more important because dramatic improvements in acuity with increasing luminance are still observed even when pupil diameter (and hence optical quality) is held constant (Shlaer, 1937). Two neural mechanisms seem to be involved. First, the shift from rod to cone activation (which accompanies an increase in light level) enhances resolution because cones are packed much more densely than rods in the central retina and because cones do

---

[6] The relationship between pupil diameter and visual acuity is actually somewhat more complicated. For large diameters (4–8 mm), any decrease in diameter improves visual acuity so long as the stimulus is fairly bright. Smaller diameters in this range are associated with higher acuity because they minimize spherical and chromatic aberrations. For bright stimuli and small diameters (1–2 mm), however, any decrease in diameter actually degrades acuity because it causes greater optical diffraction due to the pupillary aperture. Therefore, these optical factors—spherical and chromatic aberrations on the one hand and optical diffraction on the other—imply that the optimal pupil diameter for resolution of bright stimuli is roughly 2–4 mm. For an interesting discussion of the relationship between pupil diameter and visual acuity for stimuli of various luminances, see Campbell and Gregory (1960).

not pool their responses at higher-level neurons as much as rods do. (We describe the theoretical relationship between receptor density, pooling, and resolution in the next paragraph.) Second, there is physiological evidence that the receptive fields of retinal neurons change with light level. Barlow, Fitzhugh, and Kuffler (1957) and Enroth-Cugell and Robson (1966) observed that the antagonistic surround of retinal ganglion cells disappeared at low light levels and, consequently, that the resolution of the cells dropped. A third mechanism is also involved. At very low luminances, the intensity discrimination capacity of the visual system is poorer than at high luminances. This fact is illustrated by the increment threshold function (see Figure 9 in Section V). The detection or discrimination of acuity targets involves intensity discrimination, so it follows that acuity should be lower for light levels where intensity discrimination is lower.

Neural factors also seem to be primarily involved in the change in visual resolution from the fovea to the far periphery. The optical quality of the eye is much worse for the retinal periphery than for the fovea, but Green (1970) has shown nonetheless that optical quality does not constrain acuity in the periphery. He measured adults' minimum separable acuity at various eccentricities under two conditions: (1) using conventional gratings viewed under normal conditions, and (2) using laser-generated gratings that were formed directly on the retina and hence were impervious to optical degradation (except for degradation due to scattering which, presumably, is similar for the fovea and periphery). His results are summarized in Figure 3. Peripheral acuity was identical for the two conditions, suggesting that optical factors, despite their poor quality, do not constrain resolution in that part of the retina. Foveal acuity was somewhat higher for the laser gratings than for the conventional gratings. So despite the relatively good quality of foveal optics, optical quality partially constrains acuity for that part of the retina. Since optical factors apparently do not cause the fall in acuity with retinal eccentricity, neural mechanisms must. Which neural mechanisms are most significant? Green (1970) showed that, once optical factors were partialed out, acuity in the central 5° of the retina could be predicted precisely from the average separation of cones.

This is a particularly important observation, so let us examine it in some detail. The retinal image is digitized in a fashion because the photoreceptors sample the image at discrete points only (Williams, 1985). It can be shown mathematically that spatial information finer than the grain of the photoreceptor mosaic cannot be transmitted without distortion (Goodman, 1965; Snyder, 1979). Stated more precisely, the sampling frequency of the receptor mosaic (the density of receptors or, more specifi-

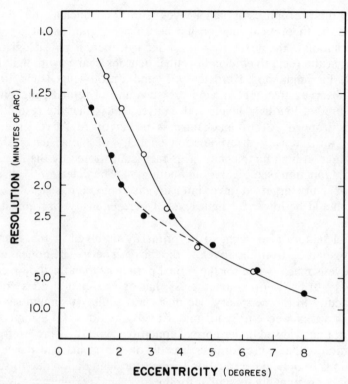

Figure 3. Adult minimum separable acuity at various positions eccentric from the fovea. The narrowest stripe width is plotted as a function of retinal eccentricity. The open circles are for laser-generated patterns that were formed directly on the retina. Filled circles are for conventional patterns. (Adapted from Green, 1970.)

cally, the reciprocal of twice the average separation between receptors) sets a limit on the highest spatial frequency (the finest pattern of stripes) that can be transmitted accurately. Consequently, it is not surprising that adults' minimum separable acuity does not exceed the limit imposed by the average separation of foveal cones. Of course, foveal acuity could be worse than the limit set by the mosaic. The fact that it is not indicates that acuity in the fovea is constrained primarily by the average separation of foveal cones and not by neural factors further upstream. Beyond 5°, Green found that acuity was actually somewhat worse than would be predicted from receptor density. The primary constraint then must be beyond the photoreceptor stage.

The neural substrates of vernier acuity are less clear than those of minimum separable acuity. For one thing, vernier thresholds can be as low as 2 sec of arc, a distance that is roughly 10 times smaller than the average separation of foveal cones! Obviously, then, simple hypotheses based on the grain of the receptor mosaic cannot account for these thresholds as they did for minimum separable thresholds. Vernier thresholds also behave differently than minimum separable thresholds in some circumstances. For instance, defocusing the stimulus reduces minimum separable acuity severely but does not influence vernier acuity much at all (Westheimer, 1979). For these and other reasons, Westheimer (1979, 1982) has argued that vernier acuity and minimum separable acuity actually tap different visual mechanisms. Barlow (1979) and Crick, Marr, and Poggio (1981) have advanced models of the neural substrates of vernier acuity that are, in fact, quite different from models of minimum separable acuity. Geisler (1984) has argued alternatively that special mechanisms are not required to explain why vernier acuity is affected by blur differently than grating acuity is.

A. Development

We now consider the development of visual acuity. There have been two fundamental motivations for studying acuity growth: (1) the expectation that such studies will provide insight into the relationship between visual performance and the optical, anatomical, and physiological development of the infant's visual system, and (2) the attempt to characterize the visual system's sensitivity to patterns at different ages. Concerning the second motivation, we will argue in the next section that acuity measurements actually do not provide a general index of pattern sensitivity. Nonetheless, visual acuity is an important aspect of pattern vision. Pattern elements that are smaller than the resolution limit cannot be detected. If such an element was the distinguishing feature of an object, the object obviously could not be correctly identified. Hence the second of the above-mentioned motivations should be stated more narrowly: acuity estimates may allow researchers to determine which high-contrast pattern elements or features are too small to be detected at different ages.

Casual observation suggests that visual acuity is quite low early in life and that it improves dramatically during the first year. For example, neonates seem to attend only to large objects whereas older infants notice quite small objects or features that even their parents have difficulty detecting. These casual observations are confirmed by the now extensive literature on infant visual acuity. The literature consists almost entirely of measurements of minimum separable acuity, but different response measures and different stimuli have been used. Consequently, one cannot summarize the literature by just stating acuity estimates for various ages because, as in adults, the estimates of acuity depend on the responses and stimuli used.

In order to keep our review of this work reasonably brief, we have chosen to describe only three studies—each with a different response measure—in detail and to present the findings of other studies as supplements. Discussion of stimulus variables will be distributed throughout this section and the next. The three response measures represented—preferential looking (PL), optokinetic nystagmus (OKN), and visually evoked potentials (VEP)—account for virtually all of the acuity studies to date (for reviews, see Dobson & Teller, 1978; Maurer, 1975).

Our primary goal is to review psychophysical work, so we will present the PL study first. Allen (1978) used the forced-choice preferential looking technique (FPL) to measure acuity in infants from $\frac{1}{2}$ to 6 months. The infants were shown simultaneously two fields of equal size, luminance, and hue. The fields differed only in that one was a stationary, high-contrast square wave grating while the other was unpatterned. An adult observer tried to identify the grating's location based on the infant's behavior. The spatial frequency of the grating was varied from 0.38 (wide stripes) to 12 (narrow stripes) c/deg. The observer's percentage correct typically varied from about 50%, which is chance performance, for high spatial frequencies, to about 100% for low spatial frequencies. Allen estimated the spatial frequency required to achieve 75% correct responding by interpolation and this value was considered as the acuity estimate. These estimates are shown in Figure 4. The acuity estimates increased monotonically from 1.3 c/deg at $\frac{1}{2}$ month to 5 c/deg at 6 months. Allen's data agree reasonably well with those of other preferential looking studies (Atkinson Braddick, & Moar, 1977a, 1977b; Banks & Salapatek, 1978; Fantz et al., 1962; Gwiazda, Brill, Mohindra, & Held, 1978; Salapatek, Bechtold, & Bushnell, 1976; Teller, Morse, Borton, & Regal, 1974). Most have found that minimum separable acuity is roughly 1 c/deg at 1 month and 6 c/deg at 6 months. As we noted earlier, however, these acuity estimates are uncertain. They only represent lower-bound estimates of infants' resolution capabilities at different ages. Consequently, we cannot be confident that the values shown represent sensory thresholds *per se* or that thresholds change with age in the manner indicated. What we would like to know, then, is whether these estimates faithfully represent sensory thresholds at different ages. This is quite difficult to ascertain, but we can use the four verification techniques outlined earlier to attempt it.

The first of the four techniques—the use of thresholds as relative rather than absolute information—is not applicable here. Those who have measured visual acuity in infants have been most interested in determining the absolute acuity at different ages rather than in determining how acuity

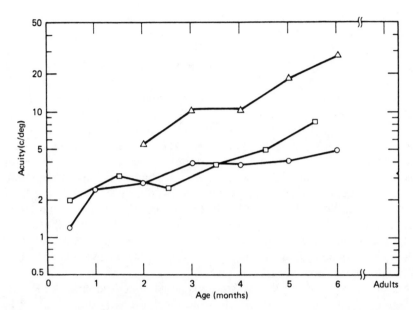

Figure 4. Minimum separable acuity estimates at different ages. The highest detectable spatial frequency is plotted as a function of age. Circles, acuity estimates from Allen's (1978) FPL experiment. Squares, acuity estimates from the Fantz, Ordy, and Udelf (1962) OKN experiment. Triangles, estimates from Sokol's (1978) VEP experiment. (From Banks, 1982.)

changes as a function of some other independent variable such as luminance. We must, consequently, concentrate on the remaining three approaches.

Some researchers have looked for stimulus convergence in infant acuity experiments (Atkinson, Braddick, & Moar, 1977c; Banks & Salapatek, 1981). They used a model of sensory mechanisms that is based on the contrast sensitivity function and linear systems analysis. Since that model is described in some detail in the next section, we will put off discussion of stimulus convergence until then.

Different response measures have been used to measure infant acuity, so we can examine the results for response convergence. If response convergence can be demonstrated convincingly, our confidence would increase that these response measures reflect the behavior of sensory mechanisms. We have chosen two studies—one that used OKN and one that used VEP—to highlight the use of different responses to measure infant acuity.

Fantz et al. (1962) used OKN to estimate acuity from birth to 6 months of age. OKN is the rhythmic pattern of slow pursuitlike eye movements followed by saccadic refixations that is elicited when a subject looks at a repetitive moving pattern. As in most OKN procedures, Fantz et al. used a moving square wave grating that covered most of the infant's visual field. The spatial frequency of the grating was varied from 0.75 to 6 c/deg. The presence or absence of OKN was judged on-line by an adult observer. The highest spatial frequency for which reliable OKN was observed was taken as the acuity estimate. We have reanalyzed their results and plotted in Figure 4 the estimated spatial frequency at which 50% of the infants in each age group would yield reliable OKN. The acuity estimates increased fairly smoothly from about 2 c/deg at $\frac{1}{2}$ month to greater than 6 c/deg at $5\frac{1}{2}$ months. These acuity values agree reasonably well with the OKN acuities observed by Enoch and Rabinowicz (1976) and Gorman, Cogan, and Gellis (1957, 1959). Dayton et al. (1964) reported OKN acuities of 4 c/deg for many newborns, a value higher than the others obtained. Banks and Salapatek (1981), however, have shown that their stimulus contained spatial frequencies lower than 4 c/deg, so Dayton et al. probably overestimated OKN acuity.

Sokol (1978) used the steady-state visually evoked potential (VEP) to measure infant acuity. The stimuli were checkerboards that reversed in phase 12 times/sec (6 Hz). Check size was varied from 7.5 to 90 min of arc and the amplitude of the VEP was noted for each size. Fifteen infants were tested, in most cases longitudinally, at monthly intervals from 2 to 6 months of age. Extrapolation to zero response amplitude on an amplitude versus check size plot allowed Sokol to estimate the threshold check size for each infant. (Campbell and Maffei, 1970, and Regan and Richards, 1971, have shown that such an extrapolation predicts adult psychophysical acuity thresholds.) The results from this experiment are also plotted in Figure 4. This figure shows the fundamental spatial frequency corresponding to threshold check size for each age. Estimated acuities increase monotonically from 5.7 c/deg at 2 months to 28 c/deg at 6 months. These results agree reasonably well with those of other steady-state VEP studies (Harris, Atkinson, & Braddick, 1976; Sokol & Dobson, 1976), sweep VEP studies (Norcia and Tyler, 1985), and of one transient VEP study (Marg, Freeman, Peltzman, & Goldstein, 1976). Other transient VEP studies have yielded lower estimates of acuity (Harter, Deaton, & Odom, 1977a, 1977b; Harter & Suitt, 1970).

Shimojo et al. (1984) have used FPL to measure vernier acuity from 2 to 9 months. They found that the smallest detectable offset was less than 3 min of arc by 6 months. Furthermore, the growth curve for vernier acuity was different than the growth curve for grating acuity. This may reflect the emergence of different resolution mechanisms.

Infant acuity experiments using different responses have often disagreed on one point: many VEP studies obtained higher acuity estimates than PL and OKN studies, particularly after 3 months of age. This discrepancy suggests that response convergence (Yonas & Pick, 1975) may not obtain and raises the question of whether behavioral techniques, such as FPL, yield meaningful estimates of visual acuity.

Dobson and Teller (1978) considered the discrepancy between VEP and PL acuity estimates in some detail. They presented a number of possible explanations, two of which suggest that the differences are more apparent than real. We describe those two explanations here.

First, the discrepancy between VEP and PL acuities might be due to differences in the stimuli used in the two techniques. Specifically, the stimuli used in VEP studies, because they were modulated temporally, may yield higher acuity estimates, regardless of the response measure used, than the static gratings used in PL studies. This hypothesis is weakened somewhat by the results of two studies that compared PL acuities for both static and nonstatic stimuli. Dobson, Teller, and Belgum (1978) used FPL to measure visual acuity in 2-month-olds with two types of stimuli: (1) phase-alternating checkerboards similar to those used in many VEP studies and (2) static square wave gratings like those used in many PL studies. Similar acuity estimates were obtained with the two patterns, which suggests that temporal modulation does not lead to higher acuity estimates. Similarly, Atkinson et al. (1977b) measured FPL acuity in 1-, 2-, and 3-month-olds using static and drifting sinewave gratings. They too found no difference between stationary and moving gratings. Before concluding that Dobson and Teller's first hypothesis is false, we should point out that data from older infants would have been more relevant to the issue at hand because VEP and PL acuities generally do not differ significantly until after 3 months. In other words, we cannot rule out the possibility that VEP estimates are higher than PL estimates after 3 months of age because of differences in the stimuli used.[7]

Second, Dobson and Teller hypothesized that the discrepancy between VEP and other estimates of acuity may be due to the different scoring techniques the measures require. They argued that in PL studies, acuity is estimated by rather strict criteria, for example, the spatial frequency required to elicit 75% correct responding. VEP acuity, on the other hand, is usually estimated with much more generous criteria, for example, the spatial frequency for which VEP amplitude will be zero or just above

---

[7] Sokol et al. (1986) showed that FPL estimates of grating acuity were increased by as much as 1 octave by flickering the square wave grating target. They observed higher acuities from 3 to 8 months, the age range tested. This finding suggests that some of the discrepancy between FPL and VEP acuity estimates may be caused by stimulus differences.

zero. They pointed out that use of more generous scoring criteria (60%, for example) in PL studies would increase acuity estimates by 1 to 1.5 octaves. In other words, much of the difference between acuities estimated by VEP and PL techniques may be attributable to differences in the scoring criteria used. Of course, this argument depends on the assumption that 75% in a PL experiment is somehow a stricter criterion than near-zero amplitude in a VEP. It is unclear to us how one would defend this assumption. PL studies provide percentage correct values as the dependent measure, while VEP studies provide changes in electrical potential. It is simply not clear how one should compare such different variables. That is to say, how many millivolts of change in electrical potential should be comparable to the 75% correct value? Until answers to such questions emerge, it will be difficult to assess response convergence in infant acuity measurements.

If we cannot compare thresholds meaningfully across response measures, how can we determine if they are tapping the same underlying mechanisms in infants? We propose that the best way is to examine whether they are influenced similarly by changes in stimulus parameters. For example, if VEP and PL acuity estimates are affected in quite different ways by changes in light level, they probably do not tap the same mechanisms. This is the most appropriate way to test for response convergence.

Unfortunately, very little is known about how various stimulus parameters affect VEP, PL, and OKN acuity estimates in infants. In the absence of such information, we resort to consultation of the adult literature for clues about the substrates of these measures. Some adult work has concluded that VEP, OKN, and psychophysical acuity estimates are, in some circumstances, affected in different ways by changes in stimulus parameters; this implies that the three responses tap somewhat different mechanisms in adults. For example, Regan (1978) has argued that VEP and psychophysical measures are affected differently by changes in stimulus parameters. Specifically, he showed that pattern-reversal VEPs in adults exhibit two components: (1) a pattern component due to the phase-reversing changes in the pattern and (2) a local flicker component due to changes in luminance over time. The relative magnitude of the two VEP components varies significantly with both the size of the pattern elements and the rate of phase reversal. Researchers using VEP to estimate acuity generally fix the rate of phase reversal and manipulate the size of pattern elements. Consequently, the choice of temporal frequency influences the estimate of acuity. Changes in temporal frequency also affect psychophysical estimates of acuity (Robson, 1966) but not in the same manner as they affect VEP estimates. In other words, spatial-temporal interactions in the VEP appear to be different than those observed in psychophysical tasks. This suggests that the two techniques may tap somewhat different mechanisms.

Cannon (1983), however, has offered a more optimistic view of the correlation between VEP and psychophysical estimates of pattern detection capabilities. He used a novel VEP technique to measure detection thresholds in adults. The details of the technique are beyond the scope of this chapter, but a few of Cannon's observations are worth mentioning here. He measured VEP and psychophysical detection thresholds but, unlike other researchers, he presented precisely the same stimulus in both tasks: a sinewave grating phase reversing 20 times/sec (10 Hz). VEP thresholds were consistently higher than psychophysical thresholds, but they were nearly perfectly correlated. Specifically, as Cannon changed a subject's optical correction or changed the spatial frequency of the stimulus (as in contrast sensitivity measurements, see Section IV), VEP and psychophysical thresholds varied in unison. These results suggest that at least one VEP technique may reveal the same mechanisms as psychophysical techniques.

One might argue from Regan's and Cannon's findings that high correlations between VEP and behavioral estimates of infant acuity would be observed if the appropriate temporal frequency for phase reversal were chosen. Unfortunately, one cannot use adult data to guide such a choice. Moskowitz and Sokol (1980) have shown that significant spatial-temporal interactions exist in infant VEPs and, most importantly, that these interactions change with age. Thus, a choice of temporal frequency based on adult work could yield an inaccurate estimate of visual acuity for the particular age tested.

Little is known of the substrates of OKN acuity in infants, so we must consult the adult literature once again for clues. Several adult studies suggest that OKN acuity reflects different visual mechanisms than psychophysical acuity. For example, Pearson (1966) and Reinecke and Cogan (1958) have shown that adults' OKN acuity estimates are not well-correlated with psychophysical estimates. Furthermore, Schor and Narayan (1981) have shown that OKN and psychophysical acuity estimates are affected differently by changes in stimulus parameters. They examined the effects of a number of stimulus parameters in eliciting involuntary OKN in adults. As in the infant studies described above, the stimulus was a drifting grating. They found that the highest velocity at which OKN could be elicited was the same as the highest detectable velocity in a psychophysical task. They also found that the acuity cutoff for OKN was well below the psychophysical acuity for some conditions.[8] Specifically, psychophysical acuity was unaffected by changes in stimulus field size, whereas OKN acuity was considerably lower for large fields than for small fields. (OKN acuity appeared to match the psychophysical acuity for the most peripheral part of the retina stimulated by the drifting grating.) To summarize, the fact that OKN and psychophysical acuities are affected differently in adults by changes in stimulus parameters implies that the two types of acuity reflect somewhat different mechanisms.

We have seen that VEP, OKN, and psychophysical estimates of adult acuity are often affected differently by variations in stimulus parameters such as rate of temporal modulation and field size. This means the three response measures may tap somewhat different visual mechanisms in adults. It is possible, however, that a careful choice of parameters, exemplified by Cannon (1983), may reveal similar underlying processes. At this stage we cannot judge whether VEP, OKN, and PL acuity estimates in infants converge. We will not be able to do so until more is learned about how various stimulus parameters, such as those examined in the adult studies mentioned above, affect the techniques' estimates of infants' visual capability. It is worth restating in this context, however, that VEP, OKN, and PL acuities do not appear to diverge until after about 3 months. Although similarity of acuity estimates is not sufficient evidence by itself, it might mean that the three response measures reflect the same mechanism early in infancy and different mechanisms later on. Stated another way, it is possible that response convergence is present before 3 months but not later.

The final verification technique that could aid the interpretation of psychophysical data on infant acuity is good performance relative to some known optimal performance. In the current context this could be demonstrated by showing that infants' visual performance approximates the best performance possible given the structural and functional quality of the young eye. We now examine this possibility. Specifically, we examine infants' performance relative to the optical quality, photoreceptor spacing, and neural processes of the young system.

First, consider optical quality. The sharpness of the retinal image depends on the quality of the cornea, lens, and other optic media. Consequently, infants' performance in acuity tasks might attain the highest level the optics allows. This hypothesis, however, does not seem to account for the data adequately (Dobson & Teller, 1978; Salapatek & Banks, 1978).

---

[8] Schor and Narayan adopted a strict definition of OKN. To distinguish involuntary OKN (the desired response) from voluntary pursuit, they computed the frequency of the fast phase. Fast phase frequencies less than 1 Hz were considered pursuit and were discarded.

Several sorts of optical errors can affect acuity: spherical aberration, chromatic abberation, diffraction due to the pupil, and clarity of the optic media, but all of these errors appear to be far too small in young infants to account for their low acuity values (see Salapatek & Banks, 1978, for details).

Infants' performance might, however, be constrained by another optical error—accommodative error. This hypothesis is plausible because accommodation, like acuity, improves notably with age (Banks, 1980). If accommodative error were an important constraint, one would expect young infants' acuity to vary with target distance. On the contrary, several investigators have shown that infants' acuity does not vary with distance (Atkinson et al., 1977a; Fantz et al., 1962; Salapatek et al., 1976). Thus, accommodative error also does not appear to be a significant limitation to infant acuity.

These considerations imply that the quality of the retinal image exceeds the acuity observed in young infants and, therefore, that acuity does not reach the optimal level expected from optical factors alone.

Another mechanism that might account for the early acuity deficit and subsequent growth is a broad class of neural mechanisms. A number of the anatomical and physiological mechanisms known to influence adult acuity are potentially involved in early acuity development. One such mechanism is the spacing of photoreceptors. Recall that the average angular separation between foveal cones predicts adults' minimum separable acuity. Smaller separations (higher density) near the center of the fovea lead to higher acuity; larger separations (lower density) in the parafovea lead to somewhat lower acuity in that part of the retina (Green, 1970). Foveal cone separation is known to decrease postnatally in humans (Abramov et al., 1982; Hendrickson & Yuodelis, 1984; Mann, 1964) and monkeys (Hendrickson & Kupfer, 1976), so receptor spacing probably contributes to age-related changes in infants' minimum separable acuity. Indeed, I. Abramov (personal communication) has estimated that the average separation of foveal cones decreases by a factor of roughly 10–20 from birth to adulthood. Furthermore, the average newborn's eye is about 33% shorter than an adult's eye (Larsen, 1971). Since the size of the retinal image (expressed in micrometers) is roughly proportional to eye length, this means that retinal images are roughly one and one-half times larger in adults than in newborns. This difference combined with the change in photoreceptor spacing predicts that neonates' acuity should be 15–30 times lower than adults'. These factors then might account for most of the roughly 45-fold increase in minimum separable acuity over the same age range. (Other evidence suggests, however, that the change in photoreceptor spacing is smaller than the 10- or 20-fold figure given by

Abramov [Yuodelis & Hendrickson, in press].) This is an exciting hypothesis, which, if correct, would imply that neonates' acuity approaches the highest level expected on anatomical grounds. Some additional information, however, is sorely needed before we can relate these numbers with confidence. No one is certain of the part of the retina infants use in acuity tasks. If they do not use the fovea, then one should not use anatomical data from the foveal region to assess the contribution of receptor spacing. Thus, measurements of minimum separable acuity as a function of retinal eccentricity are needed, along with more quantitative estimates of receptor density for different eccentricities, before one can evaluate the receptor spacing hypothesis in infants. Unfortunately, nothing is known of the relationship between infants' minimum separable acuity and retinal eccentricity. Lewis, Maurer, and Kay (1978) found that newborns could detect a narrower light bar against a dark background when it was presented near the fixation point than when it was presented in the periphery, but their task measured minimum visible acuity, which is in general not predictable from the dimensions of the receptor mosaic.

A broad class of neural mechanisms may also constrain acuity early in life: the spatial tuning of neurons at different levels of the visual system. The size of a neuron's receptive field limits its spatial resolution, larger fields exhibiting lower acuity (e.g., Enroth-Cugell & Robson, 1966). The size of retinal ganglion cell receptive fields decreases significantly postnatally in cats (Rusoff & Dubin, 1977), so one would expect a concomitant increase in visual acuity. Mitchell, Giffin, Wilkinson, Anderson, and Smith (1976) have shown that kittens' acuity improves considerably postnatally, but no quantitative links between ganglion cell receptive fields and behavioral acuity have been drawn. The spatial resolution of lateral geniculate and cortical neurons also improves postnatally in cats and monkeys (e.g., Blakemore & Vital-Durand, 1980; Derrington & Fuchs, 1979). This too should affect visual acuity. There are, of course, no physiological data on receptive field sizes in developing humans, but several lines of evidence suggest that receptive field development may be similar in human and macaque infants (Boothe, 1981).

We have considered the issue of how meaningful psychophysical estimates of infant acuity are. In particular, we examined whether response convergence is observed and concluded that it is too early to know. We also examined whether infants' performance attains the optimal levels expected on optical, anatomical, and physiological grounds. Preliminary evidence suggests that neonates' performance approaches the optimal level predicted given the spacing of photoreceptors and the length of the eye at that age. Additional experimentation is needed, however, to confirm this.

B. Summary

One form of visual acuity—minimum separable acuity—is by all accounts quite poor early in life and grows steadily until at least 6 months of life. The acuity estimates at different ages can be used to calculate roughly which high-contrast objects or features in the environment are too small to be resolved. Unfortunately, different response measures yield different estimates of acuity, particularly after 3 months. It is possible that the measures tap different visual mechanisms in infants, but more experimental and theoretical attention must be devoted to this issue before firm conclusions can be drawn.

Various neural factors such as the grain of the photoreceptor mosaic and the spatial tuning of retinal, geniculate, and cortical receptive fields may determine early visual resolution and its subsequent development. Not enough is known currently to pinpoint which of these are the major determinants. Nonetheless, it appears that the primary limitation to early acuity is not the quality of the retinal image but rather the nervous system's ability to process that image.

IV. CONTRAST SENSITIVITY

Measurements of visual acuity index the visual system's ability to resolve small objects at high contrast. This is an important aspect of the system's pattern detection capabilities, but most visual scenes actually consist of objects of many different sizes at varying contrast levels. Hence acuity measurements alone are a poor index of the visual system's ability to detect ordinary pattern information. This point is substantiated by the observation that many visual functions do not require fine pattern information at all. For example, the use of visual information to regulate posture is unaffected when the information is defocused (Leibowitz, Schupert-Rodemer, & Dichgans, 1979). A better index of the ability to detect pattern information is provided by the contrast sensitivity function (CSF). This function represents the visual system's sensitivity to everything from very coarse to very fine spatial patterns. Specifically, the CSF relates the contrast required to just detect a sinewave grating (a repeating series of stripes whose luminance varies sinusoidally) to the grating's spatial frequency (the number of stripes per degree of visual angle).

The top half of Figure 5 shows a sinewave grating whose spatial frequency increases from left to right and whose contrast increases from top to bottom. Note that your ability to detect the grating varies with spatial frequency; intermediate frequencies are the easiest to detect. The

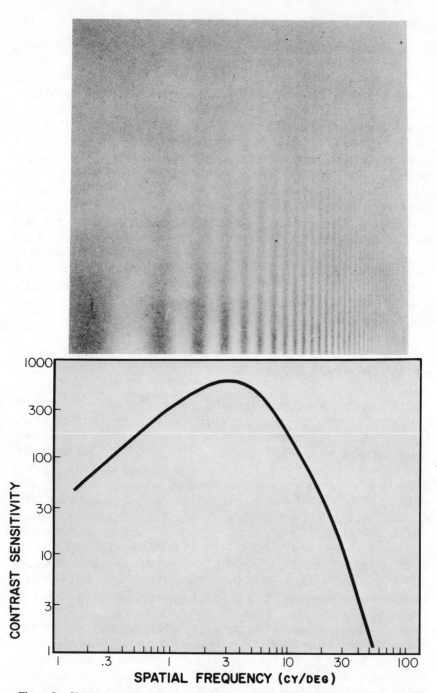

Figure 5. Sinewave grating and typical adult contrast sensitivity function (CSF). Top, a sinewave grating whose spatial frequency increases from left to right and contrast increases from bottom to top. Bottom, a typical adult CSF. Contrast sensitivity, the reciprocal of contrast at threshold, is plotted as a function of spatial frequency. (Adapted from Banks & Salapatek, 1981.)

lower half of Figure 5 represents the CSF of a typical adult. It shows how sensitivity varies with spatial frequency. Notice the bandpass characteristic: sensitivity is higher to intermediate than to low or high spatial frequencies.

The CSF has been extremely useful to the study of adult pattern vision. There are two reasons for this. First, the CSF can be used in conjunction with Fourier's theorem and linear systems analysis to characterize the visual system's sensitivity to a wide variety of patterns. Fourier's theorem implies that any two-dimensional pattern can be represented by its spatial frequency content (see Banks & Salapatek, 1981; Cornsweet, 1970; Gaskill, 1978). Thus, even a complex pattern such as the picture of a face can be exactly reproduced by combining a set of sinewave gratings of various spatial frequencies, contrasts, phases, and orientations. Linear systems analysis utilizes this fact to allow, in principle, the prediction of sensitivity to any pattern once the CSF of a visual system is known. The validity of linear systems analysis depends, however, on certain assumptions about the system under study. The adult visual system does not satisfy these assumptions in detail but, with certain restrictions, the approach has been very successful in predicting sensitivity to quite a variety of patterns (Banks & Salapatek, 1981; Cornsweet, 1970). This generalization capability has allowed researchers to synthesize a wide variety of observations.

The second reason that CSFs have been useful is related to the first. CSFs can reveal the properties of some important aspects of pattern vision. These include visual acuity, intensity discrimination, low-frequency attenuation, and multiple feature-selective channels. We will describe each of these below.

Many of the infant studies concerning CSFs have been designed to capitalize on the generalizability afforded by linear systems analysis and to reveal the properties of the above-mentioned aspects of pattern vision. In other words, the theoretical background for much of the infant work is based on rules and phenomena uncovered in previous adult work. We outline this background here by presenting a few illustrative examples from the adult literature.

The CSF has been a useful index of adults' visual acuity. The point at which the high-frequency side of the CSF intersects the abscissa is called the high-frequency cutoff and is an estimate of visual acuity. Are acuity estimates derived from the CSF in this manner more useful than other measures of acuity? Yes, because one can use the CSF to predict accurately adults' ability to resolve various sorts of acuity targets. The converse is not true. An example of how the CSF approach can be used to predict resolution thresholds for a variety of targets illustrates this. Adults exhibit remarkable resolution when the acuity target is a single black line on a white background (minimum visible acuity). The narrowest detectable line in this case is only a few seconds of arc wide (Hecht & Mintz, 1939). On the other hand, the high-frequency cutoff of the adult CSF is about 45 c/deg, so the narrowest resolvable stripes in a sinewave grating are roughly $\frac{2}{3}$ min wide (Campbell & Green, 1965). Despite this apparent contradiction between minimum visible and minimum separable acuities, Campbell, Carpenter, and Levinson (1969) showed that the narrowest detectable single line can actually be predicted from a straightforward application of the CSF and linear systems analysis.

Bodis-Wollner (1972) provided a striking example that illustrates how the CSF may pick up visual dysfunctions that measurements of acuity do not. He reported case histories of patients who were experiencing great difficulty reading and performing other pattern recognition tasks. These perceptual problems were apparently caused by cortical pathology. The visual acuity of these people was normal and hence suggested no dysfunction. Their CSFs, however, revealed a large deficit for intermediate spatial frequencies. These deficits probably caused the reading disturbances because, subsequent to treatment, the midfrequency deficit lessened and normal reading ability returned.

The CSF has also been a useful indicant of intensity discrimination in adults. Intensity differences generally define patterns in the first place, so the discrimination of intensities is a fundamental aspect of pattern vision. Each point on the CSF represents the contrast necessary to just detect that an intensity difference is present. Is the CSF a better index of this capacity than other measures? Again a positive answer is justified. Adult psychophysical studies have revealed that no single value can characterize intensity discrimination capabilities. For example, discriminability depends critically on stimulus size and on illumination level (Vos, Lazet, & Bouman, 1956). Van Meeteren (1967) has shown, however, that CSFs measured at different illumination levels can be used to predict intensity discrimination thresholds for various background illumination levels and spots of various sizes.

Yet another important property revealed in CSF measurements is low-frequency attenuation. The attenuation of sensitivity to low spatial frequencies seems to reflect lateral inhibitory processes in early stages of the visual system. These processes serve to attenuate the visual system's response to gradual intensity changes and thereby emphasize sudden or sharp intensity changes (e.g., an edge). Consider the function of lateral inhibition in pattern vision. In order to simplify processing of the astronomical amount of information entering the eye, the visual system must filter out certain types of information. Lateral inhibitory networks tend to filter out gradual intensity changes (diffuse shadows, gradual changes in lighting, etc.). Hence the pattern information that passes through lateral inhibitory networks appears to be the most "valid" information, namely the position and shape of contours which define patterns in the first place. The argument that the low-frequency falloff of the CSF reflects lateral inhibitory processing is supported by several physiological and psychophysical studies. For example, physiological experiments have found that the sensitivity of lateral inhibition among retinal ganglion cells is less for low than for high luminances (Barlow et al., 1957). Adult psychophysical experiments have shown that the slope of the low-frequency CSF falloff is also less for low than for high luminances (Van Nes & Bouman, 1967). Stated another way, at high luminances where lateral inhibition is strong, the low-frequency falloff of the adult CSF is pronounced. At low luminances where inhibition is weak, the low-frequency falloff is much less distinct.

A. Development

The utility of the CSF in adult work has led developmental researchers to measure these functions in infants as well. Three laboratories have published reports of CSF development during early infancy (Atkinson et al., 1977a; Banks & Salapatek, 1978; Pirchio, Spinelli, Fiorentini, & Maffei, 1978). The methods of the three differ, so we will describe them briefly.

Atkinson et al. (1977a) used the FPL technique (and a first fixation measure) to test 1-, 2-, and 3-month-olds. On each trial sinewave gratings appeared on one of two oscilloscopes; the other oscilloscope presented a uniform field of the same hue and average luminance. Each display subtended 15°. The gratings were either stationary or drifting. The results—the contrast necessary to elicit 70% correct responding as a function of spatial frequency—revealed a large increase in contrast sensitivity, primarily at high spatial frequencies, from 1 to 2 months and essentially no change from 2 to 3 months. The low-frequency falloff in sensitivity that is characteristic of adult CSFs was not observed consistently at 1 month but was at 2 and 3 months.

Banks and Salapatek (1978) used the first fixation version of the preferential looking technique to measure CSFs in 1-, 2-, and 3-month-olds. They used a projection system to present much larger stimuli (48° × 40°) than Atkinson et al. (1977a). The grating and uniform fields were again equal in hue and average luminance, but they were adjacent to one another. The observer always waited until the infant was fixating midline before presenting the stimuli. Consequently, the grating in the Banks and

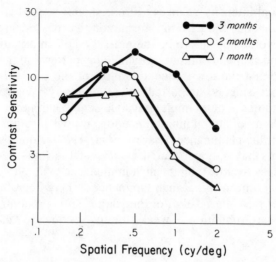

Figure 6. Average CSFs for 1-, 2-, and 3-month-old infants as reported by Banks and Salapatek (1978). Average contrast sensitivity is plotted as a function of spatial frequency. (From Banks & Salapatek, 1978.)

Salapatek study would, when first presented, have appeared close to the infant's fixation point. The sinewave gratings were always static. The results are shown in Figure 6. Again there is an increase with age in contrast sensitivity, primarily at high spatial frequencies, but not as large an increase as observed by Atkinson et al. The low-frequency falloff was again not observed consistently at 1 month but was at 2 and 3 months.

These two behavioral experiments agree substantially on the shape and height of the CSF at 2 and 3 months of age. They also agree on the shape of the CSF at 1 month but disagree on the overall sensitivity at that age. The disagreement may be due to the differences in the field sizes employed. This argument is supported by findings that 1-month-olds do not appear to process pattern information presented within a frame (e.g., Milewski, 1976, 1978). Moreover, Atkinson et al. (1983) observed higher grating acuities in 1- and 2-month-old infants when the targets were large rather than small.

The infant functions in Figure 6 are quite distinct from the adult CSF in Figure 5. Clearly, infant CSFs are shifted to a lower band of spatial frequencies. Infants also appear to have a substantial deficit in overall contrast sensitivity relative to adults. These differences prompt an important question: to what extent are the early deficits due to nonsensory factors such as motivation? We use the four verification techniques outlined earlier to explore this question.

First, note that the shape of the CSF depends on relative threshold values. Thus, shape comparisons obey our first verification technique: the use of thresholds as relative rather than absolute information. We believe, then, that comparisons of CSF shape are not as susceptible to contamination by nonsensory factors as comparisons of contrast thresholds at a given spatial frequency might be.

Second, consider whether response convergence exists. Evoked potential measurements are useful in this regard because they presumably are not as subject to motivational factors as behavioral techniques might be. Pirchio et al. (1978) used steady-state VEPs to measure CSFs in one infant from $2\frac{1}{2}$ to 6 months of age. They also measured two points on the CSF (the high-frequency cutoff and the peak) in a number of infants from 2 to 10 months. The sinewave gratings were presented in 7 to 25° fields, depending on the infant's age. The gratings were flickered in counterphase fashion at a rate of 8 Hz. Pirchio et al. estimated threshold by plotting VEP amplitude versus contrast and extrapolating to find the contrast yielding zero amplitude. The results for the infant tested longitudinally are shown in Figure 7. Results from other infants (not shown in Fig. 7) indicated that the high-frequency cutoff increased from 2 c/deg at 2

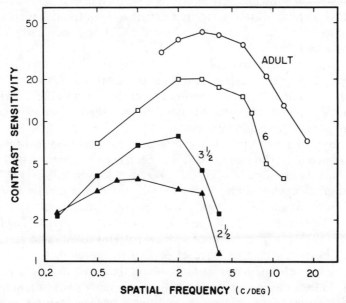

Figure 7. CSFs for one infant and one adult as reported by Pirchio, Spinelli, Fiorentini, and Maffei (1978). The infant's age in months is shown to the right of each of the infant functions. (From Banks, 1982.)

months to about 20 c/deg by 10 months and that peak contrast sensitivity improved from 4 to about 40 over the same age range.

The findings of Pirchio et al. are both similar and dissimilar to those of the behavioral studies (Atkinson et al., 1977a; Banks & Salapatek, 1978). They are dissimilar in the absolute contrast sensitivity values observed; Banks and Salapatek, for example, reported a peak sensitivity of 13 for 2-month-olds while Pirchio et al. observed a peak sensitivity of only 4. One really should not, however, expect the absolute sensitivity values to agree between two response measures for reasons described in Section III on visual acuity. The VEP and behavioral studies are similar in the relative sensitivity values reported, that is, the shapes of the CSFs and spatial frequencies at which sensitivity is highest are nearly identical. They are also similar in that the peak sensitivity of adult functions is roughly 20 times higher than those of 2- and 3-month functions. In other words, infants' sensitivity deficits, expressed relative to adult sensitivity values, are about the same in behavioral and electrophysiological studies.

Harris et al. (1976) have also found clear similarities between VEP and FPL measures. They actually measured CSFs in one 6-month-old using both techniques. Despite differences in some of the stimulus parameters and the obvious differences in response measures, the two techniques yielded similar estimates of the CSF. It should be noted that the 6-month-old's CSF exhibited only a twofold deficit in high-frequency sensitivity relative to adults. It appears, then, that the CSF may be nearly adultlike by 6 months.

Comparisons of behavioral and VEP measurements thus suggest that response convergence exists for indices of contrast sensitivity. This bolsters the argument that the sensitivity deficits young infants exhibit in behavioral experiments are due in large part to sensory factors rather than to nonsensory, motivational factors.

We can also ask if stimulus convergence exists for contrast sensitivity measurements. Recall that the CSF has been used in adult work to predict acuity thresholds for a variety of targets. Atkinson et al. (1977c) and Banks and Salapatek (1981) demonstrated that similar predictions can be drawn from infant CSFs. Banks and Salapatek reanalyzed two experiments—Dayton et al. (1964) and one described by Fantz, Fagan, and Miranda (1975)—which had used atypical patterns to estimate visual resolution. These experiments were of particular interest because both obtained higher resolution values than others that used more conventional stimuli. In both cases, application of linear systems analysis and the CSF for the appropriate age group revealed that higher acuities were actually predictable given the patterns they used. Hence the results of Dayton et al. and Fantz et al. were actually consistent with other investigators' estimates.

Atkinson et al. (1977c) developed a unique measure of acuity using facial photographs. Two faces, one focused and one defocused to varying degrees, were presented to 1- to 3-month-olds in a discrimination task. When one face was badly defocused, infants preferentially fixated the focused version. Atkinson and colleagues varied the amount of defocus to find the point at which infants preferred the focused face on 70% of the trials. Once they obtained these thresholds, the experimenters used CSF measurements from another experiment (Atkinson et al. 1977a) in an attempt to predict the amount of just-detectable defocus. The predictions were quite accurate given the inherent variability of infant data. Thus, the CSF and a simple application of linear systems analysis allowed the prediction of a unique estimate of visual acuity. The success of this experiment argues that the use of "nonecological" stimuli such as sinewave gratings has not badly misrepresented infants' visual sensitivity.

These two reports (Atkinson et al. 1977c; Banks & Salapatek, 1981) illustrate that stimulus convergence is observed among stimuli that probe the visual acuity of young infants. Banks and Stephens (1982) have examined stimulus convergence in another situation. Specifically, they used the CSF approach to predict contrast sensitivity for patterns coarser than the resolution limit. They measured 10-week-olds' contrast thresholds for five types of rectangular wave gratings. The spatial frequency of the gratings was always 1 c/deg, but the gratings differed in duty cycle (the relative widths of light and dark stripes). An adult was also tested with rectangular wave gratings of 7 c/deg. Figure 8 summarizes Banks and Stephens' infant and adult results and shows some of the stimuli employed. The infant and adult results were very similar except for a large difference in contrast sensitivity. In both cases, sensitivity varied systematically with duty cycle. Banks and Stephens used linear systems theory to derive predicted contrast sensitivities as a function of duty cycle. The predicted functions—the solid lines—fit the infant and adult data very well. The close match between the predicted and observed functions illustrates that stimulus convergence holds for stimuli coarser than the resolution limit of young infants. It also exemplifies the utility of linear systems analysis and the CSF in predicting infants' contrast thresholds for various sorts of grating patterns.

We have shown that both response convergence and stimulus convergence are present in measures of infants' contrast sensitivity. These observations corroborate the view that these CSF measurements reveal the behavior of sensory mechanisms rather than nonsensory, motivational factors. To the extent that this view is correct, we can conclude that the pattern information to which young infants are sensitive is only a fraction of the information available to adults. This fraction increases steadily from birth to 6 months, when contrast sensitivity approaches adult val-

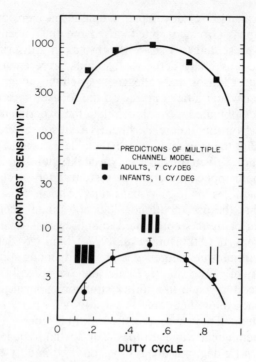

Figure 8. Average contrast sensitivity for rectangular wave gratings differing in duty cycle. Infant data are represented by circles. The sensitivity values are for 1c/deg gratings. Adult data are represented by squares. Those sensitivity values are for 7 c/deg gratings. The two curves represent linear systems predictions assuming multiple channel processing. They are identical in shape but have been shifted vertically for best fit. (Adapted from Banks & Stephens, 1982.)

ues. (This conclusion is more justifiable for the shape of the CSF than for its height, but the similarity across response measures of infant-adult differences in CSF height argues that the estimates of overall sensitivity cannot be badly in error.)

It is interesting to note that Boothe, Williams, Kiorpes, and Teller (1980) examined CSF development in macaque monkeys, a species whose mature visual system is very similar structurally and functionally to that of human adults (Boycott & Dowling, 1969; DeValois, Morgan, & Snodderly, 1974). Boothe et al. reported age-related changes very similar to those observed in humans, except that CSF development occurs more rapidly in macaques.

An important question concerning CSF development is, are the observed age differences determined primarily by changes in optical quality or by changes in neural mechanisms? An optical quality explanation is somewhat attractive because young infants' deficits are most pronounced for high spatial frequencies, and high-frequency sensitivity suffers more from optical aberrations and accommodative errors than does low-frequency sensitivity (Green, Powers, & Banks, 1980). Nonetheless, it is very unlikely that optical aberrations or accommodation contribute significantly to early contrast sensitivity deficits. The reasoning behind this conclusion was detailed in the previous section, in which we considered whether optical aberrations or accommodative errors constrain visual resolution to its low levels early in life. Age differences in the CSF, therefore, are most likely determined by neural development.

Before discussing the implications of CSF development to the growth of visual perception, we should make an important qualification. The CSFs reported in the infant literature were generally measured using stationary gratings of moderate luminance. It is quite possible, even likely, that the use of flickering, high-luminance gratings would yield higher contrast sensitivity (Dobson et al., 1983; Sokol et al., 1986). Given this, we should apply the existing CSF data to the visibility of static stimuli of moderate luminance only.

To summarize the infant CSF work reviewed thus far, the evidence is reasonably persuasive that the young infant is sensitive to a much lower and perhaps more restricted range of spatial frequencies than the adult visual system is. Similarly, the range of contrasts to which infants are sensitive is quite restricted early on. The ranges of detectable frequencies and of detectable contrasts increase steadily during the first half-year. Neural mechanisms appear to be more responsible than optical structures for the early deficits and subsequent growth. It appears, then, that the young visual system is sensitive initially to only a fraction of the information to which the adult system is sensitive and that this fraction increases steadily through at least the first half-year of life.

Banks and Salapatek (1981) have referred to the fraction of pattern information to which young infants are sensitive as their "window." Evidently the window is quite restricted early in life, but before concluding that young infants must be virtually blind, two points should be kept in mind.

1. Concerning infants' low overall contrast sensitivity relative to adults': the contours of many common objects have contrasts greater than the threshold contrasts indicated in Figures 6 and 7. Faces, for example, often exhibit contrasts of 0.7 to 0.8 between the skin and hair, a value high enough to be detected by young infants. Thus, even though infants' contrast sensitivity is quite low relative to adults', it is sufficient for the detection of many typical intensity gradients in the environment. Further-

more, as Atkinson and Braddick (1982) point out, one should not conclude from poor sensitivity in a threshold task that contrasts well above
threshold must look much fainter to infants than to adults. A contrast
sensitivity deficit does not necessarily imply a drop in apparent contrast
for suprathreshold stimuli. This point is illustrated by the work of George-
son and Sullivan (1975) with normal adults and Hess and Bradley (1980)
with amblyopic adults.

2. Concerning the shift of infants' sensitivity to low spatial frequencies
relative to adults': the spatial frequencies of the sinewave components in
an object change systematically with viewing distance. As the object is
brought closer, its angular subtense increases and the major components
are translated toward lower frequency values. The infants' low-frequency
window is best suited for perceiving objects in the immediate rather than
the distant visual environment. As the window grows with age, infants'
ability to perceive distant objects (or small near objects) should increase
correspondingly. Interestingly, Ginsburg (1978) has demonstrated that
adult pattern recognition is not affected significantly when high spatial
frequencies are deleted. His demonstrations emphasize the utility of low-
frequency information in the recognition of all but very small objects
(e.g., fine print).

As mentioned earlier, the CSF allows one in principle to predict sensitivity to a variety of patterns. It also reveals three important aspects of
pattern vision: visual acuity, intensity discrimination, and low-frequency
attenuation. We now discuss these points in the context of infant work.

We have already described work that shows that infant and adult CSFs
allow quite accurate predictions of acuity thresholds for various kinds of
targets. CSFs thus appear to provide a flexible, reasonably general index
of the growth of visual resolution.

The CSF also reveals the intensity discrimination capacity of the visual
system. Each point on the function represents the intensity difference (or
contrast) necessary for an infant to detect the presence of nonuniformity.
Peeples and Teller (1978) measured intensity discrimination in 2-month-
olds. They found that 2-month-old infants could discriminate stripes
(square wave gratings) whose intensity differed by only 12% from the
background intensity. This corresponds to a contrast sensitivity of 17.5.
The predicted contrast sensitivity, based on Banks and Salapatek's (1978)
CSF data from 2-month-olds, is 14.0, a reasonably close match consider-
ing the differences in procedures. Clearly, however, a single value cannot
portray the contrast sensitivity or intensity discrimination ability of the
developing visual system because those abilities depend highly on stimulus size and shape. For example, Banks and Stephens (1982) showed that

the contrast sensitivity of 10-week-olds varies with the relative widths of light and dark stripes in a pattern.

The third aspect of pattern vision revealed in CSFs is low-frequency attenuation. Recall that this attenuation is a product of contour-enhancing lateral inhibitory processing. Figure 6 suggests that low-frequency attenuation develops between 1 and 2 months. Atkinson et al. (1977a) examined this by testing a number of 1- to 3-month-olds at three low spatial frequencies. The results clearly showed that the low-frequency falloff is generally not present before 2 months of age. The implication is that lateral inhibition is not functional until that age. This hypothesis is supported by two observations. First, physiological studies have established that the magnitude of lateral inhibition among retinal ganglion cells is less for low than for high luminances (Barlow et al., 1957). Consequently, if the low-frequency falloff in the CSF is caused by lateral inhibition, one would expect the falloff to become shallower at low luminances. Banks and Salapatek (1981) tested this in 2-month-olds. They measured CSFs at two luminances and found a shallower falloff slope at the lower luminance. Second, physiological studies of kitten retinal ganglion cells have found that lateral inhibitory mechanisms are not adultlike until 8 to 9 weeks, which is considerably delayed relative to the development of excitatory mechanisms (Hamasaki & Sutija, 1979; Rusoff & Dubin, 1977). A similar developmental sequence has been observed in rabbit ganglion cells (Bowe-Anders, Miller, & Dacheux, 1975). Thus, the contour-enhancing properties of early visual processing may not emerge in humans until about 2 months after birth.

Another fundamental property of pattern vision that can be revealed in CSF experiments is the existence of multiple, feature-selective channels. All sensory systems possess many parallel pathways, each specialized to carry information about a particular type of stimulus. In the visual system, different sorts of pattern information from the same location in the visual field are signaled by different neurons. For instance, different cells in the visual cortex respond selectively to stimuli of different orientations (Hubel & Wiesel, 1962, 1968). Furthermore, such cells respond selectively to different sizes (or bands of spatial frequency), one cell responding to large pattern elements (low frequencies) and another to small pattern elements (high frequencies) (Albrecht, DeValois, & Thorell, 1980). A number of psychophysical experiments in adults have suggested that pattern information is processed in parallel by "channels" analogous to the cortical cells mentioned above. Different channels appear to be tuned to different orientations and spatial frequencies (reviewed by Braddick, Campbell, & Atkinson, 1978). The evidence for spatial frequency tuning among these channels lies in the fact that spatial frequencies interact in detection, adaptation, and masking experiments, but only if they lie within about 1 octave (a factor of two) of each other. Importantly, these channels appear to be involved in the perception of size (Blakemore & Sutton, 1969).

Despite the importance of these processes to pattern recognition (Ginsburg, 1978; Marr, 1982) and the electrophysiological evidence that channel specificity develops postnatally in kittens (Derrington & Fuchs, 1981), the development of spatial frequency and orientation channels in humans has only recently been investigated. Banks, Stephens, and Hartmann (1985) used a masking paradigm to measure the frequency bandwidth of channels in $1\frac{1}{2}$-month-olds, 3-month-olds, and adults. They found at all ages that a narrowband noise masker whose spatial frequency was similar to the frequency of a sinusoidal test grating caused an increase in the grating's threshold. However, when the masker and grating differed in frequency by 2 octaves (a factor of four), the grating's threshold was unaffected by the masker in 3-month-olds and adults. This indicates that pattern information whose frequency content differs by 2 octaves is processed by separate channels and, therefore, constitutes evidence for multiple spatial frequency channels. In $1\frac{1}{2}$-month-olds, the masker affected the grating's threshold even when they differed by 2 octaves and, consequently, separate channels were not demonstrated over this range of frequencies. Banks et al. used their data to estimate channel bandwidth as a function of age. The estimates were ± 1.3 octaves for 3-month-olds and adults. A bandwidth could not be estimated for $1\frac{1}{2}$-month-olds because no frequency-selective masking was observed. The results imply that the spatial frequency tuning (or size tuning) of such channels is quite broad early in life and becomes adultlike by 3 months. A second experiment, using a different paradigm, substantiated this age-related shift (Banks et al., 1985).

Stephens and Banks (1985) examined the development of contrast constancy, a perceptual phenomenon that is characteristic of the mature visual system. As the term contrast constancy implies, adults are able to judge the contrast of an object and its features veridically as the object undergoes changes in distance. Models of contrast constancy assume the presence of narrowband spatial frequency channels. An implication of the findings of Banks et al. (1985) is that contrast constancy should not be present at $1\frac{1}{2}$ months but may be at 3 months. Stephens and Banks used a preference procedure to test this implication. Indeed, 3-month-olds exhibited contrast constancy and $1\frac{1}{2}$-month-olds did not.

In mature animals, spatial frequency-tuned responding is not observed before the level of the visual cortex. Therefore, the results of Banks et al. (1985) and Stephens and Banks (1985) may reflect cortical development in humans. If spatial frequency channels are broadly tuned early in life, one might expect the ability to discriminate patterns according to size to improve correspondingly with age. Unfortunately, no data on the development of size discrimination *per se* exist, so this hypothesis cannot be evaluated. One might also expect various pattern recognition and stereovision capabilities to improve with age, but such expectations depend on the precise role spatial frequency channels are assumed to serve (e.g., Ginsburg, 1978; Marr, 1982; Pollen, Lee, & Taylor, 1971).

B. Summary

The CSF and linear systems analysis have only recently been applied to the study of visual development. Already the CSF has proven to be a useful general index of pattern detection capabilities. It has also illuminated several important aspects of pattern vision and how they change with age.

Several important questions remain to be explored. For one, how do spatial-temporal interactions influence infants' detection of pattern? This is an important question which we consider in our discussion of temporal vision. Another important question for future research concerns the encoding of spatial relations among detected contours. The potential importance of this is illustrated by an example from the adult amblyopia literature. (Amblyopia is a developmental anomaly in which visual acuity and some pattern discrimination capabilities are reduced.) Frequently one cannot predict adult amblyopes' acuity for letters (Snellen acuity) from their CSFs. Specifically, the Snellen acuity is usually worse than predicted. Pass and Levi (1982) may have discovered why. They measured conventional CSFs in amblyopic adults and found a small but reliable high-frequency deficit relative to normal adults. They also measured thresholds for the identification of spatial relations among detectable patterns. The amblyopes exhibited a large deficit in this task. This suggests that, in addition to a contrast sensitivity deficit, amblyopes also have a spatial encoding deficit. Similar sorts of experiments in infants might reveal important properties of the developing visual system.

Finally, one wonders how useful contrast sensitivity measurements might be to the study of pattern discrimination. Recently two laboratories (Banks & Ginsburg, 1985; Banks & Salapatek, 1981; Gayl, Roberts, & Werner, 1983) have used the CSF and linear systems analysis to investigate suprathreshold pattern preferences. Generally, the results exhibit close correlations between predicted and observed preferences and thus offer hope that this approach may be useful in this arena as well.

V. LIGHT AND DARK ADAPTATION

Up to this point we have considered infants' visual capabilities at fixed levels of illumination. Of course, the environment actually presents stimuli across an extremely large range of light levels. The mature visual system is able to maintain reasonably proficient pattern vision for a substantial portion of this range. Ripps and Weale (1969) have estimated that the useful range of light levels is 10 log units. In other words, we can still discern patterns when the light is 10,000,000,000 times more intense than the smallest amount of light detectable in the dark. This remarkable feat is accomplished by adjusting the visual system's sensitivity according to the ambient level of illumination. Such adjustments are usually not obvious subjectively because they occur so efficiently. They become obvious only when light level changes suddenly and drastically. On those occasions, the visual system is temporarily blinded but readapts fairly rapidly so that pattern vision is possible once again. The processes of adapting to increases and decreases in illumination are called light and dark adaptation, respectively.

Before describing research on light and dark adaptation, let us discuss the perceptual task of recognizing objects presented under different levels of illumination. An appreciation of this task is important to understanding adaptation. An object is generally defined by differences in intensity (or hue) between the object and its background or between features within the object. The apparent brightness or luminance of an object or a feature within an object depends both on its reflectance (the percentage of incident light reflected) and the amount of light falling on it. Consequently, two adjacent parts of an object with different reflectances will always differ in luminance and form a contour, if they are bathed in the same light. If the amount of light falling on the object is changed, the *ratio* of the luminances does not change. So, the luminance ratio defining the contour would be the same under sunlight or moonlight. The mature visual system capitalizes on this invariance: light and dark adaptation operate to insure that the visual system responds to luminance ratios rather than absolute luminances. In this way, contours remain approximately equally visible for a large range of illumination levels.

This property is illustrated by Weber's Law, which states that the smallest intensity increment needed for a target to be detected against an otherwise uniform background is a constant percentage of the background's intensity. Weber's Law is illustrated by the increment threshold function (ITF), which plots the logarithm of the just-detectable increment intensity against the logarithm of the background intensity. The lower function in Figure 9 is a typical adult increment threshold function.

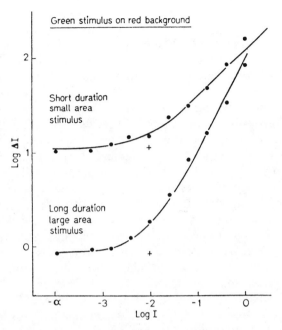

Figure 9. Adult increment threshold functions for different stimulus conditions. Both functions plot the logarithm of increment intensity at threshold as a function of the logarithm of background intensity. The lower curve represents thresholds when the test spot is 55 min in diameter and 1 sec in duration. The upper curve represents thresholds when the test spot is 5.2 min in diameter and 7 msec in duration. The separation of the functions has been reduced by 1 log unit for ease of presentation. (From Barlow, 1972.)

Weber's Law holds where the slope of this function is 1.0; thus it appears to hold over a large range of intensities in adults.

Several mechanisms contribute to adaptation in adults (see Barlow, 1972). First, pupillary changes modulate the amount of light falling on the retina in an appropriate, albeit insignificant, manner. The area of the adult pupil in bright light is about $\frac{1}{16}$th its area in darkness. Therefore, pupillary changes aid adaptation but are really quite insignificant given the total dynamic range of the visual system. Second, the presence of two types of photoreceptors, rods and cones, aid adaptation by dividing the total dynamic range roughly in half. Rods are about 4 log units (10,000-fold) more sensitive than cones, so they function over the range of dim light levels while cones operate at high levels. Even this staggering of sensitivity cannot fully account for light adaptation in adults. Additional photochemical and neural mechanisms must, therefore, contribute (Barlow, 1972).

Adult psychophysical research has shown that several properties of the visual system change when luminance is raised or lowered. These changes are presumably byproducts of the neural mechanisms of light and dark adaptation. For instance, the temporal summating properties of the visual system change with luminance; the highest detectable flicker rate (critical flicker frequency) increases from roughly 2 Hz at scotopic levels of illumination to about 60 Hz at photopic levels (Hecht & Verrijp, 1933; Kelly, 1961). This implies that the visual system summates (or integrates) inputs over longer durations at low light levels than at high light levels. The spatial summating properties of the visual system also change with luminance. This is exemplified by the large increases in visual acuity that accompany higher levels of illumination (Shlaer, 1937). Thus, the visual system seems to summate (or integrate) inputs over larger spatial intervals at scotopic light levels than at photopic levels.

These changes in temporal and spatial summation aid adaptation by increasing sensitivity at low light level, where input signals are relatively weak, and by decreasing sensitivity at high light levels, where input signals are so strong that they would otherwise saturate neural responses. The effect of increasing temporal and spatial summation at low light levels is illustrated by the two increment threshold functions (ITFs) of Figure 9. The upper curve shows an adult's ITF when the stimulus is a small (5.2-min diameter), short-duration (7 msec) spot on an otherwise uniform background. The lower curve is the ITF when the stimulus is a large (55-min diameter), long-duration (1 sec) spot on a uniform background. Because one spot is small and short in duration, it impedes the visual system's ability to summate an input over space and time. That is not the case for the other spot. The figure shows the impact of this difference on visual performance. At low background intensities, when temporal and spatial summation are needed to enhance sensitivity, thresholds for the small, brief spot are much higher than thresholds for the large, long spot. At high background intensities, when temporal and spatial summation are normally not so useful, thresholds are similar. Notice also that Weber's Law holds for the large, long-duration stimulus but not for the small, short one. This means that Weber's Law is valid for certain conditions only. In everyday settings, those conditions should correspond to relatively large, nonflickering features.

A. Development

Developmentalists have only recently studied the effects of illumination changes on pattern vision. Consequently, the experimental questions to date have been elementary. We describe some experiments that explored the development of light adaptation directly. We also describe experiments that provide circumstantial evidence that neural mechanisms involved in adaptation change with luminance.

Two studies have directly examined light adaptation in infants using increment threshold functions. Hansen and Fulton (1981) and Dannemiller and Banks (1983) measured increment threshold functions at a number of ages in order to examine the extent to which adaptation occurs to different levels of illumination. Hansen and Fulton measured increment thresholds in the scotopic range (low light levels at which rods operate) using the FPL procedure. Although only one infant was tested at each age, two developmental trends were evident. First, increment thresholds at all background intensities decreased with age. Second, thresholds decreased more at low background intensities than at high, so the slopes of the increment threshold functions increased steadily from about 0.62 at 2 weeks to an adultlike value of 0.90 at 12 weeks. Thus, adultlike adaptation (Weber's Law) did not appear, at least for scotopic stimuli, until 12 weeks of age.

Dannemiller and Banks (1983) presented both scotopic and photopic (cone vision) levels to a much larger number of infants. They also used the FPL procedure. Their results are summarized in Figure 10. They observed the same two developmental trends. First, increment thresholds declined in general with age. Second, increment threshold function slopes increased with age; slopes of 0.56 and 0.79 were observed at 7 and 12 weeks, respectively. Adult slopes in the same apparatus over the same luminance range were 0.88 on the average, fairly close to Weber's Law.

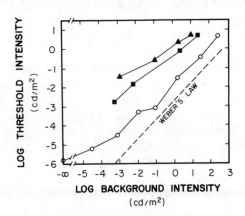

Figure 10. Increment threshold functions for 7-week-olds, 12-week-olds, and adults as reported by Dannemiller and Banks (1983). The logarithm of increment intensity at threshold is plotted as a function of the background intensity. Weber's Law is illustrated by the dashed line. Circles, adult increment threshold function. Squares, 12-week functions. Triangles, 7-week functions. (Adapted from Banks, 1982.)

Hence, the two groups of investigators concur that adultlike changes in visual sensitivity with changes in background intensity do not occur until 3 to 4 months of age.

Dannemiller and Banks considered several explanations for the postnatal changes in increment threshold function slopes they and Hansen and Fulton observed. First, adaptation mechanisms *per se* may be immature at birth and improve up to 3 to 4 months. Dannemiller and Banks argued that this account is possible but unlikely. Specifically, immaturities in most adaptation mechanisms should cause neural responses to saturate at high light levels. Saturation would cause an increase rather than a decrease in ITF slope. A second possibility is that adaptation mechanisms are mature before 3 to 4 months but other sensory and/or nonsensory factors that can affect increment threshold functions may change. They favored the second class of explanations. In particular, Dannemiller and Banks considered two hypotheses to be reasonable explanations of the shallower slopes observed in infant increment threshold functions.[9]

First, they considered the possibility that the spatial and temporal properties of the stimulus may have affected the ITF slopes. Recall that the slope of the adult ITF is shallower for small, short-duration test spots than for large, long-duration spots. The test spot in the Dannemiller and Banks experiment was very long in duration, so this probably did not lower ITF slopes. The test spot was also fairly large, but data from Hamer and Schneck (1984) suggest that infants' spatial summation areas are quite large, so perhaps the Dannemiller and Banks (and Hansen and Fulton) stimulus was small for infants. If this explanation is correct, the slopes of infant ITFs for relatively large test spots should be similar to adult slopes for smaller spots. A comparison of Figures 9 (the upper curve for small test spots) and 10 supports this explanation.

Dannemiller and Banks' second explanation for the shallower infant slopes involves differences in the relationship between stimulus intensity and response magnitude among retinal neurons (Dowling & Ripps, 1971; Naka & Rushton, 1966). A lower gain on this function would elevate absolute threshold and prolong the portion of the ITF in which threshold is unaffected by background luminance. These effects would produce a shallower slope. Both of these effects are compatible with known infant visual psychophysics: ITF slope is apparently lower in infants than in adults, and Powers et al. (1981) have reported that 1- and 3-month-olds'

---

[9] They tentatively rejected the hypothesis that nonsensory factors caused the slope changes because their psychometric data did not support that idea. Specifically, there was no evidence for different contributions of nonsensory factors at different background intensities.

absolute thresholds are roughly 2.0 and 1.0 log units higher, respectively, than adults'.

Both of these explanations—one based on large spatial summation areas and one on a shallow intensity–response function—are reasonably consistent with current data on early adaptation. The first explanation is supported by Dannemiller's (1983) observations. If age-related changes in summation area are responsible for the reduced slopes of infant ITFs, then ITF slopes should be 1.0 at all ages when large test spots are used. Dannemiller (1983) observed adultlike slopes when 6- and 12-week-olds were tested with large, 8° diameter test spots. The same infants exhibited lower slopes when tested with smaller, 2° test spots. Brown (1984) also observed adultlike slopes with large test spots. These results favor the hypothesis that light adaptation mechanisms are reasonably mature early in life because Weber's Law holds once stimulus size is sufficiently large. Further research is required to ascertain whether changes in the intensity–response function also contribute to changes in the infant's ITF. Physiological experiments with infrahuman species may be the only means of testing the intensity–response function account.

Some circumstantial evidence exists that neural mechanisms of adaptation are functional early in life. In adults, adaptation is accompanied by several changes in visual function. For example, spatial and temporal resolution both decrease as the visual system adapts to lower luminance levels. If neural mechanisms of adaptation were reasonably mature early in life, we would expect to see such adaptive, luminance-related changes in young infants. The temporal and spatial summating properties of the 2-month-old's visual system actually do seem to change with luminance in much the same way as they do in adults.

Three research groups have examined the relationship between luminance and critical flicker frequency (CFF), an index of temporal resolution. Heck and Zetterström (1958) and Horsten and Winkelman (1962, 1964) used flicker electroretinography and Regal (1981) used a behavioral technique. The results of these experiments all suggested that CFF increases as luminance is raised by 2 months of age, if not earlier. Indeed, the relationship between luminance and CFF appeared quite adultlike by 2 months.

Dobson, Salem, and Carson (1983) have examined the relationship between luminance and visual acuity in 2-month-olds. They observed a 1-octave increase in acuity as luminance was raised from 0.10 to 10.0 candelas per meter squared (cd/m^2). These changes in acuity with increasing luminance were very similar to those observed in adults. Similarly, Fiorentini, Pirchio, and Spinelli (1980) have studied the luminance dependence of infants' spatial CSFs. As luminance was diminished from 6.0 to

0.06 cd/m^2, a threefold reduction in acuity and a diminution of the low-frequency falloff was observed for infants younger than $4\frac{1}{2}$ months. Adults showed a similar diminution of the low-frequency falloff but a larger, 10-fold reduction in acuity.

These studies indicate that adaptive changes in temporal and spatial summation probably accompany changes in luminance by 2 months of age, if not earlier.

We now consider what is known about dark adaptation processes in early infancy. Only two studies have examined dark adaptation in infants less than 6 months of age. Hansen, Fulton, Leitzman, and Harris (1984) used pupillography to study the kinetics of dark adaptation. They found that the rates of dark adaptation (presumably for the rod system) were similar in young infants and adults. Dannemiller (1985) used a psychophysical technique to demonstrate that the very early phase of dark adaptation (from 0 to 5 sec) yielded very similar reductions in threshold for 6- and 12-week-olds and adults. This too implies that the rate of early dark adaptation is similar in young infants and adults. The early phase of dark adaptation is significant because it is probably controlled by neural mechanisms rather than by the photopigment regeneration kinetics responsible for the later stages of dark adaptation. Taken together, these two studies suggest that dark adaptation, like light adaptation, may be adultlike by 3 months, if not earlier.

B. Summary

Experiments on the development of light adaptation suggest that, for whatever reason, detection thresholds (expressed relative to background intensity) are affected more by changes in background intensity during the perinatal period than afterward. At 1 month, the increment intensity required for the detection of small spots is a much higher percentage of the background intensity at low light levels than it is at high levels. At 3 to 4 months, however, increment threshold is nearly a constant percentage of background intensity across a large range of light levels. Evidence suggests that younger infants' increment thresholds are also nearly a constant percentage of background intensity so long as large spots are used. Thus, very early in life, the visual system appears to capitalize on the invariance of relative intensities in the environment by responding to luminance ratios. The early phase of dark adaptation also appears to be mature soon after birth.

Studies of the development of light and dark adaptation are in their infancy. There are several aspects of adaptation that have not been investigated developmentally. However, our current sketchy understanding is that some aspects of light and dark adaptation are adultlike by 1 to 2 months of age, if not earlier.

VI. TEMPORAL VISION

Most research on infant vision has disregarded or at least minimized the time-varying or temporal aspects of visual stimulation. In reality, the eye picks up information in a series of eye movements moving from one object to another, and those objects are frequently not stationary themselves. Consequently, from moment to moment, the eye may pick up entirely different distributions of light. Some temporal resolution is required to encode such distributions separately. For this reason, the temporal response properties of the visual system are important to the perception of patterns in everyday situations. We will consider two aspects of temporal vision: the perception of flicker and the effects of spatial-temporal interactions on perception. Both of these topics have been examined extensively in adults (for reviews, see Kelly, 1972; Sekuler, 1975). In keeping with our general organization, we will first review some basic findings in the adult literature before turning to developmental work.

The temporal resolution of the mature visual system is, in a sense, rather poor. Consider, for example, the picture we perceive on a television screen. Each spot on the screen is illuminated by an electron beam that scans the whole screen 60 times a second. Thus, each spot is briefly illuminated once every 1/60 sec or 17 msec. The fact that we perceive a nonflickering picture rather than a single moving spot shows that the visual system integrates light over time periods of 17 msec or longer. The integration time of the visual system is exemplified by Bloch's Law. This law states that the light intensity of a stimulus required to evoke a threshold response is inversely proportional to stimulus duration, so long as the duration is less than some critical duration. Stated another way, the visual effect for brief, near-threshold flashes depends on the product of intensity and duration. The critical duration is roughly 30 msec for photopic stimuli and 100 msec or longer for scotopic stimuli (Roufs, 1972). Thus, the adult visual system appears to pool information in 30-msec bins for bright stimuli and in bins of 100 msec or longer for dim stimuli. This observation accounts for the apparent stability of flickering television images.

Another index of the temporal summating properties of the visual system is the critical flicker frequency (CFF), which is the highest rate of flicker that can be perceived as time varying. CFF in adults depends on experimental conditions, but it is roughly 60 Hz under optimal conditions. As with Bloch's critical duration, CFF depends critically on stimulus

luminance. It increases roughly linearly with the logarithm of intensity
from values near 2 Hz at very dim levels to about 60 Hz at bright, photopic levels (Hecht & Shlaer, 1936). Thus, temporal resolution is considerably better under photopic conditions.

Measurements of CFF index the visual system's ability to resolve very
rapid, high-contrast flicker. This is an important aspect of temporal vision, but real visual scenes actually produce varying rates of flicker at
varying contrasts. A more general index of temporal processing is provided by the temporal analog of the spatial contrast sensitivity function—
the temporal contrast sensitivity function (temporal CSF). This function
represents an observer's sensitivity to unpatterned, sinusoidally flickering
stimuli as a function of flicker frequency. The adult temporal CSF varies
with experimental conditions, but, in most cases, it exhibits a bandpass
characteristic. This is illustrated by Figure 11 which shows adult temporal
CSFs for a wide range of average illuminances. At most illuminances,
sensitivity is greater at intermediate frequencies (5–20 Hz) than at low or
high frequencies. Sensitivity, particularly at high frequencies, is higher
for high illuminances than for low illuminances. The temporal CSFs in

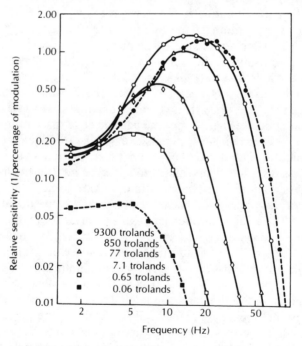

Figure 11.   Adult temporal contrast sensitivity functions for different illuminances. Contrast sensitivity is plotted as a function of flicker frequency. (From Cornsweet, 1970.)

Figure 11 have proven useful for two reasons. First, they have revealed some important properties of the visual system. For example, the temporal delay of lateral inhibition is revealed by the low-frequency falloff of these functions (Kelly, 1971). Second, these temporal CSFs have been used successfully in conjunction with linear systems analysis to predict sensitivity to a wide variety of temporal stimuli. For example, DeLange (1958) showed that sensitivity to stimuli flickering in square-wave or rectangular-wave fashion could be predicted from these sinusoidal data. Cornsweet (1970) also demonstrated that stimulus durations for which Bloch's Law is valid are predictable from temporal CSFs. This means that temporal CSFs provide a useful general index of temporal processing for unpatterned stimuli. We consider temporal processing of patterned stimuli later on in our discussion of spatial-temporal interactions.

A. Development

We now turn to the development of temporal vision. First, we consider the development of flicker perception. Infant CFFs have been examined in both electrophysiological and behavioral studies. Even though behavioral studies are generally emphasized in this chapter, we will review both electrophysiological and behavioral work in this section and look for correlations among the two measures.

The most informative of the electrophysiological studies have used the electroretinogram (ERG), a measure of changes in electrical potential in the retina when it is exposed to light (for details, see Armington, 1974; Maurer, 1975). The ERG in adults exists at quite high flicker frequencies. Indeed, CFFs measured psychophysically and with the ERG correspond quite well so long as relatively intense stimuli are used (Dodt & Wadensten, 1954; Heck, 1957). In infants, the ERG has been used mostly to examine the response to single flashes, but a few studies have used flickering stimuli to measure the CFF. Heck and Zetterström (1958) measured CFFs in 1-day-old to 2-month-old infants. The stimulus field, which was large and unpatterned, was flashed on and off at various rates. Their results are shown in Figure 12. They found ERGs in response to a large flickering stimulus at all ages tested. CFF increased both with age and luminance. At the highest luminance, CFF improved from about 15 Hz at 1 day of age to 65 Hz, or nearly adultlike performance, by 2 months. CFF increased monotonically with luminance at all ages.

Horsten and Winkelman (1964) also used the ERG to investigate CFF at a number of ages. They too observed an increase of the CFF with increasing luminance for all ages tested. Surprisingly, however, no differences across age were reported. CFF at the highest luminance was about 70 Hz

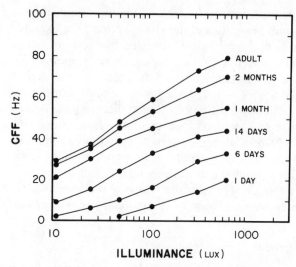

Figure 12. Critical flicker frequency as a function of flash illuminance as reported by Heck and Zetterström (1958). The highest flicker frequency to elicit a recordable ERG is plotted as a function of both flash illuminance and age. (From Banks, 1982.)

from birth to adulthood. The difference in their findings from those of Heck and Zetterström is most probably due to differences in recording technique, since the stimuli and subject populations appeared quite similar between the two experiments.

In summary, flicker ERG experiments disagree on the state of temporal resolution during the neonatal period but agree that adultlike resolution occurs by 2 months. Hence the retina is able to signal rapid temporal changes with adultlike precision by 2 months of age. This does not tell us, however, what the young visual system as a whole is capable of resolving.

The VEP has been used to investigate the temporal resolution of stages beyond the infant's retina (Ellingson, 1960; Vitova & Hrbek, 1972). The VEP, unfortunately, may not be a good index of temporal resolution. Regan (1972) has noted that the range of temporal frequencies that elicits a strong VEP in adults is different than the range of frequencies that the same adults perceive as flickering. In particular, the highest flicker frequency that elicits a VEP does not generally correspond with an adult's psychophysical CFF. Consequently, we will not review VEP work concerned with the development of temporal resolution.

Two behavioral studies of infant flicker perception have appeared. Nystrom, Hansson, and Marklund (1975) tested two age groups: 6-week-olds and 10-week-olds. They employed a preference paradigm. Two unpatterned, flickering stimuli were presented on every trial. In general, all possible pairings of 1, 5, 10, 20, and 100 Hz were presented to each infant.

The 100 Hz stimulus was assumed to appear nonflickering because it was well above adults' CFF. Nystrom et al. observed that both groups of infants preferentially fixated the higher of the two frequencies presented, with one notable exception: When the 100 Hz stimulus was presented, the other frequency was always preferentially fixated (the younger group also preferred 10 to 20 Hz). This one finding shows that infants as young as 6 weeks can demonstrate behaviorally the ability to detect flicker frequencies of at least 20 Hz. Unfortunately, frequencies between 20 and 100 Hz were not presented, so this study shows only that CFF is 20 Hz or higher at a young age.

Regal (1981) conducted a more systematic investigation in order to estimate CFF as a function of age. He tested 1-, 2-, and 3-month-olds cross-sectionally and longitudinally using the FPL technique. On each trial, two unpatterned, flickering stimuli were presented. One was always flickered at 75 Hz, a value higher than the adult CFF and, presumably, higher than the infant CFF, too. The observer judged the location of the lower frequency stimulus on each trial. The average luminance of the flickering stimuli and the background was 34 cd/m². The results are summarized in Figure 13. Correct responding rates of 75% were achieved on

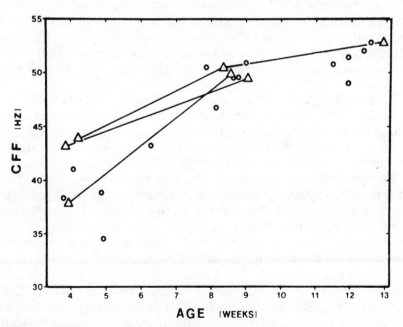

Figure 13. Critical flicker frequency as a function of age as reported by Regal (1981). The highest flicker frequency to elicit 75% correct responding in a behavioral paradigm is plotted. O, Cross-sectional data; △, longitudinal data. (From Regal, 1981.)

the average at 41 Hz for 1-month-olds, 50 Hz for 2-month-olds, 51 Hz for 3-month-olds, and about 53 Hz for adults. Consequently, Regal concluded that CFF is essentially adultlike by 2 months of age. This astonishing result is an example of good performance relative to an expected optimum. In this case, quite young infants' performance in a behavioral task approaches that of well-motivated, practiced adults. Consequently, such a finding suggests that FPL provides meaningful estimates of flicker thresholds. It also tends to bolster confidence that FPL is a sensitive index of sensory thresholds in general.

Regal (1981) also examined the influence of stimulus luminance on CFF. Specifically, he tested three 2-month-olds at two different luminances. CFF fell from 50 Hz at 34 cd/m^2 to 34 Hz at 3.4 cd/m^2. These values were quite similar to those obtained in adults under the same luminance conditions. This suggests that the relationship between stimulus luminance and temporal resolution may be adultlike by 2 months. Of course, this relationship would have to be examined over a wider range of luminances before this statement could be made with confidence.

Note that response convergence has been observed rather convincingly for these flicker experiments. Specifically, ERG recordings (which are presumably not affected by motivational factors) and behavioral investigations agree that adultlike temporal resolution is present by 2 months and perhaps that resolution changes with luminance in an adultlike fashion at that age. This observation, in conjunction with the finding of good performance relative to an optimum, implies that behavioral measures provide reasonably accurate estimates of temporal resolution early in life.

To date, no infant work has examined sensitivity to flicker rates well below the CFF. Of course, this could be accomplished by measuring the temporal CSF of infants. As in adult work, such measurements may be useful for revealing important properties of the visual system and for predicting sensitivity to a wide variety of temporal stimuli.

The temporal vision studies reviewed thus far have concerned infants' perception of very simple, unpatterned temporal stimuli. However, as we mentioned above, most of the temporal variation in visual stimulation is associated with motion of one pattern(s) with respect to another. Thus, in the remainder of this section we consider how spatial-temporal interactions affect perception in human infants.

Visual scientists have examined spatial-temporal interactions by combining sinewave grating and sinewave flicker stimuli. The resulting stimulus is a sinewave grating whose contrast flickers in counterphase fashion. Robson (1966) used such stimuli to demonstrate complex spatial-temporal interactions in adults. For high spatial frequencies, the greatest sensitivity occurred at fairly low temporal frequencies. For low spatial frequencies, sensitivity was greatest at higher temporal frequencies.

Kelly (1979) has argued that counterphase flickering gratings represent an unnatural situation. In most everyday situations, pattern information of different spatial frequencies moves across the retina at a constant velocity rather than at a constant flicker rate. Accordingly, Kelly measured adults' contrast sensitivity to sinewave gratings drifting at fixed velocities. He found that one sensitivity profile fit the data for a wide range of velocities. He concluded from this and other results that the visual system is designed to respond to drifting rather than flickering pattern information.

Researchers have examined infants' processing of both simple spatial-temporal interactions and moving stimuli. Moskowitz and Sokol (1980), for example, measured VEPs from 2 to 6 months using counterphase flickering checkerboards. Check size and flicker rate were varied orthogonally to ascertain the character of spatial-temporal interactions. They found that the spatial response function depended on flicker rate. That is, at high flicker rates, VEP amplitude was greatest for large checks but, at low flicker rates, it was greatest for smaller checks. Moskowitz and Sokol also observed that this spatial-temporal interaction changed with age. Most notably, the largest VEP amplitude was observed for higher temporal and higher spatial frequencies with increasing age. Their data for 3- and 4-month-olds are both similar and dissimilar from their adult data. For large check sizes, the temporal frequency at which the maximum VEP response occurs is 3–5 Hz for both 3- to 4-month-olds and adults. For smaller check sizes, however, the peak response occurs at a flicker frequency of 5 to 6 Hz in 3- to 4-month-olds and 3 Hz in adults. Thus, the Moskowitz and Sokol results for large check sizes are congruent with the above-mentioned flicker studies using unpatterned stimuli. Smaller check sizes, however, reveal a dissimilarity between infant and adult temporal selectivity.

Caution is required before using such VEP data to infer what the development of spatial-temporal interactions may be for visual thresholds measured using other techniques. As Regan (1972) has argued for adult VEPs, the observed spatial-temporal interactions may be caused by the peculiar temporal summating properties of the VEP itself. For this reason, Karmel, Lester, McCarvill, Brown, and Hoffmann (1977) explored the relationship between visual preference and VEP for flickering patterns. In their preference experiment, they presented simultaneously two identical checkerboards flickering in an on-and-off fashion at different rates to 3-month-olds. They found the longest fixation durations for a flicker frequency of about 5 Hz. In the VEP experiment, only one checkerboard was present at a time. The largest VEP amplitude was for 5-Hz flicker, suggesting a link between the VEP and visual preference. Unfortunately, check size in the VEP study was only about one-half the check size in the preference study, so the two experiments were not directly comparable.

Our knowledge of the development of motion perception *per se* is quite limited. Many researchers have reported that infants prefer to fixate moving as opposed to static patterns (e.g., Carpenter, 1974), but few have examined this in detail. Atkinson et al. (1977b) compared 1-, 2-, and 3-month-olds' contrast sensitivity and visual acuity for static and drifting sinewave gratings. The drifting gratings were moved so as to produce a local flicker rate of 3 Hz. Therefore, velocity and spatial frequency were inversely proportional. Thresholds under the two temporal conditions were estimated using FPL for a low spatial frequency grating (0.2 c/deg), a midfrequency grating (0.4 c/deg for 1-month-olds and 0.9 c/deg for 2- and 3-month-olds) and for the highest detectable frequency (the visual acuity cutoff). The results revealed higher sensitivity at all ages to drifting than to static gratings for low and intermediate spatial frequencies. In contrast, the acuity cutoffs for drifting and static gratings were similar. The adults yielded qualitatively similar results: drift enhanced sensitivity to 0.2 to 0.9 c/deg but did not to 4.8 c/deg, a spatial frequency similar to the acuity cutoffs of 2- and 3-month-olds.

It is tempting to conclude that movement enhances the visibility of coarse but not fine patterns in infants. Unfortunately, these data may not be conclusive on this point. Since Atkinson et al. used a constant local flicker rate of 3 Hz to set the drift rate of their gratings, the *velocity* of drift was quite low for higher spatial frequencies, like those at the acuity cutoff. Consequently, we do not know if higher velocities would have yielded higher sensitivities. Future research in this area might follow Kelly's (1979) observation that measurements of contrast sensitivity at a constant local flicker rate represent an unnatural situation because different spatial frequencies are tested at different velocities. In the real world, all of the spatial frequency components of a moving object move at the same velocity. Thus, we might learn more about basic elements of motion perception if velocity, rather than flicker rate, were held constant in such experiments.

B. Summary

The investigation of the development of temporal vision has just begun but already interesting observations have appeared. For example, temporal resolution, unlike spatial resolution, appears to be essentially mature by 2 or 3 months of life. Preliminary evidence, however, suggests that spatial-temporal interactions are not mature by this age. This latter finding is not surprising given the deficits 2- and 3-month-olds exhibit in pattern vision *per se*. The development of motion perception is an important topic that warrants more experimental attention.

VII. CONCLUSIONS

We have discussed a wide variety of topics in this chapter. We do not intend to provide a comprehensive summary here. Rather, two points are made that are based on much of the foregoing material. One point concerns the meaningfulness of psychophysical data in infants and the other concerns the relationship between infant and adult visual capabilities.

Despite the obvious virtues of psychophysical approaches to the study of visual development, we argued in the psychophysics section above that threshold estimates relying on behavioral techniques are ambiguous. The reason is that poor performance (negative results) is weak evidence that a stimulus is undetectable and threshold estimation requires information about which stimulus levels are undetectable. The resulting ambiguity hampers not only the interpretation of data at one age but also the interpretation of age effects. These are serious problems that must be addressed in infant psychophysical work.

We presented four verification techniques that might aid the interpretation of infant psychophysical data. They were: (1) the use of thresholds as relative rather than absolute information, (2) stimulus convergence, (3) response convergence, and (4) good performance relative to some known optimal performance. We described how each of these techniques has been used to assess how well infant psychophysical data reflect the behavior of sensory mechanisms. In many cases, use of the techniques yielded confirmatory evidence. For example, response convergence and stimulus convergence appeared to obtain in contrast sensitivity measurements. A cautious reader, however, may have found the arguments concerning response and stimulus convergence somewhat circular. A hypothetical example illustrates this potential circularity. Suppose we measure a sensitivity function using a technique (say FPL) whose validity is unknown. If we measure the same function using another technique (say VEP) whose validity is also unknown, what can we hope to achieve? In other words, why should similar results from the two techniques increase our confidence in the techniques unless we already know that one of them is valid? We believe that the presence of response convergence between two previously uncertain techniques tends to substantiate the validity of both techniques. The reasoning is as follows. If the two techniques are quite different at the output end (which FPL and VEP are), then one would expect that nonsensory variables such as motivation would influence the techniques quite differently. When similar rather than dissimilar findings emerge, the most plausible interpretation is that both techniques are measuring sensory rather than nonsensory effects. It also implies that one's model of how the two techniques are related (e.g., do they tap the same mechanisms?) must be reasonably valid. A similar line of reasoning applies to stimulus convergence. Any time such linkages are found, all components of the linkage become more believable.

The second point we describe here concerns the relationship between the development of pattern vision and temporal vision. We have reviewed a number of psychophysical findings concerning these visual capabilities. By all accounts, pattern vision capabilities early in life are quite poor by adult standards. Visual acuity, for example, is roughly 45-fold lower in 1-month-olds than in adults. Furthermore, acuity continues to improve until at least 6 months of age. In contrast, temporal resolution is very good in 1-month-olds and essentially adultlike one month later. The conjunction of poor spatial resolution and good temporal resolution that exists during the first several months is analogous to what is observed in the peripheral retina of the adult visual system (Banks, 1982). Specifically, at retinal eccentricities of 20 to 30°, adults' minimum separable acuity is about 2 c/deg, yet their temporal resolution (CFF) is about the same as for the fovea. This analogy between infant vision and adult peripheral vision, if correct, may mean that postnatal visual development is most marked for the fovea and parafovea. Further study is required, however, to assess the validity of this analogy.

ACKNOWLEDGMENTS

Preparation of this chapter was supported by NIH Research Grant HD-12572 and by NIMH Research Scientist Development Award MH-00318 to M.S.B. The authors thank Bill Geisler for comments on the section on psychophysical techniques and Dick Aslin for general editorial comments.

REFERENCES

Abramov, I., Gordon, J., Hendrickson, A., Hainline, L., Dobson, V., & LaBossiere, E. (1982). The retina of the newborn human infant. *Science, 217,* 265–267.
Albrecht, D. G., DeValois, R. L., & Thorell, L. G. (1980). Visual cortical neurons: Are bars or gratings the optimal stimuli? *Science, 207,* 88–90.
Allen, J. (1978). *Visual acuity development in human infants up to 6 months of age.* Unpublished doctoral dissertation, University of Washington, Seattle.

Armington, J. C. (1974). *The electroretinogram.* New York: Academic Press.

Atkinson, J., & Braddick, O. (1982). Sensory and perceptual capacities of the neonate. In P. Stratton (Ed.), *Psychobiology of the human newborn.* New York: Wiley.

Atkinson, J., Braddick, O., & Moar, K. (1977a). Development of contrast sensitivity over the first 3 months of life in the human infant. *Vision Research, 17,* 1037–1044.

Atkinson, J., Braddick, O., & Moar, K. (1977b). Contrast sensitivity of the human infant for moving and static patterns. *Vision Research, 17,* 1045–1047.

Atkinson, J., Braddick, O., & Moar, K. (1977c). Infants' detection of image defocus. *Vision Research, 17,* 1125–1126.

Atkinson, J., Pimm-Smith, E., Evans, C., & Braddick, O. (1983). The effects of screen size and eccentricity on acuity in infants using preferential looking. *Vision Research, 23,* 1479–1483.

Awaya, S., Miyake, Y., Amaizumi, Y., Shiose, Y., Kanda, T., & Komuro, K. (1973). Amblyopia in man suggestive of stimulus deprivation amblyopia. *Japanese Journal of Ophthalmology, 17,* 69–82.

Banks, M. S. (1980). The development of visual accommodation during early infancy. *Child Development 51,* 646–666.

Banks, M. S. (1982). The development of spatial and temporal contrast sensitivity. *Current Eye Research, 2,* 191–198.

Banks, M. S., Aslin, R. N., & Letson, R. D. (1975). Sensitive period for the development of human binocular vision. *Science, 190,* 675–677.

Banks, M. S., & Ginsburg, A. P. (1985). Early visual preferences: A review and new theoretical treatment. In H. W. Reese (Ed.), *Advances in child development and behavior.* New York: Academic Press.

Banks, M. S., & Salapatek, P. (1978). Acuity and contrast sensitivity in 1-, 2-, and 3-month-old human infants. *Investigative Ophthalmology & Visual Science, 17,* 361–365.

Banks, M. S., & Salapatek, P. (1981). Infant pattern vision: A new approach based on the contrast sensitivity function. *Journal of Experimental Child Psychology, 31,* 1–45.

Banks, M. S., & Stephens, B. R. (1982). The contrast sensitivity of human infants to gratings differing in duty cycle. *Vision Research, 22,* 739–744.

Banks, M. S., Stephens, B. R., & Hartmann, E. E. (1985). The development of basic mechanisms of pattern vision. Spatial frequency channels. *Journal of Experimental Child Psychology, 40,* 501–527.

Barlow, H. B. (1972). Dark and light adaptation: Psychophysics. In D. Jameson & L. Hurvich (Eds.), *Handbook of sensory physiology: Vol. 7, Pt./4. Visual psychophysics.* Berlin & New York: Springer-Verlag.

Barlow, H. B. (1979). Three theories of cortical function. In R. D. Freeman (Ed.), *Developmental neurobiology of vision.* New York: Plenum.

Barlow, H. B., Fitzhugh, R., & Kuffler, S. W. (1957). Dark adaptation, absolute threshold and Purkinje shift in single units of the cat's retina. *Journal of Physiology (London), 137,* 327–337.

Berry, R. N. (1948). Quantitative relations among vernier, real depth, and stereoscopic depth acuities. *Journal of Experimental Psychology, 38,* 708–721.

Blakemore, C., & Sutton, P. (1969). Size adaptation: A new aftereffect. *Science, 166,* 245–247.

Blakemore, C., & Vital-Durand, F. (1980). Development of the neural basis of visual acuity in monkeys. Speculation on the origin of deprivation amblyopia. *Transactions of the Ophthalmological Societies of the United Kingdom, 99,* 363–368.

Bodis-Wollner, I. (1972). Visual acuity and contrast sensitivity in patients with cerebral lesions. *Science, 178,* 769–771.

Boothe, R. G. (1981). Development of spatial vision in infant macaque monkeys under conditions of normal and abnormal visual experience. In R. N. Aslin, J. R. Alberts, &

Goodman, J. W. (1965). *Introduction to Fourier optics.* New York: McGraw-Hill.

Gorman, J. J., Cogan, D. G., & Gellis, S. S. (1957). An apparatus for grading the visual acuity of infants on the basis of opticokinetic nystagmus. *Pediatrics, 19,* 1088–1092.

Gorman, J. J., Cogan, D. G., & Gellis, S. S. (1959). A device for testing visual acuity in infants. *Sight-Saving Review, 29,* 80–84.

Green, D. G. (1970). Regional variations in the visual acuity for interference fringes on the retina. *Journal of Physiology (London), 207,* 351–356.

Green, D. G., Powers, M. K., & Banks, M. S. (1980). Depth of focus, eye size, and visual acuity. *Vision Research, 20,* 827–835.

Gwiazda, J., Brill, S., Mohindra, I., & Held, R. (1978). Infant visual acuity and its meridional variation. *Vision Research, 18,* 1557–1564.

Hamasaki, D. I., & Sutija, V. G. (1979). Development of X- and Y-cells in kittens. *Experimental Brain Research, 35,* 9–23.

Hamer, R., & Schneck, M. E. (1984). Spatial summation in dark-adapted human infants. *Vision Research, 24,* 77–85.

Hansen, R. M., & Fulton, A. B. (1981). Behavioral measurement of background adaptation in infants. *Investigative Ophthalmology & Visual Science, 21,* 625–629.

Hansen, R. H., Fulton, A., Leitzman, D., & Harris, S. (1984). *Pupillographic assessment of rhodopsin regeneration in human infants.* Paper presented at the Association for Research in Vision and Ophthalmology, Sarasota.

Harris, L., Atkinson, J., & Braddick, O. (1976). Visual contrast sensitivity of a 6-month-old infant measured by the evoked potential. *Nature (London), 264,* 570–571.

Harter, M. R., Deaton, F. K., & Odom, J. V. (1977a). Maturation of evoked potentials and visual preference in 6–45 day old infants: Effects of check size, visual acuity, and refractive error. *Electroencephalography and Clinical Neurophysiology, 42,* 595–607.

Harter, M. R., Deaton, F. K., & Odom, J. V. (1977b). Pattern visual evoked potentials in infants. In J. E. Desmedt (Ed.), *Visual evoked potentials in man: New developments.* London & New York: Oxford University Press (Clarendon).

Harter, M. R., & Suitt, C. D. (1970). Visually-evoked cortical responses and pattern vision in the infant: A longitudinal study. *Psychonomic Science, 18,* 235–237.

Hecht, S., & Mintz, E. U. (1939). The visibility of single lines at various illuminations and the basis of visual resolution. *Journal of Genetic Physiology, 22,* 593–612.

Hecht, S., & Schlaer, S. (1936). Intermittent stimulation by light. V. The relation between intensity and critical frequency for different parts of the spectrum. *Journal of General Physiology, 19,* 965–979.

Hecht, S., Schlaer, S., & Pirenne, M. H. (1942). Energy, quanta, and vision. *Journal of General Physiology, 25,* 819–840.

Hecht, S., & Verrijp, D. C. (1933). The influence of intensity, color and retinal location on the fusion frequency of intermittent illumination. *Proceedings of the National Academy of Sciences of the U.S.A., 19,* 522–535.

Heck, J. (1957). The flicker electroretinogram of the human eye. *Acta Physiologica Scandinavica, 39,* 158–166.

Heck, J., & Zetterström, B. (1958). Analyse des photopischen Flimmerelektroretinogramms bei neugeborenen. *Ophthalmologica, 135,* 205–210.

Hendrickson, A., & Kupfer, C. (1976). The histogenesis of the fovea in the macaque monkey. *Investigative Ophthalmology, 15,* 746–756.

Hendrickson, A. & Yuodelis, C. (1984). The morphological development of the human fovea. *Ophthalmology 91,* 603–612.

Hess, R. F., & Bradley, A. (1980). Contrast perception above threshold is only minimally impaired in human amblyopia. *Nature (London), 287,* 463–464.

Horsten, G. P., & Winkelman, J. E. (1962). Electrical activity of the retina in relation to histological differentiation in infants born prematurely and at full term. *Vision Research, 2,* 269–276.

Horsten, G. P. M., & Winkelman, J. E. (1964). Electro-retinographic critical fusion frequency of the retina in relation to the histological development in man and animals. *Ophthalmologica, 18,* 515–521.

Hubel, D. H., & Wiesel, T. N. (1962). Receptive fields, binocular interaction and functional architecture in the cat's visual cortex. *Journal of Physiology (London), 160,* 106–154.

Hubel, D. H., & Wiesel, T. N. (1965). Binocular interaction in striate cortex of kittens reared with artificial squint. *Journal of Neurophysiology, 28,* 1041–1059.

Hubel, D. H., & Wiesel, T. N. (1968). Receptive fields and functional architecture of monkey striate cortex. *Journal of Physiology (London), 195,* 215–243.

Karmel, B. Z., Lester, M. L., McCarvill, S. L., Brown, P., & Hoffmann, M. J. (1977). Correlation of infants' brain and behavior response to temporal changes in visual stimulation. *Psychophysiology, 14,* 134–142.

Kelly, D. H. (1961). Flicker fusion and harmonic analysis. *Journal of the Optical Society of America, 51,* 917–918.

Kelly, D. H. (1971). Theory of flicker and transient responses. I. Uniform fields. *Journal of the Optical Society of America, 61,* 537–546.

Kelly, D. H. (1972). Flicker, In D. Jameson & L. M. Hurvich (Eds.), *Handbook of sensory physiology: Vol. 7, Pt. 4. Visual psychophysics.* Berlin & New York: Springer-Verlag.

Kelly, D. H. (1979). Motion and vision. Stabilized spatio-temporal threshold surface. *Journal of the Optical Society of America, 69,* 1340–1349.

Kessen, W., Haith, M. M., & Salapatek, P. H. (1970). Human infancy: A bibliography and guide. In P. H. Mussen (Ed.), *Carmichael's manual of child psychology* (3rd ed.,). Vol. 1, New York: Wiley.

Larsen, J. S. (1971). The sagittal growth of the eye. IV. Ultrasonic measurement of the axial length of the eye from birth to puberty. *Acta Ophthalmologica, 49,* 873–886.

Leibowitz, H. W., Shupert-Rodemer, C., & Dichgans, J. (1979). The independence of dynamic spatial orientation from luminance and refractive error. *Perception and Psychophysics, 25,* 75–79.

Levitt, H. (1971). Transformed up-down methods in psychoacoustics. *Journal of the Acoustical Society of America 49,* 467–477.

Lewis, T. L., Maurer, D., & Kay, D. (1978). Newborns' central vision: Whole or hole? *Journal of Experimental Child Psychology, 26,* 193–203.

Mandelbaum, J., & Sloan, L. L. (1947). Peripheral visual acuity: With special reference to scotopic illumination. *American Journal of Ophthalmology, 30,* 581–588.

Mann, I. C. (1964). *The development of the human eye.* London: British Medical Association.

Manny, R. E. & Klein, S. A. (1985). A three-alternative tracking paradigm to measure vernier acuity of older infants. *Vision Research 25,* 1245–1252.

Marg, E., Freeman, D. N., Peltzman, P., & Goldstein, P. J. (1976). Visual acuity development in human infants: Evoked potential measurements. *Investigative Ophthalmology, 15,* 150–153.

Marr, D. (1982). *Vision: A computational investigation into the human representation and processing of visual information.* San Francisco, CA: Freeman.

Maurer, D. (1975). Infant visual perception: Methods of study. In L. B. Cohen & P. Salapatek (Eds.), *Infant perception: From sensation to cognition: Vol. 1. Basic visual processes.* New York: Academic Press.

McKee, S. P., Klein, S. A., & Teller, D. Y. (1985). Statistical properties of forced-choice psychometric functions: Implications of probit analysis. *Perception and Psychophysics 37,*

Milewski, A. E. (1976). Infants' discrimination of internal and external pattern elements. *Journal of Experimental Child Psychology, 22,* 229–246.

Milewski, A. E. (1978). Young infants' visual processing of internal and adjacent shapes. *Infant Behavior and Development, 1,* 359–371.

Mitchell, D. E., Giffin, F., Wilkinson, F., Anderson, P., & Smith, M. L. (1976). Visual resolution in young kittens. *Vision Research, 16,* 363–366.

Moskowitz, A., & Sokol, S. (1980). Spatial and temporal interaction of pattern-evoked cortical potentials in human infants. *Vision Research, 20,* 699–707.

Naka, K., & Rushton, W. (1966). S-potentials from luminosity units in the retina of fish (Cyprinicae). *Journal of Physiology (London), 185,* 587–599.

Norcia, A. M. & Tyler, C. W. (1985). Spatial frequency sweep VEP: Visual acuity during the first year of life. *Vision Research 25,* 1399–1408.

Nystrom, M., Hansson, M. B., & Marklund, K. (1975). Infant preference for intermittent light. *Psychological Research Bulletin, Lund U., 15,* 1–11.

Pass, A. F., & Levi, D. M. (1982). Spatial processing of complex stimuli in the amblyopic visual system. *Investigative Ophthalmology & Visual Science, 23,* 780–786.

Pearson, R. M. (1966). The objective determination of vision and visual acuity. *British Journal of Physiological Optics, 23,* 107–127.

Peeples, D. R., & Teller, D. Y. (1978). White-adapted photopic spectral sensitivity in human infants. *Vision Research, 18,* 49–59.

Pirchio, M., Spinelli, D., Fiorentini, A., & Maffei, L. (1978). Infant contrast sensitivity evaluated by evoked potentials. *Brain Research, 141,* 179–184.

Pollack, I. (1968). Methodological determination of the PEST (Parametric Estimation by Sequential Testing) procedure. *Perception and Psychophysics, 3,* 285–289.

Pollen, D. A., Lee, J. R., & Taylor, J. H. (1971). How does the striate cortex begin the reconstruction of the visual world? *Science, 173,* 74–77.

Powers, M. K., Schneck, M., & Teller, D. Y. (1981). Spectral sensitivity of human infants at absolute visual threshold. *Vision Research, 21,* 1005–1016.

Regal, D. M. (1981). Development of critical flicker frequency in human infants. *Vision Research, 21,* 549–555.

Regan, D. (1972). *Evoked potentials in psychology, sensory physiology and clinical medicine.* London: Chapman & Hall.

Regan, D. (1978). Assessment of visual acuity by evoked potential recording: Ambiguity caused by temporal dependence of spatial frequency selectivity. *Vision Research, 18,* 439–443.

Regan, D., & Richards, W. A. (1971). Independence of evoked potentials and apparent size. *Vision Research, 11,* 679–684.

Reinecke, R., & Cogan, D. (1958). Standardization of objective visual acuity measurements. *Archives of Ophthalmology, 60,* 418–421.

Riggs, L. A. (1965). Visual acuity. In C. H. Graham (Ed.), *Vision and visual perception.* New York: Wiley.

Ripps, H., & Weale, R. A. (1969). Visual adaptation. In H. Davson (Ed.), *The eye* (Vol. 2). New York: Academic Press.

Robson, J. G. (1966). Spatial and temporal contrast-sensitivity functions of the visual system. *Journal of the Optical Society of America, 56,* 1141–1142.

Rose, R. M., Teller, D. Y., & Rendleman, P. (1970). Statistical properties of staircase estimates. *Perception and Psychophysics, 8,* 199–204.

Roufs, J. A. J. (1972). Dynamic properties of vision. I. Experimental relationships between flicker and flash thresholds. *Vision Research, 12,* 261–278.

Ruff, H. A., & Birch, H. G. (1974). Infant visual fixation: The effect of concentricity, curvilinearity, and the number of directions. *Journal of Experimental Child Psychology, 17,* 460–473.

Rusoff, A. C., & Dubin, M. W. (1977). Development of receptive-field properties of retinal ganglion cells in kittens. *Journal of Neurophysiology, 40,* 1188–1198.

Salapatek, P., & Banks, M. S. (1978). Infant sensory assessment: Vision. In F. D. Minifie & L. L. Lloyd (Eds.), *Communicative and cognitive abilities—Early behavioral assessment.* Baltimore, MD: University Park Press.

Salapatek, P., Bechtold, A. G., & Bushnell, E. W. (1976). Infant visual acuity as a function of viewing distance. *Child Development, 47,* 860–863.

Schor, C., & Narayan, V. (1981). The influence of field size upon the spatial frequency response of optokinetic nystagmus. *Vision Research, 21,* 985–994.

Sekuler, R. (1975). Visual motion perception. In E. C. Carterette & M. P. Friedman (Eds.), *Handbook of perception: Vol. 5, Seeing.* New York: Academic Press.

Shimojo, S., Birch, E. E., Gwiazda, J., & Held, R. (1984). Development of vernier acuity in infants. *Vision Research 24,* 721–728.

Shlaer, S. (1937). The relation between visual acuity and illumination. *Journal of General Physiology, 21,* 165–188.

Snyder, A. W. (1979). The physics of vision in compound eyes. In H. Autrum (Ed.), *Handbook of sensory physiology: Vol. 7, Pt. 6A. Vision in invertebrates.* Berlin & New York: Springer-Verlag.

Sokol, S. (1978). Measurement of infant acuity from pattern reversal evoked potentials. *Vision Research, 18,* 33–40.

Sokol, S., & Dobson, V. (1976). Pattern reversal visually evoked potentials in infants. *Investigative Ophthalmology, 15,* 58–62.

Sokol, S., Augliere, R., & Moskowitz, A. (1986). *Preferential looking estimates of infant visual acuity for stationary and phase-alternating gratings.* Paper presented at the meeting of the Association for Research in Vision and Ophthalmology, Sarasota.

Stephens, B. R., & Banks, M. S. (1985). The development of contrast constancy. *Journal of Experimental Child Psychology, 40,* 528–547.

Teller, D. Y. (1979). The forced-choice preferential looking procedure: A psychophysical technique for use with human infants. *Infant Behavior and Development, 2,* 135–153.

Teller, D. Y., Morse, R., Borton, R., & Regal, D. (1974). Visual acuity for vertical and diagonal gratings in human infants. *Vision Research, 14,* 1433–1439.

van Meeteren, A. (1967). *Spatial sinewave response of the visual system* (Institute for Perception TNO Rep. No. IZF-1966-7).

Van Nes, F. L., & Bouman, M. A. (1967). Spatial modulation transfer in the human eye. *Journal of the Optical Society of America, 57,* 401–406.

Vitova, Z., & Hrbek, A. (1972). Developmental study on the responsiveness of the human brain to flicker stimulation. *Developmental Medicine and Child Neurology, 14,* 476–486.

Vos, J. J., Lazet, A., & Bouman, M. A. (1956). Visual contrast thresholds in practical problems. *Journal of the Optical Society of America, 46,* 1065–1068.

Westheimer, G. (1979). The spatial sense of the eye. *Investigative Ophthalmology & Visual Science, 18,* 893–912.

Westheimer, G. (1982). The spatial grain of the perifoveal visual field. *Vision Research, 22,* 157–162.

Wetherill, G. B., & Levitt, H. (1965). Sequential estimation of points on a psychometric function. *British Journal of Mathematical and Statistical Psychology, 18,* 1–10.

Wiesel, T. N., & Hubel, D. H. (1965). Comparison of the effects of unilateral and bilateral eye closure on cortical unit responses in kittens. *Journal of Neurophysiology, 28,* 1029–1040.

Williams, D. R. (1985). Aliasing in human foveal vision. *Vision Research 25*, 195–2.
Yonas, A., & Pick, H. L. (1975). An approach to the study of infant space perception. In L.
    B. Cohen & P. Salapatek (Eds.), *Infant perception: From sensation to cognition: Vol.
    2. Perception of space, speech, and sound.* New York: Academic Press.
Yuodelis, C. & Hendrickson, A. (in press). A qualitative and quantitative analysis of the
    human fovea during development. *Vision Research.*

4

Infant Color Vision and Color Perception

DAVIDA Y. TELLER
Department of Psychology
University of Washington
Seattle, Washington 98195

MARC H. BORNSTEIN
Department of Psychology
New York University
New York, New York 10003

> Even as the soul thirsts for ideas, so the eye of the child thirsts for light.
>
> (John Locke, attributed by Tracy & Stimpfl, 1909)

I. INTRODUCTION

In the last few years infant research has advanced considerably in many areas of sensation and perception, as the present volume attests. Thus, today we have a better, though certainly not complete, understanding than at any time previously of the nature of a variety of sensory abilities and functions near the beginning of life. This chapter is concerned with the early development of sensory, perceptual, and cognitive aspects of color vision. We begin with some general and historical considerations of the developmental study of color vision. The nature of color vision and its photochemical and physiological substrates are next briefly described. The main parts of the chapter then report current knowledge concerning spectral sensitivity, wavelength discrimination, hue preference, hue categorization, and memory for color in infants.

Interest in the ontogeny of color vision and color perception has been sustained both among parents and among experimental and developmental psychologists (see Bornstein, 1978a, for a historical review).

185

HANDBOOK OF INFANT
PERCEPTION, VOLUME 1

Indeed, that history began over a century ago with Charles Darwin's (1877) biographical speculations about the visual capabilities of his infant son Doddy. Immediately following Darwin, several well-known investigators, including developmental biologists (e.g., Preyer, 1890), psychologists (e.g., Nagel, 1906), and developmental psychologists (e.g., Baldwin, 1893, 1895) examined and commented on the early development of color vision, usually in their own children.

These investigators used many different and ingenious techniques to study the ontogeny of color vision. Unfortunately, for reasons that will be discussed below, it has proved extremely difficult to conduct methodologically sound research on color vision in infants or to achieve adequate stimulus control and specification in infant experiments. Virtually all of the studies published prior to 1975 are today of historical interest only. The fascination of this topic, however, is amply demonstrated by continuing activity in the field; in 1974 and 1975 alone, for example, several different research groups independently published attempts at a conclusive demonstration of color vision in infants.

Why have so many people been fascinated by the ontogeny of color vision? We would propose at least three reasons. First, from a purely subjective and introspective point of view, color is an aesthetically and intellectually impressive aspect of our perceptual world. Colors are known to possess influential affective qualities. Colors are attractive and are thought to elicit and to maintain our visual attention—to induce vigilance. Colors influence our moods and have come to have specific connotations, as for example of weight, size, temperature, or distance (Payne, 1964). Colors also clarify and accentuate features of our environment. In wondering about the perceptual world of infants, then, it is entirely natural for us to wonder about its color qualities for infants and their value to infants. Even if we still thought of the infant's world as a "blooming, buzzing confusion," we would want to know, "Does it bloom in technicolor, or just in monotone?"

Second, color is a major and important carrier of information about the physical world. Color assists identification and coding, aids in the visual differentiation of surfaces, helps to mediate object recognition, and facilitates visual search. In this sense, color is a highly important perceptual attribute of things. The human factors literature suggests that we can detect and locate stimuli more readily and accurately on the basis of our knowledge of their color than on the basis of alternative visual cues such as size or shape (see, e.g., Christ, 1975; L. G. Williams, 1967). Color enhances common visual functions, including intrinsic contrasts, visibility, object evaluation, and constancy, in different species that possess it. Further, color represents more than an immediate perceptual cue; it functions both as a system of classification and as a symbolic code. Thus, it is of interest to know how soon infants have this important source of information at their disposal as they build their perceptual and cognitive worlds, and how soon their color vision capabilities become like those of adults, both in broad outline and in quantitative detail.

Third, the study of color vision is especially interesting from psychophysical and physiological viewpoints. In the study of adult color vision, certain behavioral facts have been, and continue to be, taken as almost incontrovertible evidence concerning the existence and detailed properties of specific elements of the physiological substrate. As will be discussed below, color vision provides a case in which behavioral facts have led historically (through some interesting logic) to physiological conclusions. If this is true for the study of adult color vision, it must also be true for the study of infant color vision, and in this way the study of the development of color vision of infants affords the potential of a rare glimpse of human neural development *in vivo*.

Many of the modern studies of infant color vision have been designed from this third, sometimes esoteric, point of view. The reasons for carrying out particular studies—for example, why discriminations among wavelengths longer than 550 nm are especially interesting—may not always be obvious to scientists entering the field of color vision for the first time. One of the principal aims of this chapter is to make the logic and results of these studies, and the conclusions to which they lead, understandable and available to researchers in the field of human infancy.[1]

II. THE STUDY OF COLOR VISION

Before we discuss the psychophysics and perception of color vision it will be advantageous, first, to define terminology and, second, to review modern conceptions of how color is processed in the retina and beyond. In this section, we briefly chart these introductory concepts.

A. Terminology

The need for color terms comes about because, in our perceptions, lights and objects differ from one another along a set of unique qualitative dimensions. In other words, color terms such as "red" and "green" have

---

[1] For more detailed treatments, see especially Boynton (1979) and Pokorny, Smith, Verriest, and Pinckers (1979). Frequent reference will be made to specific sections of Boynton (1979) where helpful background and supplementary material can be found.

an important linguistic function as descriptors of the subjective experiences of human beings, or as characteristics attributed by human beings to lights or surfaces. These perceptually descriptive usages of color terms are indispensable in human communication, and it is important to protect and maintain them.

On the other hand, when color phenomena are studied in the laboratory, there is a need for physical specification of the stimuli used. Physical analysis shows that differences in the perceived colors of lights and objects are often correlated, albeit roughly and imperfectly, with differences in the wavelength composition of the light reaching the eye. Since variations in wavelength composition are often closely correlated with variations in subjective color perceptions, it has been tempting to specify light with color names, as in a "blue–green light." Technically this usage is incorrect, and we have attempted to avoid it, replacing it with physical descriptions of stimuli (e.g., "a light of 495 nm"). Occasionally, when physical specification is cumbersome, we do use color terminology as a shorthand language for the physical specifications of a light. It is our intention that in all such instances the necessary physical specifications can be deduced to an adequate degree of precision from the immediate context.

This convention, already firmly established in adult psychophysical and perceptual studies, is particularly necessary and appropriate in cases where subjective descriptions encounter especially formidable barriers, as, for example, when subjects other than human adults are being studied. It is easy to understand the conceptual question of whether or not an infant can discriminate between two lights of different wavelengths, but to ask whether an infant has color vision in the subjective sense is to invoke the necessity for a much more complex interpretative structure. For this reason, throughout this chapter we avoid the use of subjective terminology in referring to the capabilities of infants. For example, instead of asking, "Do infants prefer more highly saturated stimuli?" we ask, "Do infants prefer stimuli which *to adults* appear more highly saturated?" Inferences about infants' subjective color perceptions will sometimes be drawn, but they will be avoided in the basic use of terms.

The definition of the term "color vision" itself has shown symptoms of the above conceptual and terminological tug of war. Thus, the field of color vision has come to include a wide range of experiments that explore the effects of wavelength composition on visual capacities, whether or not the stimuli appear colored, even to adults. Studies of scotopic and photopic spectral sensitivity, discussed in Section III, are examples of this usage. In the animal literature the question, "Does a particular organism have color vision?" has come to mean, "Can the organism discriminate between at least two lights that differ in wavelength composition *on the basis* of the difference in wavelength composition?'' Studies of wavelength discrimination, discussed in Section IV, exemplify this kind of question. And finally, the original concept of color vision as a descriptor of a set of perceptual and cognitive dimensions is still preserved. Questions in this realm are treated in Section V.

B. Photopigments and Receptors: The Funnel Analogy

In order to interact with matter, light must be absorbed by matter. A substance that absorbs light in the visible region of the electromagnetic spectrum (approximately 400–700 nm) may be called a *photopigment*. The probability that a quantum of light will be absorbed by a photopigment varies with the wavelength of the light; that is, the photopigment has a *spectral sensitivity* curve. The normal human retina contains four kinds of photoreceptors, one kind of rod and three kinds of cones. Each receptor type contains a different photopigment, and each has a different spectral sensitivity curve, as shown schematically in Figure 1a. See Boynton (1979, pp. 149–153) for a detailed discussion of the exact shapes of these curves.

The rods function alone at low light levels, and signals resulting from the absorption of light in the rods form the basis of nighttime (*scotopic*) vision. The three cone types function together at higher light levels and act jointly to subserve daytime (*photopic*) vision, of which color vision is an integral part. The three cone types have been called short-wavelength-sensitive (SWS), middle-wavelength-sensitive (MWS), and long-wavelength-sensitive (LWS), or in less formal but more memorable terminology, blue, green, and red cones, respectively.

In addition to its spectral sensitivity curve, any single photopigment, and hence any set of receptors containing the same photopigment, has a second interesting property. It happens that the absorption of a quantum, regardless of its wavelength, always makes the same change in the photopigment molecule. Thus, when a quantum is absorbed, all information concerning the wavelength of the quantum is lost by the photopigment, and hence by the receptor. In visual science, this fact is called the *principle of univariance*. An individual photoreceptor is, at best, a quantum counter; it does not preserve wavelength information. (A third property—*invariance under chromatic adaptation*—will be discussed below.)

These two fundamental properties of photoreceptors may be intuitively understood and remembered by making an analogy to a funnel (Figure 1b). To use the analogy, one must imagine vertical curtains of marbles of different colors (quanta of different wavelengths) located perpendicular to

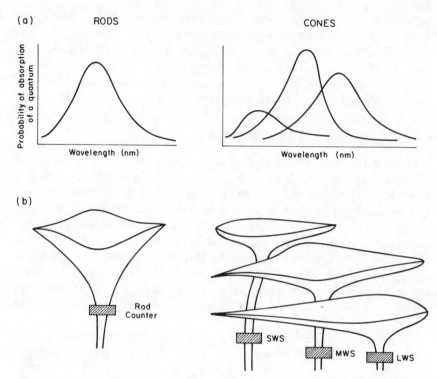

Figure 1. (a) The four receptor types. For each receptor type, the probability that an incoming quantum of light will be absorbed varies with the wavelength of the light; that is, each receptor has a *spectral sensitivity* curve. (b) The funnel analogy. Once a quantum is caught, all information about its wavelength is lost. Receptors thus function as quantum counters. (See text for details.)

the plane of the figure. These curtains of marbles rain down upon the funnel (the photopigment molecule). The width of the funnel varies along the wavelength axis, and hence by analogy the probability that a quantum will be caught varies with its wavelength. However, once caught, all marbles roll down together through the funnel. At the output of each funnel the number of marbles is counted without regard for their colors.

A given count could be produced by virtually any wavelength of light, simply by an adjustment of the intensity of the light or, indeed, by an infinite number of combinations of wavelengths and intensities. At the earliest stage of visual processing, then, wavelength information passes through a formidable bottleneck—or rather, four bottlenecks—each one of which, taken individually, would produce a complete loss of wavelength information.

Behaviorally, however, we know that in the light-adapted state much wavelength information is preserved. For example, color-normal adults can discriminate among nearly all visible spectral wavelengths, even when their relative intensities are varied over a wide range. This result comes about because, even though each cone type by itself loses wavelength information, each different wavelength of light is absorbed by all three cone photopigments in a ratio specific to that wavelength. In the funnel analogy, if the counts on the three counters could be read off and compared to each other, the wavelength of the stimulus could be deduced. It is in this fashion—by the *relative* activations of the three cone types—that wavelength information passes through the earliest stage of visual information processing.

The existence of three cone types, each of which follows the principle of univariance, was deduced originally from behavioral data (see Section IV,A). The deduction is often attributed to Helmholtz (but see Brindley, 1970), and the statement that there are three cone types is often called the Helmholtz or Young–Helmholtz theory of color vision. In modern times, converging evidence from several disciplines confirms it as fact. The peak sensitivities of the SWS, MWS, and LWS cones are now known to occur near 430, 530, and 560 nm (Boynton, 1979, Chap. 5).

C. The Neural Processing of Wavelength Information

Another early theorist, Hering (1878/1964), hypothesized that the neural substrate of color vision includes a set of three *opponent processes,* that is, neural elements that take on either of two mutually exclusive polarities of response. One of the three opponent processes was assumed to code for green and red, a second for blue and yellow, and a third for white and black. Today, there is much evidence that the signals from the three kinds of cones undergo a major recombination within the early neural layers of the retina—probably at the horizontal cell or bipolar level. Information from two or more kinds of cones is combined additively to yield what are called L-type (achromatic) channels, and subtractively to yield two kinds of C-type (chromatic) channels (see Boynton, 1979, p. 213). When inputs from two receptor types are combined subtractively, different wavelength ranges evoke different directions of physiological response: for example, a hyperpolarization for long wavelengths and a depolarization for middle wavelengths. Thus, the C-type channels appear to code wavelength information in a fashion that resembles the opponent processes postulated by Hering.

There is physiological evidence that chromatic opponency persists in cells throughout the retina, in the lateral geniculate nucleus (LGN), and in the earliest cortical level (striate cortex). For example, DeValois and his colleagues (see DeValois & DeValois, 1975) have identified statistically in the LGN of monkey three main classes of cells. Of these, two classes are C-types, called R/G and Y/B; they increase their firing rate in response to light from one spectral region and decrease their firing rate in response to light from another spectral region. Depending upon the spectral regions that excite and inhibit the cell, these cells are called $+R-G$ and $+Y-B$, and their complements $+G-R$ and $+B-Y$. The third class of cells is L-type and fires (or inhibits) to all wavelengths in a broadband fashion $(+W-B$ or $+B-W)$.

Many properties of color vision have been modeled successfully on an opponent process account (e.g., Boynton, 1979; DeValois & DeValois, 1975; Jameson & Hurvich, 1972). Hue is usually thought to be coded in the relative strengths and directions of response of C-type opponent cells. For example, green is said to be signaled by excitation in $+G-R$ cells, blue by excitation in the $+B-Y$ cells, and blue-green by excitation of both $+G-R$ and $+B-Y$ cells. Saturation is usually thought to be coded by the degree of concomitant activity in the L-type cells, with hues appearing more saturated the lower the activity level of the L-type cells with respect to the C-type cells.

The processing of wavelength and color at cortical levels is currently the subject of intensive research efforts, considerable controversy, and little consensus. To date, no formal models linking modern conceptions of cortical color coding to the psychophysics of adult color vision have been proposed.

Two final notes about neural models of color vision. First, the criterion of success or acceptability of such models rests on their power to explain various color phenomena. The foregoing physiological model is broad but not omniscient (i.e., it can account reasonably well for phenomena such as unique hues, wavelength discrimination, perceived saturation, simultaneous and successive contrast, and color-vision deficiences, but it is not so good with nonspectral hues, for example). Second, information about wavelength and hue must pass through all links of a causal chain through the nervous system in order to be expressed as behavior; thus, models of hue perception can be made from cells at *any* level. No one location has any obvious priority over the others.

D. Summary

The retina contains four receptor types, rods and three kinds of cones. The sensitivity of each receptor varies with the wavelength of light, but each receptor has a single univariate output regardless of the wavelength of light absorbed. Wavelength information is thus lost by each individual photoreceptor but encoded in light-adapted vision in the *relative* outputs of the three cone types. Beyond the photoreceptors, the resulting signals are combined additively and subtractively by later neural elements, with the subtractive operation providing the color-opponent processes inferred by Hering a century ago.

Many of the characteristics of these neural elements were originally discovered by inference from adult behavioral studies. Part of the interest of studying infant color vision is the possibility that behavioral studies at various ages will allow inferences concerning the ontogeny of these neural elements.

III. SPECTRAL SENSITIVITY

To separate the study of color vision from the study of other perceptual domains, and to separate the study of hue from other dimensions of color, especially brightness, it is necessary to study variations in the sensitivity of the visual system to different wavelengths of light. In this section, we discuss data on spectral sensitivity under neutral daytime and nighttime conditions, as well as under conditions of chromatic adaptation. We also discuss possible ontogenetic differences in spectral sensitivity.

A. Scotopic Spectral Sensitivity

If an organism possessed only a single class of photoreceptors, its vision would necessarily be dictated by the properties of a single photopigment. The visual sensitivity of the organism would vary with wavelength, in correspondence with the spectral sensitivity of its single photopigment,[2] and the organism would be incapable of discriminating among wavelengths of light matched to produce equal quantum catches.

When fully dark-adapted, human adult vision is characterized by these two properties. Psychophysically measured spectral sensitivity has a shape typical of a single photopigment absorption curve, and lights of all spectral compositions are reduced in appearance to colorless variations of white, grey, and black. The coincidence between the characteristics of dark-adapted human vision and the logical properties of a single-photopigment system lead to an inference that is very difficult to doubt: adult scotopic vision is subserved by a single photopigment. In fact, this photo-

---

[2] Various ancillary factors, such as differential absorption of light of different wavelengths by the lens of the eye, make this statement true only to a first approximation. Such factors are discussed further in Section III,C.

pigment, rhodopsin, has been isolated chemically, and its spectral sensitivity agrees well with the dark-adapted human spectral sensitivity curve.

If scotopic spectral sensitivity in infancy were similar to that in maturity, and if dark-adapted infants were incapable of discriminating among wavelengths of light, one could similarly infer that infant scotopic vision is subserved solely by rods. One could also infer that the rod system and its necessary central connections are already functional in young infants.

The scotopic spectral sensitivity of young infants has been assessed twice, once by recording the visually evoked cortical potential (VEP) and once behaviorally. Werner (1982) carried out a VEP study on eight subjects, of whom two were 4- to 5-month-old infants. The subjects were dark adapted for 10 min at the beginning of the experiment and were then presented with a series of narrow-band wavelengths of light. The stimuli subtended 42° of visual angle and flickered at 8 cycles/sec. For each wavelength, the physical intensity of the light was increased gradually over time, and a running average of the amplitude of the VEP was recorded. A criterion VEP amplitude, selected separately for each subject, was applied across all wavelength records to derive a spectral sensitivity curve. For much of the visible spectrum—about 450 to 580 nm—the data from the infants agreed well with data from adults tested under the same conditions. Above about 580 nm, data from all subjects showed cone intrusion. Below 450 nm, one of the two infants continued to resemble the adults; the other showed a systematic elevation in relative sensitivity above adult values.

Powers, Schneck, and Teller (1981) carried out a behavioral study of both spectral sensitivity and absolute sensitivity in 1- and 3-month-old infants. They used the forced-choice preferential looking (FPL) technique (Teller, 1979; Teller, Morse, Borton, & Regal, 1974). Infants were dark-adapted for at least 15 min and then confronted with a stimulus display consisting of a 17° test field presented in either a left or right position. An adult observer, blind to the position of the stimulus, watched the infant's eye movements and fixation patterns. On this basis, the observer had to judge the location of the stimulus on each trial. For each wavelength, a criterion percentage correct (75%) on the part of the observer was used to define the infant's detection threshold.

For the 3-month-olds, nine narrow-band stimuli were used, spanning the spectrum from 410 to 650 nm. At all wavelengths, excellent agreement was found between infants' relative spectral sensitivity and that of young adults tested in the same apparatus (Figure 2). The 1-month-olds were tested with only five wavelengths, and they showed a slightly elevated sensitivity below 430 nm.

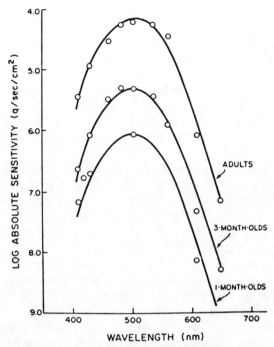

Figure 2. Behaviorally measured scotopic spectral sensitivity curves for dark-adapted 1-month-olds, 3-month-olds, and adults. (From Powers, Schneck, & Teller, 1981.) The solid curves are the CIE scotopic curve, the standard scotopic spectral sensitivity curve for adult vision, shifted vertically for best fit to each data set. At each age, the CIE curve provides a good fit to the data. It therefore seems highly likely that the same receptor type—the rods—which subserves adult scotopic vision is present and functioning in young infants.

Powers et al. also found that in absolute terms fully dark-adapted infants, like adults, are exquisitely sensitive to light. The adults detected the light at an intensity so dim that only about 1 quantum/1000 rods/sec was falling on the retina. The 3-month-old infants tested were no more than a log unit (a factor of 10) less sensitive than the adults, and the 1-month-olds were about 1.7 log units (a factor of 50) less sensitive than the adults. In other words, a signal initiated by the absorption of only a few hundred quanta of light passes all the way through the infant's visual system and is translated into the behavioral act of staring at the position of the light. This is a remarkable level of reliability for a system whose capacities have until recently been thought to be extremely limited.

B. Photopic Spectral Sensitivity

In the simplest case, one might expect that the organism's sensitivity to any given wavelength of light under photopic conditions would be determined by the sensitivity of whichever cone type is itself the most sensitive at that wavelength. Under that assumption, if we could place the three *relative* spectral sensitivity curves of Figure 1a at their appropriate *absolute* levels, a line running along the tops of the three curves should describe the organism's overall photopic spectral sensitivity, as shown in Figure 3a.

Such an *upper-envelope* model implies that the three cone types function as independent detectors. This model has represented a useful way to think about photopic spectral sensitivity, and it holds to a first approximation under many conditions. However, one can imagine many more complex ways in which the signals from the three cone types could be combined—for example, they could inhibit one another—and modern color theorists disagree about the rules of their joint action (Boynton, 1979, chap. 6). Further, it is easy to imagine that the three curves could shift independently up and down in absolute sensitivity, with consequent changes in their overall upper envelope.

Given these complexities, it is not surprising to learn that there is no such thing as "the" photopic spectral sensitivity curve. As illustrated in Figure 3, adult functions vary considerably with the technique of measurement, the size of the test field, the region of retina assessed, and a variety of other factors, and they vary enormously with the state of adaptation of the eye. In the face of such fluidity, photopic spectral sensitivity would seem to present itself as a poor starting point for the study of infant color vision.

There is, however, a fundamental reason why it is a necessary starting point. As will be discussed below, proof that infants have any form of color vision requires ruling out brightness artifacts; this, in turn, requires an assessment of brightness as a function of wavelength. Although brightness and spectral sensitivity are not identical in adult vision (LeGrand, 1972), in practice one is often a good predictor of the other, and if infant photopic spectral sensitivity were known in a given situation, it might be used to provide a first approximation to infant brightness matches in that situation. In particular, if the photopic spectral sensitivity of infants were known to be similar to that of adults tested under the same conditions, one might use adult brightness matches *in situ* as a first approximation for infant values. The search for proofs of infant color vision has therefore enticed several investigators to tackle the difficult topic of photopic spectral sensitivity. The question has been addressed using both VEP and behavioral techniques.

In the first modern study of infant spectral sensitivity, Dobson (1976) used the VEP to compare the photopic spectral sensitivity of five 2-month-old infants and two adults (20 and 23 years of age) tested under identical conditions. The stimulus used was a 16° circular field, divided into four quadrants by a fixation cross made of black lines subtending 1°. The field was flashed for about 300 msec once every 1.5 sec. Seven wavelengths were used, ranging from 448 to 658 nm. For each wavelength, an averaged evoked potential was recorded at each of a series of intensities. From each such record, a measure of "implicit time"—the time between stimulus onset and the first major positive deflection of the VEP—was abstracted, and the implicit time was plotted as a function of intensity. Data for all wavelengths were fitted with curves of the best-fitting common slope, and the horizontal displacements needed to bring all curves together on the intensity axis were used to indicate the subject's relative sensitivities to the various wavelengths of light.

Dobson's results are shown in Figure 4. Three major aspects may be noted. First, the median spectral sensitivities are similar for the two age groups, infants and young adults. Second, in this sample, the relative sensitivity of the median infant seems to be systematically about 0.3 log unit higher than that of the median adult in the short-wavelength region of the spectrum, below about 525 nm. Third, the range of individual differences is large at both ages—a full log unit at 448 nm in infants, to take the extreme example—and infant and adult populations clearly overlap. Thus, it is difficult to know whether the differences in short-wavelength sensitivity found between the median infant and the median adult arise from sampling noise or from true age differences.

In a second VEP implicit-time study, Moskowitz-Cook (1979) tested groups of five to seven infants in several age ranges, from 3 to 6 weeks to 19 to 22 weeks postnatal, and a group of three adults (24–29 years). Ten wavelengths were used, ranging from 415 to 670 nm. The stimulus was a phase-alternated checkerboard, subtending 12.3° of visual angle, with each individual check having a subtense of 45'. Stimuli were superimposed on a dim white background field.

The data from this study were presented as group averages. Data from the 19- to 22-week-old group agreed closely with average data obtained from adults. The three youngest age groups (3–6, 7–10, and 11–14 weeks), however, showed a consistent elevation of perhaps 0.5 log unit of relative sensitivity in the short-wavelength region, below about 500 nm. The data thus confirm Dobson's earlier findings for 2-month-olds and

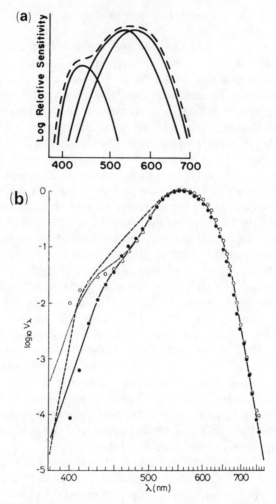

Figure 3. Photopic spectral sensitivity and its complexities. (a) An "upper envelope" model that might describe the overall spectral sensitivity of an organism using three independent receptor types simultaneously. (b) Examples of adult photopic spectral sensitivity (luminosity) curves. The data points were taken with flicker photometry (○) and step-by-step matching (●) and illustrate the variation in results across psychophysical techniques. The theoretical curves show three different adult standards that have been proposed: the CIE Standard Observer (—), the modification proposed by Judd in 1951 (. . . . .), and the CIE Supplementary Observer proposed for large test fields (- - - -). Note that virtually all of the disagreement is in the short wavelength ("blue") region of the spectrum. (From Le-Grand, 1972.) (c) Example of the influence of test field size on photopic spectral sensitivity. (From Sperling & Lewis, 1959.) (d) The influence of chromatic adaptation. When spectral sensitivities are measured against chromatic backgrounds, enormous changes in spectral sensitivity can occur. (From Wald, 1945.)

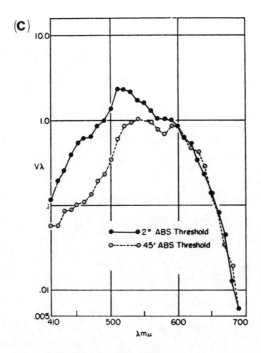

(c)

Vλ

— 2° ABS Threshold
------ 45' ABS Threshold

λmμ

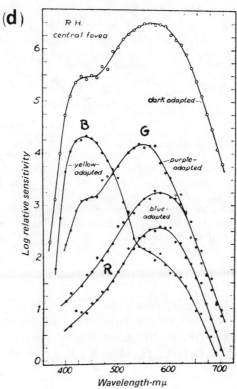

(d)

R. H.
central fovea

dark adapted

B   G

yellow-
adapted

purple-
adapted

blue-
adapted

R

Log relative sensitivity

Wavelength-mμ

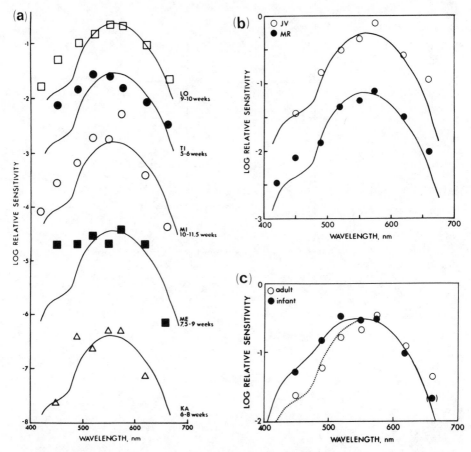

Figure 4. Photopic spectral sensitivity for 2-month-old infants and adults, measured with the visual evoked potential (Dobson, 1976). (a) Five infants. (b) Two adults. (c) Averages for the five infants (●) and two adults (○). The solid curves in a and b and the dotted curve in c show adult foveal spectral sensitivity, and the solid line in c shows parafoveal spectral sensitivity, all from Wald (1945). Infant and adult photopic spectral sensitivities are similar in this and other studies. Note, however, the slight elevation of infant sensitivities for short wavelengths in the averaged curves (c), and the large individual differences in this wavelength range in the individual data sets (a).

suggest that, whatever the cause of this difference, it has disappeared by about 20 weeks postnatal.

Peeples and Teller (1978) used the FPL technique to assess white-adapted spectral sensitivity behaviorally in two 2- to 3-month-old infants and in three adults. Six narrow-band stimuli were used, spanning the spectrum from 458 to 637 nm. The stimulus field consisted of a set of three

$3° \times 22.5°$ vertical stripes, moving across a $2.0 \log \text{cd/m}^2$ fluorescent white background. They found excellent agreement in relative sensitivity between the two infants and the three adults at all wavelengths tested. As in the Powers et al. (1981) scotopic study, the adults were about a factor of 10 more sensitive than the infants in absolute terms. Overall, the spectral sensitivity curves of both infants and adults were quite broad and relatively flat, a common finding under conditions of white adaptation (e.g., Sperling & Harwerth, 1971).

C. Second-Order Effects

In the sections on scotopic and photopic spectral sensitivity above, we noted that several (but not all) investigators have found some small but systematic deviations between infant and adult spectral sensitivity curves. In three out of five studies, infants showed spectral sensitivities as much as 0.5 log unit higher than adults in the short-wavelength (blue) region of the spectrum, below about 500 nm. There is an embarrassingly large number of ways in which such systematic deviations could come about. For example, (a) the differences could be caused by differing small samples from highly variable populations; (b) young infants could have less dense lens or macular pigmentation than adults (but see Ruddock, 1972; Werner, 1982); (c) especially for photopic vision, it could be that different retinal regions or combinations of receptor types are being sampled at different ages and by the different techniques; (d) the VEP of young infants could be unduly influenced by short-wavelength light; or (e) any combination of the above may occur.

Two of these factors especially deserve further consideration. The first is lens pigmentation. Werner (1982) found that some infants had higher relative scotopic sensitivity than adults below 430 nm, and he concluded that the pigmentation of infants' lenses is significantly less dense than that of adults. His conclusion is, however, not strongly supported by his own data, which show wide, overlapping interage variation and no systematic change in average lens density from 1 month—the youngest age tested—through 30 years of age. Powers et al.'s behavioral study shows a slight elevation of sensitivity at 410 and 430 nm for 1-month-olds, but excellent agreement between 3-month-old infant and adult scotopic spectral sensitivity over the whole spectrum down to 410 nm. These results suggest that infant and adult lenses, on the average, have highly similar absorption characteristics by 3 months postnatal.

The second factor concerns the differences between electrophysiological and behavioral studies. It is interesting to note that the three studies in which infants appear relatively more sensitive than adults in the short-wavelength region have all employed VEP techniques, whereas those showing closer infant–adult agreement have used behavioral measures. This procedural difference could submit to the following explanation. In general, the scattering of light is inversely proportional to its wavelength raised to the fourth power; thus, much of the scattered light in the eye is light of short wavelengths. Evoked potentials tend to reflect the summation of signals from the entire retina, and they can thus be strongly influenced by even a dim veil of scattered light. Optical analyses show that there is more scattered light in infant monkey eyes than in adult monkey eyes (R. Williams & Boothe, 1981), and the same may well be true for human beings. Thus, our current speculation is that the elevation of infant spectral sensitivity in the blue, so far reported in three VEP studies and less prominent or absent in two behavioral ones, will turn out to be more a consequence of VEP recording than a real property of infant vision. In any case, much systematic work will be needed to sort out these questions, and the known individual differences in preretinal absorption and scatter will make it necessary to use substantial sample sizes in such studies. As stated above, photopic spectral sensitivity is one of the most complex topics in adult color vision, and there is no reason to expect that it will yield up its ontogenetic secrets without a struggle.

D. Chromatic Adaptation

If chromatic rather than neutral backgrounds are used, enormous changes occur in the shapes of adult spectral sensitivity curves (see Figure 3d and Boynton, 1979, Chap. 6). To a first approximation, these effects can be modeled by assuming that the absolute sensitivities of each of the three cone types shift up and down independently over a range of several log units, with the sensitivity of each cone type becoming increasingly depressed as more light is absorbed by that cone type. With the use of different chromatic backgrounds, the envelope of the three cone curves will change dramatically in shape. In the extreme, the sensitivities of two of the three cone types can be so depressed that a curve resembling the spectral sensitivity of a single remaining cone type can be traced out over a broad wavelength range.

Furthermore, because of the principle of univariance, the spectral sensitivity of an individual photopigment cannot change differentially with different wavelengths of chromatic adaptation. Different chromatic backgrounds can cause different changes in the shape of an organism's spectral sensitivity curve only if at least two photopigments contribute to that curve. Thus in color vision theory, changes in the shapes of spectral sensitivity curves are taken as strong evidence for the existence and contributions of at least two photoreceptor types.

To date only one chromatic-adaptation study has been carried out on infants, in a search for the SWS (blue) cone system (Pulos, Teller, & Buck, 1980). The FPL technique was used to assess infant and adult spectral sensitivity under two conditions of chromatic adaptation. Broadband blue- and yellow-adapting backgrounds of luminances of about 1.5 log cd/m^2 were used. For 2-month-old infants and adults, clear changes in spectral sensitivities were found with changes in the wavelength composition of the background, thus indicating the participation of at least two receptor types. In adults tested under yellow adaptation, the data traced out a classical SWS cone curve, peaking at about 440 nm. In contrast, in the two most extensively studied infants, both 2-month-olds, the curve obtained under yellow adaptation was flat or rising between 440 and 500 nm, and it bore a greater resemblance to a rod curve than to a SWS cone curve. Additional 2-month-olds failed to give evidence of a mature SWS cone system. By 3 months, however, the resemblance to adults had increased for most subjects. These data suggest that the SWS cone system may be relatively insensitive at 2 months postnatal, and they invite the speculation that very young infants may be found to resemble adults who have deficits in their blue cone systems. This suggestion arises again in Section IV,D below. (For a discussion of the paradox that infants may be relatively more sensitive than adults at short wavelengths, but still have relatively insensitive SWS cones, see Pulos et al., 1980).

E. Summary

As a result of recent research, some of the properties of infant spectral sensitivity may be taken as known. The scotopic spectral sensitivity of even very young infants, measured electrophysiologically or behaviorally, is similar to that of adults. There can be little doubt that, under dark-adapted conditions, infant vision is mediated by rhodopsin and by the single photoreceptor class—the rods—that contains it. There can also be little doubt that, at least across the rather broad range of conditions and techniques represented by three electrophysiological and two behavioral studies, infant relative photopic spectral sensitivity under neutral adaptation is reasonably represented by adult values over most of the spectrum.

Considerable uncertainty remains concerning the short-wavelength region of the spectrum in very young infants. On the one hand, they sometimes show elevated short-wavelength sensitivity; on the other hand, the SWS cone system of young infants has thus far proven difficult to find under conditions of chromatic adaptation that reveal it in adults, although it has been shown by other techniques (see below).

These studies provide partial justification for the use of adult brightness matches as first approximations for equating brightness for infants, at least above about 500 nm. Their usefulness will become apparent in the discussion of infant wavelength discrimination in Section IV,C.

IV. WAVELENGTH DISCRIMINATION

We turn now to the second definition of color vision, wavelength discrimination. As has been discussed, any system based upon a single photopigment must fail to preserve wavelength information. This is so because any two lights of different wavelength compositions can be adjusted in relative intensity to produce equal quantum catches—equal counts on a single counter in the funnel analogy (Figure 1). All wavelength information is thus lost in scotopic vision, and it would also be lost if photopic vision were based on only a single kind of cone. As discussed in Section II, photopic vision is subserved by three kinds of cones, and wavelength information passes through the receptors encoded in the relative outputs of the three cone types.

A. Trichromacy and Dichromacy

It is important to realize that even in photopic vision the preservation of information about the wavelength composition of light is imperfect. The mapping of wavelength compositions into color sensations is a many-to-one affair, in the sense that many stimuli that differ in wavelength composition can give identical color appearances. Physically different stimuli that are subjectively indistinguishable are called *metamers*. To take a common example, complementary colors are pairs of wavelengths which when mixed together appear white. Many complementary pairs exist. Thus, a patch of light that appears white may have any of a very large number of different wavelength compositions, and an observer cannot know which one from its appearance. These white patches constitute a set of metamers, and *information about their differences in wavelength composition has been lost by the visual system.* Virtually any color sensation (a specific shade of red, yellow, green, or blue, any of their desaturated cousins, or any shade of white) can be produced by many different physical stimuli, and sets of different physical stimuli that produce equivalent perceptions are called metameric sets. Wavelength information is preserved to the extent that any stimulus from one metameric set (e.g., a particular shade of white) is readily distinguished from any stimulus from another metameric set (e.g., a particular shade of red), but it is lost within metameric sets.

These failures to preserve wavelength information may be described by a single empirical law, trichromacy. The law of trichromacy, informally stated, is that any light may be matched (i.e., any color sensation may be produced) by some mixture of three primaries (such as, for example, narrow-band spectral lights of 444, 526, and 644 nm). Red metamer sets will require more of the long-wavelength primary, green metamer sets more of the middle-wavelength primary, whitish hues more nearly equal amounts of all three primaries, and so forth, but any light can be matched. (For an excellent introduction to the law of trichromacy, see Cornsweet, 1970; for a formal statement, see Brindley, 1970.)

The law of trichromacy implies the existence of *three* cone photopigments. It is not, of course, obvious why this should be so. Briefly, the proof involves derivation of a set of simultaneous equations, one to describe the total quantum catch of each photopigment system (the count on each funnel in Figure 1). N photopigments generate N equations. Each photopigment catches quanta from each of the M primaries, and the total quantum catch for each receptor type is simply the sum of the catches from the M primaries. Thus, a set of N simultaneous equations in M unknowns is generated; the unknowns are the intensities of the primaries. Algebraically, a system of N simultaneous equations in M unknowns is solvable if $M = N$. For this reason, the minimum number of photopigments present in any organism's visual system may be deduced from the number of primaries needed in color-mixture experiments. Our belief in the existence of three cone types came about almost 200 years ago (Brindley, 1970) because of the *behavioral* fact of trichromacy, not because of any information provided by chemistry or physiology.

Not all human adults are trichromats. A few individuals have fewer distinguishable color sensations and larger metamer sets than do trichromats. For some of these individuals, called *dichromats*, mixtures of two primaries are sufficient to match all other lights. Thus, dichromats are generally believed to have only two of the trichromat's three photopigment systems. Different kinds of dichromats are conceived of as having lost different pigment systems. Those thought to be missing the LWS, MWS, and SWS systems are called *protanopes, deuteranopes,* and *tritanopes,* respectively. Each different kind of dichromat has a different, predictable pattern of loss of wavelength information with respect to the normal trichromat (see Boynton, 1979, Chap. 10). These patterns of loss will be described further below.

To demonstrate color vision, a researcher moving into the field of infant vision would naturally begin by asking two fundamental questions. First, "Can infants make any discriminations on the basis of wavelength?" If so, infants must have at least two functional cone types. Second, "Can infants be shown to be trichromats?" If so, they must have all three.

B. The Brightness Problem

The demonstration of true wavelength discrimination in infants is a difficult task. It is easy to show, and has been shown many times, that infants of various ages can discriminate between lights or objects that differ in color for adults (for a review, see Bornstein, 1978a). For example, an infant will track a field of light of one color moving within a field of a second color (Chase, 1937) or stare at a heterochromatic checkerboard in preference to a homochromatic field (Fagan, 1974). The logical difficulty in showing wavelength discrimination lies in proving that the discrimination is based on a true preservation of wavelength information, rather than just on a difference in *brightness*,[3] that is, on differences stemming only from the differential absorption of various wavelengths of light by a system that does not preserve wavelength information.

An analogy may help to make this clear. In a black and white photograph of an everyday scene, objects are still clearly visible; a red ball and a white ball are still distinguishable from each other because the white ball looks white and the red ball looks grey. There would exist some exact shade of grey ball which, in the photograph, would be indistinguishable from the red ball, but we could only find the right shade for the grey ball by trial and error, or by knowing the spectral characteristics of the two balls and the photographic film. Similarly, even a totally colorblind infant would see a red and white checkerboard as checkered unless the squares happened to be perfectly matched in brightness *for that infant*.

The problem of how to confront an infant with a brightness match is a complex one, the logic of which will be discussed abstractly in the following paragraphs. The reader who prefers to start with a concrete description of the actual studies should move on to Section IV,C below.

All sophisticated studies of infant color vision begin at a common starting place: the need for an initial estimate of infants' brightness matches between stimuli differing in wavelength composition. It is this conceptual framework that motivated the studies of infant photopic spectral sensitivity reviewed in Section III,B. The common finding of those studies is that infant and adult relative photopic spectral sensitivities tested under similar conditions are similar *to a first approximation*. Also, for adults under many conditions, measures of spectral sensitivity correlate with measures of the photopic brightness of chromatic stimuli (see LeGrand, 1972). Thus, in the absence of a better alternative, adult brightness equalizations—either standardized by physical calibrations or made by color-

---

[3] Since brightness is a subjective variable, the use of the term here is actually inappropriate. It is used as a shorthand notation in this context in the color vision literature because variations in the intensity of light are often perceived as variations in brightness by adults.

normal adults *in situ*—have been used almost universally to provide an initial first approximation to infant matches.[4]

Three main paths to the demonstration of infant wavelength discrimination have diverged from this common starting point. The first and weakest approach is simply to use a pair of chromatic stimuli, A and B, matched in brightness by an adult standard. One then assumes that the brightnesses of the stimuli are adequately matched for infants; that is, that the infants could not respond differentially to the two stimuli on the basis of any residual brightness difference. Then, one concludes that any differential responding on the part of the infant must be caused by the preservation of wavelength information. Such conclusions are, of course, open to question because adult brightness matches provide only a first approximation to infant brightness matches and because we have until recently had little

---

[4] There is no general answer to the question of *which* adult standard should be used to provide the first approximation to infant brightness matches. Choice of a standard is particularly difficult when short wavelengths of light are involved, both because individual differences and variations among adult standards are largest in this region, and because differences between infants and adults are sometimes reported here (Section III).

Three different choices of adult standards have most commonly been made in infancy research. The first, and in many ways the simplest, is to use purchasable physical stimuli, such as Munsell chips, with built-in direct adult heterochromatic brightness matches (equal Munsell values). Such broad-band stimuli have a limited range of flexibility, but they are simple to use and avoid the need for sophisticated equipment and calibrations. It is particularly important to realize that the adult matches in this solution are strictly valid only under the conditions of illumination specified by the manufacturer, and unless a light source with the right spectral composition is used, stimulus specification becomes very complex.

The second approach is to use lights set equal in luminosity with reference to a standardized adult photopic luminosity curve, such as the curves in Figure 3. The advantages to this approach are that a specifiable physical standard is being used, that standard sets of different luminosity coefficients are available for stimuli of different sizes and different retinal locations, and that new adult functions do not have to be measured *in situ*. The disadvantages are that sophisticated calibrations are needed and the stimulus values used will be wrong if calibration errors are made. If an adult luminosity standard is to be used, it is probably better to use either Judd's (1951) modification of the CIE standard observer or the CIE supplementary observer (the dotted and dashed lines respectively in Figure 3b) than the original CIE standard observer (the solid line in Figure 3b). The former two curves are higher than the latter in the short-wavelength region of the spectrum since it is believed that CIE originally underestimated in the blue.

The third approach is to use adults' heterochromatic brightness matches made *in situ*. The advantages of this approach are that the stimuli used are not affected by physical calibration errors, that the adult matches are made under the stimulus and adaptation conditions in use in the experiment, and that adult brightness matches, rather than the more abstract adult luminosity functions, are being used. The main disadvantage is that such adult matches are subjectively difficult and are characterized by relatively high intra- and inter-subject variability.

None of these solutions will stand scrutiny on its own. All must be used in acceptable experimental paradigms as described in the text.

idea how large the residual brightness differences are, nor how sensitive infants might be to them.

The second and third techniques for solving the brightness problem are more compelling. Both involve the use of a series of luminances of the stimuli, rather than just a single luminance of each. The second technique, taken from the animal literature (e.g., Boothe, Teller, & Sackett, 1975; DeValois, Morgan, Polson, Mead, & Hull, 1974), involves the unsystematic variation, or "jitter", of luminances from trial to trial. An approximation to the infant's brightness match—for example an adult brightness match—is first set up between two chromatic stimuli, A and B. The relative luminances of the two stimuli are then varied unsystematically from trial to trial, over a wide range around the initial approximation to the infant's brightness match. Provided that the initial approximation was reasonably good, the infant will be confronted with stimulus pairs in which stimulus A is sometimes brighter and sometimes dimmer than stimulus B, with more or less equal probabilities. If the infant responds on the basis of brightness (e.g., always stares at the brighter stimulus), the infant's responses would be haphazard with respect to wavelength composition. Systematic responding by the infant to one of the two chromatic stimuli, collapsed over all luminance pairings, cannot be carried out on the basis of brightness, and discrimination can therefore be attributed to the preservation of wavelength information.

The third solution to the brightness problem consists of the systematic variation of luminance. As in the previous cases, an approximation to the infant's brightness match—for example, an adult brightness match—is set up. The infant is shown many trials of each of a series of several relative luminances of two chromatic stimuli, A and B, centered around the initial estimate of the infant's brightness match. Provided that the range of relative luminances used encompasses the infant's true brightness match, at least one of the relative-luminance pairings used will be likely to confront the infant with luminances of A and B which differ indiscriminably in brightness. The third approach, then, is the same as the first, except that the experimenter has several chances, rather than just one, to confront the infant with a brightness match. If the infant can respond to stimulus A for *all* the relative luminances of A and B, one can conclude with increased certainty that the infant must be able to preserve wavelength information.

The rigor of the third technique can be further enhanced by asking two important preliminary questions and by employing answers to them in the experimental design. The first question is, "How good *is* the initial estimate of the infant's brightness match?" If, for example, we believe that the infant's match is within 0.2 log unit of the adult standard used, we can make the luminance series span more than ±0.2 log unit around the adult match. In so doing, we ensure that the match falls within the range of luminances used.

The second question is, "How finely must the luminance series be spaced in order to be sure that the infant's brightness match does not escape by falling between two of the luminances of the series?" This question is subject to empirical investigation, by a control study of the infant's *luminance (brightness) discrimination function*. To determine the luminance discrimination function, one would test the infant with two lights of the same wavelength composition, under the same conditions to be used in the color experiment, and see to how small a luminance difference, ΔI, the infant can in fact respond. The value of ΔI then provides the spacing needed in the luminance series for the color experiment because in a series of luminances of stimulus A spaced two ΔI apart there will exist at least one luminance that falls ΔI or less away from the infant's brightness match to stimulus B.

Two different criteria of discrimination—*absolute performance* and *curve shape*—can be used in relation to the third approach to avoiding the brightness problem. The absolute performance criterion was described above: if the infant can perform better than chance on a chromatic discrimination task for *all* of the luminances in a finely spaced series, the infant must be preserving wavelength information. The second criterion involves comparisons of curve shape between the luminance discrimination function and the chromatic discrimination functions (see Figure 7). Even if the infant's performance falls toward chance at one or more luminances of the chromatic stimulus, the shape of the chromatic discrimination curve may or may not be identical to the shape of the luminance discrimination function. For example, the minimum in the chromatic discrimination function may be narrower or shallower than the minimum in the luminance discrimination function. Any difference in curve shape between chromatic and luminance functions implies some preservation of wavelength information, while highly similar curve shapes (as in Figure 7) suggest that luminance cues control the infant's performance in both tasks; that is, that wavelength information is not preserved.

It is interesting to note that in some instances the first and third techniques converge. In adults, ΔI—the smallest detectable change in luminance—varies enormously with the conditions under which it is measured. It is smallest when two fields are contiguous in space and time and presented in a homogeneous, noise-free context, and it gets progressively larger as the fields are separated in space or time or presented in the midst of noise. The larger ΔI, the fewer the luminance steps that will be needed in the use of the third technique described above. More fundamentally, the larger ΔI, the higher the probability that any single rough approximation to the infant's brightness match will be within the infant's ΔI of the infant's match. Hence, one can improve the *a priori* value of experiments generated by the first technique—using only a single luminance of each stimulus, matched to the others by an adult standard—by separating the stimuli in space and time or by camouflaging them in a noisy background. Even better, one can measure ΔI empirically within such an experimental context. In the extreme, if one can show that ΔI is very large, an adult standard would indeed provide close enough brightness matches among spectral stimuli for infants, and the infant's discrimination among stimuli so matched would constitute proof of color vision.

One final note. It has sometimes been popular to write off all demonstrations of infant color vision on the grounds that the brightness problem is unsolved, or perhaps even unsolvable. Although the former conclusion is correct for most or all of the literature prior to 1975, recent studies cannot be so lightly discarded. We now know how to provide a reasonable first approximation to infant brightness matches and how to choose a reasonable range of relative luminances to explore. Appropriate luminance discrimination data—ΔI—can be made available as a control. In addition, in general, any residual brightness mismatches will tend to increase regularly with differences in wavelength between two stimuli, and it will thus become difficult to explain complex patterns of infants' successes and failures (as, for example, those described below) on the basis of presumed brightness mismatches alone. Thus, in the case of carefully controlled modern studies, the burden of proof of any claim that an infant's discrimination between chromatic stimuli is based on a brightness artifact has shifted to the critic.

C. Demonstrations of Wavelength Discriminations in Infants

Among older studies of color vision in infants, Chase's (1937) experiment must be considered a treasured antique. It provides an example of the first technique discussed above—use of an adult brightness match—in combination with an attempted brightness control. Chase showed 1- to 3-month-old infants a stimulus display in which a field of one color (approximately 10°) moved within a field of another color (approximately 45°). He used four broad-band stimuli, a red centered at 640 nm, a yellow at 570 nm, a green at 530 nm, and a blue at 470 nm, in all combinations. The colors were matched in brightness by adult standards to within 0.1 log unit. As a control for brightness mismatches, Chase also used a grey field within a 0.1 log unit brighter grey field. Chase watched the infants and observed that they tracked the moving field when a color difference was present but did not track in the brightness control conditions. On this basis he concluded that the infants possessed color vision. Unfortunately, his study is not quite conclusive because the colors used could well have differed in brightness to the infant by a larger amount than the brightness control used. Furthermore, it has since been demonstrated in an experiment modeled after Chase's technique (Peeples & Teller, 1978) that infants will track brightness differences much smaller than the 0.1 log unit difference used in Chase's control. Nonetheless, Chase's explicit consideration of the brightness problem and his inclusion of an attempted brightness control make his study exemplary; it was unexcelled until modern times.

Schaller (1975) used the second technique—unsystematic variation of brightness—in an operant paradigm to test the capacity of 3-month-old infants to discriminate red from green. The infants were shown a display consisting of broad-band red–black and green–black checkerboards in interchangeable left–right positions. Each checkerboard could take one of eight different luminance values across a very wide luminance range (more than 2 log units). For four stimulus pairs, the red was of a higher luminance than the green, and for the other four pairs, the green was of a higher luminance than the red, by adult standards. The infant was showered with auditory, visual, tactile, and/or gustatory reinforcers for staring in the direction of one color (red for some infants and green for others). Averaged across all luminances, most infants learned to stare more at the reinforced than the nonreinforced color, providing definitive evidence that 3-month-olds have some form of color vision.

Peeples and Teller (1975) used the third technique—systematic luminance variation—in combination with measurements of ΔI, to demonstrate a red–white discrimination in 2-month-old infants. The FPL technique was used. The infants were shown a white screen in which either a broad-band red (dominant wavelength, 633 nm) or white bar ($14° \times 1°$) could be embedded. Using the white bar, Peeples and Teller traced out infants' luminance discrimination functions (Figure 5). They found that summing ΔI above and below the luminance of the screen, the luminances of the bar which made it indistinguishable from the screen covered a total range of only about 0.1 log unit; thus, under these conditions at least, infants are exquisitely sensitive to small brightness mismatches.

The red bar was then presented, embedded in the white screen, at each of a series of 12 luminances. The series was distributed across ± 0.4 log unit, centered around the adult brightness match, in steps so small (0.08 log unit) that at least one of the steps must have confronted the infant with a red–white brightness match. The infants discriminated the red bar from the white field at *every* luminance step (Figure 5), including by inference

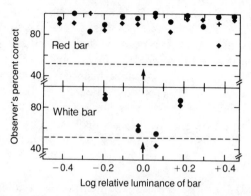

Figure 5. Demonstration of wavelength discrimination in 2-month-old infants. (From Peeples & Teller, 1975.) The ordinates show the observer's percentage correct. The abscissae show the intensity of a bar of red or white light embedded in a white surround. The dashed lines represent chance performance. The arrow marks the intensity of the bar at which the bar matched the screen in brightness *for adults*. The intensities of the red bar spanned a range of ±0.4 log unit. Since infants' spectral sensitivity is similar to that of adults, infants' red–white brightness matches should fall within this range. The lower data sets, taken with a white bar, provide a brightness control (see text) and show that the spacing in the intensity series is fine enough to have confronted the infant with a brightness match. In the upper data sets, the observer's percentage correct remained above chance for *all* intensities, including by inference the infant's brightness match, and hence the infant can make at least one discrimination based solely upon wavelength differences.

the brightness match. Thus, this study provides definitive evidence that 2-month-olds, like 3-month-olds, have some form of color vision.

A study by Oster (1975) provides an example of the convergence of the first and third techniques for solving the brightness problem. Oster adapted a "noise" or brightness "camouflage" method previously used by the ethologist von Frisch (1964) with bees. Two-month-old infants were presented with pairs of stimulus cards (17° subtense), each containing a three-by-three-unit matrix of small squares (3° subtense). One card contained nine greys of different brightnesses; the other contained eight greys and a central, saturated blue, green, yellow, or red square whose brightness fell within the range of the grey series by adult standards. The infants tended to stare at the card containing the chromatic square. It is likely both *a priori* and on the basis of Oster's brightness control data, that ΔI is very large in this case; that is, that the brightness of the central chromatic square would have to deviate greatly from the brightnesses of the surrounding "noise" matrix to attract the infant's attention solely on the basis of its brightness. Hence, the conclusion that the infants detected at least some of the chromatic stimuli on the basis of wavelength information seems strong.

A preference study by Bornstein (1975) probably also falls into the definitive category *a priori,* particularly in the condition in which individual chromatic stimuli were presented successively (see Section V below). Finally, by providing empirical brightness control data taken in a habituation paradigm closely similar to that used in a series of infant color studies (see Section V below), Kessen and Bornstein (1978) firmly established this series of studies as definitive demonstrations of wavelength discriminations in infants.

In summary, during 1975 publications from different laboratories, using several different techniques and behaviors, converged on convincing demonstrations that very young human infants can make at least some discriminations among visual stimuli on the basis of wavelength composition, and hence must have some form of color vision. The two most closely controlled studies had shown that 2-month-olds discriminate red from white, and 3-month-olds discriminate red from green. Since that time, many additional wavelength discriminations have been demonstrated, as described below.

To reiterate: if an organism preserves any information about wavelength, at least two photopigment systems must function in that organism. Thus, the demonstration that infants can discriminate between *any* two stimuli of differing wavelength composition solely on the basis of the difference in wavelength composition constitutes proof that at least two photopigment systems must be functional. Infants must possess at least two cone types and the neural machinery necessary to process and preserve the wavelength information encoded by their joint action. The next question is, "Can they be shown to possess all three?"

D. Are Infants Trichromats?

As described above, adult dichromats—protanopes, deuteranopes, and tritanopes—discriminate fewer colors and have larger metamer sets than do adult trichromats (Boynton, 1979, chap. 10; Pokorny et al., 1979). These patterns of wavelength information loss have several particularly simple and striking characteristics that can be considered diagnostic of the various dichromacies in adults. Three of these diagnostic signs— *Rayleigh discriminations, tritan discriminations,* and *neutral points*— have been exploited as tests for the presence of the various cone types in infants.

First, a *Rayleigh discrimination* is a discrimination between any two properly brightness-matched lights of wavelengths above 550 nm. For trichromats, lights from this spectral region vary in hue from green–yellow through yellow and orange to red; no two spectral lights (except the nearest of neighbors) fall in the same metamer set. Both protanopes (who are thought to lack functional LWS cones) and deuteranopes (who are thought to lack functional MWS cones) fail to make Rayleigh discriminations. Protanopes and deuteranopes are for this reason often informally called "red–green colorblinds." The capacity to make Rayleigh discriminations is diagnostically important because SWS cones are not active in the wavelength region above 550 nm. Since two receptor types are needed for wavelength discrimination, successful Rayleigh discriminations therefore imply the functional presence of both MWS and LWS cones.

Second, for tritanopes there exist pairs of spectral lights, termed *tritan pairs,* which when properly equated for luminance, are indiscriminable. The capacity to make tritan discriminations is theoretically important because (as it turns out) the members of a luminance-matched tritan pair yield equal quantum catches for MWS cones and also for LWS cones. Hence, a tritan discrimination cannot be made by a subject with only MWS and LWS cones, and a tritan discrimination thus implies the functional presence of a third receptor type, presumably SWS cones, in addition to MWS and/or LWS cones.

Third, trichromats can distinguish all spectral lights from white light, whereas for all dichromats there must exist at least one wavelength band—the *neutral point*—that is indistinguishable from white. For classical protanopes and deuteranopes the neutral point falls in the blue–green region of the spectrum, between 490 and 500 nm, whereas for classical tritanopes it falls in the yellow region, near 575 nm. If infants have a neutral point in either of these spectral regions, they might well be missing one of the three standard cone classes. If they have a neutral point in some other spectral region, interpretation is more complex (see below). If they have no neutral point, they must have three classes of cones.

Bornstein (1976a) incorporated two of these characteristics—Rayleigh discriminations and neutral points—into experiments designed to determine whether 3-month-olds could make discriminations not made by protanopes and deuteranopes. A habituation–dishabituation paradigm was used. In the first experiment, infants were tested for a neutral point in the blue–green region of the spectrum. Thirty infants were tested. Each infant was exposed to a series of blue–green stimuli (10° subtense) varying randomly in wavelength across the range of 490 to 500 nm. The luminances of the stimuli were also varied randomly from trial to trial over a range of 0.8 log unit. As a group the infants habituated to (stared less and less at) 12 repeated presentations of the blue–greens, and they dishabituated (increased their staring behavior) when, on trials 13–14, the blue–greens were replaced by a white matched by adult standards to the aver-

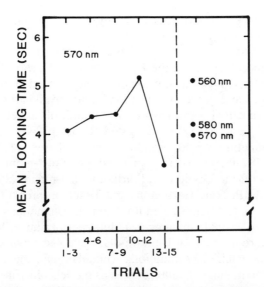

Figure 6. Demonstration that 3-month-old infants can discriminate among some wavelengths above 550 nm, taken with a habituation-test technique. (From Bornstein, 1976a.) Mean looking times are plotted for successive triplets of trials. A 570-nm light was presented repeatedly on trials 1–15. The infants habituated (looked less) to the 570-nm light on trials 13–15 and dishabituated to 560 nm relative to 570 and 580 nm which were all intermixed in the succeeding nine test trials (plotted at T on the abscissa).

Adults who are red–green color blind (protanopes and deuteranopes) cannot discriminate among any wavelengths longer than 550 nm. Since the infants discriminated 560 nm from 570 nm, they cannot be protanopes or deuteranopes.

age brightness of the blue–green series. Thus, infants discriminated chromatic stimuli in the region of the protanopic and deuteranopic neutral points from white.[5]

In the second experiment, a group of eight infants who were habituated to a 570-nm light dishabituated to a 560-nm light matched to the 570-nm light in luminance by adult standards (see Figure 6). This discrimination between two spectral stimuli of wavelengths greater than 550 nm provides

[5] The use of a neutral-point test is subject to at least two complexities. First, the exact neutral point is affected by the exact choice of the comparison white light used. Teller et al.'s (1978) white, for example, was in fact a yellowish white, and their green stimuli may provide a better match to this white than did their blue–green stimuli for dichromats. Second, white light contains some short wavelengths. Thus, the wavelength composition of the white at the level of the receptors is affected by preretinal absorption. Individual differences in preretinal absorption affect the exact neutral point in adult dichromats and presumably would do so in infant dichromats as well.

In any case, as discussed in the text, the demonstration of discriminations among stimuli with wavelengths above 550 nm proves conclusively that infants are not classical protanopes nor deuteranopes. The neutral point test provides supplementary evidence.

virtually incontrovertible evidence that 3-month-old infants are not classical protanopes or deuteranopes.

Both of Bornstein's (1976a) results have been confirmed and elaborated in a different laboratory, using the FPL technique. First, Teller, Peeples, and Sekel (1978) investigated neutral points and showed discrimination of blue, blue–green, and green stimuli (dominant wavelengths of 486, 496, and 512 nm respectively) from white in 2-month-olds. Second, Hamer, Alexander, and Teller (1982) investigated Rayleigh discriminations and showed discrimination of both broad-band red and green (550 nm) targets from a yellow (589 nm) surround in just under half of 1-month-olds, about three-quarters of 2-month-olds, and virtually all 3-month-olds.

More recently, Packer, Hartmann, and Teller (in press) have investigated the effects of test field size on Rayleigh discriminations. They found that test field size strongly influences infants' performance. When stimuli as large as 8° were used, even 1-month-olds gave some evidence of being able to make Rayleigh discriminations. Cumulatively, these studies rule out classical protanopia and deuteranopia as models of infant color vision and strongly suggest the presence of functional MWS and LWS cones in infants 2 months of age or younger.

The possibility remains that infants are tritanopes, or dichromats of some nonstandard type. As stated above, dichromats must exhibit neutral points, but trichomats ordinarily do not. This fact allows one to test the possibility that an organism is not a dichromat of *any* type, standard or nonstandard. If an organism can discriminate *every* wavelength of light from white light, it by definition does not have a neutral point, and must be a trichromat. Using this approach (see Boothe et al., 1975; DeValois et al., 1979), Teller et al. (1978) explored the capacities of 1-month-old infants to discriminate 13 stimuli (1° × 14°) of various broad-band wavelength compositions from white. They found that infants readily discriminated adult red, orange, blue–green, blue, bluish purple, and reddish purple from white but failed to demonstrate a discrimination of yellow–greens (Figure 7) and mid-purples from white. Thus, this approach has failed, to date, to document the presence of trichromacy in 2-month-old infants.

Some aspects of these results are puzzling, however. Neutral zones in the yellow–green and mid-purple are not predicted by any of the standard dichromacies. However, the tritanopic neutral point—a yellow of about 575 nm—is close to the border of the yellow–green neutral zone exhibited by the infants tested. Thus, the failures of wavelength discrimination shown by these 2-month-olds perhaps mimic a tritan deficiency more closely than either of the red–green deficiencies, and they are thus suggestive of a weakness or anomaly of the SWS cone system very early in life. This interpretation is also consistent with the results of the chromatic

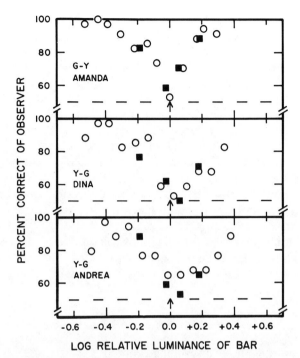

Figure 7. Failures of wavelength discrimination by 2-month-old infants. Paradigm same as Figure 5, with white (■) and broad-band yellow-green (○) stimuli embedded in a white surround. (From Teller, Peeples, & Sekel, 1978.) For each infant, the two data sets are highly similar, suggesting that for both stimuli the infants are responding to the same (brightness) cue and that wavelength information is not being preserved. The squares are plotted correctly with respect to the adult brightness match (arrow); the circles have been shifted laterally to achieve a best fit to the squares for each infant. Lateral shifts needed were only 0.05 to 0.11 log unit. The fact that only small shifts were needed provides converging evidence that infant and adult brightness matches are highly similar.

adaptation experiments (Pulos et al., 1980) described earlier (see Section III,D). However, several other interpretations of the results are plausible. For example, adults perceive a saturation minimum in the yellow–green region of the spectrum. A model assuming that infants are standard trichromats who are less sensitive than adults to differences in saturation is also consistent with the data.

Varner, Cook, Schneck, McDonald, and Teller (1984) have used tritan pairs to examine the question of infant tritanopia more directly. Varner et al. found that most infants as young as 5 weeks clearly made the tritan discrimination, and even 4-week-olds gave some evidence of being able to do so. These results rule out the possibility that young infants are tritanopes, since they demonstrate that infants as young as 4 to 5 weeks code wavelength information in a way that necessitates the functional presence of SWS cones. The use of larger field sizes might well reveal the capacity of even younger infants to make tritan discriminations.

Finally, it should be emphasized that the chromatic discrimination *failures* that infants sometimes show in these studies have some intrinsic interest. First, when they occur, they sometimes bear a close resemblance to the infant's brightness discrimination function (see Figure 7). As discussed above, such data support the interpretation that the infant is not preserving information about the wavelength differences present in the stimuli; that is, at all relative luminances at which the infant can do so, he or she is basing the discrimination on a luminance or brightness cue. Second, the point at which the observer's FPL performance dips toward chance indicates the luminance at which the brightness cue fails for the infant, *viz.*, the infant's brightness match. These discrimination failures usually occur close to the adult brightness match. Thus, data of this kind constitute converging evidence that adult heterochromatic brightness matches made *in situ* can provide a very reasonable first approximation to infant matches.

E. Summary

Two-month-old infants discriminate among a variety of chromatic stimuli on the basis of wavelength composition and in the absence of brightness cues. They have succeeded on a variety of diagnostic tests, including Rayleigh discriminations and tritan discriminations. Their Rayleigh discriminations imply the functional presence of MWS and LWS cones, and their tritan discriminations imply the functional presence of SWS cones. One-month-old infants also give some evidence of being able to make these discriminations. Taken together, these studies imply that even very young infants possess three functional cone types and three subsequent neural pathways capable of preserving and comparing their signals. Although the development of color perception in infancy is doubtless not complete in all respects, these findings strongly suggest that the color space of young infants is broadly trichromatic in nature.

V. ATTENTION, PERCEPTION, AND COGNITION

The study of color vision divides into considerations of sensory psychophysics at one level and considerations of attention, perception, and cognition at another. The relationship between these two spheres of investigation is asymmetrical in the sense that a knowledge of sensory functions (e.g., spectral sensitivity) is integral to the study—and hence understanding—of perceptual ones (e.g., preference): assurance that infants prefer, organize, or remember *hue* (or any other single dimension of color) depends critically on the initial experimental separation of hue from other dimensions of color, such as brightness. In Sections III and IV of this chapter, we focused on psychophysical aspects of the study of infant color vision. Against the background of data on sensory topics like spectral sensitivity and wavelength discrimination, we now turn our attention to the study of perception and cognition in infant color vision.

In this section, we focus on the subjective dimensions of color vision. After a brief description of these dimensions in adult vision, we address two questions. First, "How can infants be asked about their perception of subjective dimensions of color vision?" That is, "How can we tell whether or when infants prefer or categorize colors?" Second, "Do infants demonstrate behavior convincingly analogous to that of adults in their responses to chromatic stimuli?" If so, we may speculate that color perception in infants may also be like that of adults.

A. The Subjective Dimensions of Color

The subjective organization of color perception is tridimensional. One dimension (which is in fact achromatic) is *brightness*. The two other dimensions, *hue* and *saturation,* are chromatic. Relationships among the three dimensions can be represented diagramatically in a "color solid" that encompasses all possible chromatic experiences. Brightness follows a vertical axis from black to white. Hue is ordered as a circular array around that axis. Saturation is represented on radii of the circle and is the subjective density of color in a mixture.

Hue is the most salient aspect of color vision, and the one on which we focus in this section. It is the closest psychological correlate of wavelength. But the correspondence is inexact, for while the physical spectrum varies continuously in wavelength, the psychological spectrum is perceived as relatively discontinuous. Most adults describe the spectrum and extraspectral reds and violets as broken up into four basic hue categories, grouped around four pure, or *unique* hues. The unique hues are commonly identified as blue, green, yellow, and (extraspectral) red. Boynton (1971, p. 346) has summarized contemporary opinion about the psychological organization of spectral stimuli into hue categories in this manner:

> It is often productive to reduce a problem to the smallest number of variables that we can and still describe it adequately. In this spirit many people have argued that only four color names are needed to describe the chromatic character of bright colors viewed in a dark surround. . . . The four basic color names are red, yellow, green and blue. Each of these names is held to describe a unique sensation. . . . There are other

hues to which color names have been given, which do not meet the criterion of uniqueness. . . . Orange does not qualify as a unique hue because—to most people at least—it can be appreciated as being made up subjectively of a mixture of red and yellow. . . . The same can be said for the simultaneous red and blue components of a purple or violet sensation and of blue–green and green–yellow blends.

The four unique hue sensations are described as having one other fundamental property. It is claimed that red and green, and yellow and blue, are *mutually exclusive* sensations; that is, that one cannot see or imagine a reddish green nor a yellowish blue. It is interesting to note that it was the existence of unique hues, divided into pairs of mutually exclusive sensations, that led Hering to believe that physiological units which could assume two mutually exclusive states were needed for the coding of hue (see Section II,C).

In discussing color categorization, a consistent vocabulary must be defined. Unique hues are singular, in the sense that they give only one percept; there is no blue, yellow, or red in unique green. Focal colors are central exemplars of a color category, and though they encompass unique hues they may also contain elements of neighboring hues; these elements are minor, however, and focal colors tend to give the dominant impression of a single hue. Nonfocal colors are poor examples of a color category and may contain larger proportions of neighboring color categories.

Subjective categories and discontinuities of hue may be described quantitatively by a psychophysical technique known as hue naming. For example, Boynton and Gordon (1965) asked adults to name wavelengths using one or pairs of the four basic hue names, blue, green, yellow, and red. Their observers produced hue-naming functions that peak around unique hues, demonstrate hue categories around focal colors, and descend to points of crossover or transition between hue categories (see bottom of Figure 9). Adults are very consistent in hue naming, and people from a wide variety of cultures and languages pick out focal colors with great consistency (Berlin & Kay, 1969).

Focal colors have special psychological properties associated with them (for a review, see Bornstein, 1981b). Adults tend to prefer focal colors, and they name, identify, learn, and classify focal colors faster than nonfocal ones (Bornstein & Monroe, 1980; Rosch, 1978). In succeeding parts of this section, we review data that speak to analogous subjective color experiences of infants.

B. Preferences

Color preference is often thought of as highly individualistic or subject to changing fashion or cultural context; yet, consistent and selective color preferences in children and adults, even in different cultures, have been uncovered. These include a general preference for focal colors and for subjectively saturated colors, especially for the blue and red spectral extremes (for a review, see Bornstein, 1978a).

In infants, preference has been studied principally by gauging the baby's attention to different stimuli, that is, by measuring looking time or pointing. The study of color vision in infants practically began as the study of infant color preference (Baldwin, 1895), and it was sustained over nearly its first century principally by investigations of preference. Unfortunately, psychophysicists with an eye toward stimulus control have not historically been interested in the question of preference, and, almost complementarily, developmentalists persistently interested in preference have not typically found the psychophysicist's penchant for stimulus control meritorious of their attention. So, for example, though infants seem to prefer brighter stimuli regardless of their wavelength composition (Schaller, 1975; Thomas, 1973), only infrequently has brightness been systematically controlled in studies of infant color preference.

Bornstein (1978a) reviewed the literature in infant color preference, and it is unnecessary to do so here again. The main conclusion of that review is that infant preferences to a large degree parallel those found in adults: infants tend to prefer stimuli that correspond to adult focal colors, saturated colors, and the spectral extremes. (The actual preference–wavelength function is complex, however, and infants' expressed preference seem to depend on the purity or monochromaticity of the stimulus in combination with its hue.)

All of these generalizations are embodied in the results of one study. Bornstein (1975) showed 4-month-olds eight monochromatic spectral lights: violet (430 nm), blue (460 nm), blue–green (490 nm), green (520 nm), green–yellow (560 nm), yellow (580 nm), yellow–red (600 nm), and red (630 nm). The stimuli (10°) were matched in brightness by adult standards (Judd's 1951 modification of CIE) at a luminance of 55 cd/m²; see Section IV,B. These eight colors span the visible spectrum and represent adult focal colors as well as examples of other between-category nonfocal colors. Four groups of babies (10 infants in a group) together saw all possible pairings of the eight stimuli; one additional group (of 10) saw random presentations of each light singly. Presentations lasted 15 sec. Twenty-four adults (mean age, 24 years) were also asked to rate the pleasantness of the same spectral lights shown to infants.

Infants in the two experimental conditions provided separate replications of the same basic relationship between looking time and wavelength. Figure 8 shows the results for both paired comparison and single stimulus groups. Overall, infants looked at colors that are focal to adults as a group

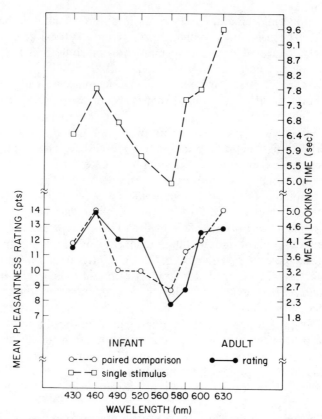

Figure 8. Wavelength (hue) preferences for 4-month-old infants and adults, taken with a preferential looking technique. (From Bornstein, 1975.) Mean looking times for infants (paired comparison and single stimulus groups) and pleasantness ratings for adults are plotted as a function of wavelength. The ordinate scales for infant paired comparisons and adult ratings have been adjusted by a double linear regression technique for best fit between data sets. The infant single stimulus data are arbitrarily displaced upward on the ordinate. The pattern of infant looking times closely resembles the pattern of adult pleasantness ratings. The data suggest that infants' hue preferences are already adultlike at 4 months.

reliably more than they looked at nonfocal colors, although not all focal colors were looked at more, and the babies preferred the saturated colors at the spectral extremes—blue and red.[6] Infant looking times also paralleled adult pleasantness ratings. Adults rated focal colors higher on the

---

[6] Infants discriminate saturation, though the degree of their capability in this dimension is not yet known. Bornstein (1978b) showed 20 4-month-olds six Munsell colors, three hues (two blues, greens, and reds with the same brightness) each at a low and high saturation. The stimuli (approximately $12° \times 16°$ subtense at 51.3 cd/m²) were exposed singly for 15-sec

average than nonfocal ones, saturated colors higher than less saturated ones, and blue and red higher than green and yellow.

The infants' demonstrated color preferences, like those of adults, can be modeled in terms of the action of lateral geniculate cells that analyze chromatic information. Color-opponent cells in the geniculate bodies fire with a maximum frequency at select spectral sites in the blue, green, yellow, and red regions of the visible spectrum, and they fire at monotonically higher rates to increasingly saturated colors (DeValois, 1973; DeValois & Marrocco, 1973). Attention (i.e., visual preference) may relate in a direct way to the activity of underlying neural tissue that is sensitive to color (see Haith, 1980, for a general model of this relationship). The developmental stability of color preferences suggests that the physiological processes that underlie color preferences are already adultlike in infants approximately 4 months after birth.

C. Categorization

To what extent is the spectrum subjectively categorical for infants as it is for adults? It is possible to study questions related to hue categorization in infants using habituation and habituation–test paradigms. In the habituation design, rates of decline in looking behavior in babies shown the same or similar stimuli repeatedly can be compared with those of babies shown a series of different stimuli; perceived stimulus variation tends to retard habituation. In the habituation–test design, babies are shown the same stimulus repeatedly until they habituate to it. Following habituation, babies dishabituate to some novel stimuli or generalize habituation to other stimuli. Dishabituation is taken to indicate that infants perceive stimulus change.

Bornstein, Kessen, and Weiskopf (1976) used a habituation–test design to study categorization of hues in 4-month-old infants. Fourteen groups of 10 infants each looked at narrow-band spectral stimuli that were selected from the four basic adult hue categories. After habituation to one wavelength over 15 repeated trials, infants were shown the original light and two new lights in a test. Two classes of groups were seen. In the test, "Boundary groups" saw the original habituation stimulus (for example, a blue of 480 nm), a second wavelength selected from the same adult hue category (a blue of 450 nm), and a third wavelength selected from a different adult hue category (a green of 510 nm). "Category groups" saw

durations, and infants saw different, counterbalanced random orders of them. The infants consistently looked at the more saturated versions of hues half again as much on the average as at the less saturated versions.

the original habituation wavelength (for example, a blue of 450 nm) and two other lights selected from the same hue category as the original (blues of 430 nm and 470 nm). For both types of groups, the new test wavelengths were equal physical distances (in nm) from the original habituation wavelength in order that any differential dishabituation to the new lights could be attributed to the psychological dissimilarity of the new and habituation stimuli. In all cases, chromatic stimuli (10°) were balanced in brightness (luminance, 3.4 cd/m²) by adult standards (Judd, 1951) (see Section IV,B). Generally, babies maintained habituation to the original habituation wavelength, generalized habituation to wavelength(s) in the same adult hue category as the habituation stimulus but dishabituated to wavelength(s) selected from another adult hue category.

Figure 9 summarizes data on infants' organization of the visible spectrum in this study and compares it with analogous adult hue-naming data (after Boynton & Gordon, 1965). This figure shows wavelength regions of

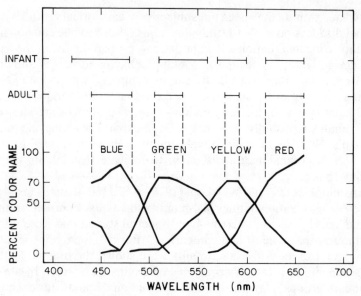

Figure 9. Wavelength groupings (i.e., hue categories) for 4-month-old infants and adults. *Bottom:* Percentage color name as a function of wavelength for the color names blue, green, yellow, and red. (After Boynton & Gordon, 1965.) The rising function at very short wavelengths is for red. *Top:* Summary results for hue categories for infants and adults. The infant summary is derived from Bornstein, Kessen, and Weiskopf (1976). The adult summary reflects a projection from the color-naming data at a psychophysical criterion of 70%. Infant and adult grouping patterns are highly similar, suggesting that by 4 months infants' hue categories are similar to those of adults.

perceived similarity and regions of probable interhue transition for infants and adults. On the whole, 4-month infants categorize wavelengths in much the same way as adults name them, but long before extensive experience or formal language training is brought to bear in development.[7]

In the wavelength discrimination study discussed above (Section IV,D), 3-month-old babies who were habituated to yellow (570 nm) dishabituated to green (560 nm)—they discriminated a stimulus from a different adult hue category—but they generalized habituation to another yellow (580 nm). Thus, 3-month-olds show a pattern similar to 4-month-olds, at least in this spectral range (Bornstein, 1976a).

The conclusion that infants categorize different wavelengths of light together does not imply that infants cannot discriminate among all wavelengths they group into categories, any more than it does in adults. In fact, within-category discriminability in infants can be demonstrated on the basis of differential rates of habituation. Bornstein (1981b), for example, found that infants habituated to the repetition of a single chromatic stimulus (476 nm) of one hue (blue) faster than they did to stimulus variation within one category (blues of 455 nm, 470 nm, 476 nm, 480 nm, 484 nm, and 490 nm). Infant habituation to stimulus variation across several categories (blue to green, or among blues, greens, yellows, and reds) is slower still (Bornstein, 1981a; Bornstein et al., 1976), suggesting again that variation in the appearance of different wavelengths within an adult hue category is not as great for the infant as is variation between or among adult hue categories.

The infant's behavioral discrimination among focal colors is apparently qualitative. Bornstein (1981a) studied patterns of dishabituation in infants who were habituated to one focal color (e.g., a blue) and then shown two other focal colors (e.g., a green and a red). Physical or quantitative distances among the stimuli proved immaterial in this study; babies dishabituated to green and red equivalently even though red is farther from blue than is green—farther in terms of physical spacing on the wavelength scale or psychological scaling around the hue circle (Boynton, 1975). The alternative explanation that dishabituation among color changes is always quantal is discouraged by other data that show that the infant's recovery to color change (e.g., Bornstein, 1981a) or to component change (e.g., Cohen, Gelber, & Lazar, 1971) can be graded; furthermore, no ceiling effect on dishabituation was observed in individual or group data in this

---

[7] Study of the human infant's perceptual categorization of the spectrum is, in principle, like the study of categorization in nonverbal species, including bees (von Frisch, 1964), pigeons (Wright & Cumming, 1971), and monkeys (Sandell, Gross, & Bornstein, 1979). However, different species see in different regions of the electromagnetic spectrum and divide it at different points.

study. Thus, for infants, focal colors, blue, green, yellow, and red, may be perceived to be roughly equivalently distinctive.

DeValois (1973; DeValois, Abramov, & Jacobs, 1966) has shown that adult hue categorization may also be modeled by the action of neurons in the central visual pathways. He proposed "an isomorphic relationship between the relative activity rates of various cell types and the hue of a given light" (DeValois et al., 1966, p. 976), showing that absolute changes in response of the four main cell types from spontaneous firing rates were in good agreement (except at short wavelengths) with Boynton and Gordon's (1965) psychophysical hue-naming data. The similarity of infant to adult hue categorization suggests at least a qualitative similarity of neural processing between the two ages.

D. Memory

Do infants retain information about the chromatic characteristics of a stimulus? For how long? Does the infant's memory correlate more closely with the wavelength characteristics of stimuli or with adult subjective hue categories? Are focal and nonfocal colors equally memorable or sensitive to interference in infants?

Modifications of the two paradigms used to study discrimination and habituation in infants have been employed to study color memory. If a well-counterbalanced design is used, the finding of different rates of habituation for different stimulus sequences implies some form of memory on the part of the infant for earlier items in the sequence. Alternatively, dishabituation to a stimulus implies that the infant discriminates that stimulus, occurring in the present, from a stimulus to which the infant has habituated and which is remembered, from the past. If the time between familiarization and test is varied, short-term or long-term recognition can be examined. (Delay time could also be filled with interference.)

Although infant recognition memory for colors has been approached using both designs several times, tests for color memory have often been confounded with changes in stimulus form or brightness. From these studies, therefore, we know little about the infant's memory capacities for chromatic variables per se. Further, physical characteristics of the chromatic stimuli have been specified only infrequently.

Two studies that have instituted appropriate stimulus control have used differences in habituation rate to assess some aspects of the infant's memory for color. Bornstein et al. (1976) tested three groups of 10 4-month-old infants. One group was habituated over 24 discrete trials to a narrow-band blue (480 nm); a second group was habituated to the same stimulus in quasi-random alternation with one other wavelength (450 nm) from the same adult hue category; and a third group was habituated to the same 480 nm in identical sequence with a wavelength (510 nm) from a different adult hue category (green). The 480-nm stimulus always appeared in the same positions in the sequence. The stimuli were 10° and were presented at a constant luminance of 3.4 cd/m². The 480–480 nm and 480–450 nm groups habituated at statistically similar rates. (Apparently, variation between two stimuli in a category is not as salient as is variation among six stimuli; see above.) Both groups habituated faster than the 480–510 nm group; indeed, the last group looked longer overall.

To investigate infant memory for broad-band focal and nonfocal colors, Bornstein (1981a) habituated one group of infants with focal blue, another with focal red, and two groups with nonfocal colors, blue–green and yellow–red, respectively. Each baby saw 12 trials of these broad-band colors at a luminance of 51.2 cd/m². An analysis of rates of habituation showed that slopes of habituation for the two focal colors were similar and significantly steeper than slopes for nonfocal colors, which themselves were similar. Neither initial preference (in this study no significant preference between focal and nonfocal emerged, probably because of the nature of the broad-band stimuli) nor absolute spectral position of the stimuli influenced these results; rather, the status of the stimuli in terms of whether or not they were focal in the category alone seems to have determined the rates at which habituation took place and, by inference, the ease with which infants developed memory for the color.

Several other experiments have used habituation–test or familiarization–novelty designs to study infant memory for color. Many experimenters (e.g., Cohen et al., 1971; Schaffer & Parry, 1969, 1970) have found that infants younger than 1 year discriminate a change in color when stimulus size and shape are held constant. Fagan (1977) studied the effects of familiarization time on the 5-month-old infant's recognition memory: relative to geometric forms, infant equivalent recognition of colors required less study time. Pancratz and Cohen (1970) found that infants failed to recognize a color after a 5-min delay; Strauss and Cohen (1980) found that 5-month-old infants could recognize both the form and color of equally salient patterns after 15 min but had forgotten the color at a 24-hr test. Bornstein (1976b) used the habituation–test design to study the effects of delay and interference on the 4-month-old infant's recognition memory for color. In that study, 3- and 5-min delays were filled with interference either on the same dimension (another color) or on a different dimension (face-to-face interaction). Independent of type of interference, infants recognized a habituation stimulus (a yellow of 570 nm) after the 3-min delays, but marginally failed a similar recognition test after the 5-min delays.

Bornstein (1981a) studied recognition memory in infants for focal (blue and red) and for nonfocal colors (blue–green and yellow–red). Groups of infants who were habituated to each kind of color were matched for retroactive interference. Although these infants looked equivalently at both kinds of colors at the beginning of habituation (broad-band stimuli were used) and at the end, and although they experienced equivalent interference, infants who were habituated to nonfocal colors recovered on the retest (they "forgot"), whereas those who were habituated to focal colors maintained habituation (they "remembered").

One further memory aspect of the habituation–test design warrants comment. In Bornstein et al. (1976), babies who were habituated to a wavelength from one adult hue category generalized habituation to different wavelengths from the same adult hue category. This finding suggests that in habituation infants may lose exact wavelength information and instead retain gross psychological information of a similar kind that binds stimuli in hue categories.

Categorical memory and the differential durability of colors in memory can also be modeled from properties of the physiological substrate. Wavelength is recoded into four major cell classes in the central pathways of the primate visual system, and the sensitivity maxima of these four cell types fall at spectral loci near focal color locations (Bornstein, 1973). The reduction of wavelength information into a cell class could account for inexactitude in the infant's behavioral coding of color—for example, false positive identification of one blue when an infant is habituated to another. Further, the peak sensitivity of these cell types at the spectral loci of focal colors could account for facility in the infant's memory for focal colors (Bornstein, 1978a, pp. 151–155, and 1981b, has elaborated on these arguments).

In summary, in infancy memory for color may be comparatively tenuous, though focal colors seem to be remembered better than nonfocal ones (even after retroactive interference) either because of their lessened information load or because of the existence of a neurophysiological template devoted to their processing. The fact that infants recognize color at all strongly suggests, first, that color memory is not totally language dependent or necessarily relational and, second, that infants may use chromatic information about a stimulus toward its future identification. Certainly recognition of physical information, such as wavelength, must be important to the growth of the infant's knowledge about the world, since the early development of object identification or recognition must depend wholly on the preverbal child's encoding and retention of the physical properties of objects. Thus, for example, color has been demonstrated to enhance young children's performance on memory tasks (e.g., Daehler,

Bukatko, Benson, & Myers, 1976) and is related to recall accuracy in later problem solving (e.g., Odom, 1972). Color also promotes attainment of concepts (Colby & Robertson, 1942; Lee, 1965).

E. Concept Formation

Farnham-Diggory and Gregg (1975) have argued that perceptual dimensions such as color function prior to and act to structure both conceptual and semantic categories characteristic of early cognitive development. In support of this proposition, they demonstrated that the young child (mean age, 5 years) classifies by color faster and more accurately than by other perceptual dimensions or more abstract properties of objects such as function or class. Given that color can function as a domain that facilitates information processing even in young children, we can ask, "When do infants or young children come to understand a concept of color?" This development must occur prior to their utilization of the dimension.

The study of conceptual development in infants is new, and it too has utilized habituation paradigms. For example, if an infant is habituated to a series of discriminable stimuli that are members of a single class and, following habituation, is shown a novel member of the class, the infant may or may not dishabituate. According to Bourne (1966), the term "conceptual" applies whenever discriminable stimuli are responded to in a similar way or classified together. By this definition, infants have been shown to be sensitive to various "concepts," inasmuch as discriminable stimulation does not always lead to dishabituation in infants. For example, Cohen (1977) and Fagan (1979) have found that infants who are familiarized with a set of discriminable faces or poses of faces of different people will generalize habituation to yet another discriminable novel face or poses of the same set.

Bornstein (1979) examined a similar example of concept formation in color. Two experiments were conducted. In the first, infants showed that they discriminate among blues, greens, yellows, and reds; in the second, infants showed that they would, under certain circumstances, generalize among colors. The infants' performance obviously depends on habituation- and test-stimulus alternatives. Data already provided in this chapter give evidence that 4-month-olds discriminate among hues. Therefore, in fulfilling the second requirement of concept formation, 16 4-month-olds were habituated to a variety of colors, including focal examples from three hue categories (e.g., blue, green, and yellow) and their mixtures (blue–green and green–yellow), but the fourth hue, red (i.e., blue–red, red, or yellow–red) was omitted from the habituation series. After the babies reached a habituation criterion, they were tested with the novel

hue (red) and with an achromatic control stimulus. Munsell colors, about
12° × 15° at 51.2 cd/m², were used, and only the babies' first looks were
recorded and analyzed. These babies generalized habituation to the novel
hue (even when the novel hue was a different shape; Bornstein, 1981a),
but they dishabituated to the neutral control. This result did not reflect
simple fatigue in the infants since they responded equally to a pretest and
posttest control. In essence, infants "know" or can learn that color is a
classification scheme. The extent to which they may make use of color
very early in perceptual and cognitive development is still, however, an
open question.

F. Summary

The literature reviewed in this section speaks to perceptual and cognitive aspects of color vision in infants. Infants, by 4 months, attend to
colors and organize the physical spectrum in ways that parallel attention
and categorization by color-normal adults. The infant's memory for color
is comparatively tenuous, although it varies with the status of the color as
focal or not. Infants, too, seem to be sensitive to color as a concept or
dimension of stimulation. Many of these effects are adequately modeled
by our current understanding of neural processing of color along the
central visual pathways of the brain, and the predictability of infant behaviors from adult hue preferences and adult hue categories suggests a
remarkable degree of maturity of neural elements at 4 months of age.

VI. REVIEW AND PREVIEW

Scientific interest in infant color vision is over 100 years old, yet the
accumulation of any genuine knowledge in this field has taken place
mostly in the last 10 years. Moreover, the growth and development of the
field in this time has been rapid. This chapter has covered the period of
infancy between approximately 1 month and 1 year, although we have
focused on the first half year; let us briefly review what has been learned
about chromatic vision and its development in this period of life.[8]

[8] The period before 1 month has received only scant attention. Neither spectral sensitivity
nor wavelength discrimination has been studied systematically in newborns. In electrophysiological studies of newborns (Barnet, Lodge, & Armington, 1965; Lodge, Armington,
Barnet, Shanks, & Newcomb, 1969), both VEPs and electroretinograms (ERGs) were recorded in response to light of two different wavelength compositions, a broad-band bluish–
white (spectrum unspecified) and a broad-band orange (dominant wavelength about 580 nm),
each presented at several different luminances. Both the VEP and the ERG response profiles

By and large, scotopic and photopic spectral sensitivities are in mature form within the first or second postnatal month. Since 2-month-olds demonstrate that they can discriminate between lights of different wavelength compositions in the absence of brightness cues, and since they can make Rayleigh discriminations and tritan discriminations, infants in the second month of life also give strong evidence that their color space is broadly color normal and trichromatic.

By the fourth postnatal month, infants give evidence that they perceive color as organized into categories that resemble adult hue groupings. Infants at this stage appear to remember focal colors best, though their memory for color is comparatively tenuous. Infants, like adults, prefer focal colors and ones that are bright and saturated. In overview, the color vision of young infants appears to be similar to that of trichromatic adults at least in broad outline.

A host of other aspects of color vision, such as wavelength discrimination, saturation discrimination, variations of color vision with retinal eccentricity, shifts of hue with intensity (Bezold–Brücke effect), contrast effects, spatial and temporal resolution capacities of the various chromatic channels, and the effects of early or continuing chromatic deficiency, remain almost totally unexplored in infants. In short, we have learned much, and yet very little, in the last few years.

At the outset we defined several functions that color serves and several explicit psychological advantages that accrue to organisms that possess color vision. The human infant's relatively precocious color vision abilities may serve him or her in these functions: some may facilitate eventual understanding of the visually complex world that newly surrounds the infant and others may facilitate perceptual or cognitive development in infancy. Perceptually, color vision subserves contrast and promotes spatial detection. Cognitively, color provides a unique type of qualitative information about the environment. At both levels color is a helpful code. Color similarities provide a basis for structuring the perceptual world, and the fact that colors may be organized by hue early in life increases their general cognitive utility and value. Aesthetically, colors control attention and please. These facts suggest, therefore, that color vision is in all probability an important component of the child's early mental machinery.

---

varied systematically with wavelength composition, as did the *change* in response profile between ERG and VEP. The authors attributed these variations to varying combinations of scotopic and photopic inputs, that is to rods and a combination of one or more cone types. Thus, even in newborns there is evidence for the existence of at least two functional receptor types and for the preservation of some wavelength information through the visual system.

NOTE ADDED IN PROOF

There are several reports of new studies of infant spectral sensitivity (see pp. 196–203). Volbrecht and Werner (1986) used a VEP technique to test the spectral sensitivities of 4- to 6-week-old infants under broad band yellow chromatic adaptation (cf. pp. 196–203). They found a spectral sensitivity curve with a maximum at about 440 nm, and thus provide the most convincing evidence to date that young infants have functional SWS cones with spectra like those of adults.

Three new studies of photopic spectral sensitivity under conditions of more neutral adaptation have also been reported. Three very different techniques were used: the locations of discrimination minima (Ankrum, Clavadetscher, & Teller, 1986), flicker photometry (Ladenheim & Gordon, 1986), and the location of a null in a complex optokinetic nystagmus task (Anstis, Cavanagh, Maurer, & Lewis, 1986). Anstis et al. showed virtual identity in spectral sensitivity between infants and adults; while Ankrum et al. and Ladenheim and Gordon agree with each other in showing that relative to adults, infants demonstrate an enhanced sensitivity to short wavelengths and a reduced sensitivity to long wavelengths. The topic of infant spectral sensitivity thus remains poorly understood, and nature is still not yielding her secrets easily in this area.

ACKNOWLEDGMENTS

Preparation of this chapter was supported by grants from The Spencer Foundation and NICHD (K04 HD00521) to Marc H. Bornstein and by an NSF Grant (BNS 78-23053) to Davida Y. Teller. We thank Russell Hamer for comments on the manuscript and Marjorie Zachow for secretarial assistance.

REFERENCES

Ankrum, C., Clavadetscher, J., & Teller, D. (1986). Chromatic discriminations and brightness matches in infants. *Invest. Ophthal. Vis. Sci. Suppl. 27(3),* 264.
Anstis, S., Cavanagh, P., Maurer, D., & Lewis, T. (1986). Early maturation of luminous efficiency for colored stimuli. *Invest. Ophthal. Vis. Sci. Suppl. 27(3),* 264.
Baldwin, J. M. (1893). Distance and color perception by infants. *Science, 21,* 231–232.
Baldwin, J. M. (1895). *Mental development in the child and the race.* New York: Macmillan.
Barnet, A. B., Lodge, A., & Armington, J. C. (1965). Electroretinogram in newborn human infants. *Science, 148,* 651–654.
Berlin, B., & Kay, P. (1969). *Basic color terms: Their universality and evolution.* Berkeley: University of California Press.
Boothe, R., Teller, D., & Sackett, G. (1975). Trichromacy in light deprived and normally reared infant monkeys (*Macaca nemestrina*). *Vision Research, 15,* 1187–1191.
Bornstein, M. H. (1973). Color vision and color naming: A psychophysiological hypothesis of cultural difference. *Psychological Bulletin, 80,* 257–285.
Bornstein, M. H. (1975). Qualities of color vision in infancy. *Journal of Experimental Child Psychology, 19,* 401–419.
Bornstein, M. H. (1976a). Infants are trichromats. *Journal of Experimental Child Psychology, 21,* 425–445.
Bornstein, M. H. (1976b). Infants' recognition memory for hue. *Developmental Psychology, 12,* 185–191.

Bornstein, M. H. (1978a). Chromatic vision in infancy. In H. W. Reese & L. P. Lipsitt (Eds.), *Advances in child development and behavior* (Vol. 12). New York: Academic Press.

Bornstein, M. H. (1978b). Visual behavior in the young human infant. *Journal of Experimental Child Psychology, 26,* 174–192.

Bornstein, M. H. (1979). Effects of habituation experience on posthabituation behavior in young infants: Discrimination and generalization among colors. *Developmental Psychology, 15,* 348–349.

Bornstein, M. H. (1981a). Psychological studies of color perception in human infants. In L. P. Lipsitt (Ed.), *Advances in infancy research* (Vol. 1). Norwood, NJ: Ablex.

Bornstein, M. H. (1981b). Two kinds of perceptual organization near the beginning of life. In W. A. Collins (Ed.), *Minnesota symposia on child psychology* (Vol. 14). Hillsdale, NJ: Erlbaum.

Bornstein, M. H., Kessen, W., & Weiskopf, S. (1976). Color vision and hue categorization in young human infants. *Journal of Experimental Psychology: Human Perception and Performance, 2,* 115–129.

Bornstein, M. H., & Monroe, M. (1980). Chromatic information processing: Rate depends on stimulus location in the category and psychological complexity. *Psychological Research, 42,* 213–225.

Bourne, L. E. (1966). *Human conceptual behavior.* Boston, MA: Allyn & Bacon.

Boynton, R. M. (1971). Color vision. In L. A. Riggs & J. Kling (Eds.), *Woodworth and Schlosberg's experiental psychology.* New York: Holt.

Boynton, R. M. (1975). Color, hue and wavelength. In E. C. Carterette & M. P. Friedman (Eds.), *Handbook of perception* (Vol. 5). New York: Academic Press.

Boynton, R. M. (1979). *Human color vision.* New York: Holt.

Boynton, R. M., & Gordon, J. (1965). Bezold-Brücke hue shift measured by color-naming technique. *Journal of the Optical Society of America, 55,* 78–86.

Brindley, G. (1970). *Physiology of the retina and visual pathways* (2nd ed.). Baltimore, MD: Williams & Wilkins.

Chase, W. (1937). Color vision in infants. *Journal of Experimental Psychology, 20,* 203–222.

Christ, R. E. (1975). Review and analysis of color coding research for visual displays. *Human Factors, 17,* 542–570.

Cohen, L. B. (1977, March). *Concept acquisition in the human infant.* Paper presented at the meeting of the Society for Research in Child Development, New Orleans, LA.

Cohen, L. B., Gelber, E. R., & Lazar, M. A. (1971). Infant habituation and generalization to differing degrees of stimulus novelty. *Journal of Experimental Child Psychology, 11,* 379–389.

Colby, M. C., & Robertson, J. B. (1942). Genetic studies in abstraction. *Journal of Comparative Psychology, 33,* 385–401.

Cornsweet, T. (1970). *Visual perception.* London: Academic Press.

Daehler, M., Bukatko, D., Benson, K., & Myers, N. (1976). The effects of size and color cues on the delayed response of very young children. *Bulletin of the Psychonomic Society, 7,* 65–68.

Darwin, C. H. (1877). A biographical sketch of a young child. *Kosmos, 1,* 367–376.

DeValois, R. L. (1973). Central mechanisms of color vision. In R. Jung (Ed.), *Handbook of sensory physiology: Vol. 7, Pt. 3A. Central processing of visual information.* Berlin & New York: Springer-Verlag.

DeValois, R. L., Abramov, I., & Jacobs, G. H. (1966). Analysis of response patterns of LGN cells, *Journal of the Optical Society of America, 56,* 966–977.

DeValois, R. L., & DeValois, K. K. (1975). Neural coding of color. In E. C. Carterette & M. P. Friedman (Eds.), *Handbook of perception* (Vol. 5). New York: Academic Press.

DeValois, R. L., & Marrocco, R. T. (1973). Single cell analysis of saturation discrimination in the macaque. *Vision Research, 13,* 701–711.

DeValois, R. L., Morgan, H. C., Polson, M. C., Mead, W. R., & Hull, E. M. (1974). Psychophysical studies of monkey vision. I. Macaque luminosity and color vision. *Vision Research, 14,* 53–63.

Dobson, V. (1976). Spectral sensitivity of the 2-month infant as measured by the visually evoked cortical potential. *Vision Research, 15,* 367–374.

Fagan, J. F. (1974). Infant color perception. *Science, 183,* 973–975.

Fagan, J. F. (1977). An attention model of infant recognition. *Child Development, 48,* 345–359.

Fagan, J. F. (1979). The origins of facial pattern recognition. In M. H. Bornstein & W. Kessen (Eds.), *Psychological development from infancy.* Hillsdale, NJ: Erlbaum.

Farnham-Diggory, S., & Gregg, L. W. (1975). Color, form and function as dimensions of natural classification: Development changes in eye movements, reaction time, and response strategies. *Child Development, 46,* 101–114.

Goodenough, F. L. (1945). *Developmental psychology.* New York: Appleton.

Haith, M. M. (1980). *Rules that babies look by.* Hillsdale, NJ: Erlbaum.

Hamer, R. D., Alexander, K., & Teller, D. Y. (1982). Rayleigh discriminations in human infants. *Vision Research, 22,* 575–587.

Hering, E. (1964). *Outlines of a theory of the light sense* (L. M. Hurvich & D. Jameson, Trans.). Cambridge, MA: Harvard University Press. (Original work published, 1878)

Jameson, D., & Hurvich, L. (Eds.). (1972). *Handbook of sensory physiology* (Vol. 7, Part 4). Berlin & New York: Springer-Verlag.

Judd, D. B. (1951). Report of the U.S. Secretariat Commission on colorimetry and artificial daylight. *CIE Proceedings 1,* 11 [Data reproduced in G. Wyszecki & W. S. Stiles, *Color science* (p. 436). New York: Wiley, 1967].

Kessen, W., & Bornstein, M. H. (1978). Discriminability of brightness change for infants. *Journal of Experimental Child Psychology, 25,* 526–530.

Ladenheim, B., & Gordon, J. (1986). Heterochromatic flicker photometry in neonates. *Invest. Ophthal. Vis. Sci. Suppl. 27(3),* 76.

Lee, L. C. (1965). Concept utilization in preschool children. *Child Development, 36,* 221–228.

LeGrand, Y. (1972). Spectral luminosity. In D. Jameson & L. M. Hurvich (Eds.), *Handbook of Sensory Physiology* (Vol. 7, Pt. 4). Berlin & New York: Springer-Verlag.

Lodge, A., Armington, J. C., Barnet, A. B., Shanks, B. L., & Newcomb, C. N. (1969). Newborn infants' electroretinograms and evoked electroencephalographic responses to orange and white light. *Child Development, 40,* 267–293.

Moskowitz-Cook, A. (1979). The development of photopic spectral sensitivity in human infants. *Vision Research, 19,* 1133–1142.

Nagel, V. A. (1906). Observation on the color-sense of a child. *Journal of Comparative Neurology and Psychology, 16,* 217–230.

Odom, R. D. (1972). Effects of perceptual salience on the recall of relevant and incidental dimensional values: A developmental study. *Journal of Experimental Psychology, 92,* 285–291.

Oster, H. E. (1975). Color perception in human infants. Doctoral dissertation, University of California, Berkeley (University Microfilms, No. 76-15, 330).

Packer, O., Hartmann, E. E., & Teller, D. Y. (1985). Infant color vision: The effect of test field size on Rayleigh discriminations. *Vision Research, 24,* 1247–1260.

Pancratz, C. N., & Cohen, L. B. (1970). Recovery of habituation in infants. *Journal of Experimental Child Psychology, 9,* 208–216.

Payne, M. C. (1964). Color as an independent variable in perceptual research. *Psychological Bulletin, 61,* 199–208.

Peeples, D. R., & Teller, D. Y. (1975). Color vision and brightness discrimination in two-month-old human infants. *Science, 189,* 1102–1103.

Peeples, D. R., & Teller, D. Y. (1978). White-adapted photopic spectral sensitivity in human infants. *Vision Research, 18,* 39–53.

Pokorny, J., Smith, C. B., Verriest, G., & Pinckers, A. J. L. G. (1979). *Congenital and acquired color vision defects.* New York: Grune & Stratton.

Powers, M. K., Schneck, M., & Teller, D. Y. (1981). Spectral sensitivity of human infants at absolute visual threshold. *Vision Research, 21,* 1005–1016.

Preyer, W. (1890). *The mind of the child.* New York: Appleton.

Pulos, E., Teller, D. Y., & Buck, S. (1980). Infant color vision: A search for short wavelength-sensitive mechanisms by means of chromatic adaptation. *Vision Research, 20,* 485–493.

Rosch, E. (1978). Human categorization. In N. Warren (Ed.), *Studies in cross-cultural psychology* (Vol. 1). London: Academic Press.

Ruddock, K. H. (1972). Light transmission through the ocular media and macular pigment and its significance for psychophysical investigation. In D. Jameson & L. M. Hurvich (Eds.), *Handbook of sensory physiology* (Vol. 7, Part 4). Berlin & New York: Springer-Verlag.

Sandell, J. H., Gross, C. G., & Bornstein, M. H. (1979). Color categories in macaques. *Journal of Comparative and Physiological Psychology, 93,* 626–635.

Schaffer, H. R., & Parry, M. H. (1969). Perceptual-motor behaviour in infancy as a function of age and stimulus familiarity. *British Journal of Psychology, 60,* 1–9.

Schaffer, H. R., & Parry, M. H. (1970). The effects of short-term familiarization in infants' perceptual-motor coordination in a simultaneous discrimination situation. *British Journal of Psychology, 61,* 559–569.

Schaller, M. J. (1975). Chromatic vision in human infants. Conditioned operant fixation to "hues" of varying intensity. *Bulletin of the Psychonomic Society, 6,* 39–42.

Sperling, H., & Harwerth, R. (1971). Red-green cone interactions in the increment-threshold spectral sensitivity of primates. *Science, 172,* 180–184.

Sperling, H. G., & Lewis, W. G. (1959). Some comparisons between foveal spectral sensitivity data obtained at high brightness and absolute threshold. *Journal of the Optical Society of America, 49,* 983–989.

Strauss, M., & Cohen, L. B. (1980). *Infant immediate and delayed memory for perceptual dimensions.* Paper presented at the International Conference of Infant Studies, New Haven, CT.

Teller, D. Y. (1979). The forced-choice preferential looking procedure: A psychophysical technique for use with human infants. *Infant Behavior and Development, 2,* 135–153.

Teller, D. Y., Morse, R., Borton, R., & Regal, D. (1974). Visual acuity for vertical and diagonal gratings in human infants. *Vision Research, 14,* 1433–1439.

Teller, D. Y., Peeples, D. R., & Sekel, M. (1978). Discrimination of chromatic from white light by two-month-old infants. *Vision Research, 18,* 41–48.

Thomas, H. (1973). Unfolding the baby's mind: The infant's selection of visual stimuli. *Psychological Review, 80,* 468–488.

Tracy, F., & Stimpfl, J. (1909). *The psychology of childhood.* Boston, MA: Heath.

Varner, D., Cook, J. E., Schneck, M. E., McDonald, M., & Teller, D. Y. (1984). Tritan discriminations by 1- and 2-month-old human infants. *Vision Research, 25,* 821–832.

Volbrecht, V., & Werner, J. (1986). Isolation of short-wave cone photoreceptors in 4–6-week-old human infants. *Invest. Ophthal. Vis. Sci. Suppl. 27(3),* 264.

von Frisch, K. (1964). *Bees: Their vision, chemical senses, and language*. Ithaca, NY: Cornell University Press.

Wald, G. (1945). Human vision and the spectrum. *Science, 101,* 653–658.

Werner, J. S. (1982). Development of scotopic sensitivity and the absorption spectrum of the human ocular media. *Journal of the Optical Society of America, 72,* 247–258.

Williams, L. G. (1967). The effects of target specification on objects fixated during visual search. *Acta Psychologica, 27,* 355–360.

Williams, R., & Boothe, R. (1981). Development of optical quality in infant monkeys (*Macaca nemestrina*). *Investigative Ophthalmology and Visual Science, 21,* 728–736.

Wright, A. A., & Cumming, W. W. (1971). Color-naming functions for the pigeon. *Journal of the Experimental Analysis of Behavior, 15,* 7–17.

5

Taste and Olfaction

CHARLES CROOK
Department of Psychology
Durham University
Durham, United Kingdom

I. INTRODUCTION

There is a long tradition of research concerning the chemical senses in early childhood; formal observations of infants' reactions to taste and smell can be found documented in the pediatric literature of the nineteenth century (e.g., Kussmaul, 1859). Perhaps a conception of the chemical senses as phylogenetically "primitive" aroused the expectation that they would be particularly important in early ontogeny. With no commitment to the logic of such an expectation, I shall suggest here that although we may regard these sense modalities as secondary in adult life, infancy is indeed a time when their function may be especially significant. As it happens, the early empirical literature provided no clear consensus regarding just how active a baby's chemical senses are, but more recent studies do greatly encourage the view that taste and smell are far from dormant in early life.

Studies of infant chemoreception will be surveyed in the present chapter and some effort will be made to evaluate the significance of these sensory systems for early development. Two features of the literature may be usefully anticipated at the outset. One concerns a disproportionate concentration of interest in the child shortly after birth. Although "infancy" will be taken here to comprise the first 2 years, research happens to be mainly concerned with infants during the earliest days of life.

237

HANDBOOK OF INFANT
PERCEPTION, VOLUME I

This is an unfortunate imbalance of effort, and one that does seem especially to characterize this particular area of infant perception research. The other feature of the literature that quickly becomes apparent is one more generally true of research into perceptual development: while there is a long history of interest in the subject, the bulk of our understanding derives from a period of remarkable empirical activity spanning the last 20 years.

The reports of earlier experimental work do indicate poor standards of design and methodology; this inevitably gave rise to a variety of contradictory findings. However, what may really distinguish recent studies of taste and smell is an application of certain advances in recording and measurement, not just a more fastidious attitude to procedure. Thus, research reported around the 1930s, notably that of Pratt, Nelson, and Sun (1930), was in fact very attentive to procedural nicety. Highly stabilized testing environments, hospital routine, and equipment were described with splendid exactness. Unfortunately, these studies cannot provide a real starting point for a contemporary survey, as they remain handicapped by unsophisticated techniques of psychological measurement. Reactions to stimuli were often assessed by eye, with little record of what was observed or how reliably it could be judged. Students active in the modern era of infancy research are more fortunate: not only may a child's reaction be easily preserved on film or videotape for subsequent scrutiny, but psychophysiological recording of more subtle responses is now quite commonplace. The present review will focus on work reported within the last 20 years; excellent summaries of earlier research have been provided by Peiper (1963) and Pratt et al. (1930).

What then, are the major questions to be posed with regard to taste and smell perception in early life? We should seek a foundation of information regarding the sensitivity and resolving power of the child's chemical senses: what capacity exists for the detection and discrimination of particular stimuli? How does such capacity vary with age? These basic psychophysical questions, along with others concerning fundamental sensory processes such as adaption and localization, are common to the developmental investigation of any modality. However, once such groundwork has been laid, does the particular topic of infant chemoreception offer any provocative theoretical problems? The scarcity of research activity might suggest not—and, indeed, there are undoubtedly no epistemological issues on the scale of those that arise in the study of infant visual perception (e.g., Ch. 4, Vol. 2). However, there do exist a family of issues relating to the child's chemical sense that are both important and challenging; unfortunately, in what follows we can often do no more than identify them and speculate a little; they have been relatively neglected by empirical research.

The relevant issues are again common to the study of other sensory systems and, broadly, they concern how the ultimate functioning of the mature sense modality may be influenced by early experiences. However, the study of chemoreception does differ from at least that of vision and audition when we consider which aspects of function are of interest with respect to a developmental history. Many authors, from Wundt onward, have stressed the strong hedonic component of taste and smell sensation. Carl Pfaffman, in particular, has argued that it is motivating or incentive properties that are significant in the chemical sense, rather than the directing or cue function we more usually investigate in stimuli from other modalities (Pfaffman, 1960). Accordingly, the significant questions concerning infant perception of taste and smell concern the discrimination of qualitative differences between stimuli and the origin of preference. What is the role of experience in the development of preferences and is the experience of early life disproportionately significant?

Questions such as these obviously bear on the development of feeding control, but the child's chemical senses are involved in other activities of psychological importance and in this review we shall touch on questions of adult–child communication and control of respiration and even draw connections with the development of representational cognition.

The two sections that follow review psychophysical studies of first taste and then smell perception. In light of this summary, a fourth section of the paper considers the general significance of chemical senses in early development. Finally, some concluding comments will be offered on the state of current research activity and possible directions for future effort.

II. REACTIONS TO TASTE STIMULI

Everyday reference to "taste" usually unites a variety of sensations mediated by quite distinct sensory systems. Technically, the term is generally reserved for the activity of certain chemoreceptors within the mouth, and this will be the convention followed here. The taste receptors exist as groups of 50 or so cells forming a "bud," buds being found mainly on the papillae of the tongue. The receptors are innervated by two cranial nerves, the seventh or facial, and the ninth or glossopharyngeal (see Figure 1). Taste buds appear early in fetal life, the adult form being apparent by the thirteenth week (Bradley & Stern, 1967); in fact, the child is as well equipped with these receptor cells at birth as at any other time in life (Arey, Tremaine, & Monzingo, 1935; Lalonde & Eglitis, 1961).

Choice of stimuli by investigators of infant taste perception has tended to reflect prevailing beliefs regarding taste "primaries." While there is some controversy over the nature of the sensory code for this modality

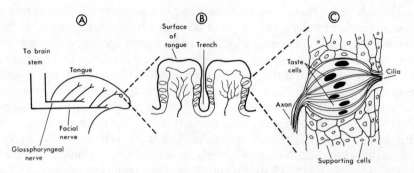

Figure 1. Schematic representation of the peripheral taste system showing afferent fibers innervating the tongue (A). The rough surface comprises papillae (B) where the taste buds (C) are located. The buds are composed of around 50 individual taste cells.

(Pfaffman, 1978), it is widely claimed that there are four basic taste sensations: sweet, salty, sour, and bitter. Thus, it is reaction to these stimuli that will be discussed here. What discussion is possible regarding more complex "taste" sensations (perhaps better described as "flavors") will be reserved for a later section. The response of newborn children will be considered first.

Earlier work in this area employed the newborn's facial expression as a measure of response to taste stimulation. There emerged no unanimity of results but some agreement that grimace-type reactions can be elicited, particularly by sour and bitter. More controversy concerned whether expressions could be elicited that were distinct and stimulus specific. Peiper (1963), in reviewing this work, doubted the evidence for such reactions and commented that he had never been able to differentiate responses himself. A number of early investigators also mentioned the occurrence of sucking responses, especially to sweet stimuli. Jensen (1932) seems to have been the first to make a mechanical record of these particular reactions and claimed the response patterns that emerged showed a degree of discrimination between milk and both salt and sweet solutions. However, the results presented are equivocal.

Interest in infant taste discrimination was revived by Nisbett and Gurwitz (1970), who manipulated taste properties of newborn bottle feedings. Intakes of differentially sweetened but isocaloric formulas were compared. Sweeter formulas were preferred, and this preference was more marked for female infants and for heavier children. Previous investigators may have been reluctant to utilize this method, whereby infants must ingest unusual fluids; however, any such qualms have evidently been dispelled in recent years, for the majority of studies have recorded some aspect of intake. It is the newborns' sensitivity to sweet taste that has been most thoroughly studied. Thus, Desor, Maller, and Turner (1973) reported greater intake of simple sugar solutions in a range up to .3 M sucrose. Rank ordering of preferences for sucrose, glucose, fructose, and lactose mirrored their relative sweetnesses as judged by adults and, again, heavier children showed the stronger preferences. Further reports by Engen, Lipsitt, and Peck (1974) and Kobre and Lipsitt (1972) confirm newborns' tendency to consume larger quantities of a sweeter fluid.

What are the changes that occur in the rhythm of sucking to mediate this increased intake? Crook (1977) compared sucking patterns for solutions of 5, 10, or 15% sucrose. The sweetness effect was most apparent in the early minutes of feeding: more concentrated solutions provoked longer bursts of sucking with shorter pauses between them. Somewhat paradoxically, the rate of sucking associated with the sweeter solutions was slower, that is, pauses between individual sucks in a burst were longer. Both Burke (1977) and Crook and Lipsitt (1976) have confirmed this observation. In addition, Burke found infants swallowed more when taking a sweeter fluid, and as a swallow causes a momentary pause in the sucking rhythm, this effect would make some contribution to an overall slower pace of response. Lipsitt (1977) has also proposed that this phenomenon may represent a kind of primitive savoring activity.

While recording intake of sugar solutions has become accepted practice, feeding children solutions characterized by the other basic tastes is a more controversial enterprise. Informal reports indicate that newborns will freely drink salt solutions when these have been mistakenly prepared as glucose (e.g., Finberg, Kiley, and Luttrel, 1963) and this has led some to question the significance of taste in early life (e.g., Gunther, 1972). One empirical study appears to support this claim. Maller and Desor (1973) contrasted intake of sodium chloride (.00312–.2 M), urea (.03–.18 M), and citric acid (.001–.012 M) with intake of pure water. No significant differences were found in 3-min feeding bouts.

Several points can be made concerning these results. They clearly need not imply that newborn babies fail to detect differences across these taste dimensions; the solution strengths may be below detection threshold or the dependent measure may not be sufficiently sensitive. Moreover, a difference may be detected but not manifest behaviorally as a preference. Desor, Maller, and Andrews (1975) have pursued the threshold possibility in a subsequent study and examined consumption of stronger solutions: .24–.48 M urea and .024–.48 M citric acid. Again intake did not differ from that of pure water. However, it may be that these tastes are hedonically negative but that ingestion can not fall below the level of the water baseline, which itself is at the lowest possible level. Thus, Desor et al.

(1975) employed .07 M sucrose as the control solution and prepared mixtures of this with urea (0.18–0.48 M) or citric acid (0.001–0.024 M) or sodium chloride (0.05–0.2 M). The sour solution suppressed intake below the (now raised) baseline condition, while there were no such effects for salty and bitter solutions.

These results certainly confirm that sour taste is functional at birth. However, it may be hasty to conclude that salt and bitter are not. By using .07 M sucrose as a diluent, these researchers aimed to raise the overall level of intake such that any suppression might be revealed, relative to a plain .07 M sucrose control. However, fuller presentation of their data (Desor, Maller, and Greene, 1977) questions the success of this strategy. The twelve experimental groups each experienced a sucrose-only control period paired with a sucrose-plus-taste period: In every group, sucking during the sucrose-only period was suppressed relative to that recorded from a thirteenth group for whom this condition was paired with plain water. This implies carry-over effects suppressing ingestion of the sucrose control, at least for those subjects who experienced experimental periods in this order. Should this have weakened the sensitivity of the method, it may be worth noting that the *direction* of results suggests that intake is suppressed by bitter solutions but possibly enhanced by salt solutions.

One conclusion that Desor et al. (1975) draw from their results is that infants may have an aversion to water. This observation suggests a connection with the adult psychophysical literature on water taste (Bartoshuk, 1968). If the adult tongue is adapted to salt solution and then stimulated with a subadapting concentration, that stimulus will generally be reported as bitter. Thus, the slightly unpleasant taste often associated with distilled water may be a consequence of the salt concentration of saliva to which the tongue is normally adapted. Moreover, neonatal salivary sodium content is up to three or four times the concentration found in adulthood, to which level it drops steadily across the first 4 months (Lawson, Saggers, & Chapman, 1967). The peculiar chemical environment of the infants' tongue may therefore influence the quality of taste sensations experienced, at least at lower intensities. However, the natural inference that newborns may not like distilled water for this reason—because it tastes bitter—would be difficult to reconcile with any apparent indifference to increasing concentrations of urea.

We may now turn to the reactions of older infants, although data in this area are scarce. One study does indicate there is no real change in the pattern of preferences for various sugar solutions across the first 6 months of life (Desor, Maller, & Greene 1977). Another study (Vazquez, Pearson and Beauchamp, 1982) has found that a group of children between 2 and

12 months (average age 9.6 months) suppressed intake for stronger solutions of urea and citric acid. These researchers also found, somewhat surprisingly, both normal and malnourished infants consumed *more* of .1 M and .2 M NaCl solutions than plain water (although there was no evidence of heightened preference for either salt or sweet taste among the malnourished children). This apparent preference for salt solutions over water has since been followed up with interesting results.

Thus, Beauchamp and his colleagues (e.g., Beauchamp and Cowert, 1985) have suggested that there may be three periods in the development of infants' reactions to salt. First, during the early months of life children are indifferent to salt taste or even fail to detect it. In this context, it should be noted that evidence from comparable animal preparations suggests a delay in the maturation of neural responsiveness to salt (Mistretta and Bradley, 1983). On the other hand, data to be discussed below does not encourage the view that newborns totally fail to detect salt stimuli. Second, from about 4 months, infants begin to show a preference for salt solutions over water (Beauchamp, Cowert and Moran, in press; Vazquez et al., 1982). So it is suggested that maturation of central or peripheral neural structures may allow the emergence of a basic unlearned acceptance of salt taste. Third, sometime within the second year a shift emerges toward increasingly rejecting salt solutions (Beauchamp and Moran, 1985; Beauchamp *et al., in press*). This account is persuasive but it does concern the manner in which taste controls *intake* and, as such, it is based upon intake measures. We shall shortly offer some qualifications to this account, following a discussion of other procedures for assessing taste discrimination.

Despite the care with which the measures of intake have been taken, this recent literature does not encourage definitive conclusions regarding the capacity of the infant to make discriminations within the taste modality. That quite small concentration differences in sugar solutions can be discriminated is not in doubt—although it does not follow that the differential intake is mediated by hedonic variations rather than simply changes in stimulus intensity. However, reactions to the other three taste dimensions might leave us wondering whether some alternative dependent measure could be more effective in demonstrating a discriminative capacity. If intake is determined by hedonic factors, then failure to find intake differences indicates the absence of a preference between stimuli and does not necessitate a failure to discriminate between them. Intake recording is unsatisfactory in other respects: different stimulus solutions can have different postingestional consequences and how these modulate intake independently of oral–sensory factors may leave intake a somewhat impure measure of taste sensitivity. It is true there are certain psychophysiological changes correlated with intake that might also serve as indices of discrimination. Thus, sucking for sweeter solutions is accompanied by higher heart rates (Crook & Lipsitt, 1976). While this observation is itself of theoretical significance (cf. Lipsitt, 1977), the magnitude of the effects reported suggest autonomic measures are not sufficiently sensitive to provide an alternative measure of sweet taste discrimination. Moreover, a central problem remains: solutions must still be presented in the context of feeding and, thus, many stimuli will be excluded from study because of potential risks associated with their ingestion. What is needed is a procedure that involves only brief presentation of a stimulus but which still provides a sensitive dependent variable.

The earliest studies aimed at this problem considered effects of brief taste stimulation upon facial expression. Can such methods be usefully revived, given the advantages of modern recording technology and more sophisticated ideas regarding behavioral categorization? Jacob Steiner has been examining the facial response of newborn children to tastes, the majority of whom he has studied prior to any feeding experience (Steiner, 1979). He has argued for the existence of *gustofacial reflexes* or intrinsic relationships between patterns of facial response and particular taste qualities. Observations suggested a differential facial reaction to sweet, sour, and bitter stimuli; salt taste has not been considered in this way. One report (Ganchrow, Steiner, & Daher 1983) details the discrete components of the facial expression in response to two concentrations of sweet and bitter stimuli. In all cases the magnitude of the reaction varied with stimulus intensity and the profile of components making up the total expression consistently differed between sweet and bitter while those for separate bitter stimuli (urea and quinine hydrochloride) were very similar. Taken together, these data therefore provide evidence for quality discriminations by newborns between sweet, sour, and bitter stimuli and intensity discriminations within at least the sweet and bitter dimensions. Steiner conceives of the gustofacial reflex as demonstrating a primitive food acceptance–rejection mechanism based upon taste information (e.g., Steiner, 1977).

It will be recalled that intake studies implied no discrimination of salt or bitter stimuli. There need be no conflict here: Steiner's experiments involved concentrations of tastants generally much greater than those used in the intake studies and it may simply be that detection thresholds are very high for these stimuli in early infancy. While the character of the response in this procedure is of great interest, the high concentrations of tastants involved may undermine its value as a psychophysical index. However, at least evidence of differential response to three of the four basic tastes has been found. Are there now other psychophysical procedures based upon brief stimulations that might prove yet more sensitive? Movements of the tongue in response to taste stimuli have been independently studied by Weiffenbach and Nowlis. Weiffenbach (1972, 1977) described a lateral movement that showed adaptation to localized surface stimulation. Following adaptation to water, response recovery occurred to drops of glucose solution; the degree of recovery was found to be a function of stimulus concentration. For psychophysical purposes, the method may be an advance on facial expression measures only in that the response is relatively easy to quantify; the concentrations required to elicit it are again very high. Nowlis (1973, 1977) recorded newborn tongue pressures at a specially designed nipple while small quantities of fluid were delivered. Sugar solutions elicited anterior tongue movements whose amplitude increased with stimulus concentration. A 10^{-4} M solution of quinine hydrochloride and .154 M sodium chloride elicited movements from the posterior region of the tongue. Nowlis identifies these distinct responses as, respectively, primitive acceptance and rejection reflexes controlling food intake. The method holds more promise as a psychophysical technique and these initial reports do suggest detection of bitter and salt taste within that range for which no effects can be found using intake measures or the gustofacial reflex.

The present author has also developed a technique that may hold promise in this area (Crook, 1978, 1982). An infant is permitted to suck on a nipple that is not delivering fluid. The "nonnutritive" sucking rhythm displays an episodic structure with bursts of activity separated by pauses. If even a very small quantity of fluid is injected through the nipple during one of these pauses, the newborn child will invariably initiate a new bout of sucking at once. The response latency is so short that it most likely reflects a reaction to the tactile component of the event. However, the number of sucks in the burst that follows has been found to be a function of chemical properties of the initiating stimulus. Specifically, sweeter solutions precipitated longer bursts and, compared to a distilled water control, salt solutions in the range .1–.6 M precipitated shorter bursts (Figure 2). The advantages of this method are that the dependent variable is easily recorded, while it is at least as sensitive as intake measures of sweet discrimination without introducing problems of uncertain postingestional influences and without creating any significant risk to the health of the child. At the same time, it does reveal perception of salt taste where intake measures have failed.

Taken together, results from these brief presentation procedures indicate that, contrary to a conclusion that might be drawn from intake studies, salt, sour, and bitter stimuli are all detected by the infant and discrimination of intensity can be made within these dimensions. The work of

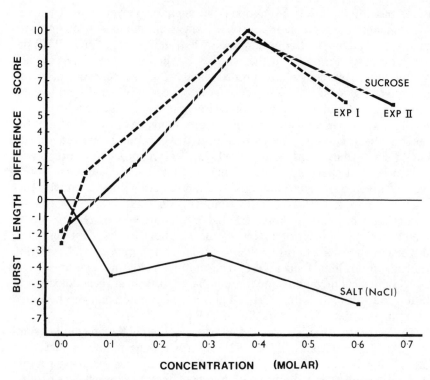

Figure 2. Effects of sweet and salt stimulation on the newborn's sucking reflex. Separate experiments show how a small volume of sucrose solution delivered to the tongue potentiates a burst of sucking. Sodium chloride solution also has this effect, but the bursts tend to be shorter. (From Crook, 1978.)

Steiner (1979), Nowlis (1977), and Crook (1978) also shows that salt, sour, and bitter stimuli can elicit responses that are different in kind from that elicited by sweet stimuli. This should satisfy any doubt that the intake-enhancing properties of increasing sweetness are related to the quality of stimulation and are not just a function of nonspecific increases in intensity of chemical stimulus input. Moreover, the character of the responses in each case imply that while sweet is hedonically positive salt, sour, and bitter are hedonically negative. It will be necessary to return to this conclusion later and attempt to reconcile the differences emerging from the intake and brief presentation methodologies, especially with regard to salt taste.

The problem of distinguishing the hedonic and intensity components of infant "judgements" is considerable. Only Nowlis and Kessen (1976) have ventured any kind of quantitative comparisons with adult psychophysical data. However, examination of all the published material on sweetness does suggest that infants' psychophysical function is very similar to pleasantness functions provided by adults, at least within a range of moderate intensities. There is even some suggestion (Crook, 1978) that there may be a peak of preference for sucrose and that the characteristic adult U-shaped preference function may be mirrored in infants (see Figure 2).

The conclusions of this review must be that, from birth, the infant discriminates between sweet, sour, salty, and bitter stimuli and can respond differentially within these taste dimensions according to stimulus intensity. With respect to affective tone, sweet appears hedonically positive, the others appear hedonically negative. Distinctive tongue and facial reflexes are elicited by stimuli representing these basic tastes and these may be considered aspects of acceptance and rejection behavior. However, actual measures of differential *ingestion* reveal that, at birth, the infant certainly has a strong sweet preference. On the other hand, sour stimuli may inhibit intake. There is apparent indifference to moderate intensity salt and bitter stimuli, but further research is required to clarify those reactions. Moreover, there may be a slight aversion to water. At least, water may define a low level of intake beneath which these taste solutions cannot readily suppress sucking. Beyond the newborn period, sweet solutions maintain their potency for enhancing intake, while intake comes to be reduced by sour and bitter. Finally, a preference develops for moderate salt solutions which reverses usually within the second year. The role taste plays in early feeding will be discussed again later, where some of the current methodological disagreements will be reconsidered.

III. REACTIONS TO ODOR

The olfactory system is unusual in that a single neuron, the olfactory cell, functions as both receptor and primary afferent fiber. A very large number of these cells are concentrated into a small area towards the top of the nasal cavity (see Figure 3). These fibers are branches of the first cranial nerve. However, it is important to note that also in this area there are free endings of the fifth (trigeminal) cranial nerve and that, therefore, most experience of smell will involve a trigeminal component. When this component is large, the sensation becomes an irritant, as in the familiar case of ammonia vapor. The relative contribution of olfactory and trigeminal stimulation to an odor experience is rarely assessed (see Silver and Maruniak, 1981); we can do no more here than bear in mind that when high concentrations of stimuli are employed with infants, as they often

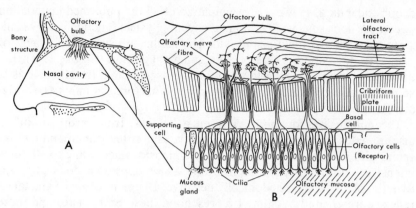

Figure 3. Schematic representation of the peripheral olfactory system. (A) shows the location of the olfactory epithelium and olfactory bulb; these areas are enlarged in (B). (From Krech and Crutchfield, 1961.)

have been, the irritant or pain component of the stimulation is likely to become increasingly significant in accounting for the response.

There have been many attempts to identify "primary" olfactory sensations comparable to those discussed above for taste, or the color primaries of vision. Numerous schemes have been proposed but none have received wide acceptance. Thus, investigators of olfactory perception in infancy have not been able to select stimuli from an organized catalog of possibilities of the kind available for taste. The variety of chemical stimuli studied has, accordingly, been very great. Choice has often been on the basis of the hedonic tone of stimuli as judged by adults or, less frequently, on the basis of an odor's hypothesized ecological significance for infants.

As with taste, facial expression in response to odor has received considerable attention, particularly in earlier research, as have other aspects of body reaction including quite specific limb movements. Physiological recording has also been employed, mainly with respect to heart rate and respiration. Some more recent research has attempted to assess overt orienting or avoidance responses to stimulation; evidently, as odors have spatial locations, this kind of measure is available for the study of olfaction where it is not for taste.

Empirical study of the olfactory sense during infancy is usually traced back as far as Kussmaul's (1859) investigations of the newborn. On the basis of facial expression and general activity he concluded that odors were perceived, but the reaction was one of disliking. For example, eyes were more tightly closed on presentation of asafoetida (often considered a "pure" stimulus for the olfactory component of smell). Responses to acetic acid and ammonia he ascribed more to the tactile than the olfactory sense.

Once more, Pratt *et al.* (1930) and Peiper (1963) provide comprehensive reviews of early research in this area. It was generally agreed that some reaction to odors occurs from shortly after birth; however, there has been considerable controversy as to how active or acute this sense modality may be. Thus, at one extreme, Canestrini (1913) concluded that smell is the least active of all senses in the newborn and that clear reactions are due more to trigeminal stimulation. Stirnimann (1936), on the other hand, believed that stimulation of the olfactory nerve was more effective than trigeminal stimulation in eliciting responses and that newborns could clearly differentiate agreeable and disagreeable odors. Much of the controversy here is doubtless rooted in varying, and often careless, approaches to methodology. In general, early investigators did not pay close attention to details that would now be considered important: for example, an infant's arousal state at the time of testing, effects of repeated stimulation, objective scaling of response, evaluation of reaction compared to control stimulation, and matching the intensity of qualitatively discriminated stimuli.

Modern work in this area is not always free from such criticism either, but some consensus has now emerged, although within a fairly limited range of research interest. As with taste, much of the more recent work involving infants has been carried out at the Child Study Center of Brown University. Engen, Lipsitt, and their collaborators have reported a series of studies on olfactory perception during the first days of life. In the typical procedure, a cotton swab saturated with a solution of an olfactory stimulus is repeatedly presented beneath the infant's nose while various measures of reaction are recorded polygraphically. Thus, Engen, Lipsitt, and Kaye (1963) related respiration, heart rate, general activity, and leg withdrawal to full strength presentation of anise oil, asafoetida, phenylethyl alcohol, and acetic acid. Observers compared by eye the polygraph record on experimental and control trials and by this method found respiratory disruption to be the most sensitive dependent variable. Clear responses occurred to all stimuli, the most marked being to acetic acid and asafoetida. Moreover, in several cases the magnitude of response declined across trials. Such a response decrement could be attributed either to fatigue at the receptor level, usually termed sensory adaption, or to a more central gating process, usually termed habituation. Engen and Lipsitt (1965) have successfully distinguished these possibilities in a study of neonates. Following a decrease in responding to an odor mixture they observed a recovery to one of the components of the mixture presented alone. Such recovery rules out explanations of their response decrement

breast pad odors by 2 weeks, but the nature of the response is not clearly specified. A choice procedure revealed clear differentiation of real and strange mother breast pads by 6 weeks. The important conclusion from both studies is that selective orientation toward particular odors may be manifest at a point surprisingly early in infancy.

Differential head turning provides one promising dependent variable for studying odor preference. These particular observations also raise the question of whether preferences exist prior to postnatal learning opportunities; head turning is the main component of the rooting reflex and early orientation to selected odors may reflect associations established through classical conditioning. The question of a suitable dependent variable for preference studies returns us to a consideration of facial expression studies, and that work has also provided results pertinent to the debate regarding the origin of early preferences and the particular role of learning mechanisms.

This debate is characterized more by differences of emphasis than vigorous disagreement. Thus, Engen (1974, 1979) represents a position that stresses associative learning as the source of olfactory preferences. His view is supported by reference to studies indicating that older children, at least up to 4 or 5 years, are virtually indifferent to many odors adults find very unpleasant (Engen, 1974; Engen & Corbitt, 1970; Peto, 1936; Stein, Ottenberg, & Roulet, 1958). Steiner (1977) on the other hand, argues for innate hedonic responses to certain odors. Examination of newborns' facial expressions to olfactory stimuli has led Steiner to identify the existence of a *nasofacial reflex*. While the presence of such a reflex at birth may be established, it is less clear whether it is reliably elicited by particular odors. The most relevant study (Steiner, 1977) claims preferences organized around food-related odors: fresh (positive response) and rotten (negative response). However, it is not clear that the infant's differential responses could not have been based on intensity differences in stimulation, rather than differences in quality. Moreover, while these responses may well serve a communicative function (Steiner, 1977), as observers can reliably distinguish them, the coding system employed in the study may have been too limited to justify strong conclusions regarding hedonic aspects of responding. Observers merely categorized a response in terms of acceptance or rejection relative to a control stimulus. Data is needed comparable to that provided for taste (Granchrow et al., 1983), in which components of the expression are cataloged and used by observers to rate stimuli varying in both qualitative and quantitative dimensions.

For the present, we can conclude that the sense of smell is active from birth: odors may induce characteristic facial expressions, increased body movements, and disturbed respiratory activity. Psychophysical intensity functions can be derived from the newborn and they have resembled those obtained from adults. Habituation occurs to repeated stimulation and odors can be localized in space. Orientation towards significant odors can occur within the first weeks but the presence of innate preferences for particular stimuli is equivocal. In the remainder of this chapter, the literature reviewed in this section and in Section II will be discussed in relation to the general significance of these two sense modalities for early development.

IV. THE PLACE OF CHEMORECEPTION IN EARLY DEVELOPMENT

The chemical senses are evidently far from dormant in early life, and it remains to be considered whether they have an important functional significance at this time. We might expect their most essential role to be their most familiar: control of feeding. This topic will, therefore, receive the closest consideration here, but attention will also be given to several other important functions in which taste and smell have been implicated.

Innate taste preferences could serve both to facilitate the ingestion of nutritious foods and to protect the infant against the harmful or toxic. Regarding the former possibility, there is no doubt that sweetness is an extremely potent stimulus for the suckling infant; indeed one of the most reliable and dramatic demonstrations in a newborn sensory psychology laboratory must be the changes induced in sucking rhythm by even slight changes in the sugar concentration of formula (Crook, 1979). It would surely be a valuable evolution to equip the species with a preference for stimulation that is such a reliable indicator of what is good to ingest. This seems to have happened; but it should be noted that the preference is not, or is no longer, perfectly matched to the food the nursing human infant will normally be offered. That is, the child's preference for sweet extends well beyond the sweetness of human milk. Insofar as there may be a peak in the preference function (Crook, 1978), it is beyond the approximately 7% lactose concentration in mother's milk and closer to the peak reported for adults.

While sweet tastes may facilitate intake, there is no evidence that other tastes are very effective protective agents. Sucking is less readily inhibited by salt, sour, or bitter tastes below a level maintained by pure water. This conclusion is in accord with anecdotes derived from accidents of formula preparation, but there are further grounds for expecting this intake "tolerance" in the newborn. However diligent experimenters are in anticipating the first feeding of their subjects, newborn infants will still have had prenatal taste experience. Radioactive tracing has demonstrated that toward the end of gestation about two-thirds of the amniotic fluid is cleared of labeled protein per day and that 80% of this is a direct result of fetal swallowing (Gitlin, Kumate, Morales, Noriega, & Arevalo, 1972). Amniotic fluid does not taste good—not, at least, to the adult palate of the present author—and so prenatal tolerance of its bitter, salty quality, for example, would predict the results of intake research on newborns. Moreover, fetal swallowing may be important; it is an additional source of protein at a time when placental supply may be taxed and it would seem also to be implicated in the regulation of amniotic fluid volume (Gitlin et al., 1972). Thus, a taste-produced mechanism for rejecting fluids would not be compatible with this aspect of early development, despite its potential for protection in other contexts.

The observations that newborns will ingest bitter and salty solutions in comparable quantities to water still needs to be reconciled with other evidence showing seemingly negative hedonic responses to these tastes when the stimulation is minimal and brief (e.g., Crook, 1978; Nowlis, 1977; Steiner, 1977). At some past point in mans' evolutionary history, taste-mediated suppression of food intake during early life may have been a very valuable survival mechanism. Man is now among the most altricial of species and, arguably, it is a highly labile sucking reflex that is most important, one that is able to derive the most from whatever sources come its way. There is abundant evidence that neonatal sucking is a well-prepared and readily elicited response (cf. Crook, 1979), and it is plausible that sensory control has been relaxed to the point where the tactile stimulation from almost any fluid in the mouth is alone sufficient to maintain sucking at a baseline burst-and-pause rhythm. It is perhaps better that the well-protected infant has a highly labile feeding response than one equipped with checks prepared for rather improbable dangers. However, when taste stimulation is not dominated by the stimulation from a continuous flow of fluid, as in laboratory tests with brief presentation methods, then rejection of sour, salt, and bitter becomes apparent with the newborn. It is only later in infancy that such stimuli gain more significant control over ingestion. The proposal is, therefore, that in very early life the hedonically negative properties of certain tastes are overridden during a feed by the potent tactile stimulation from fluid in the mouth. If the newborn infant initiates sucking at all, then this fluid stimulation will maintain a baseline level of the response that is difficult to suppress in the motivated infant.

What is being suggested by this account is that the infant's feeding response becomes less labile over the first months of life and this is reflected in more effective control of taste over intake. However, an alternative view (e.g., Beauchamp and Cowert, 1985) might be that some kind of neural maturation is occurring during this period, and it is this that underlies the observed changes in ingestion. The infant simply becomes more sensitive to taste stimulation.

Of course, these positions are not incompatible. However, what the brief presentation methods with newborns do reveal is that *some* sensitivity to the basic tastes is present at birth, whether or not significant neural maturation is yet to occur. The positions seem less easily reconciled when we consider assessments of hedonic tone for the various tastes. Brief presentation procedures with newborns suggest bitter and sour are hedonically negative, and this is indeed consistent with suppressed intake to these tastes later. However, the same comparison for salt suggests the newborn is responding negatively, but the 4-month old infant is responding positively (ingesting more salt solutions). For the present, we may only note that the concentrations employed in the ingestion studies are moderate (up to 0.2 M NaCl) whereas in brief presentation methods they have often been much higher [e.g., up to 0.6 M in Crook's (1978) study]. Clearly, the nature of reaction to salt in the newborn period must be pursued further.

Brief reference was made above to the sweetness of human milk: are an infant's chemical senses responsive to other constituents of milk? Is intake controlled by the more complex experience of "flavor," to which both taste and olfactory systems are jointly contributing? Unfortunately, no more than speculation is possible at present. From what is known regarding passage of complex molecules from maternal ingestion into milk (Knowles, 1966) there is every reason to suspect human milk has distinctive flavor characteristics reflecting the mother's diet. Such characteristics may vary both between mothers and within mothers across feeding episodes; they thus have at least a potential for modulating a nursing child's intake. There are also systematic changes in milk composition in the course of any normal feeding period at the breast (Hall, 1975), and it is possible that taste-correlated aspects of such changes contribute to factors that cause the termination of sucking.

Data concerning within and between individual variation in taste or flavor properties of human milk would be most valuable. Even if the chemical senses are found not to be involved in intake control at the breast, the experience they provide at that time may contribute to events that occur later, at weaning.

Unfortunately, very little is known regarding the details of contemporary feeding practices involving solids (cf. Fomon & Anderson, 1972), but there is abundant anecdotal evidence that from the early stages of weaning children will manifest preferences and aversions for particular foods (e.g., Beal, 1957). Indeed a good proportion of early feeding problems are claimed to stem from this fact (cf. Harris & Chan, 1969). If taste and flavor properties of foods underlie this finickiness, what is the origin of such preferences and aversions? The sensory experiences associated with earlier milk feedings may be involved in the answer to this question. Certainly, evidence from the study of other mammals encourages this speculation. Thus, it has been shown that flavors experienced by suckling rats in their mother's milk are subsequently preferred at weaning (Capretta & Rawls, 1974; Galef & Henderson, 1972). Correspondingly, a human infant's taste preferences may be indirectly shaped by the mother's diet. A more general possibility is that the greater variety of taste experience gained by the nursing infant will leave that child easier to wean than a bottle-fed peer. Again, animal parallels encourage this reasoning: infant rats are more likely to accept unfamiliar foods if they have had prior experience with a wide range of different flavors (Capretta, Petersik, & Stewart, 1975).

What mechanisms might operate in the development of selectivity and underlie effects of experience such as those discussed above? Recently, considerable attention has been given to the way in which associative mechanisms modulate the palatibility of foods. This interest stems from studies of conditioned taste aversions in which aversive but delayed postingestional consequences of distinctively flavored foods lead to very rapid avoidance learning for the flavors involved (e.g., Garcia, Hankins, & Rusiniak, 1974). It might pay to examine more closely events at weaning, when an infant's chemical senses are first introduced to a rich variety of stimulation. One seemingly testable notion would be that, occasionally, illness during infancy is coincidently preceded by the introduction of a new food and from this chance pairing a conditioned taste aversion develops. In rodents, at least, the relevant associative mechanism is first manifest around the time of weaning (Bures & Buresova, 1977), and conditioned taste aversions have been induced in children only a little older (Bernstein, 1978). Moreover, it is now argued that such learning is far more general than might be implied by the existing emphasis of research on poison effects under laboratory conditions; associative learning based upon taste and the positive postingestional consequences of feeding may also be a mechanism involved in the development of appetite (Booth, 1978). Indeed, the possible strength of such early associative effects based upon a carbohydrate intake has been cited as particular reason for vigilance in the overfeeding of starchy or sugary foods in early life (Booth, Stoloff, & Nicholls, 1974).

The foregoing models emphasize the role of learning in flavor preferences and aversions. A certain resistance to this position might be derived from Davis' (1939) studies of infants at weaning age, who were allowed to chose freely from a variety of foods presented in cafeteria style. Unaided, each child evolved a selective but balanced diet. However, this emerged from an initial period of extensive sampling and Davis herself interprets the children's behavior in terms of the association of sensory experience with feelings of "comfort and well being that followed eating" as opposed to " 'instinct' pointing to the 'good' or 'bad' in food" (Davis, 1939, p. 261).

The olfactory system plays a major part in what we casually refer to as "taste," but the evidence on unlearned olfactory preference is limited and, at best, equivocal. Moreover, the idiosyncratic nature of many children's flavor preferences and aversions reinforce the view that they are unlikely to be biologically prepared. While reactions to the basic tastes are in some sense innate, there remains a great range of individual variability to be accounted for. Tests with older children indicate that there is negligible heritability for the variation in preference functions for sucrose and sodium chloride (Greene, Desor, & Maller, 1975). It is an important issue to determine how far individual differences in taste and flavor preference have their origin during this early period of life. We have already speculated that factors associated with nursing experience may prove relevant: Could aspects of feeding strategy in the period after weaning also exert influence? Animal experimentation does encourage the search for effects based upon aspects of familiarity (e.g., Wywricka, 1981). Moreover, it is apparent that tastes generally regarded as very unacceptable to adults, such as the sour tamarind fruit, can sometimes be quite palatable to those whose experience seems to stem from an early age (Moskowitz, Kurmraiah, Sharma, Jacobs, and Sharma, 1975).

So far, there is only limited information on such matters as they relate to human infancy. Beauchamp and Moran (1982) have investigated preferences for sugared water at birth and, for the same children, at six months—in the light of information regarding the children's feeding experiences. They found that infants took significantly more of the sweet water at 6 months if some form of such a fluid had been a more regular part of their normal diet. However, these researchers note that this result may not represent the cultivation of a *generalized* preference for sweet. More specifically, it has been argued (Beauchamp and Cowert, 1985) that early dietary experience may serve to define appropriate food-related contexts for encountering basic tastes such as sweet and salt. Thus, sweetened water may be one such context for some children, and those familiar with it do indeed show a preference for sweetness encountered in this form; however, they may not be exceptional in their reactions to sweetened soft drinks, for example. Salty water, on the other hand, would be a rather unfamiliar context for salt and so older infants do generally come to reject it in this form (Beauchamp and Cowert, 1985), while welcoming it in its (familiar) form as an addition to other foods.

The clinical significance of excessive sugar and salt intake suggests that tracing possible origins in infancy of "sweet tooth" or "salt tooth" is an important enterprise. The particular possibility that generalized preferences may develop at this time should still be carefully considered. Some data pertaining to infant salt preference finds a correlation implying generalization of this kind for salt (Harris and Booth, 1985).

A further protective function for the taste system has been raised in another context. Sucking, swallowing, and breathing are smoothly integrated during feeding; it has been argued that a source of the feedback coordinating these responses comes from extralingual taste receptors (Johnson & Salisbury, 1977). Evidence suggests that stimulation of chemoreceptors in the newborn's upper airway can function to control breathing patterns during ingestion. Thus, taste stimuli may be involved not only with the modulation of intake but also with the defence of the airway during feeding.

It is not solely in connection with feeding that the chemical senses may be significant during infancy. They may also serve a more general cue function. As yet, few efforts have been made to study how olfaction may control infant attention. However, available evidence that olfactory stimuli do acquire signal properties for very young children strongly encourages this line of inquiry. There is a long history of speculation on the use of olfaction by infants to identify adults, particularly the nursing mother, around them (Peiper, 1963). It is certainly the case that the young of other mammalian species employ olfaction in this manner (e.g., Kaplan, Cubicciotti, & Redican, 1977; Rosenblatt, 1972). There is now evidence that human infants can recognize, within the first weeks of life, odors associated with their own particular feeding experiences (e.g., Macfarlane, 1975). Olfaction may, thus, be involved in the infant's growing recognition of familiar features of the environment—including other people—perhaps before the visual system becomes really effective in this function. The traditional speculation that the olfactory system is implicated in recognition processes during human infancy has been shown to deserve serious empirical study.

Before concluding this section, some consideration is due to the possible place of chemoreception in the more general development of affect: taste and smell often receive no mention at all in treatments of this more global topic (e.g., Lewis & Rosenblum, 1978). The emergence of affective representations appropriate to particular stimuli is undoubtedly an important point of early development. Things come to be known as pleasant or unpleasant, and the chemical senses are involved in the earliest of these affective distinctions. Nowlis has elaborated upon his own observations of taste-elicited acceptance and rejection tongue reflexes (Nowlis, 1977) to make the interesting suggestion that palatability reactions may mediate the earliest affective representations. For example, the response to a discrete bitter stimulus is a "rejecting" upward movement of the posterior tongue. This reflex is eventually suppressed by forebrain inhibitory functions and it is this neural activity that may come to represent the affective information, but in a now covert form. If this notion of reflexes transformed to representations is correct, then palatability reflexes with their afferents deriving from the chemical senses could well provide good model systems for controlled study of the transformation.

At least the spirit of this suggestion is realized in an experiment by Kobre and Lipsitt (1972) in which the taste system was exploited to reveal in newborn infants a familiar phenomenon from the motivation literature: behavioral contrast. When sucrose solution was alternated with plain water, the intake of fluid during water periods was significantly suppressed by comparison with a water-only control group. This would appear to demonstrate at the very beginning of life an important motivational principle: the acceptability of a stimulus is not intrinsic but, among other things, may be determined by the context of other stimuli in which it occurs. Possibly it is in part through pleasures, and otherwise, of feeding that such processes are cultivated. Responses to taste and smell certainly provide a valuable system in which they may be studied.

V. CONCLUDING REMARKS

Both taste and olfaction are functional senses in the newborn child. Their stimulation may elicit or modulate a variety of reflexes including stereotyped facial expressions, movements of the tongue, swallowing, and sucking. Some of these reactions, together with other effects on respiration and general activity levels, have allowed quite rigorous psychophysical studies of these senses very early in life. While some conception of the basic operating characteristics has emerged, a more sizable volume of the resulting research has been concerned with questions of hedonic functions: what the infant likes and does not like.

Understanding the nature and origins of preferences offers the most important challenge to research on these senses during infancy. Likes and dislikes are by no means trivial aspects of development; those established in early life may have lasting influences on the health and well-being of the child. In this paper emphasis has been placed on sensory factors controlling feeding although, unfortunately, little more has been possible than to indicate that the chemical senses are active in this context and to speculate regarding the mechanisms through which they influence behavior. Much more research is required to clarify these issues. To underline the importance of the matter, it should be noted that behavior at recognized meal times is not the sole item of concern. The function of chemoreception in signaling danger is well known; as the infant becomes more autonomous with respect to putting things into his/her mouth, the effectiveness of taste and olfaction as final censors for the digestive system becomes increasingly vital. Children do not only eat under the supervision of adults. It is curious that when practical suggestions are made for combating accidental poisonings in childhood, the relevance of the chemical senses is not always acknowledged (e.g., Jackson, Walker, & Wynne, 1968). Fortunately, some research has been initiated (Engen, 1974) and it does suggest that taste, rather than the olfactory system, may be employed to deter young children from ingesting harmful substances. Epidemiological data indicate that the problem is not a serious one until the second year of life, although this is the time at which it is also most prevalent (Deeths & Breeden, 1971). Thus, information on children in this age range is most important; but, at present it is scarce.

It must be said that data on infant chemoreception beyond the first days of life is generally in short supply. If there is to be understanding of functional development in these sensory systems, investigations must examine events beyond the newborn period. It has been argued here that there are important and interesting issues to be faced with respect to taste and olfaction during infancy, but they are largely developmental issues and must be studied in that framework. Without doubt, much progress has been made in this area, but much that has been reported with confidence in this review concerns, or stems from, research on the newborn child. The single most important task for future students of this area is to broaden their study beyond the earliest days of life and create a truly developmental perspective.

REFERENCES

Arey, L. B., Tremaine, M. J., & Monzingo, F. L. (1942). The numerical and topographical relations of taste buds to human circumvallate papillae throughout the life span. *Anatomical Record, 64,* 9–25.

Bartoshuk, L. M. (1968). Water taste in man. *Perception and Psychophysics, 3,* 69–72.

Beal, V. A. (1957). On the acceptance of solid foods, and other food patterns, of infants and children. *Pediatrics, 20,* 448–457.

Beauchamp, G. K., & Moran, M. (1982). Dietary experience and sweet taste preference in human infants. *Appetite, 3,* 139–152.

Beauchamp, G. K., & Moran, M. (1985). Acceptance of sweet and salty tastes in 2-year-old children. *Appetite, 5*, 291–305.

Beauchamp, G. K., & Cowart, B. J. (1985). Congenital and experiential factors in the development of human flavor preferences. *Appetite, 6*, 357–372.

Beauchamp, G. K., Cowert, B. J., & Moran, M. Developmental changes in salt acceptability in human infants. *Developmental Psychobiology*, in press *19*.

Bernstein, I. L. (1978). Learned taste aversions in children receiving chemotherapy. *Science, 200*, 1302–1303.

Booth, D. A. (1978). Acquired behavior controlling energy intake and output. *Psychiatric Clinics of North America, 1*, 545–579.

Booth, D. A., Stoloff, R., & Nicholls, J. (1974). Dietary flavor acceptance in infant rats established by association with effects of nutrient composition. *Physiological Psychology, 2*, 313–319.

Bradley, R. M., & Stern, I. B. (1967). The development of the human taste bud during the foetal period. *Journal of Anatomy, 101*, 743–752.

Bures, J., & Buresova, O. (1977). Physiological mechanisms and conditioned food aversions. In N. W. Milgran, L. Krames, & T. M. Alloway (eds.), *Food aversion learning.* New York: Plenum.

Burke, P. M. (1977). Swallowing and the organization of sucking in the human newborn. *Child Development, 48*, 523–531.

Canestrini, S. (1913). Ueber das sinnesleben des neugeborenen. *Monographien aus dem Gesamtgebiete der Neurologie und Psychiatrie*, 104.

Capretta, P. J., Petersik, J. T., & Stewart, D. J. (1975). Acceptance of novel flavors is increased after early experience of diverse tastes. *Nature (London), 254*, 689–691.

Capretta, P. J., & Rawls, L. H. (1974). Establishment of a flavor preference in rats: Importance of nursing and weaning experience. *Journal of Comparative and Physiological Psychology, 86*, 670–673.

Crook, C. K. (1977). Taste stimulation and the temporal organization of neonatal sucking. In J. M. Weiffenbach (ed.), *Taste and development: The ontogeny of sweet preference* (pp. 146–158). Washington, DC: U.S. Government Printing Office.

Crook, C. K. (1978). Taste perception in the newborn infant. *Infant Behavior and Development, 1*, 49–66.

Crook, C. K. (1979). The organization and control of infant sucking. In H. Reese & L. P. Lipsitt (Eds.), *Advances in child development and behavior* (Vol. 14, pp. 209–251). New York: Academic Press.

Crook, C. K. (1982). Modulation of the sucking reflex by olfaction and taste. In J. Steiner & J. Ganchrow (Eds.) *Determination of behaviour by chemical stimuli.* London: IRL press.

Crook, C. K., & Lipsitt, L. P. (1976). Neonatal nutritive sucking: Effects of taste stimulation upon sucking rhythm and heart rate. *Child Development, 13*, 469–472.

Davis, C. (1939). Results of the self-selection of diet by young children. *Canadian Medical Association Journal, 41*, 257–261.

Deeths, T. M., & Breeden, J. T. (1971). Poisoning in children—a statistical study of 1,057 cases. *Journal of Pediatrics, 78*, 299–305.

Desor, J. A., Maller, O., & Andrews, K. (1975). Ingestive responses of newborns to salty, sour and bitter stimuli. *Journal of Comparative and Physiological Psychology, 89*, 966–970.

Desor, J. A., Maller, O., & Greene, L. S. (1977). Preference for sweet in humans: Infants, children and adults. In J. M. Weiffenbach (Ed.), *Taste and development: The ontogeny of sweet preference* (pp. 161–172). Washington, DC: U.S. Government Printing Office.

Desor, J. A., Maller, O., & Turner, R. (1973). Taste acceptance of sugars by human infants. *Journal of Comparative and Physiological Psychology, 84,* 496–501.

Engen, T. (1965). Psychophysical analysis of the odor intensity of homologous alcohols. *Journal of Experimental Psychology, 70,* 611–616.

Engen, T. (1974). Method and theory in the study of odor preferences. In A. Turk, J. W. Johnston, & D. G. Moulton (Eds.), *Human responses to environmental odors* (pp. 121–141). New York: Academic Press.

Engen, T. (1979). The origin of preferences in taste and smell. In J. H. A. Kroeze (Eds.), *Preference behaviour and chemoreception* (pp. 263–273). London: Information Retrieval Limited.

Engen, T., & Corbitt, T. E. (1970). *Feasibility of olfactory coding of noxious substances to assure aversive responses in young children* (Publication ICRL-RR-69-6). Washington DC: Injury Control Research Laboratory, U.S. DHEW Public Health Service.

Engen, T., & Lipsitt, L. P. (1965). Decrement and recovery of responses to olfactory stimuli in the human neonate. *Journal of Comparative and Physiological Psychology, 69,* 312–316.

Engen, T., Lipsitt, L. P., & Kaye, H. (1963). Olfactory responses and adaption in the human neonate. *Journal of Comparative and Physiological Psychology, 56,* 73–77.

Engen, T., Lipsitt, L. P., & Peck, M. B. (1974). Ability of newborn infants to discriminate sapid substances. *Developmental Psychology, 10,* 741–746.

Finberg, L., Kiley, J., & Luttrel, C. N. (1963). Mass accidental salt poisoning in infancy. *Journal of the American Medical Association, 184,* 121–124.

Fomon, S. J., & Anderson, T. A. (1972). *Practices of low-income families in feeding infants and small children with particular attention to cultural subgroups* (U.S. DHEW Publ. No. (HSM) 72:5605). Washington, DC: Supt. of Documents, U.S. Government Printing Office.

Galef, B. G., & Henderson, P. W. (1972). Mother's milk: A determinant of the feeding preferences of weaning rat pups. *Journal of Comparative and Physiological Psychology, 78,* 213–219.

Ganchrow, J. R., Steiner, J. E., & Daher, M. (1983). Neonatal facial expressions in response to different qualities and intensities of gustatory stimuli. *Infant Behavior and Development, 6,* 189–200.

Garcia, J., Hankins, W. G., & Rusiniak, K. W. (1974). Behavioral regulation of the *milieu interne* in man and rat. *Science, 185,* 824–831.

Gitlin, D., Kumate, J., Morales, C., Noriega, L., & Arevalo, N. (1972). The turnover of amniotic fluid protein in the human conceptus. *American Journal of Obstetrics and Gynecology, 113,* 632–645.

Graham, F. K., & Jackson, J. C. (1970). Arousal systems and infant heart rate responses. In H. Reese & L. P. Lipsitt (Eds.), *Advances in child development and behavior* (Vol. 5, pp. 60–111). New York: Academic Press.

Greene, L. S., Desor, J. A., & Maller, O. (1975). Heredity and experience: Their relative importance in the development of taste preferences in man. *Journal of Comparative and Physiological Psychology, 89,* 279–284.

Gunther, M. (1972). *Infant feeding.* Harmondsworth: Penguin.

Hall, B. (1975). Changing composition of human milk and early development of appetitional control. *Lancet, 1,* 779–781.

Harris, G., & Booth, D. (1985). Sodium preference in food and previous dietary experience in 6-month-old infants. *IRCS Medical Science, 13,* 1177–1178.

Harris, L. E., & Chan, J. C. M. (1969). Infant feeding practices. *American Journal of Disease in Childhood, 117,* 483–492.

Jackson, R. H., Walker, J. H., & Wynne, N. A. (1968). Circumstances of accidental poisoning in childhood. *British Medical Journal, 4,* 245–246.

Jensen, K. (1932). Differential reactions to taste and temperature stimuli in newborn infants. *Genetic Psychology Monographs, 12,* 363–479.

Johnson, P., & Salisbury, D. M. (1977). Preliminary studies on feeding and breathing in the newborn. In J. M. Wieffenbach (ed.), *Taste and development: The ontogeny of sweet preference* (pp. 111–124). Washington, DC: U.S. Government Printing Office.

Kaplan, J. N., Cubicciotti, D., & Redican, W. K. (1977). Olfactory discrimination of squirrel monkey mothers by their infants. *Developmental Psychobiology, 10,* 447–453.

Kearsley, R. B. (1973). The newborn's response to auditory stimulation: A demonstration of orienting and defensive behavior. *Child Development, 44,* 582–590.

Knowles, J. A. (1966). Excretion of drugs in milk: A review. *Journal of Pediatrics, 66,* 1068–1082.

Kobre, K. R., & Lipsitt, L. P. (1972). A negative contrast effect in newborns. *Journal of Experimental Child Psychology, 14,* 81–91.

Krech, D., & Crutchfield, R. (1961). Elements of Psychology. New York, NY: Alfred Knopf.

Kussmaul, A. (1859). *Untersuchunger uber das Seelenleben des Neugenborenen Menschen.* Tubingen: Moser.

Lalonde, E. R., & Eglitis, J. A. (1961). Number and distribution of taste buds on the epiglottis, pharynx, larynx, soft palate and uvula in a human newborn. *Anatomical Record, 140,* 91–95.

Lawson, D., Saggers, B. A., & Chapman, M. J. (1967). Screening for cystic fibrosis by measurement of unstimulated parotid saliva sodium levels. *Archives of Disease in Childhood, 42,* 689–690.

Lewis, M., & Rosenblum, L. A. (1978). *The development of affect.* New York: Plenum.

Lipsitt, L. P. (1977). Taste in human neonates: Its effect on sucking and heart rate. In J. M. Weiffenbach (Ed.), *Taste and development: The ontogeny of sweet preference* (pp. 125–140). Washington, DC: U.S. Government Printing Office.

Lipsitt, L. P., Engen, T., & Kaye, H. (1963). Developmental changes in the olfactory threshold of the neonate. *Child Development, 34,* 371–376.

Macfarlane, A. (1975). Olfaction in the development of social preferences in the human neonate. *Ciba Foundation Symposium, New Series, 33,* 103–113.

Maller, O., & Desor, J. A. (1973). Effect of taste on ingestion by human newborns. In J. F. Bosma (Ed.), *Fourth symposium on oral sensation and perception: Development in the fetus and infant* (pp. 279–303). Washington, DC: U.S. Government Printing Office.

Mistretta, C. M., & Bradley, R. M. (1983). Developmental changes in taste responses from glossopharyngeal nerve in sheep and comparisons with chorda tympani responses. *Developmental Brain Research, 11,* 107–117.

Moskowitz, H. R., Kumaraiah, V., Sharma, K. N., Jacobs, H. L., & Sharma, S. D. (1975). Cross cultural differences in simple taste preferences. *Science, 110,* 1217–1218.

Nisbett, R. E., & Gurwitz, S. B. (1970). Weight, sex and the eating behavior of human newborns. *Journal of Comparative and Physiological Psychology, 73,* 245–253.

Nowlis, G. H. (1973). Taste-elicited tongue movements in human newborns: An approach to palatability. In J. F. Bosma (Ed.), *Fourth symposium on oral sensation and perception* (pp. 292–303). Washington, DC: U.S. Government Printing Office.

Nowlis, G. H. (1977). From reflex to representation: Taste-elicited tongue movements in the human newborn. In J. M. Weiffenbach (Ed.), *Taste and development: The ontogeny of sweet preference* (pp. 190–204). Washington, DC: U.S. Government Printing Office.

Nowlis, G. H., & Kessen, W. (1976). Human newborns differentiate differing concentrations of sucrose and glucose. *Science, 191,* 865–866.

Peiper, A. (1963). *Cerebral function in infancy and childhood.* New York: Consultants Bureau.

Peto, E. (1936). Contributions to the development of smell feeling. *British Journal of Medical Psychology, 15,* 314–320.

Pfaffman, C. (1960). The pleasures of sensation. *Psychological Review, 67,* 253–268.

Pfaffman, C. (1978). The vertebrate phylogeny, neural code, and integrative processes of taste. In E. C. Carterette and M. P. Friedman (Eds.), *Handbook of Perception* (Vol. 6A, pp. 51–123). New York: Academic Press.

Pratt, K. C., Nelson, A. K., & Sun, K. H. (1930). The behavior of the newborn infant. *Ohio State University Studies, Contributions to Psychology,* No. 10.

Rieser, J., Yonas, A., & Wikner, K. (1976). Radial localization of odors by human newborns. *Child Development, 47,* 856–859.

Rosenblatt, J. S. (1972). Learning in newborn kittens. *Scientific American, 227,* 18–25.

Rovee, C. K. (1969). Psychophysical scaling of olfactory response to the aliphatic alcohols in human neonates. *Journal of Experimental Child Psychology, 7,* 245–254.

Russell, J. M. (1976). Human olfactory communication. *Nature (London), 260,* 520–522.

Silver, W. L., & Maruniak, J. A. (1981). Trigeminal chemoreception in the nasal and oral cavities. *Chemical Senses, 6,* 295–305.

Stein, M., Ottenberg, P., & Roulet, N. (1958). A study of the development of olfactory preferences. *AMA Archives of Neurology and Psychiatry, 80,* 264–266.

Steiner, J. E. (1977). Facial expressions of the neonate infant indicating the hedonics of food-related chemical stimuli. In J. M. Weiffenbach (Ed.), *Taste and development: The ontogeny of sweet preference* (pp. 173–189). Washington, DC: U.S. Government Printing Office.

Steiner, J. E. (1979). Human facial expressions in response to taste and smell stimulation. In H. Reese & L. P. Lipsitt (Eds.), *Advances in child development and behavior* (Vol. 13, pp. 257–293). New York: Academic Press.

Steiner, J. E., Daher, M., & Ganchrow, J. R. (1980). The intensity-dependent character of taste induced facial expressions (gustofacial reflex) in the neonate infant.

Stirnimann, F. (1936). Le gout et l'odorat du nouveau-né. *Revue Francaise Pediatrie, 12,* 453–485.

Vazquez, M., Pearson, P. B., & Beauchamp, G. K. (1982). Flavor preferences in malnourished Mexican infants. *Physiology and Behavior, 28,* 513–519.

Weiffenbach, J. M. (1972). Discrete elicited motions of the newborn's tongue. In J. F. Bosma (Ed.), *Third symposium on oral sensation and perception* (pp. 391–399). Springfield, IL: Thomas.

Weiffenbach, J. M. (1977). Sensory mechanisms of the newborn's tongue. In J. M. Weiffenbach (Ed.), *Taste and development: The ontogeny of sweet preference* (pp. 205–213). Washington, DC: U.S. Government Printing Office.

Wolff, P. H. (1966). The causes, controls and organization of behavior in the neonate. *Psychological Issues, 5*(1, Whole No. 17).

Wyrwicka, W. (1981). *The development of food preferences.* Springfield, IL: Thomas.

6

Touch, Motion, and Proprioception

JUDITH E. REISMAN

Program in Occupational Therapy
Department of Physical
*   Medicine and Rehabilitation*
University of Minnesota
Minneapolis, Minnesota 55455

I. INTRODUCTION

We think of infants as helpless but they are born with some exquisitely tuned sensory abilities. Although sight is still fuzzy and hearing muted, the neonate is equipped with a sense of touch that accurately homes in on the source of its meals, a sense of motion that triggers reflexes to protect it from falls, and a sense of its body parts that allows the infant to mold its body comfortably to that of its caretakers. Although these sensory systems are often neglected in favor of the study of the infant's "higher senses," one can readily see that these early-maturing systems are the basis for survival in an otherwise very immature organism.

This chapter will consider in sequence systems concerned with touch, pain, temperature, vestibular, and proprioceptive sensitivity. Each section begins with an introduction to the anatomy and physiology of a system, followed by an overview of its prenatal development. Next, for each sensory system infant sensitivity to stimulation is described. Then the effects of age, state, sex, stimulus magnitude, and conditioning upon responses in each modality are discussed. A final section describes the results of applying a combination of stimuli in attempts to either soothe or stimulate infants.

HANDBOOK OF INFANT
PERCEPTION, VOLUME 1

C. Perception of Light Touch

The studies of infant perception of tactile stimulation may be roughly divided according to the CNS divisions mentioned. Studies activating the spinothalamic system use filaments, brushes, or air puffs as light touch stimuli; electric shock, pins, or circumcision as painful stimuli; and hot and cold objects and liquids as temperature stimuli. Object manipulation opportunities generate information which is principally carried by the lemniscal (and spinocerebellar) tracts. This section will deal with changes in response to light touch as a function of age, state, body part, and sex of the infant. Studies of habituation patterns are also included.

1. Age

By birth, defensive movements to light touch have faded, and feeding reflexes such as rooting and sucking are easily elicited, but reflex maturation continues. Prechtl (1958) observed that the infant at birth makes sweeping side-to-side head movements (seemingly in search of the nipple) in response to touch anywhere in the perioral area. After a few days the receptive field response configuration changes so that the point touched dictates the direction of head turn. Prechtl (1958) suggests a test of how discrete the receptive field for this reflex has become. The examiner can run a finger slowly around the mouth area of an infant and observe the precisely directed head-following that results.

Another receptive field change was reported by Langworthy (1932b). He observed the plantar reflex and found that it can be initially elicited by touching any part of the infant's leg. Gradually, the receptive field becomes limited to just the plantar surface of the foot, perhaps, he suggests, as a result of increasing cortical inhibition.

Defensive movements are not entirely missing from the infant's repertoire, however. Lewkowicz, Gardner, and Turkewitz (1979) found that preterms exhibit more head turns away from perioral stimulation than fullterms, perhaps a demonstration of CNS immaturity. Secondly, fullterms (with good neurological status) make persistent arm, trunk and head movements to clear the nose and mouth of a diaper placed over the face. Lipsitt (1977) conjectures that these reflex responses to a life-threatening obstruction may form the basis for learning to keep one's airways clear. Since the reflex disappears between 2 and 4 months he proposes that some Sudden Infant Death Syndrome casualties (which usually occur between 2 and 4 months of age) may be babies who are relatively insensitive to this obstructive form of tactile stimulation. They do not get the benefit of practice in clearing responses before the support of the reflex fades.

Rose, Schmidt, and Bridger (1976) compared the tactile sensitivity of sleeping full- and preterm infants by touching their abdomens with Semmes–Weinstein filaments of three different diameters. Using heart rate change and limb movement as response measures, they found that only fullterms showed the expected heart rate acceleration to stimulation. In addition, the responsive limb movements of fullterms were more vigorous than those of preterms. The results seem to indicate higher thresholds to tactile sensation in gestationally younger infants; however, preterms tend to be hypotonic (Dubowitz, 1969) and display higher resting heart rate (Rose et al., 1976). Field, Dempsey, Hatch, Ting, and Clifton (1979) found initial increases in heart rate in both term and preterm infants to a slightly stronger tactile stimulus (thicker filament) applied to the abdomen. This lends support to the theory that preterm infants have higher stimulus thresholds. In addition, the preterm infants showed no heart rate deceleration in response to repeated stimulus applications, an indication of lack of habituation or presence of CNS immaturity.

Using an airpuff above the umbilicus as the stimulus, Gray and Crowell (1968) investigated infants at 2 days, 6 weeks, and 11 weeks to see if heart rate response to this stimulation changes with age. They found that newborns and 6-week-olds responded with heart rate acceleration, the response usually seen when the nervous system attempts to inhibit or block out noxious stimulation. By 11 weeks the response was one of deceleration, indicating an orienting response to an event of interest. Although they concluded that infants had learned by this age that "sudden, peripheral stimulation is not usually painful or noxious," one must remember that an airpuff above the tender umbilicus of a 2-day-old may indeed have been a noxious stimulus. In addition, as Gray and Crowell (1968) suggest, there is a greater likelihood that 11-week-olds will be awake during stimulation. As will be discussed below, differences in state have a profound effect upon type of heart rate response to tactile stimulation.

2. State

Prechtl and Beintema (1964) first outlined a uniform method of observing behavioral state in infants. Several studies followed which further elaborated the differences among the states. Lewis, Dodd, and Harwitz (1969), measuring heart rate responses to a filament drawn across the cheek, found a response difference between sleep and awake states in infants 2 to 6 weeks old. The sleeping infants showed heart rate acceleration and return to baseline while the awake infants showed heart rate deceleration in the same period of time (approximately 10 sec).

Yang and Douthitt (1974) recorded heart rate change to an air puff to the abdomens of newborns in both quiet (QS) and active sleep (AS). Heart rate acceleration occurred in both states. Rose, Schmidt, and Bridger (1978) replicated this result using filaments applied to the abdomen instead of air puffs. They found, however, that this effect only held for the first cycle of AS and QS. By the time the infants were in the second sleep cycle they were unresponsive to (this) stimulation, indicating that sensory threshold changes, not just as a function of state, but also as a function of time asleep. They postulated an inverted U-shaped curve for threshold, the highest point being approximately 1 hr after the infant falls asleep. While this time estimate of threshold sensitivity may be accurate, separating sleep cycle from amount of time asleep, as Rose *et al.* (1978) suggest, will indicate which factor is primary in determining sensitivity.

Some researchers have investigated the influence of state on tactile sensitivity using measures other than heart rate. For example, Lenard, von Bernuth, and Prechtl (1968) found that the exteroceptive reflexes such as the palmar, plantar, and Babkin are absent in QS, only occasionally present in AS, but almost always available when the newborn is quietly awake (QA). Lastly, Martinius and Papousek (1970) were able to obtain habituation to an airpuff to the eyelid (five consecutive no-blink responses) only when the newborn was in QS. In AS complete habituation was never accomplished. (The awake states were not examined.)

In summary, the infant's state has a profound effect on tactile responses. Heart rate decelerates to stimuli when the infant is awake but accelerates when asleep (in the first sleep cycle). Touch-elicited reflexes are absent in QS, but the infant can most easily habituate, at least to an airpuff to the eyelid, in this state.

3. Body Area

Another group of studies examined tactile sensitivity as a function of area of the body stimulated. Turkewitz (1977) acknowledges that head position to the left or right may influence responses to facial tactile input but found that even when the head was immobilized at midline for 15 min prior to stimulation a stroke on the right cheek more reliably elicited an ipsilateral head turn response than a stroke on the left. Passive immobilization for this short period of time, however, seems only a first step in neutralizing the influence of head position. A controversy in the literature has been attempting to resolve whether this effect is due to a sensory bias, motor bias, or some interaction between the two (Liederman & Kinsbourne, 1980a, 1980b; Turkewitz, 1980). Although Liederman and Kinsbourne propose an innate neural asymmetry that produces a tonic motor bias, they do not seem to disagree with Turkewitz' theory of multiple sensory and motor mechanisms producing the rightward head turning bias. Since all of these mechanisms are as yet unknown, further research must supplement these conjectures.[1]

While studies have mapped the thresholds to tactile stimulation in the adult (Weinstein, 1968), lack of verbal ability has prevented this type of study in infants. Denisova and Figurin (1977) have attempted to overcome this difficulty by making use of reflex responses to map the most sensitive body areas in the newborn. These "reflexogenic areas" in descending order of sensitivity are (1) the facial area, especially around the eyes, eyelids, nose, and lips as seen by squints, grimaces, and hand movements which seem to be precursors of rubbing an irritated spot; (2) the hands, which respond with flexion to palm and extension to dorsum input; (3) the soles, with the Babinski reflex; and (4) the abdomen, with its abdominal skin reflexes. Other areas of the body are assumed to be less sensitive since only diffuse movements or no response is seen to tactile stimulation. While Denisova and Figurin (1977) seem intuitively correct in their assessment of the most sensitive areas and replicate Peiper's (1963) results with painful and tickling stimuli, it is possible that an infant may be sensitive in an area that is not "wired" to make a reflexive response. Perhaps the use of somatosensory evoked potentials (SEP) holds promise for mapping not only the thresholds of newborns but any changes in thresholds with developmental or state changes. Only state differences have been recorded thus far using this method. Desmedt and Manil (1970) recorded different SEP patterns in newborns who were awake, in REM sleep, and in slow wave sleep using mild electric current applied to the fingertips as the stimulus.

4. Sex

The search for infant sex differences in tactile sensitivity has generally produced conflicting results confounded by such variables as weight, "chubbiness," and method of feeding (Bell & Costello, 1964). Jacklin, Snow, and Maccoby (1981) used the standard Semmes–Weinstein filaments and found no sex differences in a large ($N = 204$) sample of newborns. Weinstein (1968), however, has documented slightly greater tactile sensitivity in adult females. Either male and female infants are equally sensitive to tactile stimuli and develop differential sensitivities during

---

[1] The innateness of these sensorimotor mechanisms has been demonstrated by Cioni and Pellegrinetti (1982). They found that those infants with familial right hand dominance spent more time with their heads turned to the right and made their first head turn to the right when released from the midline position. Those infants with familial left hand dominance or ambidexterity showed no preference.

ontogenetic development or current tests of infant tactile sensitivity are not fine enough to discriminate among very subtle threshold differences.

The use of habituation techniques, on the other hand, has revealed clear sex differences. For example, Moreau, Helfgott, Weinstein, and Milner (1978) found female newborns required fewer trials to habituate to perioral stimulation than males. In even younger subjects Leader, Baillie, Bahia, and Elsebeth (1982) investigated age of onset of habituation to vibrotactile stimulation (electric toothbrush to mother's abdomen) in fetuses by means of ultrasound monitoring. They found that females showed habituation 2 weeks earlier (25–26 weeks) than males (28 weeks), although all showed it by 30 weeks gestational age. While one cannot conclude that this is evidence for sex differences in sensitivity to tactile stimuli, it points to the greater nervous system maturity of females, the mechanism assumed to underlie the ability to habituate.

5. Habituation

Several researchers have investigated other aspects of habituation to tactile input. Moreau (1976) found that newborns can habituate (as demonstrated by no significant change in heart rate) to a repeated stroke of one cheek. Attempts to elicit dishabituation by stroking the contralateral cheek were unsuccessful. Either the neonate does not discriminate between the two sides or perceives that the stimulation carries essentially the same (nonthreatening) information. Perhaps dishabituation would occur if another body area was stimulated on either the ipsilateral or contralateral side. This has not yet been investigated.

Despite the lack of contralateral dishabituation, there seem to be differences between the two sides. Moreau *et al.* (1978) found that the number of infants making ipsilateral head turns to left-side perioral stimulation decreased significantly over repeated trials compared to the number of infants making ipsilateral head turns to the right. The left-side response seems to habituate sooner, although the rightward motor bias discussed above (Liederman & Kinsbourne, 1980b) cannot be discounted.

Two research groups have looked at the course of habituation. Moreau, Birch, and Turkewitz (1970) recorded a significant decrease in the number of infants showing heart rate acceleration to cheek stroke on trial two versus trial one and viewed this as evidence of habituation. Pomerleau-Malcuit, Malcuit, and Clifton (1975), however, found no significant attenuation of heart rate acceleration on trials two through eight versus trial one. They question Moreau *et al.*'s (1970) interpretation and suggest that perhaps the response seen in trial one in both studies was a startle to the "sudden onset of an unexpected stimulus." Whatever the cause for the difference between the first two trials, simply defining habituation as the "first point in the sequence of repeated stimulations at which the number of infants responding was significantly less than that on the first trial" (Moreau et al., 1970) seems to focus on a result that is not consonant with the *pattern* of data presented. While it is true that in the Moreau et al. (1970) study a significantly fewer number of infants responded to tactile stimulation on trial two versus trial one, the majority of the 40 trials contained a large number of infants who responded by heart rate acceleration. The pattern across trials is quite jagged, with no more than two consecutive trials containing either large or small numbers of infants with heart rate acceleration. The data from Pomerleau-Malcuit et al.'s (1975) study seem to indicate that habituation to tactile stimulation as measured by heart rate change occurs slowly. Perhaps the use of mean heart rate is the more useful measure in exploring the course of habituation to tactile stimulation in a population with such individual trial by trial variability.

To summarize, the habituation literature suggests that (1) females habituate before males (at least up to newborn age); (2) the left perioral side habituates sooner than the right; (3) habituation to stimulation on one cheek may generalize to the other; and (4) in general, habituation to tactile stimulation occurs slowly.[2]

D. Perception of Pain

Sensitivity to the stimulation of pain and, to a lesser degree, all tactile stimuli is a difficult area of study in both adult and infant subjects. "Pain is a private experience" influenced not only by physiological states but also by psychological variables (Chapman, 1976). To study pain in infants one needs to control the level of arousal including time since feeding, the ability to quiet oneself, and other temperamental measures, as well as the influence of maternal medication and related perinatal factors. Because infants cannot give verbal responses, one must find behavioral and physiological measures that correlate with the application of a painful stimulus. This introduces the problem of immaturity in the response systems apart from the sensory systems' receptivity. In addition, the nature of the stimulation is limited by ethical considerations unique to this area of study.

The survival value of pain sensitivity is clear. Those without it are unable to judge whether the intensity of any type of sensory stimulation is too extreme and thus dangerous. Even in sleep one is protected. Lenard

---

[2] An interesting study (Ganchrow & Steiner, 1984) using tactile stimulation (forehead stroking) as the conditioned stimulus demonstrated the ease with which very young infants could be conditioned. The choice of stroking seemed successful as a stimulus because it is "biologically meaningful" and appropriate to a newborn's perceptual maturation.

et al. (1968) demonstrated that unlike the tendon and exteroceptive reflexes the nociceptive reflexes, those that respond to skin irritation, are present in all sleep and waking states.

Physicians are reluctant to impose pain needlessly and instead report behaviors observed in unavoidable painful situations (circumcision, burns, illness). Stoddard (1982), for example, characterizes the infant's reactions to burn pain as crying and body movement, followed (in cases of extended pain) by "withdrawal, a sad facial expression, eating and sleeping disturbances, and failure to respond positively to caretakers" (p. 737). He recommends the use of the caregiver for emotional support and analgesics to reduce pain and increase responsiveness to the caregiver.

These observations highlight the practical aspects of pain and pain management in children. The psychophysical questions, on the other hand, have generally been studied by psychologists who have focused on such variables as age, area stimulated, intensity of stimulation, and CNS intactness. For the most part they have recorded the behavioral responses of body movement and state change (crying). A newer set of studies has examined the physiological responses to circumcision and will also be briefly reviewed.

Perhaps the first systematic studies of pain in infants were those by the Shermans (Sherman & Sherman, 1925; Sherman, Sherman, & Flory, 1936). By applying pinpricks and small electric shocks to the cheeks and legs of newborns they were able to document an increase in pain sensitivity at least up to 4 days of age. In addition, they found that the face was consistently more sensitive than the leg, as it is in tactile sensitivity experiments (Weinstein, 1968).

An interesting pattern of response to facial pinprick stimulation was seen by the Shermans. Over one-third of the responses involved moving the contralateral hand to that area stimulated on the cheek. This "crossed flexor reflex" may be the beginning of the scratch response discussed by Peiper (1963) and seen as well in Crudden's (1937) temperature experiments. Scratching or rubbing an irritated spot serves to block the irritating sensation with a more neutral tactile one. A correlation between stimulus intensity and type of response was also seen. As the Shermans increased stimulus intensity, the incidence of these local "prescratching" responses diminished. They were replaced by more generalized startles and cries indicating at least a rudimentary response gradient.

Others have looked at pain sensitivity in newborns using electric shock stimuli and found essentially the same result. Over the first 4 days of life sensitivity increases, whether it is the big toe (Lipsitt & Levy, 1959) or calf (Kaye & Lipsitt, 1964) that is stimulated. This change in sensitivity may be partly influenced by an increase in skin conductance (Kaye, 1964) but Kaye and Lipsitt (1964) propose the second-order variables of maternal drugs, birthing effects, and state changes to account for at least a portion of the observed responses.

McGraw (1941) applied pinprick stimuli to a wide age range of subjects (0–4 years) and found a gradient of responsiveness and response behaviors with age change. Infants were increasingly responsive up to 10 to 30 days after birth. By 1 month body movements were less intense, perhaps indicating decreasing responsiveness as a result of increasing cortical inhibition and perhaps indicating increasing motor differentiation. The reflex withdrawal response seen in early infancy was replaced by deliberate withdrawal of the area pricked and gaze, when possible, to that area, an indication of improved voluntary motor ability and cognitive maturity. McGraw (1941) and Kauffman (1980) both found other evidence that the response to pain becomes mediated by cognitive processes. Up to about 1 year of age infants cry and otherwise react at the moment of painful stimulation. Older children, however, cry when they perceive the source of the pain (for example, the hypodermic needle) (Kauffman, 1980) and make deliberate attempts to protect themselves from the impending pain (McGraw, 1941).

The usefulness of such studies from any but a psychophysical perspective may be suspect until one turns to the work of Graham (1956; Graham, Matarazzo, & Caldwell, 1956). She compared the pain thresholds of normal and at-risk (for example, anoxic) fullterm infants in the first 5 days of life, using leg and other movements in response to shock just below the knee. The normal infants produced a slightly skewed bell-shaped sensitivity curve with the greatest percentage of infants responding to very mild painful stimuli. The high-risk infants were not only significantly less sensitive to stimulation but produced a bimodal curve of wide distribution. One peak was in the same range as that of the normal subjects while the second peak fell far below the lower limit of the normal curve, indicating that more intense stimuli were required to elicit threshold responses for some high-risk infants. If pain sensitivity can be taken as a measure of CNS responsiveness it may be a useful tool for discriminating among children with potentially compromised nervous systems. One must consider, however, that high-risk infants may have motor response systems which are also compromised and thus prevent researchers from accurate detection of pain and other sensitivities.[3]

Perhaps because limb movement is difficult to quantify and perhaps

---

[3] They may be similar to premature infants who do not cry or show generalized body movements as do fullterms. D'Apolito (1984) advises that one look instead for eye rolling, seizures, breath holding, vomiting, and chemical changes.

because ethics committees are reluctant to approve studies that deliberately inflict pain, there are new directions in pain-related research. The newer studies take advantage of the practice of circumcision as a painful stressor and measure physiological responses. Of course, these researchers do not claim to be investigating pain *per se* and recognize that circumcision entails many interacting types of stress such as delay in feeding, physical restraint, and tissue damage (Gunnar, Fisch, Korsvik, & Donhowe, 1981), but while the earlier studies had "cleaner" stimuli these later studies may claim more easily quantified response measures.

Emde, Harmon, Metcalf, Koenig, and Wagonfeld (1971) recorded the respiratory rate, EEG, and eye movements of infants on the nights before and immediately after circumcision. On the first night postsurgery circumcised infants showed differences in non-REM sleep characterized by shorter latency to, increased number of, and increased duration of non-REM sleep episodes when compared to noncircumcised infants. Emde et al. (1971) hypothesize that these sleep changes are an adaptive response to painful stress since sensory thresholds in non-REM sleep are higher than in any other state. Anders and Chalemian (1974) found increased wakefulness instead of increased non-REM sleep but unfortunately only sampled for three of the 10 hr in the period used by Emde et al. (1971). A replication using the full 10-hr period may help clarify these data. To aid in settling the question of whether sleep is disturbed as a result of pain or as a consequence of the tissue repair process Emde et al. (1971) suggest a comparison of groups circumcised with and without local analgesics. This design, however, will isolate the variable of pain only as long as the analgesic is present. Care must also be used in selecting analgesics that do not themselves produce drowsiness or state changes.

Other studies have found correlations between circumcision and plasma cortisol levels with sharp rises recorded during and 20–40 min after the procedure (Gunnar et al., 1981; Talbert, Kraybill, & Potter, 1976). However, the corresponding change in behavioral state accompanying circumcision is also correlated with raised levels of cortisol (Gunnar et al., 1981; Tennes & Carter, 1973), making it difficult to tease apart primary and secondary effects. Perhaps this is a moot point since state changes will always be confounded with intense pain.

In summary, pain sensitivity appears to increase in the first month of life (and perhaps longer). Responses then diminish or become more differentiated and come increasingly under cognitive control. This makes assessment of absolute sensitivities difficult. The later circumcision studies document physiological changes in response to the procedure, but pain sensitivity *per se* can only be inferred. Comparisons of age and state effects with circumcision are as yet minimal (Gunnar et al., 1981).

E. Perception of Temperature

The studies dealing with infant temperature perception may be divided into those using changes in ambient temperature as the stimulus and those using changes in the temperature of objects applied to local areas of the body. Of course, the newborn is sensitive to ambient temperature since it must start regulating its body temperature at birth. The mechanism for accomplishing this maintenance of relatively high body temperature (approximately 98.6°F) compared to relatively cool ambient temperature (usually 72–78°F) is not fully mature for a few days (Spears & Hoyle, 1967). One- to 5-day-olds exposed to ambient cold undergo a drop in body temperature (Mestyan & Varga, 1960), indicating imperfect thermoregulation. This immature mechanism is one of the main reasons for carefully controlling the environments of preterm and newborn infants.[4]

Sensitivity to ambient temperature change may be demonstrated by simply uncovering a newborn. This usually results in respiratory changes, movement, and perhaps even crying (Denisova & Figurin, 1977). Mestyan and Varga (1960) examined the behavior and oxygen consumption of fullterm and preterm newborns exposed to a drop in ambient temperature and found that the infants tended to awaken, engage in restless movements, and increase oxygen consumption. The restlessness is thought to be an adaptive behavior designed to increase heat production. Since oxygen consumption decreased when the infants fell asleep, its use was most likely in response to the needs of moving muscles. Generally, all babies exposed to ambient cold exhibit these behaviors. By 6 days of age the combination of a more mature thermoregulatory mechanism and body movement keeps the infant's body temperature at an optimum level.

The response to a rise in ambient temperature has been investigated in two studies. Cooke (1952) recorded the caloric and fluid intake in babies up to 6 months old exposed to 81°F and 91°F environments. His results show that while mean caloric intake fell from 120 to 105 calories/day, total fluid intake was unchanged. As the ambient temperature rose water intake increased and milk intake decreased. Since one of the main functions of caloric intake is to provide fuel for the maintenance of body temperature it seems adaptive for the infants to limit caloric intake when the demands for heating the body are lessened.

Harpin, Chellappah, and Rutter (1983) increased the ambient temperature in the incubators of fullterm and preterm infants by 1 to 2°C increments every 30 min. Monitoring physiological and behavioral signs, they

---

[4] For an excellent review of the thermoregulatory mechanisms of premature infants and issues to consider in control of the NICU thermal environment, see Moffat and Hackel (1985).

278   JUDITH E. REISMAN

observed that (1) preterms are not able to sweat and thus do not yet have access to this cooling mechanism and (2) that both pre- and fullterm newborns do not pant when hot. Harpin et al. (1983) conclude that this panting behavior is limited to adults and animals (but children were not investigated in this study). Virtually all babies showed skin reddening, indicating that peripheral vasodilation operates as a cooling mechanism. In addition, almost all the babies became less active and, if awake, fell asleep regardless of time since last feeding. At all gestational ages babies assumed the "sunbathing" posture, moving from flexed to extended positions, thereby exposing as much body surface as possible in an adaptive attempt to cool off. These researchers note that observation of common body postures may be a good clue for caretakers in determining whether babies are too cold or hot. The above studies provide information about infant responses to changes in ambient temperature. One of the most common errors caretakers make, however, is over- or underdressing infants. A practical addition to the existing literature would be a study varying ambient temperature with amount of clothing.

To summarize, the infant's behavioral responses to changes in ambient temperature include (1) waking and movement to cooling temperatures and (2) decreased caloric intake, sleep, peripheral vasodilation, and "sunbathing" postures to warming. Sweating and panting behaviors seem to mature more slowly.

Studies of infant responses to local stimulation, while performed some 40 years ago, are still good demonstrations of temperature sensitivity. Crudden (1937) provides an excellent review of the methods and results of this research up to 1937. Some of the earliest studies examined the effect of changes in milk temperature. Pratt, Nelson, and Sun (1930) and Jensen (1932) found that infants sucked most vigorously when milk was at body temperature. In addition, while Pratt et al. (1930) found that infants responded less strongly (i.e., sucking was less disturbed) to milk above body temperature than milk below body temperature, Jensen (1932) found that infants showed similar disturbance of sucking patterns with both hot and cold extremes. A replication may help clarify this result.

Crudden (1937) adopted for his research a method that isolated temperature from tactile stimulation. A hollow tube was affixed to the leg of sleeping infants and water of different temperatures was piped through it. Recording respiratory changes, limb movement, reaction time, and state changes Crudden found responses to temperature changes as small as 5 to 6°C. Schendell (1944, cited in Peiper, 1963) provides a replication with essentially the same results, using a water tube attached to the chest. Infants responded to temperature changes as small as 6 to 7°C, especially in the range 43–30°C. As in the milk temperature experiment (Pratt et al.,

1930) cold elicited more reaction than warm. In general, all changes moving away from neutral (body temperature) to hot or cold evoked more response than stimuli returning to neutral (Crudden, 1937). Yet adaptation to each new temperature must have occurred quite rapidly because even when returning to neutral some response was noted (Crudden, 1937).

State change in response to temperature stimulation in sleeping infants was found to consist of a short awakening at the moment of stimulation followed by a rapid return to sleep (Crudden, 1937). When the stimulus was not sufficient to provoke full awakening Schmidt and Birns (1971) found that responsiveness was a function of sleep state and cycle. As in the Rose et al. (1978) study using tactile stimuli, infants in the first sleep cycle were more responsive to temperature stimuli than in later cycles. Within the first cycle those in QS usually responded with a jerk or startle to a cold disc applied to the abdomen, but in AS a simple increase in general activity was seen. While the cold disc is clearly temperature and tactile stimulation its sudden application to the abdomen must have been noxious to the sleeping infants. A control condition using a disc at body temperature would help to isolate temperature from abrupt tactile stimulation.

Spatially directed responses to temperature change may be seen even at very young ages (1–2 days). Crudden (1937) observed that some infants made contralateral leg movements against the tube in a seeming attempt to "scratch" the disturbing stimulus. Sometimes these movements were incomplete or anticipatory and at other times so successful that the tube had to be replaced. In another demonstration of spatially directed responses, Stirnimann (1939, cited in Peiper, 1963) held warm and cold glass tubes to the cheeks of 1-day-olds. He observed mouth opening and head turning toward the warm tube and restlessness and head turning away from the cold tube, clear evidence of temperature discrimination. Schendell (1944, cited in Peiper, 1963) elaborated this study by controlling for the hunger state of his subjects. He found that when a heat source was held near but not touching the cheek of a hungry infant s/he turned toward the source. After feeding most of the infants did not turn. The adaptive significance of this behavior is evident. The spatially directed response to temperature seems very effective in helping the infant find a meal.[5]

One last study of temperature perception seems to clarify the nature of the stimulus eliciting the palmar grasp reflex. Far from being an obligatory reflex to tactile stimulation of the palm, Stirnimann (1939, cited in Peiper,

[5] Bushnell (1986) demonstrated that 6-month-olds can reliably discriminate temperature changes in objects. Following a familiarization period, they touched and looked longer at the object of novel temperature.

1963) found that infants responded on the basis of temperature discrimination. When the temperature of a small tube pressed to the palms of the infants was 28°C all 30 infants grasped the tube. At 23°C only 15 did. Five responded when the tube was 16°C and none of the 30 infants grasped a 10°C tube. It is intriguing to think that at this young age there is already some perceptual discrimination influencing the strength of this reflex.

In summary, the infant's response to local temperature stimuli may be characterized as (1) possibly more reactive to cold but responsive to both cold and heat, (2) affected by state and sleep cycle, and (3) spatially directed.

F. Haptic Perception

The last group of studies to be reviewed in this section will deal with the more complex kind of information gained from manipulation. The questions researchers ask in this area are how early and how efficiently can infants use the tactile–proprioceptive information available to them. The research paradigm employed is generally one of familiarizing the infant with one object, either visually or hapticly and recording the amount of manipulation and/or looking time to the novel versus familiar object.

Gottfried, Rose, and Bridger (1977) attached a shape to a pacifier and placed it in the mouths of 1-year-old subjects for a period of familiarization. In the test period the subjects looked at and reached for the *novel* object significantly more than the familiar object. In 1979, Meltzoff and Borton performed the same type of experiment using 1-month-old subjects. In the test phase the majority of these subjects fixated the *familiar* object significantly longer than the novel object. E. Gibson and Walker (1984) used the same experimental technique with 1-month-olds but investigated substance (spongy versus rigid) instead of shape. They found that infants in the test phase looked longer at the *novel* display. One-year-olds given a chance to manipulate the objects in their hands in the substance experiments (E. Gibson & Walker, 1984) subsequently looked more at the *familiar* test display. The fact that each age group fixated different test displays (novel versus familiar) and that within each age group a different display was fixated in each study is puzzling. E. Gibson and Walker (1984) propose several possible explanations. Nevertheless, the results of each study indicate that subjects were able to gain information through haptic exploration.

The above experiments provided opportunity for tactile familiarization but used a strictly visual test phase. Gottfried and Rose (1980) allowed 1-year-olds to see the familiarization shape they manipulated but conducted the test phase in the dark. They found that even here infants were able to discriminate the novel shape by the haptic information alone as measured by the amount of time spent manipulating the novel versus familiar object. Infants younger than 1 year (6- and 9-month-olds) were unable to perform this task (Gottfried, Rose, & Bridger, 1978). Gottfried *et al.* (1978) suggest that the act of manipulation by these younger subjects may interfere with the ability to gain shape information even though they can see the shape.

Lastly, two experiments demonstrate that infants can detect and use tactile information without visual cues in either familiarization or test phases. When the entire study was conducted in the dark, Rose, Gottfried, and Bridger (1981) found that 1-year-olds showed form discrimination, as evidenced by their longer manipulation of the novel test objects. Soroka, Corter, and Abramovitch (1979) provided younger infants (8.5–10.5 months) with a similar task and found that those infants given the novel shape in the test phase manipulated it almost twice as long as those infants given the familiar shape in the test phase. This experiment helps pinpoint one source of the infants' difficulty in the Gottfried *et al.* (1978) study. Concurrent visual, haptic, and motor cues tax the ability of these subjects to process all this information. Eliminating the visual information eases the processing burden, freeing the infants to attend to the haptic form cues. Given suitable tasks, then, it appears that young infants are able to use haptic information to discriminate shapes.[6]

III. THE VESTIBULAR SYSTEM

The vestibular system is one of the sensory systems designed to register head motion and the often accompanying body motion. It is also the system that registers the pull of gravity. Each time the head is turned or moved through space in any manner as, for example, in nodding the head, sitting down, walking, or riding in a vehicle, the receptors of the vestibular system are activated. While the sensing of head and self motion is relatively easy to comprehend, it is a little more difficult to understand a mechanism that senses something as pervasive and constant as the pull of gravity. As Holt (1975, p. 2) explains, "gravity cannot be seen. Consequently it is very easy to overlook the important influence of this strong force. (But) many of the earliest activities of infants are concerned with achieving and holding stable postures against the influence of gravity."

---

[6] Two studies (Rose, Gottfried, & Bridger, 1983; Bushnell, 1986) demonstrate that length of tactual familiarization time affects 6- and 12-month-old (respectively) infants' ability to make visual–tactual matches. In addition, Ruff (1984) found that both 9- and 12-month-olds employ different manipulation techniques, presumably to gain information about object characteristics, when texture, shape, and weight are varied.

Beginning with the righting reflexes (which align the head and body with the pull of gravity and are first seen in utero) and progressing to the equilibrium reactions [which "help one maintain or regain a given posture" (Ayres, 1973)] the developing human body continually strives to keep itself in the best possible position for locomotion and/or skilled movement. While adults can often use visual cues to compensate for vestibular problems, infants and children so affected show "loss of postural control and delay of gross motor function" (Kaga, Suzuki, Marsh, & Tanaka, 1981). This makes the study of normal vestibular system functioning a necessary prelude to diagnosis and intervention for vestibular problems.

Anatomically, the vestibular system consists of a pair (one set per ear) of fluid-filled structures. In each inner ear are three semicircular canals oriented in three different planes and sensitive to angular acceleration and deceleration in those planes. A swelling at one end of each canal, the ampulla, contains cilia embedded in a gelatinous mass, the cupula. When the head (and its attached body) moves, the endolymph presses against the cupula. This in turn bends the cilia, triggering nerve impulses signifying movement. Two sacs, the utricle and saccule, register linear acceleration, including the pull of gravity, and head tilt with respect to gravity. Tiny calcium carbonate crystals or otoliths, denser than the surrounding endolymph, rest on and bend the nerve hair cells in these sacs stimulating them to signal both the tonic pull of gravity and static head position as well as phasic changes in the position of the head as it moves through space (Howard, 1973). Impulses arising in the semicircular canals, utricle, and saccule are carried along the vestibular portion of the eighth cranial nerve to the brain stem vestibular nuclei and to the cerebellum. It is here that sensations from many sensory systems are integrated (Ayres, 1973). Some of the brain stem-initiated impulses then travel down the vestibulospinal tract to the extensor or antigravity muscles to adjust muscle tone as the body moves in and out of equilibrium. Other messages travel by way of the medial longitudinal fasciculus to the cranial nerve nuclei innervating the extraocular eye muscles. These signals mediate the compensatory eye movements made in response to head movement. All of this is accomplished smoothly, automatically, and for the most part, below the level of conscious awareness.

A. Prenatal Development

The vestibular system develops very early and is almost completely mature at birth. In fact, the first weak responses to movement stimulation may be seen in a fetus as young as 10 weeks gestational age (Minkowski,

1928, cited in Humphrey, 1970). By 12 weeks the first vestibulo-ocular reflexes are present although they are not reliably established until the twenty-fourth week (Hamilton & Mossman, 1972). By the fifth fetal month the system is almost as responsive as that of an adult, as several behaviors demonstrate. For example, a Moro reflex is seen to sudden movement by the mother (Wyke, 1975) and the fetus can orient itself in the amnion by "labyrinthine-activated kicking" (Elliott & Elliott, 1964). This ability to orient is important in ensuring that the head down or vertex presentation is assumed for birth. While births in other positions are not unknown, the incidence of abnormal births is significantly elevated under conditions affecting the fetal ear (for example, deafness) and presumably the labyrinths (Barton, Court, & Walker, 1962).

Structurally, the vestibular end organs have started to form by 7.5 weeks gestational age (Bradley & Mistretta, 1975). At 16 weeks, when myelination of the CNS begins, the first point of myelination is the vestibular nerve. In fact, two of the first three central tracts to myelinate carry vestibular messages, the vestibulospinal tract and the medial longitudinal fasciculus (Langworthy, 1932a). One can only speculate on the importance of a sensory system that matures 4 months before birth in an organism that has so many other immature systems at birth.

B. Eye Movement Responses

By far the greatest number of studies of the infant vestibular system have involved measuring eye movement responses to rotation. Even before electronystagmography (ENG) was in use, observations were made that documented the presence of nystagmus in neonates (Heck, 1952; Laurence & Feind, 1953). With the advent of ENG techniques, recording could be done in the dark, thus eliminating fixation and optokinetic effects. Tibbling (1969) compared the response of newborns (0–5 days) to older children (3 months to 15 years) and found developmental differences. Most newborns responded to rotation with sustained eye deviation in the direction of the slow component of what will become nystagmus. The 3-month-old subjects displayed adultlike perrotary nystagmus of the same duration as the newborns' eye deviation. Since for the most part the slow phase is peripherally controlled and the fast phase centrally controlled, Tibbling (1969) proposes that the response in newborns is a function of relatively mature peripheral receptors but immature CNS function.

The simple presence of nystagmus (versus eye deviation), then, may be used as an index of CNS maturity. This was investigated further by the Eviatars (Eviatar, Eviatar, & Naray, 1974) using the torsion swing and ice-cold caloric methods. Like Tibbling (1969) they found mainly eye deviation in newborns but by 20 to 30 days 84% of normal-weight fullterms had developed nystagmus to both types of stimulation. This was in contrast to only 24% of smaller-than-normal fullterms and none of the premature infants. Upon retesting 3–4 months later all the infants exhibited nystagmus. This seems to implicate birth weight and accompanying CNS maturity as crucial elements in the development of nystagmus.

In a second study (Eviatar, Miranda, Eviatar, Freeman, & Borkowski, 1979) a comparison was made of the magnitude of the nystagmus response among fullterm large (LGA), appropriate (AGA), and small (SGA) for gestational age and premature infants using the same torsion swing and ice-cold caloric methods of stimulation. In the 0–3 month age group the largest responses evoked were in the largest babies (LGA) with magnitude of response diminishing as a function of birth weight and gestational age. By 6 months the groups' responses were similar and by 1 year indistinguishable. Low birth weight and prematurity seem to accompany a pronounced but transient delay in the appearance of nystagmic responses to vestibular stimulation. The Eviatars caution, therefore, that the absence of nystagmus in the first 6 months should not be interpreted as pathology but as nervous system immaturity.

A replication by Rossi et al. (1979) produced the same results but with one interesting addition. "During the 45th week the percentage of positive responses by AGA infants increased as gestational age decreased" (p. 220). Fourteen of 16 fullterm AGAs born at 38 to 39 weeks showed nystagmus at 45 weeks while only 10 of 25 born at 41 to 42 weeks did. Once a certain critical period of development is reached extrauterine environmental stimulation seems to foster CNS maturity. Even though premature infants show delayed responses compared to fullterms, it would be interesting to investigate whether those born 6 weeks early, for example, will show nystagmus responses sooner than preterms born 3 weeks early. As Rossi et al. (1979) suggest, studies that correlate the age of first appearance of this vestibular response with later developmental gains and delays may be useful as a first step in identifying vestibular system deficits.

Several researchers have observed the response to rotation of infants and children and documented developmental changes in the specific components of nystagmus (slow and fast phase velocity, duration, amplitude, and frequency). There is some evidence (Henriksson, 1955; Tibbling, 1969) that slow component speed is most related to peripheral vestibular responsiveness, while slow component amplitude depends in large part upon when the slow phase is interrupted by the fast and is, therefore, a measure of central function (Tibbling, 1969). These two qualities of nystagmus may be used, then, in comparing central and peripheral functions when charting both normal developmental changes and pathology.

In general, the trend is for the components to diminish in magnitude with increasing age. This is true for both slow and fast phase velocities as well as slow phase amplitude (Ornitz, Atwell, Walter, Hartmann, & Kaplan, 1979; Tibbling, 1969). The rate of change, however, is not linear. Ornitz et al. (1979) found that while there is a decrement in response (to rotary stimulation) up to at least age seven the greatest changes occur prior to 30 months of age. Using the ice-cold caloric test Eviatar et al. (1979) found the reverse trend. The speed of the slow component and its amplitude both increased in preterm and fullterm infants over the course of the first year. One wonders if this unilateral, intense stimulation would continue to produce the same trend in results after 1 year of age or whether the vigor of the response would decline as central maturation and inhibition increase.

C. Muscle Tone

The developing vestibular system also influences muscle tone. Although early researchers were unable to observe changes in the newborn's muscle tone in response to vestibular stimulation, Antonova and Vakhrameeva (1973) have been able to do so by recording the Hoffman reflex (H-reflex). This monosynaptic reflex indicates the excitability of the motor neuron pool being stimulated. Infants in the QA state were tested during the first 6 days of life, some longitudinally. Vestibular stimulation was applied by raising and lowering an infant seat from horizontal to 52° above horizontal with electrical nerve stimulation applied at various points in the arc. Muscle tone responses to this stimulation were recorded electromyographically with the following results: (1) the H-reflex is less stable in newborns than adults; (2) on the first day of life only inhibitory vestibulospinal influences on the H-reflex can be recorded; and (3) by the second day facilitory as well as inhibitory vestibulospinal influences may be seen. The vestibular system, therefore, does play a role in regulating muscle tone in the neonate.

D. State

Although the above subjects were studied in one behavioral state, muscle tone and state do interact (Prechtl, Vlach, Lenard, & Grant, 1967). Further investigation might demonstrate whether infants in other behavioral states respond to vestibular stimulation with the same type and magnitude of muscle tone changes.

In other studies the influence of subject state is seen upon eye movement responses to vestibular stimulation. Sleeping or drowsiness abolishes both the perrotary (Eviatar & Eviatar, 1978) and postrotary (Laurence & Feind, 1953) nystagmus responses. The vestibulo-ocular reflex (compensatory eye movements in response to head movement), on the other hand, is preserved at the same high amplitude in the awake and AS states, but is diminished in amplitude or abolished in the QS state (von Bernuth & Prechtl, 1969). The mechanism for this effect is not yet clear (von Bernuth & Prechtl, 1969).

Pomerleau and Malcuit (1981) have replicated earlier findings (Pomerleau-Malcuit & Clifton, 1973) that heart rate responses to vestibular stimulation are dependent upon state. In the sleeping infant rocking causes a sharp rise in heart rate, while the awake infant responds with deceleration (Pomerleau-Malcuit & Clifton, 1973) or no heart rate change (Pomerleau & Malcuit, 1981). While these studies provide preliminary data concerning the influence of state on initial heart rate response to vestibular stimulation, the effect of one type of vestibular stimulation, no matter how "biologically significant," cannot be taken as the prototypical response to all types of vestibular stimulation. Studies that vary the duration, angle, intensity, and rhythmicity of stimulation with state of the infant will provide a more complete picture of this system's responsiveness. Some of these studies are discussed in a later section of this review.

E. Conditioning

A final group of studies attempted to determine whether movement is an effective conditioned stimulus. Soviet psychologists propose a developmental order in which various conditioned stimuli become effective (Kasatkin, 1969). The list begins with vestibular (and progresses through auditory, tactile, olfactory, gustatory, and thermal) stimulation. Between the tenth and twenty-seventh day of life the first naturally occurring conditioned reflex is seen in response to the infant's being placed in the feeding position (Denisova & Figurin, 1925, cited in Kasatkin, 1969). This evokes anticipatory head and mouth movements. The stimulus, however, combines vestibular, tactile, and proprioceptive inputs. To test the effectiveness of a vestibular stimulus alone Nemanova (1935, cited in Kasatkin, 1969) paired rocking with an airpuff to the eyelid and rocking with sucking on a milk bottle. She found that by 13 to 15 days of age the onset of rocking alone was sufficient to trigger a blink response. Similarly, sucking movements in the absence of the bottle were seen in response to rocking by the time infants were 21–24 days old. An even finer discrimination was made by infants near the end of the second and beginning of the third month of life (Nemanova, 1935, cited in Kasatkin 1969). They showed the ability to discriminate between side-to-side and up–down rocking as seen in a conditioned blink response to movement in one direction but not the other! The conditioning paradigm presents problems in young infants because of the variable states and responsiveness of the subjects and the time necessary to achieve results, but when such clear evidence of discrimination can be shown it seems worthwhile.

One other study has been performed using the conditioning paradigm. Evans (1980) paired movement of the bassinet of newborns with presentation of dextrose for 20 trials. The control group received the same amount of movement and dextrose but in randomly ordered presentations. Number of sucks was recorded during extinction trials in which the bassinet was moved but no dextrose was presented. The experimental group made significantly more sucks than the control group in this period, particularly just after each movement stimulus. Evans (1980) postulated that babies have an organization at birth that pairs movement with "enhancement of sucking during feeding." Whether this is true, it seems evident that movement is a powerful stimulus in conditioning experiments.

In summary, the early-maturing vestibular system has a pervasive influence on many of the most fundamental operations of the body—the sensing of motion, the maintenance of equilibrium, the control of eye movements. Further study on the relationship between normal and abnormal functioning and later achievement is clearly warranted.

IV. THE PROPRIOCEPTIVE SYSTEM

A. Introduction

Classically, proprioception refers to sensory information from within the body that indicates where the body parts are, how they are moving, and how much effort to use in particular movements. For example, proprioception provides information without one's looking as to whether one's arm is straight or bent, whether one's foot is swinging or still, and just how much effort to use in holding a Styrofoam cup without dropping or crushing it. The behaviors seen in a newborn that indicate s/he is using proprioceptive information are the reflex patterns called "active postural adjustments" (Casaer, 1979). Although one is not usually aware of proprioception unless attention is focused upon it, proprioception aids in maintaining normal muscle tone and in controlling both reflexive and skilled movement. Thus, as the infant develops, proprioception forms the substrate for such purposeful movements as reaching, imitation, and locomotion.

The receptors for proprioception consist mainly of the joint receptors, muscle spindles, and Golgi tendon organs. These respond to changes in the joint angles as well as changes in muscle length and tension. Because some muscles are always stretched even when the body is at rest, proprioceptive impulses are continually occurring. These help in monitoring the muscle tone needed to maintain body position and posture. Impulses arising from the proprioceptors travel by way of the lemniscal and spinocerebellar tracts to the brain stem and cerebellum and from there to the thalamus and neocortex. Integration with other senses occurs at each level, but even in the neocortex most of the sensations are processed in areas below the level of consciousness (Ayres, 1979).

B. Prenatal Development

Developmentally, effects of proprioception can be detected soon after the tactile and vestibular systems have become responsive. Langworthy (1932b) observed that the first proprioceptive reflex pattern is actually that of muscle tone. By 2 months gestational age an extremity passively moved will return to its original position (Minkowski, 1928, cited in Langworthy, 1932b). In addition, Fitzgerald and Windle (1942) report that when the limb of an 11-week-old fetus is flipped (i.e., stretched) a reflex limb movement results. As in the adult, these tendon and muscle responses are local and not the same as the total body patterns seen at this age to light touch stimulation (Humphrey, 1953).

Anatomically, the muscle spindle begins to differentiate between the eleventh and twelth gestational week, although functional maturity is not reached until the twenty-fourth to thirty-first week (Bergstrom & Bergstrom, 1963, cited in Wyke, 1975). The Golgi tendon organ, on the other hand, does not start to differentiate until the fourth month. The joints at this time still contain only free nerve endings but no specialized receptors (Hromada, 1960, cited in Humphrey, 1964). Full structural maturity for the proprioceptors does not occur until some time after birth (Casaer, 1979).

C. State

State has a profound effect on proprioceptively controlled behaviors, as several researchers have documented. The tendon reflexes—knee jerk, biceps jerk, ankle clonus—are as strong in QS (Casaer, 1979), as they are in the QA state (Prechtl et al., 1967). In AS the proprioceptive reflexes are greatly diminished or absent (Lenard et al., 1968), probably as a result of descending inhibition. This inhibition acts on the alpha motor neurons to the muscles as well as the gamma loop system carrying neural impulses from the muscles. The result is not only a decrease in motor activity but a diminished sensitivity to limb motion and stretch (Casaer, 1979). Thus both the afferents carrying the stimulation and the efferents carrying the response to the stimulation are inhibited in the AS state.

D. Conditioning

Support for the effectiveness of proprioception as a conditioned stimulus is seen in the work of the Russian psychologists. The study by Denisova and Figurin (1925, cited in Kasatkin, 1969) already mentioned in the vestibular section is relevant here. In that study the movement to a feeding position (the conditioned stimulus for sucking movements) involved proprioceptive as well as vestibular input. Other researchers paired arm movement (Kaye, 1965) and foot movement (Kasatkin, 1949, cited in Kasatkin, 1969) with elicitation of feeding reflexes and found stable responses by 3 to 4 months. Perhaps the most striking demonstration of the early effectiveness of proprioception in conditioning is a set of studies by Vakhrameeva (1958, 1964, cited in Kasatkin, 1969). She paired arm motion with the presentation of an airstream to the eyelid. When the infant's arm had moved from the fully extended to the fully flexed position the air stream stopped. In the test phase application of the air stream resulted in the infant voluntarily moving his/her arm! This was a stable response as early as 1.5 to 2 months.

E. Proprioception and Life Skills

The investigation of how infants use proprioception in mastering the natural tasks of infancy has produced some ingenious studies. Proprioception is involved in tasks which require that the infant coordinate his/her unseen movements with a visual display. Von Hofsten and Lindhagen (1979) found infants as young as 4 months amazingly effective in making hand contact with a moving object. Even though infants this young are not skilled in grasping, they could contact an object moving at speeds up to 30 cm/sec. To do this "the infant not only has to correctly perceive the spatial parameters of the surrounding space and the motion characteristics of the moving object, but must correctly judge his own capacities when acting in this situation" (von Hofsten & Lindhagen, 1979, p. 170). These capacities depend upon the coordination of proprioceptive and efferent messages that enable the infant to stabilize the trunk and shoulder and to reach to a certain point at a certain speed with the hand and arm.[7]

Another instance of the skilled use of proprioceptive information was documented by Bigelow (1981) in a study of toddlers' visual self-recognition. Eighteen-month-olds confronted with a mirror or videotaped image of themselves spontaneously engaged in repetitive body movements while intently watching the visual display. To master the cognitive task of visual self-recognition they needed to perceive the match between the proprioceptive information from body movement and simultaneous visual information from the mirror. The fact that children recognized the *moving* images of themselves sooner than stationary photographs attests to the salience of this proprioceptive information. While Bigelow (1981) used subjects who were 18 months old, Dixon (1957) has seen similar movement-testing behavior in children as young as 7 months. It is common knowledge that children handle objects to gain haptic information; it appears also that they purposefully move their body parts in order to gain proprioceptive information.

The ability to maintain upright posture, another "life skill," depends upon the ability to interpret and respond to information about body sway. When the body sways, several sensory systems are activated. Because the head moves through space the vestibular system is called into play. The stretch on the muscles and change in joint angles activate the proprioceptors. Finally, as the head moves forward and back on the swaying body, changes in the visual field give visual information about movement and posture (Lee & Aronson, 1974). To the conventional definition of proprioception as information about the body from the muscles and joints, Lee and Aronson (1974) add this visual information about the body and name it visual proprioception. To test the dominance of the two types of proprioception, mechanical and visual, infants stood (Lee & Aronson, 1974) or sat (Butterworth & Hicks, 1977) in a specially constructed room whose suspended walls could swing above the stationary floor. Because the floor was stationary traditional proprioceptive and vestibular information indicated the body was stable. However, when the suspended walls were gently moved visual information specified a swaying body and caused a real disruption of equilibrium. The majority of subjects in the first study (Lee & Aronson, 1974) responded with a sway, stagger, or fall as a result of making compensatory responses to the misleading visual

---

[7] The maturation of this visual-proprioceptive ability is explored in two studies demonstrating adjustment in hand orientation as infants reach to objects in different orientations (Lockman, Ashmead, & Bushnell, 1984; von Hofsten & Fazel-Zandy, 1984). Infrared filming of infants in darkness as they reach for a glowing rod in different orientations would separate the influence of visual from proprioceptive guidance in this task.

information. The majority of subjects in the second study (Butterworth & Hicks, 1977) also responded to the visual cues but mainly with a sway from the more stable sitting posture. These results indicate that infants rely heavily upon visual proprioception in the maintenance of stable postures.[8,9]

In summary, proprioception forms a substrate of information upon which movement, both reflexive and skilled, operates.

V. SOOTHING AND STIMULATION STUDIES

Most of the studies reviewed thus far have examined either the infant's sensory threshold or the infant's ability to make use of sensory information. In the past 15 years there has been a growing number of studies concerned with the effects of application of suprathreshold stimulation on both short-term and long-term behavior and development (Schaefer, Hatcher, & Barglow, 1980). These studies may be divided into those investigating attempts to soothe infants and those investigating attempts to stimulate them.

A. Soothing

The ability to calm a crying infant is seen by professionals and parents alike as a sign of caregiver effectiveness. With the increase in reported cases of child abuse more studies have focused on defining some of the specific skills that parents and others can use in order to avert or interrupt the abuse cycle. Soothing with resultant cessation of crying and induction of sleep is a prime area of study. Researchers now agree (Brackbill & Fitzgerald, 1969; Schmidt, 1975) that it is not so much the decrease or absence of stimulation that is soothing, as the application of continuous or monotonous stimulation. Many parents have applied this principle, perhaps intuitively. Wrapping a baby in a soft blanket provides continuous tactile input; rocking or jiggling the child provides rhythmic vestibular stimulation.

Those who have studied swaddling (Brackbill, 1971, 1973; Brackbill & Fitzgerald, 1969) have found it the most effective stimulus for soothing

---

[8] Two later studies demonstrate that even younger infants (2- to 4-month-olds) make compensatory head movements in response to changes in moving (Pope in Butterworth, 1983) and static (Jouen, 1984) visual displays.

[9] For an excellent review of the factors involved in the development of walking, see Thelen (1984).

1-month-old infants when compared to auditory (heart beat sound), visual (a 400-watt light), or temperature (increase) stimulation. Additionally, they have shown that combining stimulation from the different modalities is more effective than a single stimulus for decreasing crying and increasing sleep. Brackbill (1973) found that the state and accompanying physiological changes of decreased heart rate and more regular respiration occurred very rapidly, most often in the first 10 min of stimulation. Furthermore, the induced sleep state remained unchanged over at least a 2-hr time period. Studies such as these help make the point that one cannot really discuss each sensory system in isolation. Intermodal effects may be seen not just for such high level tasks as form perception but also for such basic functions as the control of state or arousal level.

Other studies have concentrated on vestibular stimulation, attempting to identify the parameters most effective in soothing infants. Korner and Thoman (1972) compared the use of contact and movement in calming crying infants. They found that not only did movement produce more soothing but that the act of lifting the infant from supine to upright at the shoulder was more effective than either lifting the infant in the horizontal position and cuddling, or moving an infant seat to and fro. Many parents seem to know this. When their baby cries they lift it to the shoulder. If crying continues, they jiggle and rock the baby or begin walking. When prolonged fussiness, such as in teething, sets in many parents report that the only thing that puts their baby to sleep is a ride in the car—a heavy dose of continuous vestibular input. Although it is clear that the assumption of the upright position was most effective in the Korner and Thoman (1972) study the contact provided was minimal compared to the intensity of swaddling in the Brackbill (1973) study. Caution must, therefore, be used in assigning greater soothing effectiveness to one type of sensory stimulation over another, at least until these comparisons can be made and such factors as individual differences in sensory responsiveness are studied.

In a search for which components of vestibular input produce calm in crying infants Pederson and TerVrught (1973; TerVrught & Pederson, 1973) rocked 2-month-olds at different amplitudes and frequencies. They found that, in general, the more intense the stimulation, the more power it had to produce soothing. Rocking through a 2-inch amplitude was effective if the infants were in a low state of arousal, but only rocking through the 5-inch amplitude inhibited activity regardless of initial state. Likewise, rocking at higher frequencies produced more sleep and less crying, with 90 cpm more effective than 60 cpm and 60 cpm more effective than 30 cpm. These results replicate the findings of Ambrose (1969) with 5-day-olds and de Lucia (1969, cited in TerVrught & Pederson, 1973) with

1-month-olds. The use of an *intensity* measure (Pederson & Ter Vrught, 1973) is especially helpful since it allows for computations that include both amplitude and frequency.

One other parameter, that of direction of movement, was investigated. Pederson (1975) rocked 2-month-olds in up–down, side-to-side, and head–toe directions; Byrne and Horowitz (1981) held newborns and rocked either horizontally or vertically (knee bends). None of these maneuvers was more effective than any other in producing a significant difference in state. Comparing intermittent (pause between movements) with continuous stimulation, Byrne and Horowitz (1981) found that only the continuous stimulation produced drowsy babies. Their suggestion that this results from stimulation at twice the frequency of the intermittent condition seems plausible.

One must be careful, however, not to assume an optimum intensity of vestibular or any other stimulation for infants. Depending upon the desired behavior, different qualities and quantities of stimulation are required in different situations. While the calming effect of rocking is desirable under some conditions, quiet alertness is needed for the infant to explore the environment and to learn. This result was achieved in the Byrne and Horowitz (1981) study upon application of intermittent vestibular stimulation. Additionally, Korner and Thoman (1970) found that holding crying newborns upright at the shoulder produced a significantly greater amount of visual alerting than any of the other activities they explored. The behaviors seen in the upright position were opening the eyes and scanning with a "bright, alert expression." Frederickson and Brown (1975) also investigated the influence of posture on visual behavior. Choosing three common positions, they observed newborns lying in a crib, sitting in an infant seat, and held to the shoulder. The on-shoulder or upright position produced a significantly greater amount of visual following of the target stimulus.

Gregg, Haffner, and Korner (1976) attempted to separate the influence of position from the vestibular stimulation involved in lifting the child to the upright position. Comparing infants in the supine position and in an infant seat angled 52° from the horizontal, they found no difference in amount of eye tracking behavior until the infants were moved. No matter what the position, it was movement that resulted in more tracking.

From the soothing studies one may conclude that swaddling, especially in combination with other sensory system inputs, and rocking, especially at higher amplitudes and frequencies, are most effective. To produce a quietly alert baby who engages in visual scanning, movement to the on-shoulder position seems best of those techniques studied.

B. Stimulation

The final group of studies are those that have examined the effect of sensory stimulation on behavior and development. Most have used premature infants as subjects and applied vestibular and tactile input in the forms of rocking and/or massage. This was generally meant to be compensatory stimulation since "birth before term deprives the infant of the regulatory influence of maternal biorhythms and the tactual, kinesthetic, and auditory stimulation that characterizes the intrauterine environment" (Rose, Schmidt, Riese, & Bridger, 1980).

The literature in this area is expanding yearly as positive results accrue. The following is a sample of the types of studies reported. Preterm infants who received additional tactile stimulation for an average of 13 days prior to testing responded like normal fullterms with increased heart rate to the application of a filament to the abdomen when asleep (Rose et al., 1980; Schmidt, Rose, & Bridger, 1980). Control group preterms showed no heart rate change. In addition, gently oscillating (water)beds reduced the number of episodes of apnea and/or bradycardia (Korner, Kraemer, Haffner, & Cosper, 1975; Korner, Guilleminault, & Van den Hoed, 1978; Tuck, Monin, Duvivier, May, & Vert, 1982), increased weight gain and head size (Kramer & Pierpont, 1976), and increased time asleep and decreased fussing and crying (Edelman, Kraemer, & Korner, 1982). Programs of rubbing and passive limb movement, sometimes accompanied by other types of stimulation, correlated with increased food intake or better utilization of calories (Leib, Benfield, & Guidubaldi, 1980) and subsequent weight gain (Solkoff, Yaffe, Weintraub, & Blase, 1969; Scarr-Salapatek & Williams, 1973; White & Labarba, 1976) in premature infants. Even the simple placing of premature infants on the textured surface of lambswool (vs. cotton sheets) produced significant weight gains (Scott & Richards, 1979). Despite the many methodological problems (Field, 1980), these and other studies have been demonstrating that tactile and vestibular–proprioceptive stimulation (of relatively short duration) is useful in enhancing the development of premature infants and possibly in averting the severity of later developmental problems (Cassler, 1965; Rice, 1977; Schaefer et al., 1980).[10,11,12]

---

[10] Studies such as these and the resultant changes in many NICU programs and nursing techniques have prompted physicians and researchers to critically examine the impact of intervention on premature infants (Wright, Hubbard, & Clark, 1979; Denhoff, 1981; Ferry, 1981; Browder, 1981; Bricker, Carlson, & Schwarz, 1981; Simeonsson, Cooper, & Scheiner, 1982; Harrison, 1985; Turkewitz & Kenny, 1985; Ferry, 1986; Russman, 1986; Hachinski, 1986). While acceptance of the criticisms of methodology of most studies seems warranted, one must take care not to discount the scientific nature of some infant stimulation programs. Dismissing them as a "ritualistic substitute for (medical) evaluation" (Hachinski, 1986) may deprive infants of potentially valuable service.

The results of two studies providing stimulation to fullterm infants have also been reported. In the Solkoff and Matuszak (1975) study newborns received 1200 min of extra stroking in the first 10 days of life. When compared to controls the stimulated group had gains of two or more points on 11 of the 26 Brazelton Neonatal Behavioral Assessment scales, while control infants had similar gains on only two scales. Because of the small sample size the trend is only suggestive but a replication would help clarify the role of extra tactile input in early life.[13] In the second study using normal infants, Clark, Kreutzberg, and Chee (1977) provided 3- to 13-month-old preambulatory infants with 16 10-min sessions of spinning. In the 1 month of the study the experimental group gained more than three times as much as the control group on tests of motor skill and reflex maturation. These two studies suggest the powerful influence of additional tactile and vestibular stimulation on the rate of normal development. Further study may help clarify the influence and limits of these supplementary stimulations.

VI. SUMMARY

To be able to consider five sensory modalities in one chapter is actually a statement about the need for further research in this area. Not only is there much work to be done in understanding changing sensitivities with age, especially in the cutaneous senses, but very little attention has been paid to the normal range of individual differences to be found in infant sensory functioning. Yet, as Sperry (1971) claims, "there is as much individual variation in (neural) circuitry as in faces."

Infants are a difficult population to study. They present many investigative "roadblocks" with their "motoric immaturity, lack of linguistic skill, and unstable behavioral state" (Whitely, 1981). Perhaps for these reasons many researchers have applied stimuli which the infant would never or

---

[11] Studies of the effect of proprioceptive–vestibular input report preterm infants who display more behaviors indicating readiness to interact with the environment (Korner, & Schneider, 1983; Pelletier, Short, & Nelson, 1985) and who have improved developmental status (Burns, Deddish, Burns, & Hatcher, 1983; Williams, Williams, & Dial, 1986).

[12] Studies of tactile-proprioceptive input report preterm infants who are more responsive to social contact (Oehler, 1985) and who are discharged 6 days sooner than control group preterms with greater weight gain and improved developmental status (Scafidi, Field, Schanberg, Bauer, Vega-Lahr, Garcia, Poirier, Nystrom, & Kuhn, 1986).

[13] Booth, Johnson-Crowley, & Barnard (1985) report no difference between fullterm infants who did and did not receive massage on Bayley scores at 4 weeks. They hypothesize that these middle class infants probably all received more intense stimulation through normal parenting than that provided in the structured one-half hour each day of the program.

rarely encounter under normal circumstances. While this is a good beginning, the "aim of research is to elucidate the psychophysiological mechanisms underlying behavior" (Hutt, Lenard, & Prechtl, 1969). It is time now to supplement the present type of research with the study of infants in natural environments responding to naturally occurring stimuli (Hutt et al., 1969). For example, what is the relationship between normal vestibular functioning and such behaviors as posture and gross motor skills (Werner & Lipsitt, 1981)? Or how does tactile sensitivity relate to the interpretation of touch as pleasant or unpleasant and how does this relate to social–emotional behavior (Ayres, 1973; Schaffer & Emerson, 1964)? Given the early functional maturity of these systems, researchers have a unique opportunity for investigating the substrate of many infant behaviors.

REFERENCES

Ambrose, A. (Ed). (1969). *Stimulation in early infancy*. New York: Academic Press.

Anders, T., & Chalemian, R. (1974). The effects of circumcision on sleep-wake states in human neonates. *Psychosomatic Medicine, 36*, 174–179.

Antonova, T., & Vakhrameeva, I. (1973). Vestibulospinal influences in early human postnatal development. *Neurosciences and Behavioral Physiology, 6*, 151–156.

Ayres, A. J. (1973). *Sensory integration and learning disorders*. Los Angeles, CA: Western Psychological Services.

Ayres, A. J. (1979). *Sensory integration and the child*. Los Angeles, CA: Western Psychological Services.

Barton, M., Court, S., & Walker, W. (1962). Causes of severe deafness in school children in Northumberland and Durham. *British Medical Journal, 1*, 351–355.

Bell, R., & Costello, N. (1964). Three tests for tactile sensitivity in the newborn. *Biologia Neonatorum, 7*, 335–347.

Bigelow, A. (1981). The correspondence between self and image movement as a cue to self-recognition for young children. *Journal of Genetic Psychology, 139*, 11–26.

Booth, C., Johnson-Crowley, N., & Barnard, K. (1985). Infant massage and exercise: Worth the effort? *MCN, 10*, 184–189.

Brackbill, Y. (1971). Cumulative effects of continuous stimulation on arousal level in infants. *Child Development, 42*, 17–26.

Brackbill, Y. (1973). Continuous stimulation reduces arousal level: Stability of effects over time. *Child Development, 44*, 43–46.

Brackbill, Y., & Fitzgerald, H. (1969). Development of the sensory analyzers during infancy. In L. Lipsitt & H. Reese (Eds.), *Advances in child development and behavior* (Vol. 4). New York: Academic Press.

Bradley, R., & Mistretta, C. (1975). Fetal sensory receptors. *Physiological Reviews, 55*, 352–382.

Bricker, D., Carlson, L., & Schwarz, R. (1981). A discussion of early intervention for infants with Down Syndrome. *Pediatrics, 67*, 45–46.

Browder, J. (1981). The pediatrician's orientation to infant stimulation programs. *Pediatrics, 67*, 42–44.

Burns, K., Deddish, R., Burns, W., & Hatcher, R. (1983). Use of oscillating waterbeds and rhythmic sounds for premature infant stimulation. *Developmental Psychology, 19,* 746–751.

Bushnell, E. (1986). The basis of infant visual-tactual functioning-amodal dimensions or multimodal compounds? In L. Lipsitt & C. Rovee-Collier (Eds.), *Advances in infancy research* (Vol. 4). Norwood, NJ: Ablex.

Butterworth, G. (1983). Structure of the mind in human infancy. In L. Lipsitt & C. Rovee-Collier (Eds.), *Advances in infancy research* (Vol. 2). Norwood, NJ: Ablex.

Butterworth, G., & Hicks, L. (1977). Visual proprioception and postural stability in infancy. A developmental study. *Perception, 6,* 255–262.

Byrne, J., & Horowitz, F. (1981). Rocking as a soothing intervention: The influence of direction and type of movement. *Infant Behavior and Development, 4,* 207–218.

Casaer, P. (1979). Postural behavior in newborn infants. *Clinics in developmental medicine* (Vol. 72). Philadelphia: J. B. Lippincott Co.

Casler, L. (1965). The effects of extra tactile stimulation on a group of institutionalized infants. *Genetic Psychology Monographs, 71,* 137–175.

Chapman, C. R. (1976). Measurement of pain: Problems and issues. In J. Bonica & D. Albe-Fessard (Eds.), *Advances in pain research and therapy* (Vol. 1). New York: Raven Press.

Cioni, G., & Pellegrinetti, G. (1982). Lateralization of sensory and motor functions in human neonates. *Perceptual and Motor Skills, 54,* 1151–1158.

Clark, D., Kreutzberg, J., & Chee, F. (1977). Vestibular stimulation influence on motor development in infants. *Science, 196,* 1228–1229.

Cooke, R. (1952). The behavioral response of infants to heat stress. *Yale Journal of Biology and Medicine, 24,* 334–340.

Crudden, C. (1937). Reactions of newborn infants to thermal stimuli under constant tactual conditions. *Journal of Experimental Psychology, 20,* 350–370.

D'Apolito, K. (1984). The neonate's response to pain. *MCN, 9,* 256–257.

Denhoff, E. (1981). Current status of infant stimulation or enrichment programs for children with developmental disabilities. *Pediatrics, 67,* 32–37.

Denisova, M., & Figurin, N. (1977). Experimental reflexological research on the newborn. In M. Cole (Ed.), *Soviet developmental psychology.* New York: M. E. Sharpe.

Desmedt, J., & Manil, J. (1970). Somatosensory evoked potentials of the normal human neonate in REM sleep, in slow wave sleep and in waking. *Electroencephalography and Clinical Neurophysiology, 29,* 113–126.

Dixon, J. (1957). Development of self-recognition. *Journal of Genetic Psychology, 91,* 251–256.

Dubowitz, V. (1969). The floppy infant. *Clinics in developmental medicine* (Vol. 31). London: Heinemann.

Edelman, A., Kraemer, H., & Korner, A. (1982). Effects of compensatory movement stimulation on the sleep–wake behaviors of preterm infants. *Journal of the American Academy of Child Psychiatry, 21,* 555–559.

Elliott, G., & Elliott, K. (1964). Some pathological and clinical implications of the precocious development of the human ear. *Laryngoscope, 74,* 1160–1171.

Emde, R., Harmon, R., Metcalf, D., Koenig, K., & Wagonfeld, S. (1971). Stress and neonatal sleep. *Psychosomatic Medicine, 33,* 491–497.

Evans, B. (1980). Learned responses to movement in neonates. *Developmental Psychobiology, 13,* 95–101.

Eviatar, L., & Eviatar, A. (1978). The normal nystagmic response of infants to caloric and perrotary stimulation. *Laryngoscope, 89,* 1036–1044.

Eviatar, L., Eviatar, A., & Naray, I. (1974). Maturation of neurovestibular responses in infants. *Developmental Medicine and Child Neurology, 16,* 435–446.

Korner, A., & Thoman, E. (1972). The relative efficacy of contact and vestibular-proprioceptive stimulation in soothing neonates. *Child Development, 43,* 443–453.

Kramer, L., & Peirpont, M. (1976). Rocking waterbeds and auditory stimuli to enhance growth of preterm infants. *Journal of Pediatrics, 88,* 297–299.

Langworthy, O. (1932a). Development of behavior patterns and myelinization of the nervous system in the human fetus and infant. *Archives of Neurology and Psychiatry, 28,* 1365–1382.

Langworthy, O. (1932b). The differentiation of behavior patterns in the foetus and infant. *Brain, 55,* 265–277.

Laurence, M., & Feind, C. (1953). Vestibular responses to rotation in the newborn infant. *Pediatrics, 12,* 300–306.

Leader, L., Baillie, P., Bahia, M., & Elsebeth, V. (1982). The assessment and significance of habituation to a repeated stimulus by the human fetus. *Early Human Development, 7,* 211–219.

Lee, D., & Aronson, E. (1974). Visual proprioceptive control of standing in human subjects. *Perception and Psychophysics, 15,* 529–532.

Leib, S., Benfield, G., & Guidubaldi, J. (1980). Effects of early intervention and stimulation on the preterm infant. *Pediatrics, 66,* 83–89.

Lenard, H., von Bernuth, H., & Prechtl, H. (1968). Reflexes and their relationship to behavioral state in the newborn. *Acta Paediatrica Scandinavica, 57,* 177–185.

Lewis, M., Dodd, C., & Harwitz, M. (1969). Cardiac responsivity to tactile stimulation in waking and sleeping infants. *Perceptual and Motor Skills, 29,* 259–269.

Lewkowicz, D., Gardner, J., & Turkewitz, G. (1979). Lateral differences and head turning responses to somesthetic stimulation in premature human infants. *Developmental Psychobiology, 12,* 607–614.

Liederman, J., & Kinsbourne, M. (1980a). The mechanism of neonatal rightward turning bias: A sensory or motor asymmetry? *Infant Behavior and Development, 3,* 223–238.

Liederman, J., & Kinsbourne, M. (1980b). Rightward turning biases in neonates reflect a single neural asymmetry in motor programming: A reply to Turkewitz. *Infant Behavior and Development, 3,* 245–251.

Lipsitt, L. (1977). The study of sensory and learning processes of the newborn. *Clinical Perinatology, 4,* 163–186.

Lipsitt, L., & Levy, N. (1959). Electrotactual threshold in the neonate. *Child Development, 30,* 547–554.

Lockman, J., Ashmead, D., & Bushnell, E. (1984). The development of anticipatory hand orientation during infancy. *Journal of Experimental Child Psychology, 37,* 176–186.

Martinius, J., & Papousek, H. (1970). Responses to optic and exteroceptive stimuli in relation to state in the human newborn: Habituation. *Neuropaediatrie, 1,* 452–460.

McGraw, M. (1941). Neural maturation as exemplified in the changing reactions of the infant to pin prick. *Child Development, 12,* 31–42.

Meltzoff, A., & Borton, R. (1979). Intermodal matching by human neonates. *Nature (London), 282,* 403–404.

Mestyan, G., & Varga, F. (1960). Chemical thermoregulation of full-term and premature newborn infants. *Journal of Pediatrics, 56,* 623–629.

Moffat, R., & Hackel, A. (1985). Thermal aspects of neonatal care. *In* A. Gottfried & J. Gaiter (Eds.), *Infant stress under intensive care.* Baltimore, Maryland: University Park Press.

Moreau, T. (1976). Modality differences in the habituation and dishabituation of cardiac responsiveness in the human newborn. *Developmental Psychobiology, 9,* 109–117.

Moreau, T., Birch, H., & Turkewitz, G. (1970). Ease of habituation to repeated auditory and somesthetic stimulation in the human newborn. *Journal of Experimental Child Psychology, 9,* 193–207.

Moreau, T., Helfgott, E., Weinstein, P., & Milner, P. (1978). Lateral differences in habituation of ipsilateral head-turning to repeated tactile stimulation in the human newborn. *Perceptual and Motor Skills, 46,* 427–436.

Oehler, J. (1985). Examining the issue of tactile stimulation for preterm infants. *Neonatal Network, 4,* 25–33.

Ornitz, E., Atwell, C., Walter, D., Hartmann, E., & Kaplan, A. (1979). The maturation of vestibular nystagmus in infancy and childhood. *Acta Oto-Laryngologica, 88,* 244–256.

Pederson, D. (1975). The soothing effect of rocking as determined by the direction and frequency of movement. *Canadian Journal of Behavioral Science, 7,* 237–243.

Pederson, D., & Ter Vrught, D. (1973). The influence of amplitude and frequency of vestibular stimulation on the activity of two-month-old infants. *Child Development, 44,* 122–128.

Peiper, A. (1963). *Cerebral function in infancy and childhood.* New York: Consultants Bureau.

Pelletier, J., Short, M., & Nelson, D. (1985). Immediate effects of waterbed flotation on approach and avoidance behaviors of premature infants. In K. Ottenbacher & M. Short (Eds.), *Vestibular processing dysfunction in children.* New York, New York: Haworth.

Pomerleau, A., & Malcuit, G. (1981). State effects on concomitant cardiac and behavioral responses to a sucking stimulus in human newborns. *Infant Behavior and Development, 4,* 163–174.

Pomerleau-Malcuit, A., & Clifton, R. (1973). Neonatal heart rate response to tactile, auditory, and vestibular stimulation in different states. *Child Development, 44,* 485–496.

Pomerleau-Malcuit, A., Malcuit, G., & Clifton, R. (1975). An attempt to elicit cardiac orienting and defense responses in the human newborn to two types of facial stimulation. *Psychophysiology, 12,* 527–535.

Pratt, K., Nelson, A., & Sun, K. (1930). Behavior of the newborn infant. *Ohio State University: Contributions in Psychology,* No. 10.

Prechtl, H. (1958). The directed head turning response and allied movements of the human baby. *Behavior, 13,* 212–242.

Prechtl, H., & Beintema, D. (1977). The neurological examination of the fullterm newborn infant. *Clinics in developmental medicine* (Vol. 63). Philadelphia: J. B. Lippincott Co.

Prechtl, H., Vlach, V., Lenard, H., & Grant, D. (1967). Exteroceptive and tendon reflexes in various behavioral states in the newborn infant. *Biologia Neonatorum, 11,* 159–175.

Rice, R. (1977). Neurophysiological development in premature infants following stimulation. *Developmental Psychology, 13,* 69–76.

Rose, S., Gottfried, A., & Bridger, W. (1981). Cross-modal transfer and information processing by the sense of touch in infancy. *Developmental Psychology, 17,* 90–98.

Rose, S., Gottfried, A., & Bridger, W. (1983). Infants' cross-modal transfer from solid objects to their graphic representations. *Child Development, 54,* 686–694.

Rose, S., Schmidt, K., & Bridger, W. (1976). Cardiac and behavioral responsivity to tactile stimulation. *Developmental Psychology, 12,* 311–320.

Rose, S., Schmidt, K., & Bridger, W. (1978). Changes in tactile responsivity during sleep in the human newborn infant. *Developmental Psychology, 14,* 163–172.

Rose, S., Schmidt, K., Riese, M., & Bridger, W. (1980). Effects of prematurity and early intervention on responsivity to tactual stimuli: A comparison of preterm and full-term infants. *Child Development, 51,* 416–425.

Rossi, L., Pignataro, O., Nino, L., Gaini, K., Sambataro, G., & Oldini, C. (1979). Maturation of vestibular responses: Preliminary report. *Developmental Medicine and Child Neurology, 21,* 217–224.

Ruff, H. (1984). Infants' manipulative exploration of objects: Effects of age and object characteristics. *Developmental Psychology, 20,* 9–20.

Russman, B. (1986). Are infant stimulation programs useful? *Archives of Neurology, 43,* 282–283.

Scafidi, F., Field, T., Schanberg, S., Bauer, C., Vega-Lahr, N., Garcia, R., Poirier, J., Nystrom, G., & Kuhn, C. (1986). Effects of tactile/kinesthetic stimulation on the clinical course and sleep/wake behavior of preterm neonates. *Infant Behavior and Development, 9,* 91–105.

Scarr-Salapatek, S., & Williams, M. (1973). The effect of early stimulation on low-birth-weight infants. *Child Development, 44,* 94–101.

Schaefer, M., Hatcher, R., & Barglow, P. (1980). Prematurity and infant stimulation: A review of research. *Child Psychiatry and Human Development, 10,* 199–212.

Schaffer, H., & Emerson, P. (1964). Patterns of response to physical contact in early human development. *Journal of Child Psychology and Psychiatry, 5,* 1–13.

Schmidt, K. (1975). The effect of continuous stimulation on the behavioral sleep of infants. *Merrill-Palmer Quarterly, 21,* 77–88.

Schmidt, K., & Birns, B. (1971). The behavioral arousal threshold in infant sleep as a function of time and sleep state. *Child Development, 42,* 269–277.

Schmidt, K., Rose, S., & Bridger, W. (1980). Effect of heartbeat sound on the cardiac and behavioral responsiveness to tactual stimulation in sleeping preterm infants. *Developmental Psychology, 16,* 175–184.

Scott, S., & Richards, M. (1979). Nursing low-birthweight babies on lambswool. *Lancet, 1,* 1028.

Sherman, M., & Sherman, I. (1925). Sensori-motor responses in infants. *Journal of Comparative Psychology, 5,* 53–68.

Sherman, M., Sherman, I., & Flory, C. (1936). Infant behavior. *Comparative Psychology Monographs, 12,* (4).

Simeonsson, R., Cooper, D., & Scheiner, A. (1982). A review and analysis of the effectiveness of early intervention programs. *Pediatrics, 69,* 635–641.

Solkoff, N., & Matuszak, D. (1975). Tactile stimulation and behavioral development among low-birthweight infants. *Child Psychiatry and Human Development, 6,* 33–37.

Solkoff, N., Yaffe, S., Weintraub, D., & Blase, B. (1969). Effects of handling on the subsequent development of premature infants. *Developmental Psychology, 1,* 765–768.

Soroka, S., Corter, C., & Abramovitch, R. (1979). Infants' tactual discrimination of novel and familiar tactual stimuli. *Child Development, 50,* 1251–1253.

Spears, W., & Hoyle, R. (1967). Sensory and perceptual processes in infants. In Y. Brackbill (Ed.), *Infancy and early childhood.* New York: Free Press.

Sperry, R. (1971). How a developing brain gets itself properly wired for adaptive function. In E. Tobach, L. Aronson, & E. Shaw (Eds.), *The biopsychology of development.* New York: Academic Press.

Stoddard, F. (1982). Coping with pain: A developmental approach to treatment of burned children. *American Journal of Psychiatry, 139,* 736–742.

Talbert, L., Kraybill, E., & Potter, H. (1976). Adrenal cortical response to circumcision in the neonate. *Obstetrics and Gynecology, 48,* 208–210.

Tennes, K., & Carter, D. (1973). Plasma cortisal levels and behavioral states in early infancy. *Psychosomatic Medicine, 35,* 121–128.

Ter Vrught, D., & Pederson, D. (1973). The effects of vertical rocking frequencies on the arousal level in two-month-old infants. *Child Development, 44*, 205–209.

Thelen, E. (1984). Learning to walk: Ecological demands and phylogenetic constraints. In L. Lipsitt & C. Rovee-Collier (Eds.), *Advances in infancy research* (Vol. 3). Norwood, NJ: Ablex.

Tibbling, L. (1969). The rotary nystagmus response in children. *Acta Oto-Laryngologica, 68*, 459–467.

Tuck, S., Monin, P., Duvivier, C., May, T., & Vert, P. (1982). Effect of a rocking bed on apnoea of prematurity. *Archives of Diseases in Childhood, 57*, 475–476.

Turkewitz, G. (1977). The development of lateral differentiation in the human infant. *Annals of the New York Academy of Sciences, 299*, 309–318.

Turkewitz, G. (1980). Mechanisms of a neonatal rightward turning bias: A reply to Lieder-man and Kinsbourne. *Infant Behavior and Development, 3*, 239–244.

Turkewitz, G., & Kenny, P. (1985). The role of developmental limitations of sensory input on sensory/perceptual organization. *Journal of Developmental and Behavioral Pediatrics, 6*, 302–306.

von Bernuth, H., & Prechtl, H. (1969). Vestibular-ocular response and its state-dependency in newborn infants. *Neuropaediatrie, 1*, 11–24.

von Hofsten, C., & Fazel-Zandy, S. (1984). Development of visually guided hand orientation in reaching. *Journal of Experimental Child Psychology, 38*, 208–219.

von Hofsten, C., & Lindhagen, K. (1979). Observations on the development of reaching for moving objects. *Journal of Experimental Child Psychology, 28*, 158–173.

Weinstein, S. (1968). Intensive and extensive aspects of tactile sensitivity as a function of body part, sex and laterality. In D. Kenshalo (Ed.), *The skin senses*. Springfield, IL: Thomas.

Werner, J., & Lipsitt, L. (1981). The infancy of human sensory systems. In E. Gallin (Ed.), *Developmental plasticity*. New York: Academic Press.

White, J., & Labarba, R. (1976). The effect of tactile and kinesthetic stimulation on neonatal development in the premature infant. *Developmental Psychobiology, 9*, 569–577.

Whitely, J. (1981). Canadian research on infant development: 1970-1980. *Canadian Psychology, 22*, 55–68.

Williams, P., Williams, A., & Dial, M. (1986). Children at risk: Perinatal events, developmental delays and the effects of a developmental stimulation program. *International Journal of Nursing Studies, 23*, 21–38.

Wright, C., Hubbard, D., & Clark, G. (1979). Observations of human fetal otoconial membranes. *Annals of Otology, Rhinology and Laryngology, 88*, 267–274.

Wyke, B. (1975). A neurological basis of movement-A developmental review. *Clinics in developmental medicine* (Vol. 55). Philadelphia: J. B. Lippincott Co.

Yang, R., & Douthitt, T. (1974). Newborn responses to threshold tactile stimulation. *Child Development, 45*, 237–242.

Index